The EVERYTHING CHRISTMAS BOOK

Sharon

Barry Littmann

Bob Adams, Inc.
Holbrook, Massachusetts

Published by Bob Adams, Inc.
260 Center Street, Holbrook, Massachusetts 02343

ISBN 1-55850-403-6

Printed in the United States of America
A B C D E F G H I J

Library of Congress Cataloging-in-Publication Data

The everything Christmas book : stories, songs, food, traditions, revelry, and more.
     p.   cm.
     Includes bibliographical references and index.
     ISBN 1-55850-403-6
     1. Christmas—United States. 2. Unites States—Social life and customs. I. Bob Adams, Inc.
     GT4986.A1E94 1994
     394.2'663'0973—dc20   94-3752
         CIP

This work is designed to provide accurate and authoritative information with regard to the subject matter covered. It has been prepared with care and thoroughness, but due to the magnitude of the database and the complexities of the subject matter, occasional errors may occur. If you should encounter an error in this work, please contact the publisher at the address above so that corrections may be made in future editions. This publication is sold with the understanding that the publisher is not engaged in rendering legal, accounting, culinary, or other professional advice. If legal advice or other expert assistance is required, the services of a qualified professional person should be sought.

This book is available at quantity discounts for bulk purchases. For information, call 1-800-872-5627.

CONTENTS

ACKNOWLEDGEMENTS ⌇

This book was a labor of love over a period of two and a half years; many good people contributed to its pages. This project would not be complete if we did not gratefully recognize the efforts of:

Janet Anastasio, Anna Botelho, Christopher Ciaschini, Nancy Collins, Richard Dey, Peter Gouck, Robin Hayden, Wayne Jackson, Kate Layzer, Nancy McGovern, Carol Tierney, Mary Toropov, Henry Tragert, Mary Tragert, Matthew Tragert, Elizabeth Tragert and the staffs of the Boston Public Library, the Holbrook Public Library, and the Flint Public Library in Middleton, Massachusetts.

INTRODUCTION

HRISTMAS BEGINS IN the mists of long-distant history and extends along the future of the human family. We identify it so closely with childhood that, in our culture at any rate, to be a young person in December is, in many a household, to *be* Christmas—for oneself, and , although one does not know it, for one's family members, too.

Our vision of Christmas is informed by countless Christmases past and the knowledge that, as long as there are children among us and a sense of tradition, there are likely to be Christmases in the future. But the true event, the true day of days, is neither an account of old customs nor a prediction of the ways in which this holiday will continue to extend its reach into countries that, not too long ago, had never heard of it. And we can give great thanks that Christmas is not—or at least, need not be—best summed up in a seasonal retail sales target that merchants either meet or miss. The true experience of Christmas is, at least for those of us who worked on this book, *wonder.*

In this book we have tried to catalogue the history of the holiday, its rituals and customs, the varying ways it is observed throughout the world, and some idea of the modern American way of celebrating the big day. We have also supplied recipes, gift ideas, local celebrations both on and off the beaten path, party ideas, poetry, fiction, and lists of good videos to rent. Everything, in short, that we considered worth remembering about December 25 is within these covers. And that sense of memory is important, because it is the basis of tradition—and what is Christmas if not one of the fundamental traditions of our time?

But what *makes* something memorable? For us simply to catalogue and include all of the various elements of the holiday would have been to fall far short of our goal. We wanted to include, not just everything vaguely related to Christmas—we could have filled ten books this size had that been our goal—but everything that inspired that sense of wonder that so typifies the season. It is, after all, wonder that permeates the eyes of a five-year-old who starts down the stairs to see the tree aglow. And, yes, it is ultimately the anticipation of wonder (and not just a certain bleary resolve) that gets her parents out of bed at the crack of dawn to watch those eyes sparkle.

Once a year, on Drecember 25, we are all reintroduced to wonder on a scale that we should never forget, but nevertheless somehow manage to on December 26. This book is intended as a celebration of that wonder. We wish you the most precious gift of the holiday: the ability to see things, for a time, through the eyes you once had on Christmas morning—and, therefore, to be amazed.

— *The Editors*

CHAPTER ONE

The History of Christmas

~

When and how did the observance of Christmas as a holiday begin? The answers are surprising! The day as we know it has been shaped by many people and many cultures … and continues to change to this very day. To find out how the early Roman festivals influence our holiday season, why Queen Victoria's wedding played such a big part in what we now consider essential for the holidays, and why Christmas was illegal for many years, read on.

~

E MAY THINK of the Christmas of trees and family togetherness and decorations and cards from loved ones as having been around forever . . . but it's actually a relatively recent development.

The celebration we recognize today took centuries to develop, and can be said to have caught on in earnest only in the middle of the nineteenth century.

Christmas as we know it did not happen overnight, but evolved over many centuries, enduring occasional tribulation, scrutiny, and abolishment along the way.

THE FIRST CHRISTMAS

One might say that Christmas has been celebrated since the very eve of Jesus' birth, when, the Bible says, the angels proclaimed his arrival on the plains of Bethlehem in an event later celebrated in a special "Christes Masse," or Christ's Mass. Though scholars are unsure of the actual day or even the month of Jesus' birth, Biblical and other records have led them to set the year at around 3 or 4 B.C.

Most of the elements of the traditional Christmas story have their origin in the Gospels of St. Matthew and St. Luke. (Both of these Nativity accounts are included in this book.) Together these books create a picture of the birth of Jesus that is beloved around the world.

Luke's Gospel offers us not only a time and place for this event but a real human and religious drama. Focusing on the trials of Joseph and Mary and the actual scene of the birth, Luke tells a story of weary travelers forced to spend the night in a stable because there was "no room for them at the inn." There their baby is born and placed in a manger, or feeding trough, in lieu of a cradle. From Luke's tale of the shepherds and angels come the ingredients for many of the world's best loved Christmas songs.

It's interesting to note that although our Christmas celebrations take place in the winter, the Nativity of Luke's story is most likely set in the spring or summer. As Luke would have known, shepherds and their flocks would not be likely to be roaming the hills at night in the winter.

"I have often thought, Sir Roger, it happens very well that Christmas should fall out in the Middle of Winter."

Joseph Addison (1672–1719)

A later passage from the same chapter of Luke describes an event that would later become a little-known religious holiday, one that in some places marks the true close of the Christmas season. According to Jewish law, a mother was to be taken to the temple to be purified forty days after the birth of her child. Mary was no exception to this rule: "The days of her purification according to the law of Moses were accomplished . . . ." This purification is remembered on February 2 in a ceremony in which candles are also blessed, giving it the name Candlemas Day. Candlemas Day observances began in the late ninth century with Pope Sergius. In some European countries it is considered bad luck to keep greenery up after this day.

The Gospel of Matthew provides us with two other important Christmas symbols: The Star of Bethlehem and the Three Wise Men. Over the years, the science of astronomy has provided some possible explanations for accounts of a magical star at the

time of Jesus' birth. Some have argued that it must have been a comet, but records of that time mark the only comets near the period at 17 B.C. (too early), and A.D. 66 (too late!). Chinese astronomers, the best in history, observed a nova in 4 B.C., but there is no way to know whether this is the "star" remembered in the story.

Another explanation comes from the fields of astronomy and astrology. In the year 6 or 7 B.C. there was an alignment of the planets Jupiter and Saturn in the constellation of Pisces, a fact confirmed by the School of Astronomy at Sippar in Babylon and by the world-renowned astronomer Johannes Kepler. Ancient astrological legend, moreover, asserts that the meeting of these planets would signify the Messiah's birth. The sign for Pisces is two fish joined by their tales; this is also the sign of the Messiah. However, if you trust recent scholarship, 6–7 B.C. is too late to be the year of Jesus' birth.

Careful reading of Matthew reveals another surprising fact: the writer never gives a definitive number of Wise Men, and he never refers to them as kings. Over the years popular culture settled on the number three, presumably because of the three gifts Matthew mentions. Their status as kings is believed to come from a passage in Psalms that refers to kings bearing gifts, though they are also referred to as Magi.

The Wise Men's visit to Jesus is commemorated on Epiphany, also known in some places as Twelfth Night or Three Kings' Eve. Originally Epiphany marked the manifestation of God to the world in the form of Jesus. Later, when the Romans began introducing Christianity to the West, they represented Epiphany as the day the Wise Men came and presented their gifts to Jesus. Tradition marks this event on January 6, also the date of Eastern Orthodox Christmas in many countries.

As the sketchiness of these Gospels indicates, much about the time, place, and circumstance of Jesus' birth cannot be known. Still, these writings do give us a rich tradition from which to draw at Christmas.

THE LONG JOURNEY TOWARD CHRISTMAS BEGINS

If Christmas celebrations had begun the year Jesus was born, the holiday would be nearing its two thousandth birthday. But don't go scouting up all those candles yet. Christmas had to wait a while before it was popularized in any meaningful way—over three hundred years, in fact.

The early days of Christianity were very different from the state of affairs today. The first Christians on record, in the second half of the first century, had their work cut out for them trying to gain converts while avoiding persecution by the religious authorities. Early leaders such as Paul of Tarsus spread the word and gradually achieved converts, but official persecution of  Christians began as early as A.D. 64 under the Emperor Nero. For the next two hundred years and more, Christians endured imprisonment and death at the hands of the Roman Empire, while the Egyptian goddess Isis, the Greek goddess Demeter, and the Persian god Mithra were worshiped freely.

Not surprisingly, widespread observance of Christmas within the Roman Empire did not occur before Emperor Constantine's conversion to Christianity in the fourth century A.D.

When Constantine came to power in 306, the prevailing religion was Mithraism, but Constantine gradually came to be converted to Christianity. As a result, Christianity became the state religion and public funds were used to build churches. It was Constantine who commissioned the building of the Church of the Nativity on a spot in Bethlehem assumed to be the exact birthplace of Christ. By the end of the fourth century, the old forms of worship had been banned, and Christianity began spreading across the land.

DECEMBER 25— AND THE WINTER SOLSTICE ~

While there is one record of Christmas being celebrated in Antioch (Turkey) on December 25 in the middle of the second century, there is no record of its being observed on that date in Rome until the year 336. In 350 Pope Julius I declared December 25 the official date, and in 529 Emperor Justinian declared Christmas a civic holiday. Further legislation by the Council of Tours in 567 officially made Advent a period of fasting and preparation; the time from Christmas to Epiphany (the twelve days of Christmas) was also declared part of the festive season.

What's so special about late December? It's the part of the year when the days finally begin to get longer.

To some the December date may seem completely arbitrary, but in fact it was a calculated choice that reflected the importance of winter solstice festivals for the cultures of pre-Christian Europe and Asia. To abolish these festivals in favor of strictly Christian forms of celebration would have been extremely unpopular. Though many early Christian leaders such as Gregory of Nazainzus spoke out against combining pagan and Christian ways, it became clear early on that rather than trying to beat the pagans, Christians would be wiser to join their game—to incorporate their most deep-rooted traditions into Christian worship and celebration.

Ancient peoples believed that the days grew shorter in December because the sun was leaving them, perhaps dying. Festivals held right before December 21, the winter solstice, featured rituals designed to appease the sun and get it to return. After the solstice, the shortest day of the year, the days got longer again, and grand celebrations were held in honor of the sun's return. Along with the idea of the physical presence of the sun were underlying themes of harvest, rebirth, and light.

Although the basic conception of the solstice festival was common to all lands, each area had its unique variations. In the Zagmuk of Mesopotamia, a convict was sacrificed in atonement for the people's sins. In a custom that may have been an ancestor of the yule log tradition, wooden representations of their god Marduk's enemies were burned in a great fire.

Persia and Babylonia had Sacaea, an event in which slaves and their owners engaged in role reversal. Sacaea also featured a tradition of liberation and execution involving a pair of criminals. As in the story of Jesus and Barabbas, with which the ritual shares striking parallels, two convicts were chosen; one went free while the other was mocked as a king and put to death, again as penance for the sins of the masses.

But the tradition that left its mark most indelibly on Christmas was the Roman Saturnalia. The Saturnalia was observed from December 17–24, and was a nominal celebration of a number of different events, among them Saturn's triumph over Jupiter. According to belief, Saturn's reign had heralded the Golden Age in Rome. Although the god later lost out to Jupiter, during the Saturnalia he was believed to return, allowing Rome to relive the Golden Age for a brief time. It is not surprising that the Romans, who associated Saturn closely with the sun, would celebrate this festival near the solstice.

During the festivities, no one worked except those whose business it was to provide food, drink, or entertainment. Masters and slaves became equals, and there was much feasting, dancing, gambling, and general revelry. Candles were used as decoration to scare away the darkness and celebrate the sun and light. Another recognizable ritual was the giving of gifts, which was done in honor of the goddess of vegetation, Strenia. The people felt that in time of darkness and winter it was important to honor someone who had a hand in the harvest. At first produce and baked goods were exchanged, but as time went on, inedible gifts became fashionable.

The Saturnalia was followed by the calends of January (the calends marked the first day of the month). Observed on January 1–3, this period meant still more parties.

The earliest of the church's many battles over the less-than-reverent nature of some solstice celebrations resulted in compromise: the adaptation of certain pagan symbols and rites to the Christmas tradition.

It's not hard to understand the Christian officials' disapproval of these festivals and their reluctance to allow them either to continue by themselves, or to be incorporated as part of Christianity. The celebrations, after all, could take on orgiastic proportions. After years of mostly futile attempts to abolish these pagan festivals and rituals, however, the church realized it would be better served by allowing them—revised so that their focus was now to honor Christ. Both church and popular interests were thus satisfied: The people got to keep their time of fun, while the church ensured that the birth of Christ would be celebrated with all due honor and festivity. In this

way, many parts of the old festivals remained, while others were reformed to honor Christ's birth. Some of the retained elements that have remained popular to this day are greenery, candles, singing, tree decorating, Yule logs, and feasting.

But why December 25? Why not the December 21 or December 22, the actual time of the solstice? The use of this date was a remnant of the Mithriac religion, a major religion of the Roman era with close similarities to Christianity. Mithra, the god of light and wisdom, was said to have been born from a rock

on December 25. Mithra, symbolizing the sun, was naturally a big part of solstice festivals, and his birth was celebrated as a major holiday by believers. In the third century (that is, in the century before Constantine's ascension), Emperor Aurelian declared December 25 *Dies Invicti Solis* (the Day of the Invincible Sun).

Although Constantine converted to Christianity, remnants of his old religion stayed around. For many, incorporating Mithraic or solstice rites into the celebration of Christmas was easy to justify: Christ represents life, triumph over death and darkness, and restored hope and light; rather than celebrating the sun as before, people would be celebrating the Son of God. Simply put, the birth of Christ replaced the birth of the sun as a cause for celebration.

The so-called "barbarian invasions" of the Roman Empire that began in the fifth century brought the Nordic and Germanic peoples in direct contact with Christianity, and thus with Christmas. In northern and western Europe, the Germanic and Celtic peoples had their own solstice rituals, which were later incorporated into Christmas. The December Julmond festival (Jul later became Yul) was a celebration of harvest and rebirth, with wheat representing life triumphing over death. Anything made of wheat, such as bread or liquor, was consumed heartily, and also given as gifts. Evergreens were used as a symbol of life, and what we would call the yule log was lit in this time of darkness to symbolize the eventual triumph of light over darkness. The festive meal was boar's head. These traditions have been presented in centuries-old carols, including wassail songs, holly carols, and boar's head carols still widely sung today.

THE DAWN OF CHRISTMAS IN EUROPE

Christianity gradually made its way across Europe, bringing Christmas with it. It came to England via St. Augustine, the first Archbishop of Canterbury, who supposedly baptized more than ten thousand English on December 25, 598.

St. Augustine was the prime architect of the early English Christmas celebration.

Acting under the direction of Pope Gregory I, Augustine was also instrumental in bringing the celebration of Christmas to that area. At the end of the sixth century the pope instructed Augustine to make the midwinter yule festival over into Christmas observances, emphasizing the importance of condoning any customs from the festival that could be found to contain Christian significance. It was a well-tested strategy, and it worked. (There are some who believe, however, that King Arthur had the first English Christmas in 521, with his Knights of the Round Table, without the input of either Augustine or Gregory.)

Christmas came to Germany in 813, via the Synod of Mainz, and was brought to Norway in the mid-900's by King Hakon the Good. By the end of the ninth century, Christmas was observed all over Europe with trees, lights, gifts, and feasts. The items that had held significance for the old religions were either tossed aside or altered to fit within a Christian context.

Today Christmas is celebrated on December 25 by Roman Catholics and Protestants, but not by most European churches, which continue to combine Epiphany and nativity celebrations on January 6. (A side note: A small portion of English believers observed the January 6 tradition until about 1950—not because of any connection with the rites of Eastern churches, but because some of their own observances followed the old Julian calendar rather than the current Gregorian.)

Over the centuries the holiday was reformed more and more to contain fewer of the old "pagan" elements. In ninth-century England, Alfred the Great declared that the twelve days between Christmas and Epiphany be reserved for seasonal festivities, thus formalizing observation of the twelve days of Christmas in England. Alfred was serious about celebrating: As part of his declaration, he made working during this period illegal.

Alfred followed his own rules, even at great cost: In 878 he refused to go to war during these twelve days. His failure to do so is said to have caused England to lose the Battle of Chippenham to the Danes.

THE BIG PARTY

The heights of Christmas extravagance and rowdiness were achieved in medieval England after 1066. Celebrating the season for the full twelve days was no problem. People would attend church, but not in the way one might think; donning masks and costumes as on Halloween, the churchgoers would sing colorful (meaning off-color) songs and even roll dice on the altar.

So: Christmas during this period was a time for a little good-natured ribbing of the solemnity of the church. A touch of comedy was added to the sermons, so serious the rest of the year. This is not to say that the festivities were entirely irreverent. There was also devout caroling and nativity plays, although in the latter Herod was often portrayed in a comic vein.

The king and court had a grand time trying to outdo each other with outrageous abundance. Henry III had six hundred oxen killed and prepared for a single feast—and that was just the main course! Merchants and other higher-ups paid their kudos to the king by giving him gifts and cash. There were guidelines for gift giving based on one's social position. The aforementioned Henry III once closed down merchants until they paid their proper dues, although in 1248 he seemed to regain a bit of his Christmas spirit when he established a custom of giving food to the needy for the holiday.

Gambling was also a big part of the festivities around the court; stories of the royalty using loaded dice to insure against losing seem to capture the spirit of the age. But royal excess at Christmas surely reached its apogee in 1377. In that year, we are told, Richard II had a Christmas feast for over ten thousand people. Records do not indicate whether the two thousand cooks employed at the feast enjoyed the holiday.

The fourteenth century also saw the beginning of widespread caroling. Carols had been used in Roman churches as early as the second century, but they came to England much later, by way of France. In the Middle Ages they were used in conjunction with Nativity plays to convey the Christmas story to those who could not read. By the 1500s the mummers, a traveling band of costumed carousers somewhat like street actors, were out and about.

Fortunately for historians and carol lovers alike, a young man named Richard Hill kept a written record of, among other things, the popular English carols of the time. Spanning the years 1500–1536, Hill's diary was extremely valuable in helping to keep alive such secular carols as "The Boar's Head Carol."

Henry VIII's renowned love of a good party set a high standard for yuletide carousals—a standard that stood for years and would come to worry many in the clergy.

In 1533 Henry VIII made himself the Supreme Head of the Church of England, taking to himself the power of regulating religious holidays, including Christmas. He then proceeded to rival Henry III in yuletide extravagance.

Under his rule Christmas became a very big deal indeed, both socially and ecclesiastically, and Christmas celebrations were filled with dancing, plays, general carousing, and, of course, food. This tradition was carried on by his daughter, Elizabeth I, and, upon the accession of James I in 1603, by the Stuarts.

*At Christmas I no more desire a rose
Than wish a snow in May's
new-fangled mirth;
But like of each thing that
in season grows.*

William Shakespeare, from
Love's Labour's Lost

CHRISTMAS'S ENEMIES EMERGE

It is not surprising that some members of the clergy objected to the way in which Christ's birth was being commemorated: Aside from the gluttony and games, they worried about observing Jesus' birth as if he were a person rather than the Incarnate God. Celebrations of the Nativity should be more spiritual, they argued, or perhaps abolished outright.

The more Christmas became established in the customs and hearts of the people, the more worried the clergy became. Old worries about the pagan elements of the celebration began to surface again, and some church officials questioned the prudence of having allowed them to continue in the first place. Should they put a halt to all this before things went too far?

With the Protestant Reformation, these objections gained the backing of an organized power. Beginning in 1517 with the posting of Luther's ninety-five theses, the Reformation attacked religious feasts and Saint's Days, among other things, as corrupt practices. Christmas was outlawed in Scotland in 1583.

The Protestants and Puritans of England also condemned the gluttony, drinking, and partying associated with Christmas celebrations and argued for all pagan customs to be done away with. Most Protestants observed Christmas as a day of quiet reflection; the Puritans, however, did not observe it at all. Strict interpreters of the Scriptures, the Puritans pointed to the commandment to devote six to days for work and one to rest. Unless Christmas happened to fall on the Sabbath, it was considered a work day.

By the middle of the seventeenth century, the holiday was under fire. The feelings of previously small pockets of objectors began to have mass impact as the political situation in England became increasingly unstable. From 1642 to 1649 the country was engaged in civil war as a result of the power struggle between the Stuart kings and Parliament; over this time England entered its Commonwealth period and was ruled by Oliver Cromwell and the Puritans. Christmas's enemies began taking the first steps toward defeating the holiday. The government issued official policies outlawing all religious festivals.

"Whereas some doubts have been raised whether the next Fast shall be celebrated because it falleth on the day which, heretofore, was usually called the Feast of the Nativity of our Saviour, the lords and commons do order and ordain that public notice be given, that the Fast appointed to be kept on the last Wednesday in every month, ought to be observed until it be otherwise ordered by both houses; and that this day particularly is to be kept with the same solemn humiliation because it may call to remembrance our sins and the sins of our forefathers, who have turned this Feast, pretending the memory of Christ, into an extreme forgetfulness of him, by giving liberty to carnal and sensual delights."

1644 English proclamation outlawing public Christmas revelries

The era of the Puritan reign was filled with such laws, updated over the years to be even more strict. At first such declarations caused a great deal of upheaval among the people, who were unprepared for such a step and objected to the idea to begin with. In the initial days of

these ordinances, the people tried to disobey, and there was even some rioting. Gradually, however, the Puritans won out.

And so Christmas was now an outlaw, as were those who celebrated it in any way. Carols were deemed illegal and churches were locked, even to clergy.

Technically, the Puritans objected to Christmas not as a Christian event but as an excessive festival with pagan roots; apparently they believed the only way to deal with such impious doings was to abolish the day and everything associated with it. They meant to banish this "wrong" not only from the country but from the hearts of its subjects. And they came very close to succeeding—but then came the Restoration.

THE ENGLISH BANS ARE LIFTED

Christmas was legitimized again when the monarchy, led by Charles II, returned to power in 1660. The holiday could be observed freely again, and people were happy. The popular sentiment of the time was expressed in this verse:

Now thanks to God for Charles' return,
Whose absence made old Christmas mourn;
For then we scarcely did it know,
Whether it Christmas were or no.

With the good will of the new leaders, and with the lifting of the formal bans instituted under the Puritans, Christmas seemed to be positioned for a comeback of titanic proportions in England. But it was not to be.

*England was merry England, when
Old Christmas was brought his
sports again.
'Twas Christmas broach'd the
mightiest ale;
'Twas Christmas told the merriest tale;
A Christmas gambol oft could cheer
The poor man's heart through
half the year.*

Sir Walter Scott

The holiday was, at the outset of the Restoration, a shadow of what it had been. The pagan excesses and riotous elements were not the only things lost to the Puritan purge; the Christmas spirit seemed to have simply left many hearts and minds.

Indeed, although the Puritans had been deposed, much of their philosophy still carried a lot of weight, and many carried on as if they were still in power. Christmas may have been legal, but it was still opposed by some powerful members of the clergy. This left a good many parishioners in a bind, and kept the holiday from making much of a public recovery from the latter part of the seventeenth century onward. The middle of the eighteenth brought still more obstacles.

*What stood in the way of the large-scale
public celebration of Christmas in
England as the Industrial Revolution
began? A good deal of the problem had to
do with the appalling social conditions
that would eventually be chronicled
by Charles Dickens.*

Surprising as it may seem, as the years passed and the era of Puritan rule became a more and more distant memory, the outlook for Christmas actually got worse, thanks to continuing resistance from some members of the clergy and a changing social climate. By the time the Industrial Revolution had begun, all thoughts had seemingly turned toward work; everything took a back seat to the quest for money and progress. In this fast-paced atmosphere, it appeared, there was simply no room for holidays.

Charles Dickens' stinging literary indictments of mindless greed and soul-crushing poverty appear not only in *A Christmas Carol*, but in much of the rest of his work as well. The numbing, inescapable want of most English workers and their families was one of the chief reasons people had a hard  time finding much to celebrate during this period.

At the end of the day, common people didn't have much to celebrate with, and they didn't have much time, either. England had entered into the era of child labor, miserable working conditions, and endless work weeks. Not that things were *all* bad: some benevolent employers actually gave their workers half the day off for Christmas.

Don't celebrate—work! In 1761, the Bank of England closed for forty-seven holidays over the course of a year; in 1834, it closed for only four. Employees of the middle nineteenth century considered themselves lucky to get a half-day off for Christmas.

Throughout this period, however, there were small, quiet groups of people who kept the holiday alive in their hearts and homes. But mass enjoyment of the holiday would not take place again until the Victorian Era.

THE GERMANS KEEP THE FLAME ALIVE

While public celebration of Christmas faced both religious objections and adverse social conditions in England, the German people were enjoying a wonderful and expansive Christmas tradition that had been building up over the centuries. It is very likely that the American love affair with Christmas that began in the late nineteenth and early twentieth centuries, so influential in the way the whole world now views the holiday, would have never occurred if it had not been for the enthusiastic influence of Christmas-loving German immigrants.

The Germans have long espoused the idea of keeping the spirit of Christmas alive inside—in one's heart, mind and spirit—and turning that feeling outward in mass celebration. The German Christmas is a Christmas of trees, gingerbread houses, cookies, feasts, and carols; most of all, it is the Christmas of childhood wonder and joy.

The Christmas season in Germany is about the longest anywhere: a month and a half. Starting with St. Andrew's Night on November 30, the country throws itself into a festive abandon that doesn't wind down until January 13, the Octave of Epiphany. Between those days, *sixteen* holidays are observed, and life is filled with both strict devotion to the Christ Child and joyous merriment. The cities are brimming with *Christkindl-markts* (Christ Child Markets), fairs, parades, and carolers. The smell of gingerbread and other delicious treats is in the air, and Christmas trees are everywhere. Other German contributions to the world's celebration of Christmas include the timeless carols *"O Tannenbaum"* ("Oh, Christmas Tree") and "Silent Night."

Many legends surround the origin of the Christmas tree, but whatever the specifics, there is no doubt that it was perfected in Germany.

The German people have had an enormous part to play in shaping Christmas into the form we know and love today. It has been said that the Germans had "such an abundance of Christmas spirit that they gave some of it to the rest of the world."

One of the beneficiaries of the German love of Christmas was Victorian England. Victoria assumed the throne in 1837 at the age of eighteen; three years later she married Prince Albert, who became Prince Consort. Prince Albert, being of German descent, brought with him to England many of the wonderful Christmas traditions of his homeland. Christmas soon became a special occasion for the Royal Family; their celebration of it emphasized the importance of family closeness and an appreciation of children, and revived the idea of the holiday meal and holiday decorations. In 1841 Prince Albert introduced the first Christmas tree to Windsor Castle; he was largely responsible for the later popularity of Christmas trees in England.

Since Victoria and her family enjoyed an astonishing popularity that verged at times on religious adoration, much of what they did was widely emulated. Newspapers and magazines such as The *Illustrated London News* provided a hungry audience with chronicles of the royals' daily activities. Anything seen in the castle, it seemed, was soon copied in homes throughout the country, providing the English Christmas with a much-needed boost.

THE VICTORIAN CHRISTMAS ∾

Gradually, over the course of Victoria's reign, the tide turned. Christmas once more had an important place in English life.

The Victorian Christmas was quaint and warm, highlighted by family togetherness. Christmas became more than a party. It commanded a special spirit, full of kindness and charity. More prevalent than the excesses of the past was the idea of giving, of concern for others, particularly those less fortunate. As Charles Dickens said, Christmas was "the only time I know of, in the long calendar of the year, when men and women seem by one consent to open their shut-up hearts freely."

Dickens himself had a large role in reviving the Christmas spirit in his countrymen. With the publication of *A Christmas Carol* in 1843, people were reminded of what the holiday truly meant, and all that it could be and bring to their lives.

The Christmas card was created during the Victorian Era, and it enjoyed great popularity. So did carols, which got their biggest boost since they had become legal again under Charles II. There was now caroling in church, caroling in homes, and bands of carolers roaming the streets. Most of the images we have today of outdoor carolers are from these times.

After all that caroling and good cheer, there were bound to be some hungry mouths to feed. The Victorian Christmas menu is doubtless the one most people envision when thinking of a "classic" Christmas dinner: turkey, goose or roast beef, mince pie, Yorkshire and plum pudding, wassail, and eggnog. To aid in digestion, there were games like Shadow

Buff, the Memory Game, Poker and Tongs, and the Minister's Cat; there was also the ubiquitous sprig of mistletoe.

The custom of giving gifts on Christmas Day did not come about until the last few decades of the century; before that, England adhered to the old Roman tradition of waiting until New Year's Day. When Christmas eventually became the day for gifts, it was England's turn to borrow from America, whose Santa Claus became the model for the English Father Christmas.

By the beginning of the twentieth century, Christmas was fully reestablished as a holiday, steeped again in tradition and spirit. The Victorians had helped to mold a Christmas tradition that would forever alter the way Christmas was celebrated in England and America.

CHAPTER TWO

The WHYS And WHEREFORES of CHRISTMAS CUSTOMS

Why do we kiss under mistletoe? Where did the
Christmas tree originate? Who printed the first
Christmas card? Why do we leave gifts in stockings?
When did Santa get his reindeer? The answers to
these and many other Christmas questions are
all here!

WHY CHRISTMAS IS ABBREVIATED AS XMAS

The "X" in Xmas stands for the Greek letter "Chi," the first letter in the Greek word for Christ. Over time, the letter "X" came to stand for the name of Christ. The practice gained very wide usage in the mass media during the twentieth century— but not, as many erroneously believe, because of any squeamishness about using the word "Christmas." Often, Xmas simply fits better in a headline.

RED AND GREEN

Why are red and green the colors of Christmas? No one really knows for sure, but there have been plenty of educated guesses. Green is the easiest of the two to theorize about; it is the color of the ever-greens that symbolize so much that is important to the meaning of the holiday. (See the earlier chapter on the history of Christmas, which gives a full account of the importance of greenery in the early Christmas festivals.) The holly berry seems to be responsible for the red: The red berry that lives through winter, symbolizing life in the face of death, represents Christ.

THE ADVENT WREATH

The season of Advent begins the fourth Sunday before Christmas. A season of preparation, it is a

solemn time to make ready for the coming of Christ and Christmas. As a way to mark the coming of Christmas, the church may use an Advent Wreath containing five candles. On the first Sunday of Advent one candle is lit; on the second, two, and so on. Finally on Christmas Eve the fifth candle is lit, representing Christ, the light of the world.

CANDLEMAS DAY

According to Jewish law, a mother had to be brought to the temple forty days after her child's birth in order to be purified. If Jesus was born on December 25, then February 2 would have been the day Mary underwent this ritual, an event that has been commemorated in the church each year on that day since the late seventh century, when Pope Sergius I began the tradition. During the ceremony, candles are also blessed, giving the day its name. In England it is considered bad luck to keep Christmas greenery up after this day.

NATIVITY SCENES

The first nativity scene was created at the church of Santa Maria Maggiore in tenth-century Rome. The custom was soon popular at other churches, each one constructing ornate mangers with gold, silver, jewels, and precious stones. Though popular among high society, such opulence was far removed from the original circumstances of Christ's birth, as well as being inaccessible to the poorer masses.

We owe the crèche to St. Francis of Assisi, who revised the gaudier displays of his time. In 1224 St. Francis of Assisi sought to remedy these problems by creating the first manger scene that was true to the Biblical account of Christ's birth. Called a crèche, the scene that St. Francis set up for the village of Greccio was made up of hay, carved figures, and live animals, capturing for the unlettered people of the town more of the spirit and the story of Christ's

birth than any splendid art treasure.

The popularity of St. Francis's crèche spread throughout the world. In Italy it is called a *presepio*; in Germany, a *Krippe*. It is a *naciemiento* in Spain and Latin America, a *jeslicky* in the Czech Republic, a *pesebre* in Brazil, and a *portal* in Costa Rica.

THE CHRISTMAS ROSE

A legend surrounds the origin of the Christmas Rose: Once there was a young girl who wanted to worship the baby Jesus, but felt she could not because she had no present. Saddened, the girl began to cry; as her tears fell to the ground, they created a bush bearing a beautiful white rose, which she gave to the Holy Infant.

FEASTS ≈

Extravagant feasts played a large part in the winter solstice festivals of ages past. Apart from being a gathering where people exchanged good will and cheer, the mere existence of these feasts displayed faith in the prosperity of the upcoming year. Holiday feasting hit its peak in medieval England, where the king and his court were constantly trying to outdo each other with outrageous quantities of food and drink. The guests at these festivities preferred their food to be presented looking as much like its animal of origin as possible. Not that the work was admired for long once it made it to the table. Conspicuous consumption was, after all, the order of the day.

By Victorian times, the boar's head, roasted oxen, and other wild beasts had been replaced by turkey,

goose, plum pudding, and Yorkshire pudding. Though there are still many traditional menu items, these days the food on the table is not as important as the idea of a gathering with family and friends, full of warmth and Christmas spirit.

CHRISTKIND ≈

This German name for the Christ Child originally referred directly to the Holy Infant Jesus himself, who was said to bring gifts to children in Germany, Austria, Switzerland, and the Pennsylvania Dutch region on Christmas Eve. (Other forms of the name are *Christkindli* and *Christkindlein*.)

≈

Although Kris Kringle has become popular as another name for the Santa Claus figure, in fact it is a variant of the German for "Christ Child."

Later the name came to stand for the embodiment of the Child's spirit, in angelic form, who brought the gifts in his place. Veiled in white, with gold wings upon his shoulders, he arrives secretly, often through an open window; when he is through with his work, he rings a bell to notify all that the presents have arrived. Over the years the name has evolved to Kris Kringle, but contrary to popular belief, the *Christkind* is *not* another form of Santa Claus.

CRADLE ROCKING ∽

Beautiful in its simplicity and intent, the custom of cradle rocking began in medieval Germany as a way to symbolize the human significance of Christ. At the midnight Mass, the priest and altar boys would gently rock the cradle of the infant Jesus, sometimes singing lullabies. Though the tradition was later outlawed during the Protestant Reformation, it endures during the holiday season in some places.

THE BIRD'S CHRISTMAS TREE ∽

Also known as the Sheaf of Grain, the Bird's Christmas Tree is a Scandinavian custom. A sheaf of grain is hung on a pole on Christmas Eve or Christmas Day as a way of sharing the Christmas spirit with the animals. Including the animals in Christmas is very important in Scandinavia, as it is believed that kindness to animals will help to insure a prosperous new year.

BELLS AND OTHER JOYOUS NOISEMAKERS ∽

A holdover from pagan times, bells and other noisemakers were believed to frighten away evil spirits. As part of the midwinter solstice festivals, bell-ringing activities were very rowdy, mixing some fun in with the serious intent. As late as the 1890s in the United States, children thought of Christmas and noisemakers as nearly synonymous. The demise of the tiny, wildly popular Christmas firecracker may have as much to do with care for parental eardrums

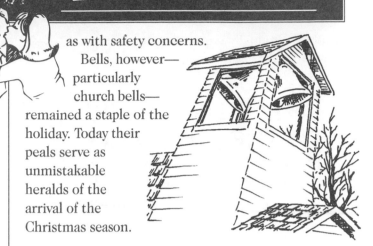

as with safety concerns.

Bells, however—particularly church bells—remained a staple of the holiday. Today their peals serve as unmistakable heralds of the arrival of the Christmas season.

THE BOAR'S HEAD ∽

According to an old English legend, there was once a philosophy student who fended off an attacking wild boar by choking the animal with a book on Aristotle. When the boar was dead, the student cut off his head to remove the book, then brought the head back to his college, where he and his friends had a grand feast. Soon boar's head was a must for every English household at Christmas.

Although this legend seeks to explain the popularity of the boar's head as part of the Christmas feast, a more likely explanation is that the custom is another remnant of pagan times. In some places, the German god Frey was considered responsible for the well-being of livestock. As Frey was symbolized by the boar, a boar was often sacrificed in hopes of a prosperous spring herd.

Like many Christmas traditions popular in medieval England, the boar's head custom eventually became impractical and died out. Boars became increasingly hard to track down and were dangerous to catch once they were found. Then, too, the week's worth of cooking and preparation required was more conducive to a well-staffed castle kitchen than that of a home. (The passing of the Christmas festival may have added to the time crunch.) The boar's head was gradually replaced by the more familiar pork, roast beef, turkey, and goose.

THE LORD OF MISRULE AND THE MUMMERS

The Lord of Misrule played a major part in the Christmas festivities in medieval England. Like the Boy Bishop, he was the leader of many holiday activities, but he also had real power, and his whims had to be obeyed by all, even the king. The Lord of Misrule was a strictly secular figure, appointed by the king and the nobility to reign over the twelve days of Christmas. The man chosen for this position, however, was generally wise enough not to abuse his power when dealing with the nobility. Much of the custom surrounding the Lord of Misrule and the mummers had parallels with the Roman Saturnalia, during which masters and slaves changed places, with general rowdiness abounding.

Out on the streets among the common people, the Lord of Misrule was head of the mummers, a traveling band of rowdy players who roamed the streets in costume performing plays, songs, and so on. Though they stuck to the streets for the most part, the mummers were sometimes known to barge into churches and disrupt the service, an act that did not sit well with church officials.

The mummers, roving street carousers all, offered just about anything that would win the attention of passersby. The classic mummer's play has a number of variations, but it always focuses on the death and revival of one of the principals.

The ancestors of street actors, the mummers did it all: plays, songs, comedy routines, and nearly any other diversion that came to mind.

Like carolers, mummers would often perform in exchange for goodies, though their performances were often disruptive and sacrilegious. When the Puritans came to power, they did away with the Lord of Misrule and his companions. Though the restored monarchy reinstated most of the Christmas traditions outlawed by the Puritans, the Lord of Misrule remained an outlaw. He and the mummers never again enjoyed the freedom and popularity they had had in medieval England.

THE BOY BISHOP

The Boy Bishop was a popular figure in medieval Christmas festivities, inspired by the life of St. Nicholas, who, while still in his teens, was appointed Bishop of Myra. In medieval times the boy chosen to be Bishop would preside over certain portions of the Christmas festivities. The Bishop's "reign" usually began on December 6, St. Nicholas' Day, and would last until December 28, the Feast of the Holy Innocents. During this time the Boy Bishop acted as a priest of sorts, blessing people, bringing up the offerings, and leading the choir. He always dressed the part, and in some countries Boy Bishop services were very elaborate.

In time, however, the innocence of this tradition was lost, as it became overshadowed by rowdiness; Boy Bishop services were often seen as an excuse to parody the church and have wild parties. The Boy Bishop had become too closely associated with the figure of the Lord of Misrule for many people's taste, and as a result was eventually outlawed by the church. The popular tradition did not die out completely, however, until Henry VIII banned him from England in 1542.

BOXING DAY

No, it has nothing to do with prizefighting. In England it was customary for churches to open their alms boxes to the poor on the first workday after Christmas in an attempt to give some cheer to those who could not afford a very merry Christmas. Out of this custom grew Boxing Day, on which service people and other workers would collect money or treats from their employers.

MIDNIGHT MASS

The most popular Christmas Mass for Roman Catholics is the midnight Mass, a tradition that began in the early 400s. Midnight Mass is important because tradition holds that Christ was born at midnight.

In Spanish and Latin countries, the midnight Mass is referred to as the Mass of the Rooster, after the legend that says the only time a rooster ever crowed at midnight was at the moment of Christ's birth. The Polish midnight Mass is called *Mass Pasterka*, (Mass of the Shepherds), in reverence to the shepherds present in accounts of the first Christmas.

THE LEGEND OF *LA BEFANA*

The legend of *La Befana* explains how this elderly woman came to be the one who brings gifts to the children of Italy on Epiphany Eve. The old woman, a very particular housekeeper, was visited one day by the Wise Men, who sought directions to Bethlehem. They offered to take the woman with them to pay homage to the Baby Jesus, but she declined, too busy cleaning her house to be bothered. In time the woman came to regret her decision and set out after the Wise Men, only to get lost herself. Though she never found the Wise Men or the Baby Jesus, she still wanders the world searching, leaving gifts with the children of each house she passes by in honor of the one child she missed.

There is a similar legend in Russia, about a woman called the *Babushka*; both women bring coal to bad children.

THE LEGEND OF THE POINSETTIA

The legend of the plant we now associate so strongly with Christmas arose years ago in Mexico, where it was traditional to leave gifts on the altar for Jesus on Christmas Eve. As the story goes, among a group of worshipers one night was a poor boy who had no present. Upset by his inability to provide a gift, the boy knelt outside the church window and prayed. In the spot where he knelt there sprung a beautiful plant with vibrant red leaves. In  Mexico this plant is called "the Flower of the Holy Night."

The first American Ambassador to Mexico (1825–1829), Dr. Joel Roberts Poinsett, was impressed by the vibrant plant Mexicans called "the Flower of the Holy Night." He brought it to America, where it was subsequently renamed in his honor.

Today, Encitas, California, is called the poinsettia capital of the world because of the large number of poinsettias found there.

STOCKINGS

The idea of hanging stockings out on Christmas Eve is believed to have come from Amsterdam, where children leave out their shoes on St. Nicholas's Eve in hopes that he will fill them with goodies. But where did the people of Amsterdam get the idea? Perhaps from St. Nicholas himself. One of the most popular stories surrounding the saint concerns his generosity to the three daughters of a poor family. It seems the daughters were of marriageable age, but could not marry because they had no dowry. Nicholas heard of their plight and set out to help them. In the middle of the night (he wanted his act to be a secret), Nicholas threw bags of gold coins down the girl's chimney. The bags landed in the girl's stockings, which they had hung out to dry. (For a more detailed account of the life of St. Nicholas, see chapter five.)

SANTA'S SLEIGH AND REINDEER

The popularity of Santa and his reindeer is largely due to Clement C. Moore, who put the two together in his wildly successful poem, "A Visit from St. Nicholas." But Moore was not the first to pair Santa with hoofed friends. Before Moore published his poem, there had been a number of less successful books that portrayed Santa flying around in a sleigh pulled by *one* reindeer. This concept had long been popular in Russia, where Father Frost arrived in the villages in a reindeer-drawn sleigh. The Norse god Wodin was said to ride his horse Sleipner through the air to make sure people were behaving; in Holland St. Nicholas rides Sleipner to this day.

Today, Rudolph, "the red-nosed reindeer," is by far the most popular of Santa's nine; he is also the youngest (or at any rate the most recent arrival). The first eight reindeer were introduced by Moore in 1823; Rudolph did not come along until 1939, in a story by Robert L. May. Rudolph's notoriety owes much to the popularity of the Gene Autry song "Rudolph the Red-Nosed Reindeer," released in 1949 and a holiday classic to this day.

CHRISTMAS ANIMALS

Along with the comparatively recent addition of reindeer, a few other animals have commonly been linked to Christmas. Camels, goats, sheep, horses,

and donkeys have all been associated with the Biblical story of the nativity, although only sheep are mentioned explicitly, and most recreations of the nativity include some, if not all, of these animals. In some countries the Camel of Jesus brings gifts to the children.

In Hamlet, *Shakespeare cites a legend of the "bird of dawning," which was said to sing the whole night through at Christmastime.*

In addition, there are abiding legends about animals having received the power to speak on the night Christ was born; some say that every year between Christmas Eve and Christmas morning this power returns and the animals speak. Another legend has the oxen kneeling every Christmas Eve at midnight.

WASSAIL

Wassail was a popular Christmas drink in England, particularly in Victorian times. The drink's name comes from the old toast expression *waes hael* (to your health), and is made of eggs, curdled cream, nuts, spices, roasted apples, and mulled ale. In  pagan times wassail was thought to provide more than just good cheer. During the agricultural festivals, groups would visit apple trees and douse them with wassail to ensure that the next apple harvest would be plentiful. This ritual also involved a great deal of noise making to ward off evil, which helped to instill a festive atmosphere. From this ritual grew wassail's association with parties. Now that its significance to the apple harvest has been more or less forgotten, wassail is considered no more than a tasty holiday drink—a rowdy eggnog.

STARS

The Star of Bethlehem, often found at the top of a Christmas tree or on a plate of Christmas cookies, is strictly Christian in origin.

The nature of the star mentioned in the Bible remains a mystery. For an account of the ongoing debate regarding its mythical or factual status, see chapter one.

THE YULE LOG

The tradition of the yule log has very deep pagan roots. Celts, Teutons, and Druids burned the massive logs in winter ceremonies in celebration of the sun. The selection of each season's yule log was of the highest importance and surrounded by ceremony, as the log was to start the celebration fires and last for the duration of the winter festival.

In the Christian era, the log was often cut on February 2 (Candlemas Day), then set outside to dry during the late spring and summer; sometimes it was soaked in spices and decorated with greenery. Often a piece of the previous year's log was used to light the new log. In Scandinavia this saved piece had the additional significance of representing good will from Thor. Scandinavians believed that Thor's lighting bolt would not strike burned wood, and that their houses were safe from lightning as long as they had this yule brand.

When Christianity emerged in Europe, the yule log remained popular in England and Scandinavia. In order to justify this pagan ritual, church officials gave it a new significance, that of the light that came from Heaven when Christ was born. The log was lit on Christmas Eve and left burning throughout the twelve days of Christmas.

In the American South, plantation slaves always tried to select the biggest possible yule log. As long as the log burned, the slaves had to be paid for any work they did.

In some parts of France the yule log was presented as the source of children's gifts. The log was covered with cloth and brought into the house, where the children whacked it with sticks, beseeching it to bring forth presents. When no presents came, the children were sent outside to confess the sins they had committed that year; when they returned, the log was uncovered, surrounded by gifts.

Changes brought by the Industrial Revolution finally made the Yule Log impractical. Few had the time or space for the preparations it required, and the small fireplaces of the city could not accommodate such a massive thing. Like the boar's head, the huge yule log became, for most people, an emblem of the past.

CANDLES

In the time of darkness surrounding the winter solstice, candles were important as a source of light and heat. During the Saturnalia, Romans lit candles to convince the sun to shine again and to ward off evil. From this pagan start the candle has gone on to become an essential part of Christmas lighting, both in church ceremonies and at home. For Christians it symbolizes Christ himself, the light of the world; candles are used during Advent to mark the days before the coming of Christmas. The Candlemas services that celebrate the purification of Mary forty days after Christ's birth (February 2) take their name from the candles that are blessed during the ceremony.

In Victorian times candles came to represent concern and good will for the poor and unfortunate during the holiday season. Candles were placed in windows over the twelve days of Christmas as a sign to needy passersby that shelter and warmth could be found within.

The first string of electric Christmas tree lights was not sold until 1903. Only the wealthy could afford them, however, and only those with indoor electric outlets could use them. Most people continued to follow the earlier (and dangerous) tradition of affixing small lighted candles to the boughs of the tree. Larger trees bore hundreds of candles.

Candles were the preferred means of lighting Christmas trees for many years. Although replaced on trees and in windows by electric replicas for the most part, real candles are still used in caroling ceremonies and church celebrations today.

GREENERY

Pagan peoples long revered evergreens for their ability to stay alive during the cold dark winters. Often considered magical, greenery in various forms adorned the inside and outside of houses during the winter solstice festivals. Church officials at first attempted to banish greenery, then decided it would better serve their purpose to translate the beloved custom to Christian terms. Evergreens came to symbolize Christ, who in his triumph over death gave the gift of everlasting life to the world.

Greenery, as a general term, refers to those trees and plants that remain green and flourishing all year round. Though cypress, box, yew, rosemary, and laurel are all considered greenery, they are not as common to Christmas as holly, ivy, mistletoe, and, of course, …

THE CHRISTMAS TREE

The Christmas tree is by far the most popular form of greenery in the United States. Indeed, it has become such an integral part of our Christmas celebration that most people cannot imagine celebrating the holiday without one in their living room. Yet the tree is, like much we associate with Christmas, a relatively recent innovation.

The decorated Christmas tree apparently had no broad popularity in colonial America; the tradition, followed by German immigrants for years, did not catch on in other parts of society until the 1830s. It is said that the Hessians defeated by George Washington in the Battle of Trenton in 1776 may have been observing the holiday in the custom of their homeland by setting lighted candles upon the boughs of a tree.

No one seems to be able to explain the reasons behind the popularity of the Christmas tree, but along with Santa it is now the most common secular entity associated with Christmas in the United States. For most of us, the tree's attractiveness needs no explanation. The beauty, the smell, the fun of decorating, the spirit, the memories of holidays past—whether of pine, fir, or cedar, there is simply nothing like a good Christmas tree.

As early as the Roman Saturnalia, trees were hung with decorations, but this custom did not become part of Christmas until the Middle Ages. Like all greenery with pagan origins, the tree has long been assigned Christian significance, but how it came to be so

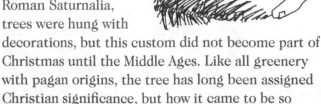

important to Christmas is the subject of much debate. The earliest record of a decorated tree is from an English book printed in 1441, which describes a tree set up in the middle of a village, decorated with ivy. The popular consensus, however, is that the Christmas tree as we know it originated in Germany.

According to one legend, St. Boniface, who helped organize the Christian church in France and Germany during the mid-700s, was responsible for the first Christmas tree. One Christmas Eve, St. Boniface was traveling through the forest and happened upon a group of people gathered around an oak tree preparing to sacrifice a child to the god Thor. In protest of this act, St. Boniface destroyed the oak, either with an ax or a single blow from his fist. In any event, when the oak was felled, a fir tree appeared in its place. St. Boniface informed the people that this was the Tree of Life, representing Christ.

Another familiar legend holds that when Christ was born, all the animals received the power to speak and the trees bloomed and brought forth fruit, despite the harsh winter. All the grand trees came forth to pay homage to the Lord, except one tiny fir tree, embarrassed by her stature. But then the Lord came down and lighted the fir tree's branches, making her sparkle, and she was no longer ashamed.

In yet another legend a poor man gave shelter and food to a needy child one Christmas Eve. The child turned out to be the Christ Child; in return for the man's generosity, the Child created a small, lighted fir tree that grew outside the house.

The most popular Christmas tree legend of all concerns Martin Luther. One Christmas Eve, as Luther was ambling through the forest, he became enraptured by the

beauty of the starlight playing off the evergreen branches. Luther chopped down a tree and brought it home, where he lit it with candles in an effort to duplicate the scene for his family. Though Martin Luther himself never mentioned this event, the legend spread throughout the land.

❧

Because of Martin Luther's supposed association with the Christmas tree, strictly Roman Catholic inhabitants of southern Germany would not have trees in their homes until the nineteenth century, when news of the custom's popularity in America traveled overseas.

❧

Though these legends are entertaining, most experts believe that the truth behind the Christmas tree is much less spectacular. In the fourteenth and fifteenth centuries, pine trees were used in Europe as part of the miracle plays performed in front of cathedrals at Christmas time. The plays detailed the birth and fall of humanity, its salvation through the death and resurrection of Christ, and Christ's promise of redemption. The pine trees, decorated with apples, symbolized the Tree of Life in the Garden of Eden.

Though such plays were later banned by the church, the tradition of this Paradise Tree, or *Paradeisbaum*, was kept alive in individual homes. People began decorating the trees with wafers to represent the Eucharist; later these wafers evolved into cookies, cakes, fruit, and other goodies. At first these foods were shaped to represent some aspect of the Nativity, but in time they came to depict anything the decorator's heart desired.

To this day, the Christmas tree enjoys incredible popularity in Germany. The decorating of the tree is one of the most anticipated events of the holiday, and in some homes each family member has his or her own tree. So beloved is the Christmas tree in Germany that the most popular carol there after "Silent Night" is *"O, Tannenbaum"* ("Oh, Christmas Tree").

By the 1800s, the Christmas tree had spread to Norway, Finland, Sweden, Denmark, and Austria. In Scandinavia, fishermen of old trimmed trees with fish nets and flags. Today it is more common in those countries to decorate with cookies, candy, fruit, lighted candles, and flags.

The most famous tree in Great Britain is a gift each year from Norway, in appreciation for Britain's help to them during World War II. When Norway was occupied by the Nazis, King Haakan set up a free

Norwegian government in London. Since 1947 Norway has, each year, presented the people of Britain with an enormous tree at least seventy feet high, which is set up in Trafalgar Square for all to enjoy.

∽

Popular with wealthy Americans around the end of the nineteenth century were combination tree-stands and music boxes; these rotated the tree and played soothing music.

∽

In America, the Christmas tree caught on in the nineteenth century and has become almost as beloved as it is in Germany. Most homes have some type of Christmas tree during the holidays; trees can be found everywhere from department stores to offices to churches. Even trees growing outside are decorated.

∽

Famous U.S. Christmas Trees:

The tree in Rockefeller Center, ninety feet high, has been a tradition since 1933.

"The Nation's Christmas Tree" is located in General Grant National Park in Sanger, California. The huge Sequoia was given this honor on Christmas Day, 1925. It measures 267 feet high and 107 feet around, and is 3,500 years old.

In Washington, a tree near the White House in Sherman Square known as "The National Living Christmas Tree" is lit every year by a member of the First Family.

The demand for trees during the Christmas season has made the tree-growing business a sizable industry. Commercial trees are grown in controlled forests. Synthetic trees have also become an option, considered by some to be less messy and safer around electric lights. Many artificial trees are sold each year; it is unlikely, however, that the aroma of old plastic will ever summon up childhood memories in quite the same way as that of a fresh-cut fir. Purists will always argue that nothing can replace the fragrance and appearance of a real tree.

The first church in this country to display a tree was that of pastor Henry Schwan in Cleveland, Ohio. President and Mrs. Franklin Pierce were the first to popularize the Christmas tree in the White House.

ORNAMENTS

The earliest Christmas ornaments consisted of edible goodies, typically fruits and nuts; eventually these made way for cookies, candy, and cakes. Flowers and paper decorations provided non-edible beauty.

The first commercial "ornaments" for Christmas trees were actually hollow, brightly colored containers that held good things to eat. The most popular of these was probably the cornucopia.

When the goodies got too heavy for the tree, German glassblowers began manufacturing the first glass ornaments. But these and other purely decorative elements would not be the main attraction of the Christmas tree for some years. (Originally, trees were the means by which presents were displayed on Christmas morning before their owners claimed them. Small toys, candies, and other treats were hung on the boughs; children would awaken and strip the tree.)

HOLLY

In ancient times holly was thought to be magical because of its shiny leaves and its ability to bear fruit in winter. Some believed it contained a syrup that cured coughs; others hung it over their beds to produce good dreams. Holly was a popular Saturnalia gift among the Romans. The Romans later brought holly to England, where it was also considered sacred. In medieval times, holly, along with ivy, became the subject of many Christmas songs. Some of these songs gave the holly and ivy sexual identities (holly is male, ivy female), while other, more religious, songs and poems portray the holly berry as a symbol of Christ.

IVY

In pagan times ivy was closely associated with Bacchus, the god of wine, and played a big part in all festivals in which he figured. English tavernkeepers eventually adopted ivy as a symbol and featured it on their signs. Its festive past has not kept ivy from being incorporated into modern Christian celebrations, however.

MISTLETOE

To this day mistletoe—a parasitic plant that grows on oak and other nonevergreen trees—is the only form of greenery not allowed inside a Christian church during the holiday season. Although other greenery was also used in pagan festivals, mistletoe was actually worshiped.

Both Druids and Romans considered the plant sacred, as a healing plant and a charm against evil. Mistletoe was thought to be the connection between earth and the heavens, because it grew without roots, as if by magic. Mistletoe was also considered a symbol of peace; warring soldiers who found themselves under mistletoe quickly put down their weapons and made a temporary truce. In a related custom, ancient Britons hung mistletoe in their doorways to keep evil away. Those who entered the house

safely were given a welcome kiss.

While the custom of kissing under the mistletoe lost popularity in most other countries, it remained popular in England and the United States. Today, most consider mistletoe an excuse for kissing and nothing more, but some people in France still brew it as a cure for stomachaches.

THE KISSING BOUGH

Though its name might suggest otherwise, the kissing bough was not made just out of mistletoe, but includes holly, ivy, and other evergreens. Shaped in a double hoop with streamers flowing from the top, the kissing bough was decorated with apples, pears, ribbon, and lighted candles. As with plain mistletoe, anyone found under the bough was to be kissed forthwith. The kissing bough was very popular, particularly in England, before the heyday of the Christmas tree.

People who celebrate Christmas in warm weather do not depend so much on greenery to decorate their holiday as Europeans and those living in colder climates. The Christmas bell (bell-shaped flowers) and the Christmas bush (little red flowers) are common Christmas sights in Australia; the poinsettia abounds in Mexico during the holiday season.

CHRISTMAS CARDS

The distinction of having created the first Christmas card is usually given to John Calcott Horsley, but there are some who disagree. Horsley printed his card in 1843 for Sir Henry Cole, the friend who had given him the idea. The card looked much like a postcard and consisted of three panels. The central panel pictured the typical English family of the day enjoying the holiday; this panel caused some controversy, as it showed a child drinking wine. The other panels depicted acts of charity, so important to the Victorian Christmas spirit. The card's inscription read "Merry Christmas and a Happy New Year to You." A thousand copies of the card were printed, selling for one shilling apiece.

But around the same time as Horsley, two other men, W. A. Dobson and Reverend Edward Bradley, were designing cards and sending them to their friends. These cards, however, were hand-created instead of printed.

Christmas cards soon became the popular means of sending holiday greetings among the Victorians. Most of the cards were not particularly religious. The onset of the "penny post" in 1840 had made it affordable for people to send greetings by mail, and the invention of the steam press made mass production of these cards possible. At one time in Britain the Post Office delivered on Christmas Day, which is when most people received their cards. As could be expected, this process soon became too much for postal workers, who eventually got the day off.

Across the water, in America, the Christmas card was popularized by the firm of Marcus Ward & Co., and later by Louis Prang, a German-born printer and lithographer. Prang first turned his talents toward Christmas cards in 1875, designing and printing them from his Roxbury, Massachusetts, shop. Prang created chromos, as he called the colored lithographs, in eight colors. His cards depicted Nativity scenes, family Christmas gatherings, nature scenes, and later, Santa. The beauty of

Prang's cards did much to ensure their popularity, but so did his marketing technique. Prang would hold contests all across the country, offering prizes for the best card designs, which spurred public interest. Prang's cards went strong until 1890, when the states began importing cheaper cards from German manufacturers. Americans reclaimed the market twenty years later.

CHRISTMAS SEALS

Like Easter, Christmas has a special seal dedicated to helping those in need. The Christmas Seal, which changes in design each year, was originated in Denmark in 1903 by postal worker Einar Holboell, who felt there should be a special stamp to benefit tuberculosis sufferers. The first seal was printed in 1904 with a picture of Queen Louise of Denmark; over four million were sold. Sweden followed suit that same year; Norway had its own seals by 1905.

The Christmas Seal is popular in America largely due to the efforts of Emily Bissell, state secretary of the Red Cross in Wilmington, Delaware. Word of the success of the seal in Scandinavia had spread to America, and Bissell sought to use such a seal to keep a local tuberculosis treatment center open. The original American Seal, designed in 1907 by Bissell, pictured holly, a cross, and the words "Merry

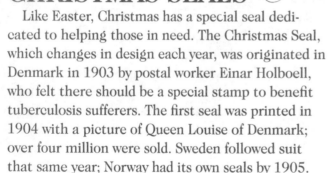

Christmas and Happy New Year." By 1908 the Christmas Seal was circulating nationwide for the benefit of various charities. In 1919 the National Tuberculosis Association (later the American Lung Association) became the seal's sole beneficiary. That same year the double-barred Cross of Lorraine became the seal's signature element.

CHRISTMAS STAMPS

Christmas stamps, not to be confused with Christmas Seals, are issued seasonally to give the mail some holiday spirit. The stamps, which benefit no organization but the United States Postal Service, also feature different religious or secular Christmas scenes each year. The very first Christmas stamps were printed in Canada in 1898; the United States did not have its own until 1962. For some years, the most popular stamp in U.S. history—until the Elvis stamp came along in the '90s—was a Christmas stamp picturing a reproduction of the Renaissance painting "The Adoration of the Shepherds," by the Italian painter Giorgione; over one billion were printed.

THE CHRISTMAS BONUS, THE CHRISTMAS TIP, AND OTHER ECONOMIC NICETIES

The Christmas bonus was first instituted by department store owner F. W. Woolworth in 1899. Woolworth, savvy to the ever-growing fiscal importance of the Christmas shopping season, decided to take steps to insure that his stores ran smoothly through the frenzied buying time. Working under the assumption that happy workers are reliable and productive workers, Woolworth gave a bonus of $5 to each employee for every year of service, bonuses not to exceed $25—quite a sum of money in those days. The holiday bonus has a cousin, the Christmas tip, extended to letter carriers, apartment complex employees, and other workers. Both are outgrowths of the English tradition of giving to the needy on Boxing Day.

In 1876, publishing magnate James Gordon Bennett, Jr., left his breakfast waiter a Christmas tip of $6,000— perhaps $200,000 in today's funds. Initially, the flabbergasted waiter gave the money to his supervisor to return, but Bennett later insisted that he had meant to leave the sum. Whether he did or not remains a matter of conjecture, but the end result was that Bennett's tip was—and is—among the most extravagant on record.

The custom of giving employees the day off for Christmas was apparently not observed in the United States until about 1875. Up until that time, most all work-  ers were expected to report as usual—unless the holiday fell on a Sunday, of course. (No matter the time of year, merchants were forbidden to sell their wares on the Sabbath, although some were arrested for trying to do so during the holiday season.) Store clerks of the era, paid not by the hour but the day, worked thousands of unpaid overtime hours during the holiday rush each year. Woolworth's later generosity toward them was the culmination in a long series of concessions by the owners of retail establishments to harried store workers.

CHAPTER THREE

CHRISTMAS PROSE

The following sample of classic Christmas story-telling runs from Dickens to Morley, and touches just about everything in between. We've included enough read-aloud holiday tales to enchant you and your family for the entire holiday season. Why not read a little a night for the entire month of December?

THE LITTLE WOMEN'S CHRISTMAS
Louisa May Alcott

Published in 1868, *Little Women* was an instant success, particularly with female readers of the time. "Little Women's Christmas" is an excerpt of the book's first two chapters, "Playing Pilgrims" and "A Merry Christmas." The little women themselves stand as a reminder to all who have endured hard times that even a penniless Christmas can be cause for celebration…if it is filled with selfless generosity, love, and faith.

"CHRISTMAS WON'T BE Christmas without any presents," grumbled Jo, lying on the rug.

"It's so dreadful to be poor!" sighed Meg, looking down at her old dress.

"I don't think it's fair for some girls to have lots of pretty things, and other girls nothing at all," added little Amy, with an injured sniff.

"We've got father, and mother, and each other, anyhow," said Beth, contentedly, from her corner.

The four young faces on which the firelight shone brightened at the cheerful words, but darkened again as Jo said sadly, "We haven't got father, and shall not have him for a long time." She didn't say "perhaps never," but each silently added it, thinking of father far away, where the fighting was.

Nobody spoke for a minute; then Meg said in an altered tone, "You know the reason mother proposed not having any presents this Christmas was because it's going to be a hard winter for every one; and she thinks we ought not to spend money for pleasure, when our men are suffering so in the army. We can't do much, but we can make our little sacrifices, and ought to do it gladly. But I am afraid I don't;" and Meg shook her head, as she thought regretfully of all the pretty things she wanted.

"But I don't think the little we should spend would do any good. We've each got a dollar, and the army wouldn't be much helped by our giving that. I agree not to expect anything from mother or you, but I do want to buy *Undine and Sintram* for myself; I've wanted it *so* long," said Jo, who was a bookworm.

"I planned to spend mine in new music," said Beth, with a little sigh, which no one heard but the hearth brush and kettleholder.

"I shall get a nice box of Faber's drawing pencils;

I really need them," said Amy, decidedly.

"Mother didn't say anything about our money, and she won't wish us to give up everything. Let's each buy what we want, and have a little fun; I'm sure we grub hard enough to earn it," cried Jo, examining the heels of her boots in a gentlemanly manner.

"I know *I* do—teaching those dreadful children nearly all day, when I'm longing to enjoy myself at home," began Meg, in the complaining tone again.

"You don't have half such a hard time as I do," said Jo. "How would you like to be shut up for hours with a nervous, fussy old lady, who keeps you trotting, is never satisfied, and worries you till you're ready to fly out of the window or box her ears?"

"It's naughty to fret, but I do think washing dishes and keeping things tidy is the worst work in the world. It makes me cross; and my hands get so stiff, I can't practice good a bit." And Beth looked at her rough hands with a sigh that any one could hear that time.

"I don't believe any of you suffer as I do," cried Amy; "for you don't have to go to school with impertinent girls, who plague you if you don't know your lessons, and laugh at your dresses, and label your father if he isn't rich, and insult you when your nose isn't nice."

"If you mean *libel* I'd say so, and not talk about *labels,* as if Pa was a pickle-bottle," advised Jo, laughing.

"I know what I mean, and you needn't be 'statirical' about it. It's proper to use good words, and improve your *vocabilary,*" returned Amy, with dignity.

"Don't peck at one another, children," said Meg.

It was a comfortable old room, though the carpet was faded and the furniture very plain, for a good picture or two hung on the walls, books filled the recesses, chrysanthemums and Christmas roses bloomed in the windows, and a pleasant atmosphere of home peace pervaded it.

Margaret, the eldest of the four, was sixteen, and very pretty. Fifteen-year-old Jo was tall, thin and brown, and reminded one of a colt; for she never seemed to know what to do with her long limbs, which were very much in her way. Elizabeth—or Beth, as every one called her—was a rosy, smooth-haired, bright-eyed girl of thirteen. Amy, though the youngest, was a most important person, in her own opinion at least.

The clock struck six; and, having swept up the hearth, Beth put a pair of slippers down to warm. Somehow the sight of the old shoes had a good effect upon the girls, for Mother was coming, and every one brightened to welcome her.

"They are quite worn out; Marmee must have a new pair."

"I thought I'd get her some with my dollar," said Beth.

"No, I shall!" cried Amy.

"I'm the oldest," began Meg, but Jo cut in with a decided—"I'm the man of the family, now Papa is away, and I shall provide the slippers, for he told me to take special care of Mother while he was gone."

"I'll tell you what we'll do," said Beth; "let's each get her something for Christmas, and not get anything for ourselves."

"That's like you, dear! What will we get?" exclaimed Jo.

Every one thought soberly for a minute; then Meg announced, as if the idea was suggested by the sight of her own pretty hands, "I shall give her a nice pair of gloves."

"Army shoes, best to be had," cried Jo.

"Some handkerchiefs, all hemmed," said Beth.

"I'll get a little bottle of Cologne; she likes it, and it won't cost much, so I'll have some left to buy something for me," added Amy.

"How will we give the things?" asked Meg.

"Put 'em on the table, and bring her in and see her open the bundles," answered Jo.

"Well, dearies, how have you got on today?" said a cheery voice at the door. "There was so much to do, getting the boxes ready to go tomorrow, that I didn't come home to dinner. Has any one called, Beth? How is your cold, Meg? Jo, you look tired to death. Come and kiss me, baby."

While making these maternal inquiries Mrs. March got her wet things off, her hot slippers on, and sitting down in the easy chair, drew Amy to her lap, preparing to enjoy the happiest hour of her busy day. The girls flew about, trying to make things comfortable, each in her own way. Meg arranged the tea table; Jo brought wood and set chairs, dropping, overturning, and clattering everything she touched; Beth trotted to and fro between parlor and kitchen, quiet and busy; while Amy gave directions to every one, as she sat with her hands folded.

As they gathered about the table, Mrs. March said, with a particularly happy face, "I've got a treat for you after supper."

A quick, bright smile went round like a streak of sunshine. Beth clapped her hands, regardless of the hot biscuit she held and Jo tossed up her napkin, crying, "A letter! a letter! Three cheers for Father!"

"Yes, a nice long letter. He is well, and thinks he shall get through the cold season better than we feared. He sends all sorts of loving wishes for Christmas, and an especial message to our girls," said Mrs. March, patting her pocket as if she had got a treasure there.

"Hurry up, and get done. Don't stop to quirk your little finger, and prink over your plate, Amy," cried Jo, choking in her tea, and dropping her bread, butter side down, on the carpet, in her haste to get at the treat.

Beth ate no more, but crept away, to sit in her shadowy corner and brood over the delight to come, till the others were ready.

"I think it was so splendid in Father to go as a chaplain when he was too old to be drafted, and not strong enough for a soldier," said Meg, warmly.

"When will he come home, Marmee?" asked Beth, with a little quiver in her voice.

"Not for many months, dear, unless he is sick. He will stay and do his work faithfully as long as he can, and we won't ask for him back a minute sooner than he can be spared. Now come and hear the letter."

They all drew to the fire, Mother in the big chair with Beth at her feet, Meg and Amy perched on either arm of the chair, and Jo leaning on the back, where no one would see any sign of emotion if the letter should happen to be touching.

Very few letters were written in those hard times that were not touching, especially those which fathers sent home. In this one little was said of the hardships endured, the dangers faced, or the home-sickness conquered; it was a cheerful, hopeful letter, full of lively descriptions of camp life, marches, and military news; and only at the end did the writer's heart overflow with fatherly love and longing for the little girls at home.

"Give them all my dear love and a kiss. Tell them I think of them by day, pray for them by night, and find my best comfort in their affection at all times. A year seems very long to wait before I see them, but remind them that while we wait we may all work, so that these hard days need not be wasted. I know they will remember all I said to them, that they will be loving children to you, will do their duty faithfully, fight their bosom enemies bravely, and conquer themselves so beautifully, that when I come back to them I may be fonder and prouder than ever of my little women."

Everybody sniffed when they came to that part; Jo wasn't ashamed of the great tear that dropped off the end of her nose, and Amy never minded the rumpling of her curls as she hid her face on her mother's shoulder and sobbed out, "I *am* a selfish pig! but I'll truly try to be better, so he mayn't be disappointed in me by and by."

"We all will!" cried Meg. "I think too much of my looks, and hate to work, but won't any more, if I can help it."

"I'll try and be what he loves to call me, 'a little woman,' and not be rough and wild; but do my duty here instead of wanting to be somewhere else," said Jo, thinking that keeping her temper at home was a much harder task than facing a rebel or two down South.

Beth said nothing, but wiped away her tears with the blue army-sock, and began to knit with all her might, losing no time in doing the duty that lay nearest her, while she resolved in her quiet little soul to be all that Father hoped to find her when the year brought round the happy coming home.

Jo was the first to wake in the gray dawn of Christmas morning. No stockings hung at the fire-place, and for a moment she felt as much disap-pointed as she did long ago, when her little sock fell down because it was so crammed with goodies. Then she remembered her mother's promise, and slipping her hand under her pillow, drew out a little crimson-covered book. She knew it very well, for it was that beautiful old story of the best life ever lived, and Jo felt that it was a true guidebook for any pilgrim going the long journey. She woke Meg with a "Merry Christmas," and bade her see what was under her pillow. A green-covered book appeared, with the same picture inside, and a few words written by their mother, which made their one present very precious in their eyes. Presently Beth and Amy woke, to rummage and find their little books also—one dove-colored, the other blue; and all sat looking at and talking about them, while the East grew rosy with the coming day.

"Girls," said Meg, seriously, looking from the tumbled head beside her to the two little night-capped ones in the room beyond, "mother wants us to read and love and mind these books, and we must begin at once. We used to be faithful about it; but since Father went away, and all this war trouble unsettled us, we have neglected many things. You can do as you please; but I shall keep my book on the table here, and read a little every morning as soon as I wake, for I know it will do me good, and help me through the day."

Then she opened her new book and began to read. Jo put her arm around her, and, leaning cheek to cheek, read also, with the quiet expression so seldom seen on her restless face.

"How good Meg is! Come, Amy, let's do as they do. I'll help you with the hard words, and they'll explain things if we don't understand," whispered Beth, very impressed by the pretty books and her sister's example.

"I'm glad mine is blue," said Amy; and then the rooms were very still while the pages were softly turned, and the winter sunshine crept in to touch the bright heads and serious faces with a Christmas greeting.

"Where is Mother?" asked Meg, as she and Jo ran down to thank her for their gifts, half an hour later.

"Goodness only knows. Some poor creeter come a-beggin', and your ma went straight off to see what was needed. There never *was* such a woman for givin' away vittles and drink, clothes, and firin'," replied Hannah, who had lived with the family since Meg was born, and was considered by them all more as a friend than a servant.

"She will be back soon, I guess; so do your cakes, and have everything ready," said Meg, looking over the presents which were collected in a basket and kept under the sofa, ready to be produced at the proper time. "Why, where is Amy's bottle of cologne?" she added, as the little flask did not appear.

"She took it out a minute ago, and went off with it to put a ribbon on it, or some such notion," replied Jo, dancing about the room to take the first stiffness off the new army-slippers.

"How nice my handkerchiefs look, don't they? Hannah washed and ironed them for me, and I marked them all myself," said Beth, looking proudly at the somewhat uneven letters which had cost her such labor.

"Bless the child, she's gone and put 'Mother' on them instead of 'M. March'; how funny!" cried Jo, taking up one.

"Isn't it right? I thought it was better to do it so because Meg's initials are 'M. M.' and I don't want any one to use these but Marmee," said Beth, looking troubled.

"It's all right, dear, and a very pretty idea; quite sensible, too, for no one can ever mistake them now. It will please her very much, I know," said Meg, with a frown for Jo, and a smile for Beth.

"There's Mother; hide the basket, quick!" cried Jo, as a door slammed, and steps sounded in the hall.

Amy came in hastily, and looked rather abashed when she saw her sisters all waiting for her.

"Where have you been, and what are you hiding

behind you?" asked Meg, surprised to see, by her hood and cloak, that lazy Amy had been out so early.

"Don't laugh at me, Jo. I didn't mean any one should know till the time came. I only meant to change the little bottle for a big one, and I gave *all* my money to get it, and I'm truly trying not to be selfish any more."

As she spoke, Amy showed the handsome flask which replaced the cheap one; and looked so earnest and humble in her little effort to forget herself, that Meg hugged her on the spot, and Jo pronounced her "a trump," while Beth ran to the window, and picked her finest rose to ornament the stately bottle.

"You see, I felt ashamed of my present, after reading and talking about being good this morning, so I ran round the corner and changed it the minute I was up; and I'm glad, for mine is the handsomest now."

Another bang of the street-door sent the basket under the sofa, and the girls to the table eager for breakfast.

"Merry Christmas, Marmee! Lots of them! Thank you for our books; we read some, and mean to every day," they cried in chorus.

"Merry Christmas, little daughters! I'm glad you began at once, and hope you will keep on. But I want to say one word before we sit down. Not far away from here lies a poor woman with a little new-born baby. Six children are huddled into one bed to keep from freezing, for they have no fire. There is nothing to eat over there; and the oldest boy came to tell me they were suffering hunger and cold. My girls, will you give them your breakfast as a Christmas present?"

They were all unusually hungry, having waited nearly an hour, and for a minute no one spoke; only a minute, for Jo exclaimed impetuously, "I'm so glad you came before we began!"

"May I go and help carry the things to the poor little children?" asked Beth, eagerly.

"*I* shall take the cream and the muffins," added Amy, heroically giving up the articles she most liked.

Meg was already covering the buckwheats, and piling the bread into one big plate.

"I thought you'd do it," said Mrs. March, smiling as if satisfied. "You shall all go and help me, and when we come back we will have bread and milk for breakfast, and make it up at dinner-time."

They were soon ready, and the procession set out. Fortunately it was early, and they went through back streets, so few people saw them, and no one laughed at the funny party.

A poor, bare, miserable room it was, with broken windows, no fire, ragged bedclothes, a sick mother, wailing baby, and a group of pale, hungry children cuddled under one old quilt, trying to keep warm. How the big eyes stared, and the blue lips smiled, as the girls went in!

"*Ach, mein Gott!* It is good angels come to us!" cried the poor woman, crying for joy.

"Funny angels in hoods and mittens," said Jo, and set them laughing.

In a few minutes it really did seem as if kind spirits had been at work there. Hannah, who had carried wood, made a fire, and stopped up the broken panes with old hats, and her own shawl. Mrs. March gave the mother tea and gruel, and comforted her with promises of help, while she dressed the little baby as tenderly as if it had been her own. The girls, meantime, spread the table, set the children round the fire, and fed them like so many hungry birds; laughing, talking, and trying to understand the funny broken English.

"*Das ist gut!*" "*Die angel-kinder!*" cried the poor things, as they ate, and warmed their purple hands at the comfortable blaze. The girls had never been called angel children before, and thought it very agreeable. That was a very happy breakfast, though they didn't get any of it; and when they went away, leaving comfort behind, I think there were not in all the city four merrier people than the hungry little girls who gave away their breakfasts, and contented themselves with bread and milk on Christmas morning.

"That's loving our neighbor better than ourselves, and I like it," said Meg, as they set out their presents, while their mother was upstairs collecting clothes for the poor Hummels.

Not a very splendid show, but there was a great deal of love done up in the few little bundles; and the tall vase of red roses, white chrysanthemums, and trailing vines, which stood in the middle, gave quite an elegant air to the table.

"She's coming! Strike up, Beth. Open the door, Amy. Three cheers for Marmee!" cried Jo, prancing about, while Meg went to conduct Mother to the seat of honor.

Beth played her gayest march, Amy threw open the door, and Meg enacted escort with great dignity. Mrs. March was both surprised and touched; and smiled with her eyes full as she examined her presents, and read the little notes which accompanied them. The slippers went on at once, a new handkerchief was slipped into her pocket, well scented with Amy's cologne, the rose was fastened in her bosom, and the nice gloves were pronounced "a perfect fit."

There was a good deal of laughing, and kissing, and explaining, in the simple, loving fashion which makes these home festivals so pleasant at the time and so sweet to remember long afterward.

Beth nestled up to her mother, and whispered softly, "I'm afraid Father isn't having such a merry Christmas as we are."

THE LITTLE MATCH GIRL

Hans Christian Andersen

Reflecting the poverty from which Andersen himself came, "The Little Match Girl" offers us a heroine who shows how faith makes it possible to transcend the hardships of everyday life. The story has become one of the timeless classics of the holidays.

IT WAS TERRIBLY COLD and nearly dark on the last evening of the old year, and the snow was falling fast. In the cold and the darkness, a poor little girl, with bare head and naked feet, roamed through the streets. It is true she had on a pair of slippers when she left home, but they were not of much use. They were very large, so large, indeed, that they had belonged to her mother, and the poor little creature had lost them in running across the street to avoid two carriages that were rolling along at a terrible rate. One of the slippers she could not find, and a boy seized upon the other and ran away with it, saying that he could use it as a cradle, when he had children of his own.

So the little girl went on with her little naked feet, which were quite red and blue with the cold. In an old apron she carried a number of matches, and had a bundle of them in her hands. No one had bought anything of her the whole day, nor had anyone given her even a penny. Shivering with cold and hunger, she crept along; poor little child, she looked the picture of misery. The snowflakes fell on her long, fair hair, which hung in curls on her shoulders, but she regarded them not.

Lights were shining from every window, and there was a savory smell of roast-goose, for it was New Year's Eve—yes, she remembered that. In a corner, between two houses, one of which projected beyond the other, she sank down and huddled herself together. She had drawn her little feet under her, but she could not keep off the cold; and she dared not go home, for she had sold no matches and could not take home even a penny of money. Her father would certainly beat her; besides, it was almost as cold at home as here, for they had only the roof to cover them, through which the wind howled, although the largest holes had been stopped up with straw and rags.

Her little hands were almost frozen with the cold. Ah! Perhaps a burning match might be some good, if she could draw it from the bundle and strike it against the wall, just to warm her fingers. She drew one out—scratch!—how it sputtered as it burnt! It gave a warm, bright light, like a little candle, as she held her hand over it.

It really was a wonderful light. It seemed to the little girl that she was sitting by a large iron stove, with polished brass feet and a brass ornament. How the fire burned! And it seemed so beautifully warm that the child stretched out her feet as if to warm them, when, lo, the flame of the match went out, the stove vanished, and she had only the remains of the half-burnt match in her hand.

She rubbed another match on the wall. It burst into flame, and where its light fell upon the wall it became as transparent as a veil, and she could see into the room. The table was covered with a snowy white tablecloth, on which stood a splendid dinner service and a steaming roast goose, stuffed with apples and dried plums. And what was still more wonderful, the goose jumped down from the dish and waddled across the floor, with a knife and fork in its breast, to the little girl. Then the match went out, and there remained nothing but the thick, damp, cold wall before her.

She lighted another match, and then she found herself sitting under a beautiful Christmas tree. It was larger and more beautifully decorated than the one which she had seen through the glass door at the rich merchant's. Thousands of tapers were burning upon the green branches, and colored pictures, like those she had seen in the show-windows, looked down upon it all. The little one stretched out her hand towards them, and the match went out.

The Christmas lights rose higher and higher, till they looked to her like the stars in the sky. Then she saw a star fall, leaving behind it a bright streak of fire. "Someone is dying," thought the little girl, for her old grandmother, the only one who had ever loved her, and who was now dead, had told her that when a star falls, a soul was going up to God.

She again rubbed a match on the wall, and the light shone round her; in the brightness stood her old grandmother, clear and shining, yet mild and loving in her appearance. "Grandmother," cried the little one, "oh, take me with you: I know you will go away when the match burns out; you will vanish like the warm stove, the roast goose, and the large, glorious Christmas tree." And she made haste to light the whole bundle of matches, for she wished to keep her grandmother there. And the matches glowed with a light that was brighter than the noon-day.

Her grandmother had never appeared so large or so beautiful. She took the little girl in her arms, and they both flew upwards in brightness and joy far above the earth, where there was neither cold nor hunger nor pain, for they were with God.

* * *

In the dawn of the morning, there lay the little one, with pale cheeks and smiling mouth, leaning against the wall; she had been frozen to death on the last evening of the year, and the New Year's sun rose and shone upon a little corpse. The child still sat, in the stiffness of death, holding the matches in her hand, one bundle of which was burnt. "She tried to warm herself," said some. No one imagined what beautiful things she had seen, nor into what glory she had entered with her grandmother, on New Year's Day.

THE GATE
Walter Ash

Based in part on an old play by K. M. Rice, Ash's "The Gate" is a Christmas tale of loss and redemption, of incalculable pain and unforeseen renewal. It traces a fateful series of events in the lives of three people— and reminds us that there are many fewer strangers in this world than we may at first be inclined to believe.

IN A BUSY RAILROAD STATION in New York City on Christmas Eve, 1911, an announcer shouted, "Boston! Boston! First track on the left!" Not all of his intended audience understood his words.

Among the uncounted travelers milling through the huge concourse that night, one could have made out a host of tired and bedraggled immigrants from the nation that loves Christmas perhaps more fervently than any other; and among these scores of German men, women, and children, one could have made out a worried-looking woman in blue who had been separated from her party and did not know where to go, who neither spoke nor understood a word of English, and who scanned the wooden benches as she led her daughter, a little girl of about four bearing a small bundle, through the station.

And one would have seen her settle at last upon a bench at the far end of the station. If one under-stood German, one would have known that the young mother told her little girl not to move, that she, the mother, would return in a moment. One would have heard the child agree. One would have

seen the mother struggle back into the crowd, rejoin her group, and, before she could frame the question she meant to ask about the train's departure time, find herself shoved, with the rest of the party, toward the track by the gate tender. One would have heard her shout for her child, still and sharp at first, then rising, like the shriek of tearing metal, but still a component of the general din.

One would have heard many shouts, many calls, some of it in one's own language, some of it not. One would have heard the gate tender bellow to someone in the party to keep the young mother in line, that he had seen her ticket and knew where she was bound. One would have seen the mother carried along with the crowd, her terrified voice reverberating and eventually dying away, as she was borne along toward the train, and one would have heard the chuffing of the engine, and an exhausted commitment of wheels, and a roar, and a grey roll toward Boston.

And one would have been able to make out, had one looked back to the far end of the station, a little blonde girl in a dark cap who, like her mother, spoke not a word of English, seated alone with her tiny bundle on her wooden bench. One would have seen her staring ahead impassively, still, waiting expectantly for her mother as the thousands of Christmas travelers walked past.

Three little schoolgirls, home for the holiday and waiting to be met by their parents, sat down next to her. The oldest marked her and said, "She's so lovely! And look, she hasn't moved a muscle this whole time."

The next oldest said, "It's as if she's posing for a picture."

The youngest said, "She's looking for something."

Then the oldest of the three girls spied their father, and they all shouted and ran away.

Still the little girl stared at the black gate.

After a time, a man and a woman passed by the bench. The man was mustachioed, in his late forties, tall and thin. His chin bore a week's stubble. His companion was a woman of about his age, short and stocky, with a tiny pinched-up face and a sneer that seemed to speak of a lifetime of discontent.

They passed nonchalantly several times, watching the little girl and pretending not to. From the bench across the aisle, a bespectacled woman looked up from her newspaper and watched them suspiciously.

"She's been left behind," the tall man said to his companion. "All those Germans boarded that train for Boston. She's abandoned."

"Would you lower your voice?" the stout woman hissed. "Do you want someone to hear you? Turn around; I think that busybody over on the other bench is watching us. Now, what if her folks come back for her?"

"Every last one of those Germans got on the Boston train, I tell you."

They stood for a moment, looking away from the benches. When the woman turned back, she saw only the girl; the woman with the newspaper was nowhere to be seen.

"Let's take her, then," the woman whispered to her companion. "Get her ticket and give it to me. Then pick her up. We'll find her a new home—and profit from it."

Quickly, almost before the little girl knew what was happening, a bony hand was at her coat. It tore off the red Immigration ticket that had been pinned there. The sound of the paper tearing was followed by the little girl's shout of surprise and fear, and a few desperate words from her in German.

The man lifted her up and held her toward his companion. "Mommy will give you something to eat," he said. "Don't cry." The tiny one was indeed sobbing now, pointing toward the black gate and shouting in inexplicable bursts.

"Would you mind telling me what you two are doing with that little girl?"

The voice was not hard, but intent, a voice that was not, perhaps, accustomed to being raised, but that could be brought to bear when the occasion demanded. It belonged to a well dressed woman in her thirties with almond-colored hair tied in a bun. Under her arm was a neatly folded newspaper. On the bridge of her nose was a small pair of spectacles.

The man withdrew the little girl, whom he was attempting to hand to his companion, and set her roughly on the bench. Without bothering to look at the stout woman with the pinched little face, he backed away from the bench.

"I'm her mother," the stout woman said unconvincingly.

The woman in spectacles knelt down to comfort the little girl. "Then you'd best tell her father that the policeman at the far end of the station is walking this way," she said. "He will be asking you a great many questions. Be sure you can answer them without contradicting one another."

In an instant the man was gone, his footsteps echoing for a time above the din of the station. The stout woman swore an oath, then turned and ran after the thin man.

The woman tried to comfort the weeping child. "Don't worry, little one," she said, trying to soothe the girl. "Don't worry. We will find your mother." The girl was chattering in weeping German, staring at the black gate and pointing. Her young cheeks were bright with tears.

"Don't bother with her, ma'am," a voice behind the woman said. She turned around to find an old railroad official in a blue uniform. "Likely enough her mother abandoned her there. These immigrants have been known to do worse, poor wretches. Down on their luck, I suppose. That was a nice piece of play-acting about the policeman, there. I suppose you'll be wanting me to call one for you now. I'm afraid it's the home for wanderers this one's bound for."

She stared at him. The little girl had begun to control her sobs, which were now tiny heaves. She would not look away from the gate.

"Thank you for the offer," came the answer. "I shall summon the police myself in a moment, once I've calmed her down. Please don't trouble yourself."

They could not understand each other. The little girl's rescuer had thought of looking for someone who could speak German, but since her young friend steadfastly refused to be moved from the spot on which she sat, finding a translator would have meant leaving the girl unattended, and that seemed unthinkable. So they sat together for a time.

Every once in a while, the little girl would point to the gate and say something in German, confidently and even with a little pride. Although she had no way to make out the words, the word "mutter" sounded repeatedly, and the woman in spectacles eventually concluded that she was being told that the little girl's mother would return momentarily. At length a

discussion (of sorts) ensued, and by revealing several times, and with broad gesticulations, that her own name was Eugenia Parsley, the woman was able, after a number of false starts, to determine that the girl's name was Ingrid. After a few moments, during which the youngster had managed to stop crying altogether, Miss Parsley withdrew a pad of paper and a pencil and began to write.

"James," (she wrote) "it has been more than an hour, and the young lady for whom we're waiting has not arrived. I have, however, encountered someone else, someone who needs both your assistance and mine. Please come to meet me near the north entrance of the terminal. I am seated on one of the benches there."

"Boy!" she called. A young lad of eight or nine years turned at the call and said, "Yes, ma'am?"

"Would you care to earn a dollar?"

"A whole dollar, ma'am?"

"Yes, indeed, a whole dollar. Take this note to my driver; you'll find him in the blue and white automobile near the front entrance. Return here with him and you shall have your payment."

The boy ran off. In a few moments, he returned with a befuddled driver and an open hand. She paid the lad, who vanished into the crowd quite unable to believe his luck. Eugenia Parsley turned to her driver, who stood waiting for his instructions. "Yes, ma'am?" he said, touching his cap.

She explained the situation and, having handed the pad and pencil to James, dictated the contents of an advertisement to be placed in every German-language newspaper in the country, and every other paper, German-speaking or otherwise, in New York and Boston.

The advertisement advised that a young German girl of about four years of age answering to the name of Ingrid had been found in Central Station in New York City on Christmas Eve, having apparently been separated from her mother, and that said mother was, in the author's estimation, likely bound for Boston despite her best efforts not to be so. The readers of the advertisement were instructed to contact Miss Eugenia Parsley at her permanent address (and here she supplied the particulars of her upstate New York abode). Anyone supplying any worthwhile information, the advertisement continued, would be eligible for a cash reward of a size to be determined after the girl was reunited with her mother. Having relayed all this to James, whose skill at such tasks was evident as his hand sped across page after page, Miss Parsley looked to the little girl. She was still staring at the black gate.

"There remains only the matter of bringing her with us, James," she said.

James pocketed the papers and the pencil and eyed the young girl warily. "Yes ma'am," he said.

He took a breath, walked to her, and attempted, rather clumsily, to pick her up. She screamed at once, and again began to cry and shout incomprehensible words and point at the black gate.

"James, I'm surprised at you," Miss Parsley said. "You act as though you've never held a little girl before. Put her down immediately."

James put her back gently.

Miss Parsley kneeled and looked the little girl in the eyes. "'Mutter'?" she said softly. "Shall we find your 'mutter'?" There was a silence. And then the little girl slid off the bench, looking all the while into Miss Parsley's hazel eyes.

The little girl took a position directly in front of her benefactress, who placed her large white hands upon the child's shoulders. "James will help you. Let's go with James," Miss Parsley said.

And in a moment Miss Parsley had hoisted the little girl into the waiting arms of the driver. They had hardly moved when a little cry came from Ingrid.

"She doesn't like me, ma'am," James said, help-lessly.

"Nonsense, James," said Miss Parsley. "You've only to look at her to see that she wants us to bring along her bundle."

Indeed, the little girl was pointing at the tiny bundle on the bench, her lower lip held steady, but vibrating a little now and then. Miss Parsley picked up the bundle and handed it to James, and together the three made their way out of the crowded and noisy station.

It was the late afternoon of Christmas Eve, 1927. In a small New York town, a woman with disheveled white hair, wearing a tattered dress, made her way down a flight of stairs with a basket on her arm, intending to have a pleasant sit on the front porch of the building in which she rented a room. She had not been long in this (or, it seemed, any) town—she had held her

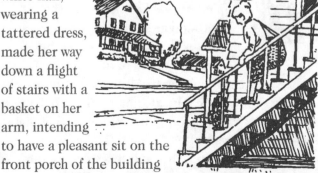

lodgings for perhaps six months. She paid her way by taking in washing, but she did not now, nor did she customarily, get much work. This may have been as a result of the fact that she was not an easy person to talk to, or to watch, and this put her at a disadvantage with potential customers. Her English was bad. She was brusque and often impatient. She put people off. She gave them the feeling that she had been too long alone and too thoroughly broken to be at ease with others. And indeed this may well have been the case.

In the distance she heard young voices singing:

Good King Wenceslas looked out
On the feast of Stephen
Where the snow lay round about
Deep and crisp and even.
Brightly shone the moon that night,
Though the frost was cruel,
When a poor man came in sight,
Gathering winter fuel.

She sighed. She had heard the song many times, and it always stirred her heart. She had learned the words in German when she herself was a child, of course, but now she knew and recognized the words as well as the tune. As the lyrics rang across the skies from the mouths of children, the old woman (her name was Eva) stared at the ground as she sat in her rocking chair. Her lips moved silently, framing the new English words of the old song.

The children came nearer. Although on this of all days she should have felt safe among the people of the neighborhood, and among children at that, habit died hard. She was, after all, (and she knew this, intuitively) considered the oddest resident of the neighborhood: Crazy Eva, the strange old German woman who never troubled herself to speak to any-

one on the street. She had come, by now, to believe she would always be so—if not Crazy Eva in this town, then another such name in another one. Before the children came into view, she hid behind the outer stair.

Presently the children were quite near the house, laughing and shouting about which song to sing next. One of them asked where they had arrived.

"This," she heard a young boy's voice say, "is where Crazy Eva lives. People call her crazy; to me she just looks sad. I saw her sitting on the porch once, although she didn't see me; she had a string of beads around her neck. I do believe she was praying. They were the kind Ingrid has, you know."

At the moment the word "Ingrid" was spoken, Eva's breath went short.

"Perhaps she'll come out for us," a little girl said. "Perhaps we should sing her a carol."

"You can't be serious," an older girl exclaimed. "It's Crazy Eva. Who knows what she'll do to us if she comes out. Let's find another house."

"I say it's Christmas for everyone, and that includes Crazy Eva," the first little girl said emphatically. "Let's sing 'God Rest Ye Merry, Gentlemen.'"

"Yes," said the little boy who had seen Eva's beads, "'God Rest Ye Merry, Gentlemen.'" The first notes rang out—and then from behind the stair an old woman's voice said, "Dat song you have been singing. Again, please. Sing dat song for me once more, please."

And Eva stepped from the shadows and stood before the children.

The older girl, the one who had wanted to move on to another house, turned white. But she did not move. None of them moved. For an instant all was silence, then the youngest girl, the one who had

insisted on staying (she was a radiant little one with jet-black hair), began to sing.

Good King Wenceslas looked out
On the feast of Stephen . .

she began, and the other children, every one of them, joined in and sang the carol through again for Eva.

At the end of the song, all the children were staring happily at Eva, who was smiling with the broadest smile she had smiled in sixteen years.

"I like dat the most oaf any song dere is," said Eva. "*Auf Deutsch*—in the German—we call it *Der Gute Konig Wenceslas.*"

The littlest one clapped her hands joyfully and said, "Oh, she likes Ingrid's song!"

Eva knelt and looked at the little girl, who for some reason did not flinch at the sight of the fearful old lady against whom she had so often been warned in recent months. Truth be told, Eva was only fifty, but the years had not been at all kind to her.

"Dis Ingrid you are speaking off," she said slowly. "Vere doss she liff?"

"Why, here in town," said the youngest girl.

"And how old, how old dis Ingrid iss?"

"Forty," said one.

"Never," said another. "She's not *that* old."

"Thirty," said another.

"You are all such geese," said the oldest girl. "Ingrid is only twenty. She told me so herself on her birthday. Actually, it was her *make-believe* birthday, for she hasn't a real one at all, you know. And she might as well not have Christmas either, for all the moping she does around it."

There was a pause. Eva took a deep breath and moved closer to the oldest girl. "Tell me please—no, no, I vill not hurt you—tell me please, how is it this Ingrid is not vit a real birthday."

"Because she forgot it, of course. Oh, she knew it once. But she was lost when she was a little girl, a foolish little girl who got separated from her own mother, you see."

"Ah."

All the little ones looked at her face; Eva stared off into the distance. A moment passed, and then the oldest girl looked round at the others. She made a motion for them to leave while Eva was in her reverie, but got no response. The girl smirked and scowled, then turned on her heel and began to walk away. She had not moved more than a step or two when she felt Eva's gentle hand on her shoulder.

"No, no, not yet, please, not yet," Eva said in a low voice, not at all frightening, but more as a child who cannot bear to have the evening bedtime story end so soon. "Please," she continued, "please, do not go yet. Tell me. Why is it you say she is sad always venn it is Christmas?"

The older girl stared at her for a moment but could not manage to get a word out. Finally from the back a voice piped: "Tell her, Louise."

"Because," Louise said at last, staring at the gentle eyes of her inquisitor, "it is like this, you see. When Ingrid was but a little girl, she was separated from her mother in New York . . ."

"Vit, vit de trains, vit de many, many trains . . ." Eva said softly, barely above a whisper.

Louise looked at her young companions, and then back at Eva.

"In a train station, yes. Why, that's it exactly."

Eva's hand stroked Louise's cheek slowly, then patted it gently, and then fell.

"Bring her here," Eva said. "Tell her dat I knew her mother."

For the first time in a very many years, Eva threw up her hands and laughed, not so much because she recognized her daughter as she walked towards her, but because she felt the familiar rhythm of the girl's approach. It is an interesting question, whether or not two people who are bonded as one, as parent and child, would, after an interval of a decade and a half, still respond with that instinctual knowledge of the other's presence that so defines their relationship. Eva's reaction to the altered-but-unaltered form, the lithe, blonde young woman whom she could just make out in the distance, that reaction was unmistakable in its joy at recognition. It was unintentional, it was obvious before even the features of the youngster's face were visible. Eva's reaction, indeed, would lead one to believe that the bond between a mother and a daughter is not broken by even a dense span of time. The halting half-smile of the young beauty herself, however, would lead one to believe that even a mother's instinctive—if quickly stifled—show of joy is not immediately obvious to the daughter who believes herself to be one stranger approaching another.

All this is by way of saying that Ingrid had appar-ently not seen this brief reaction of Eva's, or if she had not seen it, had not been much moved by it. Ingrid walked with a young man of about her own age (whom Eva imagined, correctly, to be a classmate), and soon drew near the house.

Eva struggled to remain calm—to be, as she felt she must be, a stranger. She knew that she would hear her daughter's young voice soon, but when the words came it was still a strange shock.

"Is it true what they say? That you knew my mother?"

Eva, who was by now sitting in her rocking chair, nodded and bade the young woman to come up onto the porch.

"Ya. It is true."

Ingrid gasped.

"Did you hear? Did you hear, Toby? She knew her!"

"I heard," the boy said warily.

"Come here, come here," Eva said. "Sit by me."

Ingrid hesitated for a moment, then drew closer. Presently she fell to her knees and looked up at the older woman. One of her young hands rested comfortably, and without apparent thought, on Eva's knee. Ingrid took a deep breath before framing with words the question she had come to pose.

"How did you know my mother?"

But Eva said nothing, only smiled and touched the blonde hair. How shiny it was!

The young woman seemed perplexed not to receive an answer; when Eva made a movement toward her, she started for a moment, and then thought better of her fear.

Eva carefully extended her hand toward the soft young neck and touched a string of beads resting there. Then without breaking the movement for an instant, she put her hand to her own neck and removed an identical string of beads.

"She gave you her beads!" Ingrid exclaimed. "I remember, oh, I remember playing with them the morning we landed in America. Hers exactly like mine! And I took hers and put them on my neck, and wound mine about hers! Oh, I remember it so well!"

"I saw you play vit dem as you say," Eva said quietly.

"Then you were on the same ship?"

Eva nodded.

"Tell me, what did Ingrid look like as a little girl?" It was the young man who posed the question. "Miss Parsley said I should ask you."

Eva thought for a moment and asked, "Did dis Miss Parsley give you also dat little bag you have brought?"

He seemed surprised at the directness of the question. "Why, yes," he said.

"Who knows what's come over her," Ingrid said wearily. "She gave him all kinds of orders on a little slip of paper, and wouldn't show me a thing."

"Den she iss a good voman."

The youngsters looked quizzically at her.

"Ingrid vass the morning she came to America wearing a leetle skirt, blue. The bag. Open it, young lady, I tink you vill find it."

He brought the bag. It was as she said. Eva stretched out her hand and took the small blue skirt that Ingrid held out to her, then held it as one would hold a baby. She looked back at Ingrid.

"What else?" the young man asked.

"A leetle bodice, cut vit an angle, lots of squares. Edges, de edges vit flowers. I saw your mother ven she sew dis."

Ingrid withdrew something from the bag, stood up, and held a flowered garment against her breast.

"Oh, you *were* there, you *did* know my mother!" Ingrid shouted. "And you say you saw her sewing this? Oh, how marvelous! Miss Parsley, when she taught me to sew, would always tell me, 'Now, Ingrid, we must sew with stitches as small as your mother's, you know.'"

"Do you haff, in dat bag, de leetle shoes?"

"Did you hear that, Toby? Of course we have the little shoes. Hand them to me, Toby."

They were wrapped in a colored neckerchief. Toby handed them to Ingrid, who handed them to Eva.

"They are lovely things, you know. They have a high front, and blue leather in the back, and . . ."

"And haf leetle brass clasps, front and back. And a deep scratch on the right shoe by de heel, one or two inches long."

There was a silence as Ingrid regarded her, then opened up the neckerchief and displayed the shoes, which were exactly as they had been described. Eva turned away, ostensibly to look out at the houses on the street, but, more evidently than she imagined, eager at this point not to have to look another in the eye.

"Diss is vat your mother told me," Eva said, still staring away.

"Toby, leave us here," Ingrid said, wiping away a tear with the back of her hand.

The boy left.

"Who are you?" The young woman's question was not pained, not insistent, nor yet even touched with longing. It was the question of one trying to make sense of the forgotten objects of a room after a long night dreaming.

"I am Crazy Eva," came the answer. "I am a woman by myself here for people to hate. I tink maybe you haff neffer news of your mother without you come on me like this, by a mistake. By an accident. So iss for dat, at least, good dat we should meet." She still would not look Eva in the eye.

"Tell me about my mother," Ingrid said. "Tell me everything you know."

"Tell *me*," said Eva. "You tell me. Vat it iss you remember." She stared down. The waving grain in the painted planks of the porch on which the two women stood ran in long, irregular patterns, rising and falling. It was as though the wooden veins, no two alike, were racing on a course that no one could predict, a course that comprehended any number of paths, a course concluded in itself at the hard seam of each board, and then began anew.

"I remember a gate, a black iron gate," Ingrid responded, as if hypnotized. "I remember a hard bench and a crowd and an iron gate, all black, that took her away."

"Notting more?"

"Nothing more."

They stared out at the cold sky.

"Dere vas more," Eva said.

"Then tell me." Ingrid spoke the words openly, with no fear, as one following a path.

"Your mother, maybe you have thought to hate her for leaving you. But I know she not mean to leave you dere. I know. She vent to ask from a friend a question. And a man at de gate ask to see her ticket. And he said 'Dot's good, go' and push her.

Denn a crowd come following a call from someone. Many bodies. She try to get back. Hard, hard, hard, she try to get back. She called you. Den she pushed on dat train, and den gone and no one to talk to.

"She called your name again and again and again.

"She vould be glad you are still called by dat name."

Ingrid stepped closer to her mother. The two were now side by side, a handswidth at most between them, staring out from the porch toward the great grey sky.

"I never hated my mother," Ingrid said softly.

Eva said nothing.

"I had no ticket. All I had was this. Half of an immigration ticket." And she knelt down and pulled from the little bag an old faded ticket.

"A new country," said Eva.

"Yes, it was," said Ingrid.

Ingrid stood up again, pocketed the ticket, and put her hand on Eva's. The older woman closed her eyes and took a deep breath.

Ingrid touched Eva's cheek. "Please look at me," she said.

They were soft, grey-blue eyes, eyes that remembered, eyes that needed, suddenly, no further summoning.

"These beads," Ingrid said, "belonged to you, I think."

And with that Ingrid removed the beads from around her neck and handed them to Eva, who took them in her hand and turned them for a moment. They were round beads, suitable for praying, for reaching beyond oneself, for touching the quiet part of the soul that we see, now and again, in ourselves and in others at Christmas time. The beads were black and round and worn, and the hand that held them seemed to draw the bright essence of life from their scratched dark surfaces.

When the two embraced, it was not difficult at all. It was extended across a gulf of time and distance and words, as true embraces often are, and so they did their best to squeeze every moment of time, every inch of distance, and every syllable of speech out of themselves, to forget such petty details as who they were or had been, and to find again what they had found in the beginning, to find it over and over and for the first time, as well. The mother and daughter in each other's arms tried to stay true to the unspoken demands of a single heart, a heart that discovers itself again quite by accident, and in a moment. They tried to touch something that could only change if you tried, like a fool, to put a word on it, to use language as though it were not, in the end, a dark black gate into which true experience often passed mysteriously and for an eon.

And for a long moment they did touch something, and it did not change.

❧

Word of what had happened spread like wildfire through the town. On Christmas Day, the children rushed to the Parsley house and cheered and pointed at Eva (no one called her by her old name any more), who was waving to them from an upper window.

Words, of course, had their place, and there were many that passed once Eva had made her way within that house. She learned, for instance, of the many efforts Miss Parsley had made to locate her, of the years of placing advertisements at Christmas time in Boston's papers and those of nearly every other city in the country. And Miss Parsley learned of the hardships and trials Eva had undergone, of her wanderings and her penury, and of her final, seemingly aimless decision to settle in the humble town in upstate New York where they now found themselves. The tellings and explainings spun themselves out like tops. At last there was a flat current of silence, and it was natural. They were free simply to stare at the exquisitely decorated tree Miss Parsley had prepared, free not to bother any more with words. Perhaps it was the season before them that explained their comfort with this state of affairs, or perhaps it was the day's remarkable events. For whatever reason, the three women seemed, at long last, to have entered a world in which neither miracles nor accidents—or the words to describe them—were possible or necessary, but only the day at hand.

There was a knock at the door. Miss Parsley rang

James's bell and, when he arrived, pointed down the flight of stairs. He nodded and walked down.

When James opened the door, he saw a small boy bearing a huge basket of fruit.

"It's for Miss Ingrid, sir, if you please," the boy chanted, as though he had rehearsed his speech a dozen times or more. "We were hoping we could come to see her this morning, myself and some of her other friends." (Here it may be mentioned that Ingrid had, and had always had, an uncommon facility with the local children, and was close to nearly every one of them who lived in the town.) James thanked the boy, asked him to wait where he was, and went upstairs to take the basket of fruit to Miss Parsley.

"I heard him, James, thank you," Miss Parsley said. She was busy writing something, and did not look up. "You may place the basket beneath the tree. Go and return to our young gift-bearer the gracious thanks of this house, and tell him to bring his friends back in half an hour. Miss Ingrid will have something to say for us all then, I believe. After you've seen him off, I want you to prepare a room for Eva. She will be living with us here now."

James nodded and exited.

"I believe it is beginning to snow," said Ingrid, who was standing by the window next to her mother.

"Clean snow, snow for de day iss good. Vash clean everyting and hold it, hold it vit big vite arms." Eva grasped her daughter's hand.

"Indeed it is," said Miss Parsley, looking up for a moment. She saw the two others staring at each other and smiling. She smiled herself, and then resumed her work.

Perhaps ten minutes passed in silence.

When Miss Parsley had finished writing, she walked to the window, and the three watched the grey sky shatter open into denser and denser fields of white snowflakes, a gateway limitlessly exposed.

Some time later the doorbell rang. Ingrid opened it and wished the children a merry Christmas, and was wished the same in return by a chorus of young voices.

"I have something important to read to you all," she said.

The children laughed and shouted. Their many voices rang out into the cold white air. "A story!" "How wonderful!" "Ingrid is going to read us a story!" "What kind of story, Ingrid?"

"I must warn you, it's a story without an ending," she answered. And she began to read what Miss Parsley had written.

"'There were two sets of travelers. The first traveler was a grimy old man, ill-shaven, ill-clad, and he often stank of whisky and old cigar smoke. He rode boxcars and begged or stole for his supper. Most people feared him and would not look him in his eye, and thought nothing of it, but the more they looked away the more he became the man they feared.

"'The second set of travelers was made up of a poor man and his wife, who was great with child. The

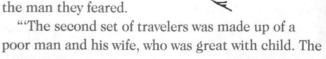

two had not a penny to their name, and the wife's time was approaching on a bitterly cold night. They had nowhere to go at the time of their greatest need, and no one to see to them. They went from inn to inn, but all the inns were full, and each innkeeper looked away from them and shut the door in their face. To be cast aside by the world at such a time! How do you imagine they felt?

"'I am afraid this is not a once-upon-a-time story. It is a once-upon-many-times story. For the first traveler travels tonight, as do any number of others, and the man and his wife traveled many centuries ago. But their journey, children, was upon the same earth we all share.

"'And our job is not to finish either story, but to begin each one, and all such stories, as that woman's child would have us begin them. With a look in the eye, unjudging and unjudged, and a hand extended in common humanity. To do so is not an ending, but a beginning, and this day we celebrate the great beginning, the great gift of our own ability to make beginnings together, in the face of adversity and happiness alike.'"

When she had finished she put away the paper, wished the children a merry Christmas, hugged them all, and sent them on their way. And she knew, as she watched them go, that new beginnings do indeed lie somewhere in all of us.

"YES, VIRGINIA, THERE IS A SANTA CLAUS"
Francis P. Church

Editor Francis P. Church's letter to Virginia O'Hanlon is one of the most touching written demonstrations of the importance in believing in what cannot be seen, touched, or proven. The letter originally appeared in the September 21, 1897 edition of The *New York Sun*. Nearly a century later, it remains a classic.

WE TAKE PLEASURE in answering at once and thus prominently the communication below, expressing at the same time our great gratification that its faithful author is numbered among the friends of the *Sun*:

DEAR EDITOR—I am 8 years old.

Some of my little friends say there is no SANTA CLAUS. Papa says 'If you see it in the Sun it's so.' Please tell me the truth, is there a SANTA CLAUS? VIRGINIA O'HANLON, 115 West Ninety-fifth street.

Virginia, your little friends are wrong. They have been affected by the skepticism of a skeptical age. They do not believe except they see. They think that nothing can be which is not comprehensible by their little minds. All minds, Virginia, whether they be men's or children's are little. In this great universe of ours man is a mere insect, an ant, in his intellect, as compared with the boundless world about him, as measured by the intelligence capable of grasping the whole of truth and knowledge.

Yes, Virginia, there is a Santa Claus. He exists as certainly as love and generosity and devotion exist, and you know that they abound and give to your life its highest beauty and joy. Alas! how dreary would be the world if there were no Santa Claus! It would be as dreary as if there were no Virginias. There would be no childlike faith then, no poetry, no romance to make tolerable this existence. We should have no enjoyment, except in sense and sight. The eternal light with which childhood fills the world would be extinguished.

Not believe in Santa Claus! You might as well not believe in fairies! You might get your papa to hire men to watch in all the chimneys on Christmas Eve to catch Santa Claus, but even if they did not see Santa Claus coming down, what would that prove? Nobody sees Santa Claus, but that is no sign that there is no Santa Claus. The most real things in the world are those that neither children nor men can see. Did you ever see fairies dancing on the lawn? Of course not, but that's no proof that they are not there.

Nobody can conceive or imagine all the wonders there are unseen and unseeable in the world.

You tear apart the baby's rattle and see what makes the noise inside, but there is a veil covering the unseen world which not the strongest man, nor even the united strength of all the strongest men that ever lived, could tear apart. Only faith, fancy, poetry, love, romance, can push aside that curtain and view and picture the supernal beauty and glory beyond. Is it all real? Ah, Virginia, in all this world there is nothing else real and abiding.

No Santa Claus! Thank God! he lives, and he lives forever. A thousand years from now, Virginia, nay, ten times ten thousand years from now, he will continue to make glad the heart of childhood.

A CHRISTMAS CAROL
Charles Dickens

With the publication in 1843 of *A Christmas Carol in Prose* (as the full title originally read), Charles Dickens bestowed a timeless message of repentance and hope to generations of readers. An aristocratic Dickens enthusiast, Lord Jeffrey, told the author that he had done "more good by this publication, fostered more kindly feelings, and prompted more positive acts of beneficence than can be traced to all the pulpits in Christendom since Christmas 1842." The 6,000-copy first printing sold out in a single day; second and third editions went almost as quickly. Over the years, Dickens' classic has been adapted into countless media, but purists will always argue that movies and plays and cartoons pale in comparison to the genuine item. What follows is a truly immortal work meant to be read aloud during the holidays.

MARLEY WAS DEAD, to begin with. There is no doubt whatever about that. The register of his burial was signed by the clergyman, the clerk, the undertaker, and the chief mourner. Scrooge signed it. And Scrooge's name was good upon 'Change for anything he chose to put his hand to.

Old Marley was dead as a doornail.

Mind! I don't mean to say that I know, of my own knowledge, what there is particularly dead about a doornail. I might have been inclined, myself, to regard a coffin nail as the deadest piece of ironmongery in the trade. But the wisdom of our ancestors is in the simile; and my unhallowed hands shall not disturb it, or the Country's done for. You will therefore permit me to repeat, emphatically, that Marley was as dead as a doornail.

Scrooge knew he was dead? Of course he did. How could it be otherwise? Scrooge and he were partners for I don't know how many years. Scrooge was his sole executor, his sole administrator, his sole assign, his sole residuary legatee, his sole friend, and sole mourner. And even Scrooge was not so dreadfully cut up by the sad event but that he was an excellent man of business on the very day of the funeral, and solemnized it with an undoubted bargain.

The mention of Marley's funeral brings me back to the point I started from. There is no doubt that Marley was dead. This must be distinctly understood, or nothing wonderful can come of the story I am going to relate. If we were not perfectly convinced that Hamlet's Father died before the play began, there would be nothing more remarkable in his taking a stroll at night, in an easterly wind, upon his own ramparts, than there would be in any other middle-aged gentleman rashly turning out after dark in a breezy spot—say Saint Paul's Churchyard, for instance—literally to astonish his son's weak mind.

Scrooge never painted out Old Marley's name.

There it stood, years afterward, above the warehouse door: *Scrooge and Marley*. The firm was known as Scrooge and Marley. Sometimes people new to the business called Scrooge Scrooge, and sometimes Marley, but he answered to both names. It was all the same to him.

Once upon a time—of all the good days in the year, on Christmas Eve—old Scrooge sat busy in his countinghouse. It was cold, bleak, biting weather: foggy withal: and he could hear the people in the court outside go wheezing up and down, beating their hands upon their breasts, and stamping their feet upon the pavement stones to warm them. The city clocks had only just gone three, but it was quite dark already—it had not been light all day—and candles were flaring in the windows of the neighboring offices, like ruddy smears upon the palpable brown air. The fog came pouring in at every chink and keyhole, and was so dense without, that although the court was of the narrowest, the houses opposite were mere phantoms. To see the dingy cloud come drooping down, obscuring everything, one might have thought that Nature lived hard by, and was brewing on a large scale.

The door of Scrooge's countinghouse was open, that he might keep his eye upon his clerk, who, in a dismal little cell beyond, a sort of tank, was copying letters. Scrooge had a very small fire, but the clerk's fire was so very

much smaller that it looked like one coal. But he couldn't replenish it, for Scrooge kept the coalbox in his own room; and so surely as the clerk came in with the shovel the master predicted that it would be necessary for them to part. Wherefore the clerk put on his white comforter and tried to warm himself at the candle, in which effort, not being a man of imagination, he failed.

"A merry Christmas, Uncle! God save you!" cried a cheerful voice. It was the voice of Scrooge's nephew, who came upon him so quickly that this was the first intimation he had of his approach.

"Bah!" said Scrooge. "Humbug!"

He had so heated himself with rapid walking in the fog and frost, this nephew of Scrooge's, that he was all in a glow; his face was ruddy and handsome; his eyes sparkled, and his breath smoked again.

"Christmas a humbug, Uncle!" said Scrooge's nephew. "You don't mean that, I am sure."

"I do," said Scrooge. "Merry Christmas! What right have you to be merry? What reason have you to be merry? You're poor enough."

"Come, then," returned his nephew gaily. "What right have you to be dismal? What reason have you to be morose? You're rich enough."

Scrooge having no better answer ready on the spur of the moment, said, "Bah!" again; and followed it up with, "Humbug!"

"Don't be cross, Uncle!" said the nephew.

"What else can I be?" returned the uncle, "when I live in such a world of fools as this? Merry Christmas! Out upon merry Christmas! What's Christmas time to you but a time for paying bills without money, a time for finding yourself a year older and not an hour richer, a time for balancing your books and having every item in 'em through a round dozen of months presented dead against you? If I could work my will," said Scrooge indignantly, "every idiot who goes about with 'Merry Christmas,' on his lips should be boiled with his own pudding, and buried with a stake of holly through his heart. He should!"

"Uncle!" pleaded the nephew.

"Nephew!" returned the uncle sternly. "Keep Christmas in your own way, and let me keep it in mine."

"Keep it!" repeated Scrooge's nephew. "But you don't keep it."

"Let me leave it alone, then," said Scrooge. "Much good may it do you! Much good it has ever done you!"

"There are many things from which I might have derived good, by which I have not profited, I dare say," returned the nephew. "Christmas among the rest. But I am sure I have always thought of Christmas time, when it has come round—apart from the veneration due to its sacred name and origin, if anything belonging to it can be apart from that—as a good time; a kind, forgiving, charitable, pleasant time; the only time I know of the long calendar of the year, when men and women seem by one consent to open their shut-up hearts freely, and to think of people below them as if they really were fellow passengers to the grave, and not another race of creatures bound on other journeys. And therefore, Uncle, though it has never put a scrap of gold or silver in my pocket, I believe that it has done me good and will do me good; and I say God bless it!"

The clerk in the tank involuntarily applauded. Becoming immediately sensible of the impropriety, he poked the fire and extinguished the last frail spark forever.

"Let me hear another sound from you," said Scrooge, "and you'll keep your Christmas by losing your situation. You're quite a powerful speaker, sir," he added, turning to his nephew. "I wonder you don't go into Parliament."

"Don't be angry, Uncle. Come! Dine with us tomorrow."

Scrooge said that he would see him—yes, indeed he did. He went the whole length of the expression, and said that he would see him in that extremity first.

"But why?" cried Scrooge's nephew. "Why?"

"Why did you get married?" said Scrooge.

"Because I fell in love."

"Because you fell in love!" growled Scrooge, as if that were the only one thing in the world more ridiculous than a merry Christmas. "Good afternoon!"

"Nay, Uncle, but you never came to see me before that happened. Why give it as a reason for not coming now?"

"Good afternoon," said Scrooge.

"I want nothing from you; I ask nothing of you; why cannot we be friends?"

"Good afternoon," said Scrooge.

"I am sorry, with all my heart, to find you so resolute. We have never had any quarrel to which I have been a party. But I have made the trial in homage to Christmas, and I'll keep my Christmas humor to the last. So, a Merry Christmas, Uncle!"

"Good afternoon!" said Scrooge.

"And a Happy New Year!"

"Good afternoon!" said Scrooge.

His nephew left the room without an angry word, notwithstanding. He stopped at the outer door to bestow the greetings of the season on the clerk, who, cold as he was, was warmer than Scrooge; for he returned them cordially.

"There's another fellow," muttered Scrooge, who overheard him. "My clerk, with fifteen shillings a week and a wife and family, talking about a merry Christmas. I'll retire to Bedlam."

This lunatic, in letting Scrooge's nephew out, had let two other people in. They were portly gentlemen, pleasant to behold, and now stood, with their hats off, in Scrooge's office. They had books and papers in their hands, and bowed to him.

"Scrooge and Marley's I believe," said one of the gentlemen, referring to his list. "Have I the pleasure of addressing Mr. Scrooge or Mr. Marley?"

"Mr. Marley has been dead these seven years," Scrooge replied. "He died seven years ago, this very night."

"We have no doubt his liberality is well represented by his surviving partner," said the gentlemen, presenting his credentials.

It certainly was; for they had been two kindred spirits. At the ominous word "liberality" Scrooge frowned and shook his head and handed the credentials back.

"At this festive season of the year, Mr. Scrooge," said the gentleman, taking up a pen, "it is more than usually desirable that we should make some slight provision for the poor and destitute, who suffer greatly at the present time. Many thousands are in want of common necessaries, hundreds of thousands are in want of common comforts, sir."

"Are there no prisons?" asked Scrooge.

"Plenty of prisons," said the gentleman, laying down the pen again.

"And the Union workhouses?" demanded Scrooge. "Are they still in operation?"

"They are. Still," returned the gentleman, "I wish I could say they were not."

"The Treadmill and the Poor Law are in full vigor, then?" said Scrooge.

"Both very busy, sir."

"Oh! I was afraid, from what you said at first, that something had occurred to stop them in their useful course," said Scrooge. "I am very glad to hear it."

"Under the impression that they scarcely furnish Christian cheer of mind or body to the multitude," returned the gentleman, "a few of us are endeavoring to raise a fund to buy the Poor some meat and drink and means of warmth. We choose this time, because it is a time of all others, when Want is keenly felt, and Abundance rejoices. What shall I put you down for?"

"Nothing!" Scrooge replied.

"You wish to be anonymous?"

"I wish to be left alone," said Scrooge. "Since you ask me what I wish, Gentlemen, that is my answer. I don't make merry myself at Christmas, and I can't afford to make idle people merry. I help to support the establishments I have mentioned—they cost enough, and those who are badly off must go there."

"Many can't go there; many would rather die."

"If they would rather die," said Scrooge, "they had better do it, and decrease the surplus population. Besides—excuse me—I don't know that."

"But you might know it," observed the gentleman.

"It's not my business," Scrooge returned. "It's enough for a man to understand his own business, and not to interfere with other people's. Mine occupies me constantly. Good afternoon, Gentlemen!"

Seeing clearly that it would be useless to pursue their point, the gentlemen withdrew. Scrooge resumed his labor with an improved opinion of himself, and in a more facetious temper than was usual with him.

At length the hour of shutting up the countinghouse arrived. With an ill will Scrooge dismounted from his stool and tacitly admitted the fact to the expectant clerk in the tank, who instantly snuffed his candle out and put on his hat.

"You'll want all day tomorrow, I suppose?" said Scrooge.

"If quite convenient, sir."

"It's not convenient," said Scrooge, "and it's not fair. If I was to stop half-a-crown for it, you'd think yourself ill-used, I'll be bound?"

The clerk smiled faintly.

"And yet," said Scrooge, "you don't think *me* ill-used, when I pay a day's wages for no work."

The clerk observed it was only once a year.

"A poor excuse for picking a man's pocket every twenty-fifth of December!" said Scrooge, buttoning his greatcoat to the chin. "But I suppose you must have the whole day. Be here all the earlier the next morning."

The clerk promised that he would; and Scrooge walked out with a growl. The office was closed in a twinkling, and the clerk, with the long ends of his white comforter dangling below his waist (for he boasted no greatcoat), went down a slide on Cornhill, at the end of a lane of boys, twenty times, in honor of its being Christmas Eve, and then ran home to Camden Town as hard as he could pelt, to play at blindman's buff.

Scrooge took his melancholy dinner in his usual melancholy tavern; and having read all the newspapers, and beguiled the rest of the evening with his banker's book, went home to bed. He lived in chambers which had once belonged to his deceased partner. They were a gloomy suite of rooms, in a lowering pile of building up a yard, where it had so little business to be, that one could scarcely help fancying it must have run there when it was a young house, playing at hide-and-seek with other houses, and have forgotten the way out again. It was old enough now, and dreary enough; for nobody lived in it but Scrooge, the other rooms being all let out as offices. The yard was so dark that even Scrooge, who knew its every stone, was fain to grope with his hands. The fog and frost so hung about the black old gateway of the house that it seemed as if the Genius of the Weather sat in mournful meditation on the threshold.

Now it is a fact that there was nothing at all particular about the knocker on the door, except that it was very large. It is also a fact that Scrooge had seen it, night and morning, during his whole residence in that place; also that Scrooge had as little of what is called fancy about him as any man in the City of London, even including—which is a bold word—the corporation, aldermen, and livery. Let it also be borne in mind that Scrooge had not bestowed one thought on Marley since his last mention of his seven-years dead partner that afternoon. And then let any man explain to me, if he can, how it happened that Scrooge, having his key in the lock of the

door, saw in the knocker, without its undergoing any intermediate process of change—not a knocker, but Marley's face.

Marley's face. It was not in impenetrable shadow, as the other objects in the yard were, but had a dismal light about it, like a bad lobster in a dark cellar. It was not angry or ferocious, but looked at Scrooge as Marley used to look, with ghostly spectacles turned up on its ghostly forehead. The hair was curiously stirred, as if by breath of hot air; and, though the eyes were wide open, they were perfectly motionless. That, and its livid color, made it horrible; but its horror seemed to be in spite of the face, and beyond its control, rather than a part of its own expression.

As Scrooge looked fixedly at this phenomenon, it was a knocker again.

To say that he was not startled, or that his blood was not conscious of a terrible sensation to which it had been a stranger from infancy, would be untrue. But he put his hand upon the key he had relinquished, turned it sturdily, walked in, and lighted his candle.

He *did* pause, with a moment's irresolution, before he shut the door; and he *did* look cautiously behind it first, as if he half expected to be terrified with the sight of Marley's pigtail sticking out into the hall. But there was nothing on the back of the door except the screws and nuts that held the knocker on, so he said, "Pooh, pooh!" and closed it with a bang.

The sound resounded through the house like thunder. Every room above and every cask in the wine merchant's cellar below appeared to have a separate peal of echoes of its own. Scrooge was not a man to be frightened by echoes. He fastened the door and walked across the hall and up the stairs, slowly, too, trimming the candle as he went.

Up Scrooge went, not caring a button for that. Darkness is cheap, and Scrooge liked it. But before he shut his heavy door, he walked through his rooms to see that all was right. He had just enough recollection of the face to desire to do that.

Sitting-room, bedroom, lumber room. All as they should be. Nobody under the table, nobody under the sofa; a small fire in the grate; spoon and basin ready; and the little saucepan of gruel (Scrooge had a cold in his head) upon the hob. Nobody under the bed; nobody in the closet; nobody in his dressing gown, which was hanging up in a suspicious attitude against the wall. Lumber room as usual. Old fireguard, old shoes, two fish baskets, washing stand on three legs, and a poker.

"Humbug!" said Scrooge, and walked across the room.

After several turns, he sat down again. As he threw his head back in the chair, his glance happened to rest upon a bell, a disused bell that hung in the room and communicated for some purpose now forgotten with a chamber in the highest story of the building. It was with great astonishment, and with a strange, inexplicable dread, that as he looked, he saw this bell begin to swing. It swung so softly in the outset that it scarcely made a sound; but soon it rang out loudly, and so did every bell in the house.

This might have lasted half a minute, or a minute, but it seemed an hour. The bells ceased as they had begun, together. They were succeeded by a clanking noise, deep down below, as if some persons were dragging a heavy chain over the casks in the wine merchant's cellar.

Scrooge then remembered to have heard that ghosts in haunted houses were described as dragging chains.

The cellar door flew open with a booming sound, and then he heard the noise much louder, on the floors below; then coming up the stairs; then coming straight toward his door.

"It's humbug still!" said Scrooge. "I won't believe it."

His color changed, though, when, without a pause, it came on through the heavy door and passed into the room before his eyes. Upon its coming in, the dying flame leaped up, as though it cried, "I know him! Marley's ghost!" and then fell again.

The same face; the very same. Marley in his pigtail, usual waistcoat, tights, and boots; and tassels on the latter bristling like his pigtail, and his coat skirts, and the hair upon his head. The chain he drew was clasped about his middle. It was long and wound about him like a tail; and it was made (for Scrooge observed it closely) of cashboxes, keys, padlocks, ledgers, deeds, and heavy purses wrought in steel. His body was transparent, so that Scrooge, observing him and looking through his waistcoat, could see the two buttons on his coat behind.

Scrooge had often heard it said that Marley had no bowels, but he had never believed it until now.

"How now!" said Scrooge, caustic and cold as ever. "What do you want with me?"

"Much!" Marley's voice, no doubt about it.

"Who are you?"

"Ask me who I *was*."

"Who *were* you, then?" said Scrooge, raising his voice. "You're particular, for a shade." He was going to say "to a shade," but substituted this, as more appropriate.

"In life I was your partner, Jacob Marley."

"Can you—can you sit down?" asked Scrooge, looking at him.

"I can."

Scrooge asked the question because he didn't know whether a ghost so transparent might find himself in a condition to take a chair; and felt that in the event of its being impossible, it might involve the necessity of an embarrassing explanation. But the ghost sat down on the opposite side of the fireplace, as if he were quite used to it.

"You don't believe in me," observed the Ghost.

"I don't," said Scrooge.

"What evidence would you have of my reality beyond that of your own senses?"

"I don't know," said Scrooge.

"Why do you doubt your senses?"

"Because," said Scrooge, "a little thing affects them. A slight disorder of the stomach makes them cheats. You may be an undigested bit of beef, a blot of mustard, a crumb of cheese, a fragment of an underdone potato. There's more of gravy than of grave about you, whatever you are!"

Scrooge was not much in the habit of cracking jokes, nor did he feel in his heart by any means waggish then. The truth is that he tried to be smart, as a means of distracting his own attention, and keeping down his terror, for the specter's voice disturbed the very marrow of his bones.

To sit staring at those fixed glazed eyes, in silence for a moment, would play, Scrooge, felt, the very deuce with him. There was something very awful, too, in the specter's being provided with an infernal atmosphere of his own. Scrooge could not feel it himself, but this was clearly the case; for though the Ghost sat perfectly motionless, its hair and skirts and tassels were still agitated as by the hot vapor from an oven.

"You see this toothpick?" said Scrooge, returning quickly to the charge for the reason just assigned, and wishing, though it were only for a second, to divert the vision's stony gaze from himself.

"I do," replied the Ghost.

"You are not looking at it," said Scrooge.

"But I see it," said the Ghost, "notwithstanding."

"Well!" returned Scrooge, "I have but to swallow this, and be for the rest of my days persecuted by a legion of goblins, all of my own creation. Humbug, I tell you; humbug!"

At this the spirit raised a frightful cry, and shook its chain with such a dismal and appalling noise that Scrooge held on tight to his chair to save himself from falling in a swoon. But how much greater was his horror when, the phantom taking off the bandage round its head, as if it were too warm to wear indoors, its lower jaw dropped down upon its breast!

Scrooge fell upon his knees, and clasped his hands before his face.

"Mercy!" he said. "Dreadful apparition, why do you trouble me?"

"Man of the worldly mind!" replied the Ghost. "Do you believe in me or not?"

"I do," said Scrooge. "I must. But why do spirits walk the earth and why do they come to me?"

"It is required of every man," the Ghost returned, "that the spirit within him should walk abroad among his fellow men, and travel far and wide; and if that spirit goes not forth in life, it is condemned to do so after death. It is doomed to wander through the world—oh, woe is me!—and witness what it cannot share, but might have shared on earth, and turned to happiness!"

Again the specter raised a cry, and shook its chain and wrung its shadowy hands.

"You are fettered," said Scrooge, trembling. "Tell me why?"

"I wear the chain I forged in life," replied the Ghost. "I made it link by link, and yard by yard; I girded it on of my own free will, and of my own free will I wore it. Is its pattern strange to you?"

Scrooge trembled more and more.

"Or would you know," pursued the Ghost, "the weight and length of the strong coil you bear yourself? It was full as heavy and as long as this seven Christmas Eves ago. You have labored on it since. It is a ponderous chain!"

Scrooge glanced about him on the floor, in the expectation of finding himself surrounded by some fifty or sixty fathoms of iron cable; but he could see nothing.

"Jacob," he said imploringly. "Old Jacob Marley, tell me more. Speak comfort to me, Jacob!"

"I have none to give," the Ghost replied. "It comes from other regions, Ebenezer Scrooge, and is conveyed by other ministers, to other kinds of men. Nor can I tell you what I would. A very little more is all that is permitted to me. I cannot rest, I cannot stay, I cannot linger anywhere. My spirit never walked beyond our countinghouse—mark me!—in life my spirit never roved beyond the narrow limits of our money-changing hole; and weary journeys lie before me!"

It was a habit with Scrooge, whenever he became thoughtful, to put his hands in his breeches' pockets. Pondering on what the Ghost had said, he did so now, but without lifting up his eyes, or getting off his knees.

"You must have been very slow about it, Jacob," Scrooge observed in a businesslike manner, though with humility and deference.

"Slow!" the Ghost repeated.

"Seven years dead," mused Scrooge. "And traveling all the time?"

"The whole time," said the Ghost. "No rest, no peace. Incessant torture of remorse."

"You travel fast?" said Scrooge.

"On the wings of the wind," replied the Ghost.

"You might have got over a great quantity of ground in seven years," said Scrooge.

The Ghost, on hearing this, set up another cry and clanked its chain so hideously in the dead silence of the night, that the Ward would have been justified in indicting it for a nuisance.

"Oh! Captive, bound and double-ironed," cried the phantom, "not to know that ages of incessant labor, by immortal creatures, for this earth must pass into eternity before the good of which it is susceptible is all developed. Not to know that any Christian spirit working kindly in its little sphere, whatever it may be, will find its mortal life too short for its vast means of usefulness. Not to know that no space of regret can make amends for one life's opportunities misused! Yet such was I! Oh! such was I!"

"But you were always a good man of business, Jacob," faltered Scrooge, who now began to apply this to himself.

"Business!" cried the Ghost, wringing its hands again. "Mankind was my business. The common welfare was my business; charity, mercy, forbearance, and benevolence were all my business. The dealings of my trade were but a drop of water in the comprehensive ocean of my business!"

It held up its chain at arm's length, as if that were the cause of all its unavailing grief, and flung it heavily upon the ground again.

"At this time of the rolling year," the specter said, "I suffer most. Why did I walk through crowds of fellow beings with my eyes turned down, and never raise them to that blessed Star which led the Wise

Men to a poor abode? Were there no poor homes to which its light would have conducted me?"

Scrooge was very much dismayed to hear the specter going on at this rate, and began to quake exceedingly.

"Hear me!" cried the Ghost. "My time is nearly gone."

"I will," said Scrooge. "But don't be hard upon me! Don't be flowery, Jacob! Pray!"

"How it is that I appear before you in a shape that you can see, I may not tell. I have sat invisible beside you many and many a day."

It was not an agreeable idea. Scrooge shivered and wiped the perspiration from his brow.

"That is no light part of my penance," pursued the Ghost. "I am here tonight to warn you that you have yet a chance and hope of escaping my fate. A chance and hope of my procuring, Ebenezer."

"You were always a good friend to me," said Scrooge. "Thank'ee!"

"You will be haunted," resumed the Ghost, "by Three Spirits."

Scrooge's countenance fell almost as low as the Ghost's had done.

"Is that the chance and hope you mentioned, Jacob?" he demanded, in a faltering voice.

"It is."

"I—I think I'd rather not," said Scrooge.

"Without their visits," said the Ghost, "you cannot hope to shun the path I tread. Expect the first tomorrow, when the bell tolls one."

"Couldn't I take 'em all at once, and have it over?" hinted Scrooge.

"Expect the second on the next night at the same hour. The third, upon the next night when the last stroke of twelve has ceased to vibrate. Look to see me no more; and look that, for your own sake, you remember what has passed between us!"

When it had said these words, the specter took its wrapper from the table and bound it round its head, as before. Scrooge knew this by the smart sound its teeth made, when the jaws were brought together by the bandage. He ventured to raise his eyes again, and found his supernatural visitor confronting him in an erect attitude, with its chain wound over and about its arm.

The apparition walked backward from him; and at every step it took, the window raised itself a little, so that when the specter reached it, it was wide open. It beckoned Scrooge to approach, which he did. When they were within two paces of each other, Marley's Ghost held up its hand, warning him to come no nearer. Scrooge stopped.

Not so much in obedience, as in surprise and fear; for on the raising of the hand, he became sensible of confused noises in the air; incoherent sounds of lamentation and regret; wailings inexpressibly sorrowful and self-accusatory. The specter, after listening for a moment, joined in the mournful dirge; and floated out upon the bleak, dark night.

Scrooge followed to the window, desperate in his curiosity. He looked out.

The air was filled with phantoms, wandering hither and thither in restless haste, and moaning as they went. Every one of them wore chains like Marley's

Ghost; some few (they might be guilty governments) were linked together; none were free. Many had been personally known to Scrooge in their lives. He had been quite familiar with one old ghost, in a white waistcoat, with a monstrous iron safe attached to its ankle, who cried piteously at being unable to assist a wretched woman with an infant, whom it saw below, upon a doorstep. The misery with them all was, clearly, that they sought to interfere, for good, in human matters, and had lost the power forever.

Whether these creatures faded into mist, or mist enshrouded them, he could not tell. But they and their spirit voices faded together; and the night became as it had been when he walked home.

Scrooge closed the window and examined the door by which the Ghost had entered. It was doubled-locked, as he had locked it with his own hands, and the bolts were undisturbed. He tried to say, "Humbug!" but stopped at the first syllable. And being, from the emotion he had undergone, or the fatigues of the day, or his glimpse of the Invisible World, or the dull conversation of the Ghost, or the lateness of the hour, much in need of repose, went straight to bed without undressing, and fell asleep upon the instant.

* * *

When Scrooge awoke it was so dark that, looking out of bed, he could scarcely distinguish the transparent window from the opaque walls of his chamber. He was endeavoring to pierce the darkness with his ferret eyes, when the chimes of a neighboring church struck the four quarters. So he listened for the hour.

To his great astonishment, the heavy bell went on from six to seven, and from seven to eight, and regularly up to twelve; then stopped. Twelve! It was past two when he went to bed. The clock was wrong. An icicle must have got into the works. Twelve!

He touched the spring of his repeater, to correct this most preposterous clock. Its rapid little pulse beat twelve and stopped.

"Why, it isn't possible," said Scrooge, "that I can have slept through a whole day and far into another night. It isn't possible that anything has happened to the sun, and this is twelve at noon!"

This idea being an alarming one, he scrambled out of bed and groped his way to the window. He was obliged to rub the frost off with the sleeve of his dressing gown before he could see anything; and could see very little then. All he could make out was that it was still very foggy and extremely cold, and that there was no noise of people running to and fro and making a great stir, as there unquestionably would have been if night had beaten off bright day and taken possession of the world. This was a great relief, because *Three days after sight of this First of Exchange pay to Mr. Ebenezer Scrooge on his order, and so forth*, would have become a mere United States security if there were no days to count by.

Scrooge went to bed again and thought and thought, and thought it over and over, and could make nothing of it. The more he thought the more perplexed he was; and the more he endeavored not to think, the more he thought.

Marley's ghost bothered him exceedingly. Every time he resolved within himself, after mature inquiry, that it was all a dream, his mind flew back again, like a strong spring released, to its first position, and presented the same problem to be worked all through: Was it a dream or not?

Scrooge lay in this state until the chime had gone three quarters more, when he remembered, on a sudden, that the Ghost had warned him of a visitation when the bell tolled one.

He resolved to lie awake until the hour was

passed; and, considering that he could no more go to sleep than go to heaven, this was perhaps the wisest resolution in his power.

The quarter was so long, that he was more than once convinced that he must have sunk into a doze unconsciously and missed the clock. At length it broke upon his listening ear.

Ding, dong!

"A quarter past," said Scrooge, counting.

Ding, dong!

"Half past," said Scrooge.

Ding, dong!

"A quarter to it," said Scrooge.

Ding, dong!

"The hour itself," said Scrooge triumphantly, "and nothing else!"

He spoke before the hour bell sounded, which it now did with a deep, dull, hollow, melancholy one. Light flashed up in the room upon the instant, and the curtains of his bed were drawn.

The curtains of his bed were drawn aside, I tell you, by a hand. Not the curtains at his feet, nor the curtains at his back, but those to which his face was addressed. The curtains of his bed were drawn aside; and Scrooge, starting up into a half-recumbent attitude, found himself face to face with the unearthly visitor who drew them; as close to it as I am now to you, and I am standing in the spirit at your elbow.

It was a strange figure—like a child; yet not so like a child as like an old man, viewed through some supernatural medium, which gave him the appearance of having receded from the view, and being diminished to a child's proportions. Its hair, which hung about its neck and down its back, was white as if with age; and yet the face had not a wrinkle in it, and the tenderest bloom was on the skin. The arms

were very long and muscular; the hands the same, as if its hold were of uncommon strength. Its legs and feet, most delicately formed, were, like those upper members, bare. It wore a tunic of the purest white; and round its waist was bound a lustrous belt, the sheen of which was beautiful. It held a branch of fresh green holly in its hand; and, in singular contradiction of that wintry emblem, had its dress trimmed with summer flowers.

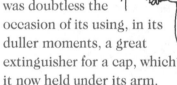

But the strangest thing about it was that from the crown of its head there sprung a bright clear jet of light, by which all this was visible; and which was doubtless the occasion of its using, in its duller moments, a great extinguisher for a cap, which it now held under its arm.

Even this, though, when Scrooge looked at it with increasing steadiness, was *not* its strangest quality. For as its belt sparkled and glittered, now in one part and now in another, and what was light one instant, at another time was dark, so the figure itself fluctuated in its distinctness, being now a thing with one arm, now with one leg, now with twenty legs, now a pair of legs without a head, now a head without a body; of which dissolving parts, no outline would be visible in the dense gloom wherein they melted away. And in the very wonder of this, it would be itself again; distinct and clear as ever.

"Are you the Spirit, sir, whose coming was foretold to me?" asked Scrooge.

"I am!"

The voice was soft and gentle. Singularly low, as if instead of being so close beside him, it were at a distance.

"Who and what are you?" Scrooge demanded.

"I am the Ghost of Christmas Past."

"Long Past?" inquired Scrooge, observant of its dwarfish stature.

"No. Your past."

Perhaps Scrooge could not have told anybody why, if anybody could have asked him, but he had a special desire to see the Spirit in his cap, and begged him to be covered.

"What!" exclaimed the Ghost. "Would you so soon put out, with worldly hands, the light I give? Is it not enough that you are one of those whose passions made this cap, and force me through whole trains of years to wear it low upon my brow?"

Scrooge reverently disclaimed all intention to offend or any knowledge of having wilfully "bonneted" the Spirit at any period of his life. He then made bold to inquire what business brought him there.

"Your welfare!" said the Ghost.

Scrooge expressed himself much obliged, but could not help thinking that a night of unbroken rest would have been more conducive to that end.

The Spirit must have heard him thinking, for it said, "Your reclamation, then. Take heed!"

It put out its strong hand as it spoke, and clasped him gently by the arm.

"Rise! And walk with me!"

It would have been in vain for Scrooge to plead that the weather and the hour were not adapted to pedestrian purposes; that bed was warm, and the thermometer a long way below freezing; that he was clad but lightly in his slippers, dressing gown, and nightcap; and that he had a cold upon him at the time. The grasp, though gentle as a woman's hand, was not to be resisted. He rose; but finding that the Spirit made toward the window, clasped its robe in supplication.

"I am mortal," Scrooge remonstrated, "and liable to fall."

"Bear but a touch of my hand there," said the Spirit, laying it upon his heart, "and you shall be upheld in more than this!"

As the words were spoken, they passed through the wall and stood upon an open country road, with fields on either hand. The city had entirely vanished. Not a vestige of it was to be seen. The darkness and the mist had vanished with it, for it was a clear, cold, winter day, with snow upon the ground.

"Good Heaven!" said Scrooge, clasping his hands together, as he looked about him. "I was bred in this place. I was a boy here!"

The Spirit gazed upon him mildly. Its gentle touch, though it had been light and instantaneous, appeared still present to the old man's sense of feeling. He was conscious of a thousand odors floating in the air, each one connected with a thousand thoughts and hopes and joys and cares, long, long forgotten.

"Your lip is trembling," said the Ghost. "And what is that upon your cheek?"

Scrooge muttered, with an unusual catching in his voice, that it was a pimple; and begged the Ghost to lead him where he would.

"You recollect the way?" inquired the Spirit.

"Remember it!" cried Scrooge with fervor. "I could walk it blindfold."

"Strange to have forgotten it for so many years!" observed the Ghost, "Let us go on."

They walked along the road, Scrooge recognizing every gate and post and tree, until a little market town appeared in the distance, with its bridge, its church, and winding river. Some shaggy ponies now were seen trotting toward them with boys upon their backs, who called to other boys in country gigs and carts, driven by farmers. All these boys were in great spirits and shouted to each other, until the broad fields were so full of merry music that the crisp air laughed to hear it.

"These are but shadows of the things that have been," said the Ghost. "They have no consciousness of us."

The jocund travelers came on; and as they came, Scrooge knew and named them every one. Why was he rejoiced beyond all bounds to see them? Why did his cold eye glisten, and his heart leap up as they went past. Why was he filled with gladness when he heard them give each other Merry Christmas, as they parted at crossroads and byways, for their several homes? What was merry Christmas to Scrooge? Out upon merry Christmas! What good had it ever done to him?

"The school is not quite deserted," said the Ghost. "A solitary child, neglected by his friends, is left there still."

Scrooge said he knew it. And he sobbed.

They left the highroad by a well-remembered lane, and soon approached a mansion of dull red brick, with a little weathercock-surmounted cupola on the roof, and a bell hanging in it. It was a large house, but one of broken fortunes, for the spacious offices were little used, their walls were damp and mossy, their windows broken, and their gates decayed. Fowls clucked and strutted in the stables, and the coach houses and sheds were overrun with grass. Nor was it more retentive of its ancient state within; for entering the dreary hall and glancing through the open doors of many rooms, they found them poorly furnished, cold, and vast. There was an earthy savor in the air, a chilly bareness on the place, which associated itself somehow with too much getting up by candlelight, and not too much to eat.

They went, the Ghost and Scrooge, across the hall to a door at the back of the house. It opened before them and disclosed along, bare, melancholy room, made barer still by lines of plain deal forms and desks. At one of these a lonely boy was reading near a feeble fire; and Scrooge sat down upon a form, and wept to see his poor forgotten self as he had used to be.

Not a latent echo in the house, not a squeak and scuffle from the mice behind the paneling, not a drip form the half-thawed waterspout in the dull yard behind, not a sigh among the leafless boughs of one despondent poplar, not the idle swinging on an empty storehouse door, no, not a clicking in the fire, but fell upon the heart of Scrooge with softening influence, and gave a freer passage to his tears.

The Spirit touched him on the arm and pointed to his younger self, intent upon his reading. Suddenly a man in foreign garments, wonderfully real and distinct to look at, stood outside the window, with an axe stuck in his belt, and leading by the bridle an ass laden with wood.

"Why, it's Ali Baba!" Scrooge exclaimed in ecstasy. "It's dear old honest Ali Baba! Yes, yes I know. One Christmas time, when yonder solitary child was left here all alone, he did come for the first time, just like that. Poor boy! And Valentine," said Scrooge, "and his wild brother, Orson; there they go! And what's his name, who was put down in his drawers, asleep, at the gate of Damascus; don't you see him? And the Sultan's groom turned upside down by the Genii, there he is upon his head! Serves him right. I'm glad of it. What business had he to be married to the Princess?"

To hear Scrooge expending all the earnestness of his nature on such subjects, in a most extraordinary voice between laughing and crying, and to see his heightened and excited face, would have been a surprise to his business friends in the city, indeed.

"There's the Parrot!" cried Scrooge. "Green body and yellow tail, with a thing like lettuce growing out of the top of his head; there he is! 'Poor Robin Crusoe,' he called him, when he came home again after sailing round the island. 'Poor Robin Crusoe, where have you been, Robin Crusoe?' The man thought he was dreaming, but he wasn't. It was the Parrot, you know. There goes Friday, running for his life to the little creek! Halloa! Hoop! Halloo!"

Then, with a rapidity of transition very foreign to his usual character, he said, in pity for his former self, "Poor boy," and cried again.

"I wish," Scrooge muttered, putting his hand in his pocket and looking about him, after drying his hands with his cuff, "but it's too late now."

"What is the matter?" asked the Spirit.

"Nothing," said Scrooge. "Nothing. There was a boy singing a Christmas carol at my door last night. I should like to have given him something; that's all."

The Ghost smiled thoughtfully and waved its hands, saying as it did so, "Let us see another Christmas!"

Scrooge's former self grew large at the words, and the room became a little darker and more dirty. The panels shrunk, the windows cracked; fragments of plasters fell out of the ceiling, and the naked laths were shown instead; but how all this was brought about, Scrooge knew no more than you do. He only knew that it was quite correct; that everything had happened so; that there he was alone again, when all the other boys had gone home for the jolly holidays.

He was not reading now, but walking up and down despairingly. Scrooge looked at the Ghost and, with a mournful shaking of his head, glanced anxiously toward the door.

It opened; and a little girl, much younger than the boy, came darting in, and putting her arms about his neck, and often kissing him, addressed him as her "Dear, dear brother."

"I have come to bring you home, Dear Brother!" said the child, clapping her tiny hands, and bending down to laugh. "To bring you home, home, home!"

"Home, little Fan?" returned the boy.

"Yes!" said the child, brimful of glee. "Home, for good and all. Home, forever and ever. Father is so much kinder than he used to be, that home's like Heaven. He spoke so gently to me one dear night when I was going to bed, that I was not afraid to ask him once more if you might come home; and he said 'Yes,' you should; and sent me in a coach to bring you. And you're to be a man," said the child, opening her eyes; "and are never to come back here; but first we're to be together all the Christmas long, and have the merriest time in all the world."

"You are quite a woman, little Fan!" exclaimed the boy.

She clapped her hands and laughed and tried to touch his head; but being too little, laughed again, and stood on tiptoe to embrace him. Then she began to drag him, in her childish eagerness, toward the door; and he, nothing loath to go, accompanied her.

A terrible voice in the hall cried, "Bring down Master Scrooge's box, there!" And in the hall appeared the schoolmaster himself, who glared on Master Scrooge with a ferocious condescension, and threw him into a dreadful state of mind by shaking hands with him. He then conveyed him and his sister into the veriest old well of a shivering best-parlor that ever was seen, where the maps upon the wall, and the celestial and terrestrial globes in the windows, were waxy with cold. Here he produced a decanter of curiously light wine and a block of curiously heavy cake, and administered installments of these dainties to the young people, at the same time sending out a meager servant to offer a glass of "something" to the postboy, who answered that he thanked the gentleman, but if it was the same tap as he had tasted before, he had rather not. Master Scrooge's trunk being by this time tied on to the top of the chaise, the children bade the schoolmaster good-by right willingly; and getting into it, drove gaily down the garden sweep, the quick wheels dashing the hoar frost and snow from off the dark leaves of the evergreens like spray.

"Always a delicate creature, whom a breath might have withered," said the Ghost. "But she had a large heart!"

"So she had," cried Scrooge. "You're right. I will not gainsay it, Spirit. God forbid!"

"She died a woman," said the Ghost, "and had, as I think, children."

"One child," Scrooge returned.

"True," said the Ghost. "Your nephew!"

Scrooge seemed uneasy in his mind, and answered briefly, "Yes."

Although they had but that moment left the school behind them, they were now in the busy thoroughfares of a city, where shadowy passengers passed and repassed, where shadowy carts and coaches battled for the way, and all the strife and tumult of a real city were. It was made plain enough, by the dressing of the shops, that here too it was Christmas time again; but it was evening, and the streets were lighted up.

The Ghost stopped at a certain warehouse door, and asked Scrooge if he knew it.

"Know it?" said Scrooge. "Was I apprenticed here?"

They went in. At sight of an old gentleman in a Welsh wig, sitting behind such a high desk, that if he had been two inches taller he must have knocked his head against the ceiling, Scrooge cried in great excitement, "Why, it's old Fezziwig! Bless his heart; it's Fezziwig alive again!"

Old Fezziwig laid down his pen and looked up at the clock, which pointed to the hour of seven. He rubbed his hands, adjusted his capacious waistcoat, laughed all over himself, from his shoes to his organ of benevolence, and called out in a comfortable, oily, rich, fat, jovial voice, "Yo ho, there! Ebenezer! Dick!"

Scrooge's former self, now grown a young man, came briskly in, accompanied by his fellow 'prentice.

"Dick Wilkins, to be sure!" said Scrooge to the Ghost. "Bless me, yes. There he is. He was very much attached to me, was Dick. Poor Dick! Dear, dear!"

"Yo ho, my boys!" said Fezziwig. "No more work tonight. Christmas Eve, Dick. Christmas, Ebenezer! Let's have the shutters up," cried old Fezziwig, with a sharp clap of his hands, "before a man can say 'Jack Robinson!'"

You wouldn't believe how those two fellows went at it! They charged into the street with the shutters—one, two, three—had 'em up in their places—four, five, six—barred 'em and pinned 'em—seven, eight, nine—and came back before you could have got to twelve, panting like race horses.

"Hilli-ho!" cried old Fezziwig, skipping down from the high desk with wonderful agility. "Clear away, my lads, and let's have lots of room here! Hilli-ho, Dick! Chirrup, Ebenezer!"

Clear away! There was nothing they wouldn't have cleared away, or couldn't have cleared away, with old Fezziwig looking on. It was done in a minute. Every movable was packed off, as if it were dismissed from public life for evermore; the floor was swept and watered, the lamps were trimmed, fuel was heaped upon the fire; and the warehouse was as snug and warm and dry and bright a ballroom as you would desire to see upon a winter's night.

In came a fiddler with a music book and went up to the lofty desk and made an orchestra of it, and tuned like fifty stomach-aches. In came Mrs. Fezziwig, one vast, substantial smile. In came the three Miss Fezziwigs, beaming and lovable. In came the six young followers whose hearts they broke. In came all the young men and women employed in the business. In came the housemaid with her cousin, the baker. In came the cook with her brother's particular friend, the milkman. In came the boy from over the way, who was suspected of not having board enough from his master; trying to hide himself behind the girl from next door but one, who was proved to have had her ears pulled by her mistress. In they all came, one after another; some shyly, some boldly, some gracefully, some awkwardly, some pushing, some pulling; in they all came, anyhow and

everyhow. Away they all went, twenty couples at once; hands half round and back again the other way; down the middle and up again; round and round in various stages of affectionate grouping; old top couple always turning up in the wrong place; new top couple starting off again, as soon as they got there; all top couples at last, and not a bottom one to help them! When this result was brought about, old Fezziwig, clapping his hands to stop the dance cried out, "Well done!" And the fiddler plunged his hot face into a pot of porter especially provided for that purpose. But, scorning rest, upon his reappearance he instantly  began again, though there were no dancers yet, as if the other fiddler had been carried home, exhausted, on a shutter, and he were a brand-new man resolved to beat him out of sight or perish.

There were more dances, and there were forfeits, and more dances, and there was cake, and there was negus, and there was a great piece of Cold Roast, and there was a great piece of Cold Boiled, and there were mince pies and plenty of beer. But the great effect of the evening came after the Roast and Boiled, when the fiddler (an artful dog, mind! The sort of man who knew his business better than you or I could have told it him!) struck up "Sir Roger de Coverley." Then old Fezziwig stood out to dance with Mrs. Fezziwig. Top couple, too, with a good stiff piece of work cut out for them, three or four and twenty pair of partners, people who were not to be trifled with, people who would dance, and had no notion of walking.

But if they had been twice as many—ah, four times—old Fezziwig would have been a match for them, and so would Mrs. Fezziwig. As to her, she was worthy to be his partner in every sense of the term. If that's not high praise, tell me higher, and I'll use it. A positive light appeared to issue from Fezziwig's calves. They shone in every part of the dance like moons. You couldn't have predicted, at any given time, what would become of them next. And when old Fezziwig and Mrs. Fezziwig had gone all through the dance—advance and retire, both hands to your partner, bow and curtsey, corkscrew, thread-the-needle, and back again to your place—Fezziwig "cut"—cut so deftly that he appeared to wink with his legs, and came upon his feet again without a stagger.

When the clock struck eleven, this domestic ball broke up. Mr. and Mrs. Fezziwig took their stations, one on either side of the door, and shaking hands

with every person individually as he or she went out, wished him or her a Merry Christmas. When everybody had retired but the two 'prentices, they did the same to them; and thus the cheerful voices died away, and the lads were left to their beds, which were under a counter in the back shop.

During the whole of this time Scrooge had acted like a man out of his wits. His heart and soul were in the scene, and with his former self. He corroborated everything, remembered everything, enjoyed everything, and underwent the strangest agitation. It was not until now, when the bright faces of his former self and Dick were turned from them, that he remembered the Ghost, and became conscious that it was looking full upon him, while the light upon its head burned very clear.

"A small matter," said the Ghost, "to make these silly folks so full of gratitude."

"Small!" echoed Scrooge.

The Spirit signed to him to listen to the two apprentices, who were pouring out their hearts in praise of Fezziwig; and when he had done so, said, "Why! Is it not? He has spent but a few pounds of your mortal money, three or four perhaps. Is that so much that he deserves this praise?"

"It isn't that," said Scrooge, heated by the remark and speaking unconsciously like his former, not his latter self. "It isn't that, Spirit. He has the power to render us happy or unhappy; to make our service light or burdensome; a pleasure or a toil. Say that his power lies in words and looks; in things so slight and insignificant that it is impossible to add and count 'em up; what then? The happiness he gives is quite as great as if it cost a fortune."

He felt the Spirit's glance, and stopped.

"What is the matter?" asked the Ghost.

"Nothing particular," said Scrooge.

"Something, I think?" the Ghost insisted.

"No," said Scrooge. "No. I should like to be able to say a word or two to my clerk just now. That's all."

His former self turned down the lamps as he gave utterance to the wish; and Scrooge and the Ghost again stood side by side in the open air.

"My time grows short," observed the Spirit. "Quick!"

This was not addressed to Scrooge, or to any one whom he could see, but it produced an immediate effect. For again Scrooge saw himself. He was older now, a man in the prime of life. His face had not the harsh and rigid lines of later years, but it had begun to wear the signs of care and avarice. There was an eager, greedy, restless motion in the eye, which showed the passion that had taken root, and where the shadow of the growing tree would fall.

He was not alone, but sat by the side of a fair young girl in a mourning dress, in whose eyes there were tears, which sparkled in the light that shone out of the Ghost of Christmas Past.

"It matters little," she said softly. "To you, very little. Another idol has displaced me; and if it can cheer and comfort you in time to come, as I would have tried to do, I have no just cause to grieve."

"What idol has displaced you?" he rejoined.

"A golden one."

"This is the evenhanded dealing of the world!" he said. "There is nothing on which it is so hard as poverty; and there is nothing it professes to condemn with such severity as the pursuit of wealth!"

"You fear the world too much," she answered, gently. "All your other hopes have merged into the hope of being beyond the chance of its sordid reproach. I have seen your nobler aspirations fall off one by one, until the master passion, Gain, engrosses you. Have I not?"

"What then?" he retorted. "Even if I have grown so much wiser, what then? I am not changed toward you."

She shook her head.

"Am I?"

"Our contract is an old one. It was made when we were both poor and content to be so, until, in good season, we could improve our worldly fortune by our patient industry. You are changed. When it was made you were another man."

"I was a boy," he said impatiently.

"Your own feeling tells you that you were not what you are," she returned. "I am. That which promised happiness when we were one in heart, is fraught with misery now that we are two. How often and how keenly I have thought of this, I will not say. It is enough that I have thought of it, and can release you."

"Have I ever sought release?"

"In words, no. Never."

"In what, then?"

"In a changed nature, in an altered spirit, in another atmosphere of life, another Hope as its great end. In everything that made my love of any worth or value in your sight. If this had never been between us," said the girl, looking mildly but with steadiness upon him, "tell me, would you seek me out and try to win me now? Ah, no!"

He seemed to yield to the justice of this supposition, in spite of himself. But he said, with a struggle, "You think not."

"I would gladly think otherwise if I could," she answered, "Heaven knows! When I have learned a Truth like this, I know how strong and irresistible it must be. But if you were free today, tomorrow, yesterday, can even I believe that you would choose a dowerless girl—you who, in your very confidence with her, weigh everything by Gain; or choosing her, if for a moment you were false enough to your one guiding principle to do so, do I not know that your repentance and regret would surely follow? I do; and I release you. With a full heart, for the love of him you once were."

He was about to speak; but, with her head turned from him, she resumed.

"You may—the memory of what is past half makes me hope you will—have pain in this. A very, very brief time, and you will dismiss the recollection of it, gladly, as an unprofitable dream, from which it happened well that you awoke. May you be happy in the life you have chosen!"

She left him and they parted.

"Spirit!" said Scrooge. "Show me no more!

Conduct me home. Why do you delight to torture me?"

"One shadow more!" exclaimed the Ghost.

"No more!" cried Scrooge. "No more. I don't wish to see it. Show me no more!"

But the relentless Ghost pinioned him in both arms, and forced him to observe what happened next.

They were in another scene and place, a room, not very large or handsome, but full of comfort. Near the winter fire sat a beautiful young girl, so like that last that Scrooge believed it was the same, until he saw her, now a comely matron, sitting opposite her daughter. The noise in this room was perfectly tumultuous, for there were more children there than Scrooge in his agitated state of mind could count; and, unlike the celebrated herd in the poem, they were not forty children conducting themselves like one, but every

child was conducting itself like forty. The consequences were uproarious beyond belief, but no one seemed to care; on the contrary, the mother and daughter laughed heartily and enjoyed it very much, and the latter, soon beginning to mingle in the sports, got pillaged by the young brigands most ruthlessly. What would I not have given to be one of them! Though I never could have been so rude, no, no! I wouldn't for the wealth of all the world have crushed that braided hair, and torn it down; and for the precious little shoe, I wouldn't have plucked it

off—God bless my soul!—to save my life. As to measuring her waist in sport, as they did, bold young brood, I couldn't have done it; I should have expected my arm to have grown round it for a punishment, and never come straight again. And yet I should have dearly liked, I own, to have touched her lips, to have questioned her, that she might have opened them, to have looked upon the lashes of her downcast eyes and never raised a blush, to have let loose waves of her hair, an inch of which would be a keepsake beyond price; in short, I should have liked to have had the lightest license of a child, and yet to have been man enough to know its value.

But now a knocking at the door was heard, and such a rush immediately ensued that she with laughing face and plundered dress was borne toward it in the center of a flushed and boisterous group, just in time to greet the father, who came home attended by a man laden with Christmas toys and presents. Then the shouting and the struggling, and the onslaught that was made on the defenseless porter! The scaling him, with chairs for ladders, to dive into his pockets, despoil him of brown paper

parcels, hold on tight by his cravat, hug him round the neck, pommel his back, and kick his legs in irrepressible affection. The shouts of wonder and delight with which the development of every package was received! The terrible announcement that the baby had been taken in the act of putting a doll's frying pan into his mouth, and was more than suspected of having swallowed a fictitious turkey, glued on a wooden platter! The immense relief of finding this a false alarm! The joy, and gratitude, ecstasy! They are all indescribably alike. It is enough that, by degrees, the children and their emotions got out of the parlor, and, by one stair at a time, up to the top of the house, where they went to bed.

And now Scrooge looked on more attentively than ever, when the master of the house, having his daughter leaning fondly on him, sat down with her and her mother at his own fireside; and when he thought that such another creature, quite as graceful and as full of promise, might have called him Father, and been a springtime in the haggard winter of his life, his sight grew very dim indeed.

"Belle," said the husband, turning to his wife with a smile, "I saw an old friend of yours this afternoon."

"Who was it?"

"Guess!"

"How can I? Tut, don't I know." She added, in the same breath, laughing as he laughed, "Mr. Scrooge."

"Mr. Scrooge it was. I passed his office window; and as it was not shut up, and he had a candle inside, I could scarcely help seeing him. His partner lies upon the point of death, I hear; and there he is alone. Quite alone in the world, I do believe."

"Spirit!" said Scrooge. "Remove me from this place."

"I told you these were shadows of the things that have been," said the Ghost. "That they are what they are, do not blame me!"

"Remove me!" Scrooge exclaimed. "I cannot bear it!"

He turned upon the Ghost, and seeing that it looked upon him with a face in which, in some strange way, there were fragments of all the faces it had shown him, wrestled with it.

"Leave me! Take me back. Haunt me no longer!"

In the struggle—if that can be called a struggle in which the Ghost, with no visible resistance on its own part was undisturbed by any effort of its adversary—Scrooge observed that its light was burning high and bright; and dimly connecting that with its influence over him, he seized the extinguisher-cap, and by a sudden action pressed it down upon its head.

The Spirit dropped beneath it, so that the extinguisher covered its whole form; but though Scrooge pressed it down with all his force, he could not hide the light, which streamed from under it, in an unbroken flood upon the ground.

He was conscious of being exhausted and overcome by an irresistible drowsiness and, further, of being in his own bedroom. He gave the cap a parting squeeze, in which his hand relaxed, and had barely time to reel to bed before he sank into a heavy sleep.

* * *

Awakening in the middle of a prodigiously tough snore, and sitting up in bed to get his thoughts together, Scrooge had no occasion to be told that the bell was again upon the stroke of one. He felt that he was restored to consciousness in the right nick of time, for the especial purpose of holding a conference with the second messenger despatched to him through Jacob Marley's intervention.

Now, being prepared for almost anything, he was not by any means prepared for nothing; and consequently, when the bell struck one and no shape appeared, he was taken with a violent fit of trembling. Five minutes, ten minutes, a quarter of an hour went by, yet nothing came. All this time he lay upon his bed, the very core and center of a blaze of ruddy light which streamed upon it when the clock proclaimed the hour, and which, being only light, was more alarming than a dozen  ghosts, as he was powerless to make out what it meant, or would be at; and was sometimes apprehensive that he might be at that very moment an interesting case of spontaneous combustion, without having the consolation of knowing it. At last, however, he began to think—as you or I would have thought at first, for it is always the person not in the predicament who knows what ought to have been done in it, and would unquestionably have done it too—at last, I say, he began to think that the source and secret of this ghostly light might be in the adjoining room, from whence, on further tracing it, it seemed to shine. This idea taking full possession of his mind, he got up softly and shuffled in his slippers to the door.

The moment Scrooge's hand was on the lock, a strange voice called him by his name and bade him enter. He obeyed.

It was his own room. There was no doubt about that. But it had undergone a surprising transformation. The walls and ceiling were so hung with living green, that it looked a perfect grove, from every part of which bright gleaming berries glistened.

"Come in!" exclaimed the Ghost. "Come in and know me better, man!"

Scrooge entered timidly, and hung his head before this Spirit. He was not the dogged Scrooge he had been; and though the Spirit's eyes were clear and kind, he did not like to meet them.

"I am the Ghost of Christmas Present," said the Spirit. "Look upon me!"

Scrooge reverently did so. It was clothed in one simple deep green robe, or mantle, bordered with white fur. This garment hung so loosely on the figure that its capacious breast was bare, as if disclaiming to be warded or concealed by any artifice. Its feet, observable beneath the ample folds of the garment, were also bare, and on its head it wore no other covering than a holly wreath, set here and there with shining icicles. Its dark brown curls were long and free, free as its genial face, its sparkling eye, its open hand, its cheery voice, its unconstrained demeanor, and its joyful air. Girded round its middle was an antique scabbard, but no sword was in it.

"You have never seen the like of me before?" exclaimed the Spirit.

"Never." Scrooge made answer to it.

"Have never walked forth with the younger members of my family; meaning (for I am very young) my elder brothers born in these later years?" pursued the Phantom.

"I don't think I have," said Scrooge. "I am afraid I have not. Have you had many brothers, Spirit?"

"More than eighteen hundred," said the Ghost.

"A tremendous family to provide for," muttered Scrooge. The Ghost of Christmas Present rose.

"Spirit," said Scrooge submissively, "conduct me where you will. I went forth last night on compulsion, and I learned a lesson which is working now. Tonight, if you have aught to teach me, let me profit by it."

"Touch my robe!"

Scrooge did as he was told, and held it fast.

Holly, mistletoe, red berries, ivy, turkeys, geese, game, poultry, brawn, meat, pigs, sausages, oysters, pies, puddings, fruit, and punch, all vanished instantly. So did the room, the fire, the ruddy glow, the hour of night, and they stood in the

city streets on Christmas morning, where (for the weather was severe) the people made a rough but brisk and not unpleasant kind of music, in scraping the snow from the pavement in front of their dwellings, and from the tops of their houses, whence it was mad delight to the boys to see it come plumping down into the road below, and splitting into artificial little snowstorms.

The house fronts looked black enough, and the windows blacker, contrasting with the smooth white sheet of snow upon the roofs and with the dirtier snow upon the ground, which last deposit had been plowed up in deep furrows by the heavy wheels of carts and wagons, furrows that crossed and re-crossed each other hundreds of times where the great streets branched off, and made intricate channels, hard to trace, in the thick yellow mud and icy water. The sky was gloomy, and the shortest streets were choked up with a dingy mist, half thawed, half frozen, whose heavier particles descended in a shower of sooty atoms, as if all the chimneys in Great Britain had, by one consent, caught fire and were blazing away to their dear hearts' content. There was nothing very cheerful in the climate or the town, and yet was there an air of cheerfulness abroad that the clearest summer air and brightest summer sun might have endeavored to diffuse in vain.

In time the bells ceased, and the bakers were shut up; and yet there was a genial shadowing forth of all these dinners and the progress of their cooking, in the thawed blotch of wet above each baker's oven, where the pavement smoked as if its stones were cooking too.

"Is there a peculiar flavor in what you sprinkle from your torch?" asked Scrooge.

"There is. My own."

"Would it apply to any kind of dinner on this day?" asked Scrooge.

"To any kindly given. To a poor one most."

"Why to a poor one most?" asked Scrooge.

"Because it needs it most."

"Spirit," said Scrooge, after a moment's thought, "I wonder you, of all the beings in the many worlds about us, should desire to cramp these people's opportunities of innocent enjoyment."

"I!" cried the Spirit.

"You would deprive them of their means of dining every seventh day, often the only day on which they can be said to dine at all," said Scrooge; "wouldn't you?"

"I!" cried the Spirit.

"You seek to close these places on the Seventh Day," said Scrooge. "And it comes to the same thing."

"I seek!" exclaimed the Spirit.

"Forgive me if I am wrong. It has been done in your name, or at least in that of your family," said Scrooge.

"There are some upon this earth of yours," returned the Spirit, "who lay claim to know us, and who do their deeds of passion, pride, ill will, hatred, envy, bigotry, and selfishness in our name, who are as strange to us, and all our kith and kin, as if they had never lived. Remember that, and charge their doings on themselves, not us."

Scrooge promised that he would; and they went on, invisible, as they had been before, into the suburbs of the town. It was a remarkable quality of the Ghost (which Scrooge had observed at the baker's), that notwithstanding his gigantic size, he could accommodate himself to any place with ease; and that he stood beneath a low roof quite as gracefully and like a supernatural creature as it was possible he could have done in any lofty hall.

And perhaps it was the pleasure the good Spirit

had in showing off this power of his, or else it was his own kind, generous, hearty nature, and his sympathy with all poor men, that led him straight to Scrooge's clerk's; for there he went, and took Scrooge with him, holding to his robe; and on the threshold of the door the Spirit smiled, and stopped to bless Bob Cratchit's dwelling with the sprinklings of this torch. Think of that! Bob had but fifteen bob a week himself; he pocketed on Saturdays but fifteen copies of his Christian name; and yet the Ghost of Christmas Present blessed his four-roomed house!

Then up rose Mrs. Cratchit, Cratchit's wife, dressed out but poorly in a twice-turned gown, but brave in ribbons, which are cheap and make a goodly show for sixpence; and she laid the cloth, assisted by Belinda Cratchit, second of her daughters, also brave in ribbons; while Master Peter Cratchit plunged a fork into the saucepan of potatoes, and getting the corners of his monstrous shirt collar (Bob's private property, conferred upon his son and heir in honor of the day) into his mouth, rejoiced to find himself so gallantly attired, and yearned to show his linen in the fashionable parks. And now two smaller Cratchits, boy and girl, came tearing in, screaming that outside the baker's they had smelled the goose and known it for their own; and basking in luxurious thoughts of sage and onion, these young Cratchits danced about the table and exalted Master Peter Cratchit to the skies, while he (not proud, although his collar nearly choked him) blew the fire until the slow potatoes bubbling up, knocked loudly at the saucepan lid to be let out and peeled.

"What has ever got your precious father, then?" said Mrs. Cratchit. "And your brother, Tiny Tim! And Martha warn't as late last Christmas Day by half an hour!"

"Here's Martha, Mother!" said a girl appearing as she spoke.

"Here's Martha, Mother!" cried the two young Cratchits. "Hurrah! There's such a goose, Martha!"

"Why, bless your heart alive, my dear, how late you are!" said Mrs. Cratchit, kissing her a dozen times, and taking off her shawl and bonnet for her with officious zeal.

"We'd a deal of work to finish up last night," replied the girl, "and had to clear away this morning, Mother!"

"Well! never mind, so long as you are come," said Mrs. Cratchit. "Sit ye down before the fire, my dear, and have a warm, Lord bless ye!"

"No, no! There's Father coming," cried the two young Cratchits, who were everywhere at once. "Hide, Martha, hide!"

So Martha hid herself, and in came little Bob, the father, with at least three foot of comforter exclusive of the fringe hanging down before him, and his threadbare clothes darned up and brushed, to look seasonable, and Tiny Tim upon his shoulder. Alas for Tiny Tim, he bore a little crutch, and had his limbs supported by an iron frame!

"Why, where's our Martha?" cried Bob Cratchit, looking round.

"Not coming," said Mrs. Cratchit.

"Not coming!" said Bob, with a sudden declension in his high spirits; for he had been Tim's blood horse all the way from church, and had come home rampant. "Not coming upon Christmas Day!"

Martha didn't like to see him disappointed, if it were only in joke, so she came out prematurely from behind the closet door and ran into his arms, while the two young Cratchits hustled Tiny Tim and bore him off into the washhouse, that he might hear the pudding singing in the copper.

"And how did little Tim behave?" asked Mrs. Cratchit, when she had rallied Bob on his credulity, and Bob had hugged his daughter to his heart's content.

"As good as gold," said Bob, "and better. Somehow he gets thoughtful, sitting by himself so much, and thinks the strangest things you ever heard. He told me, coming home, that he hoped the people saw him in the church, because he was a cripple, and it might be pleasant to them to remember upon Christmas Day who made lame beggars walk, and blind men see."

There never was such a goose. Bob said he didn't believe there ever was such a goose cooked. Its tenderness and flavor, size and cheapness, were the themes of universal admiration. Eked out by apple sauce and mashed potatoes, it was sufficient dinner for the whole family; indeed, as Mrs. Cratchit said with great delight (surveying one small atom of a bone upon the dish), they hadn't eaten it all at last! Yet every one had had enough, and the youngest Cratchits, in particular, were steeped in sage and in onion to the eyebrows! But now the plates being changed by Miss Belinda, Mrs. Cratchit left the room—too nervous to bear witness—to take the pudding up and bring it in.

Suppose it should not be done enough! Suppose it should break in turning out! Suppose somebody should have got over the wall of the back yard, and stolen it, while they were merry with the goose—a supposition at which the two young Cratchits became livid! All sorts of horrors were supposed.

Hallo! A great deal of steam! The pudding was out of the copper. A smell like a washing day! That was the cloth. A smell like an eating house and a pastry cook's next door to each other, with a laundress's next to that! That was the pudding! In half a minute Mrs. Cratchit entered—flushed, but smiling proudly—with the pudding, like a speckled cannon ball, so hard and firm, blazing in half-a-quartern of ignited brandy, and bedight with Christmas holly stuck into the top.

Oh, a wonderful pudding! Bob Cratchit said, and calmly, too, that he regarded it as the greatest success achieved by Mrs. Cratchit since their marriage. Mrs. Cratchit said that now the weight was off her mind, she would confess she had her doubts about the quantity of flour. Everybody had something to say about it, but nobody said or thought it was at all a small pudding for a large family. It would have been flat heresy to do so. Any Cratchit would have blushed to hint at such a thing.

At last the dinner was all done, the cloth was cleared, the hearth swept, and the fire made up. The compound in the jug being tasted, and considered perfect, apples and oranges were put upon the table, and a shovel full of chestnuts on the fire. Then all the Cratchit family drew round the hearth, in what Bob Cratchit

called a circle, meaning half a one; and at Bob Cratchit's elbow stood the family display of glass: two tumblers and a custard cup without a handle.

These held the hot stuff from the jug, however, as well as golden goblets would have done; and Bob served it out with beaming looks, while the chestnuts on the fire sputtered and cracked noisily. Then Bob proposed, "A Merry Christmas to us all, my dears. God bless us!"

Which all the family re-echoed.

"God bless us every one!" said Tiny Tim, the last of all.

He sat very close to his father's side, upon his little stool. Bob held his withered little hand in his, as if he loved the child and wished to keep him by his side and dreaded that he might be taken from him.

"Spirit," said Scrooge, with an interest he had never felt before, "tell me if Tiny Tim will live."

"I see a vacant seat," replied the Ghost, "in the poor chimney corner, and a crutch without an owner, carefully preserved. If these shadows remain unaltered by the Future, the child will die."

"No, no," said Scrooge. "Oh, no, kind Spirit! Say he will be spared."

"If these shadows remain unaltered by the Future, none other of my race," returned the Ghost, "will find him here. What then? If he be like to die, he had better do it, and decrease the surplus population."

Scrooge hung his head to hear his own words quoted by the Spirit, and was overcome with penitence and grief.

"Man," said the Ghost, "if man you be in heart, not adamant, forbear that wicked cant until you have discovered What the surplus is, and Where it is. Will you decide what men shall live, what men shall die? It may be that, in the sight of Heaven, you are more worthless and less fit to live than millions like this poor man's child. Oh, God! To hear the Insect on the leaf pronouncing on the too much life among his hungry brothers in the dust!"

Scrooge bent before the Ghost's rebuke and, trembling, cast his eyes upon the ground. But he raised on hearing his own name.

"Mr. Scrooge!" said Bob; "I'll give you Mr. Scrooge, the Founder of the Feast!"

"The Founder of the Feast, indeed!" cried Mrs. Cratchit, reddening. "I wish I had him here. I'd give him a piece of my mind to feast upon, and I hope he'd have a good appetite for it."

"My dear," said Bob; "The children! Christmas Day."

"It should be Christmas Day, I am sure," said she, "on which one drinks the health of such an odious, stingy, hard, unfeeling man as Mr. Scrooge. You know he is, Robert! Nobody knows it better than you do, poor fellow!"

"My dear," was Bob's mild answer. "Christmas Day."

"I'll drink his health for your sake and the Day's," said Mrs. Cratchit, "not for his. Long life to him! A merry Christmas and a happy New Year! He'll be very merry and very happy, I have no doubt!"

The children drank the toast after her. It was the first of their proceedings which had no heartiness in it. Tiny Tim drank it last of all, but he didn't care twopence for it. Scrooge was the Ogre of the family. The mention

of his name cast a dark shadow on the party, which was not dispelled for full five minutes.

After it had passed away, they were ten times merrier than before, from the mere relief of Scrooge the Baleful being done with. Bob Cratchit told them how he had a situation in his eye for Master Peter's being a man of business; and Peter himself looked thoughtfully at the fire from between his collar, as if he were deliberating what particular investments he should favor when he came into the receipt of that bewildering income. Martha, who was a poor apprentice at a milliner's, then told them what kind of work she had to do, and how many hours she worked at a stretch, and how she meant to lie abed tomorrow morning for a good long rest; tomorrow being a holiday she passed at home. Also how she had seen a countess and a lord some days before, and how the lord "was much about as tall as Peter"; at which Peter pulled up his collar so high that you couldn't have seen his head if you had been there.

All this time the chestnuts and the jug went round and round; and by the by they had a song about a lost child traveling in the snow, from Tiny Tim, who had a plaintive little voice, and sang it very well indeed. There was nothing of high mark in this. They were not a handsome family; they were not well dressed; their shoes were far from being waterproof; their clothes were scanty; and Peter might have known, and very likely did, the inside of a pawnbroker's. But they were happy, grateful, pleased with one another, and contented with the time; and when they faded, and looked happier yet in the bright sprinklings of the Spirit's torch at parting, Scrooge had his eye upon them, and especially on Tiny Tim, until the last.

By this time it was getting dark and snowing pretty heavily; and, as Scrooge and the Spirit went along the streets, the brightness of the roaring fires in kitchens, parlors, and all sorts of rooms, was wonderful. Here, the flickering of the blaze showed preparations for a cozy dinner, with hot plates baking through and through before the fire, and deep red curtains, ready to be drawn to shut out cold and darkness. There, all the children of the house were running out into the snow to meet their married sisters, brothers, cousins, aunts, and to be the first to greet them. Here, again, were shadows on the window blinds of guests assembling, and there, a group of handsome girls, all hooded and fur-booted, and all chattering at once, tripped lightly off to some near neighbor's house, where, woe upon the single man who saw them enter—artful witches, well they knew it—in a glow.

But if you had judged from the numbers of people on their way to friendly gatherings, you might have thought that no one was at home to give them welcome when they got there, instead of every house expecting company, and piling up its fires half-chimney high. Blessings on it, how the Ghost exulted! How it bared its breadth of breast, and opened its capacious palm, and floated on, outpouring, with a generous hand, its bright and harmless mirth on everything within its reach! The very lamplighter, who ran on before, dotting the dusky streets with specks of light, and who was dressed to spend the evening somewhere, laughed out loudly as the Spirit passed, though little kenned the lamplighter that he had any company but Christmas!

And now, without a word of warning from the Ghost, they stood upon a bleak and desert moor, where monstrous masses of rude stone were cast about as though it were the burial of giants; and water spread itself wheresoever it listed; or would have done so, but for the frost that held it prisoner; and nothing grew but moss and furze and coarse, rank grass. Down in the west the setting sun had left a streak of fiery red, which glared upon the desolation for an instant like a sullen eye, and frowning lower, lower, lower yet, was lost in the thick gloom of darkest night.

"What place is this?" asked Scrooge.

"A place where miners live, who labor in the bowels of the earth," returned the Spirit. "But they know me. See!"

A light shone from the window of the hut, and swiftly they advanced toward it. Passing through the wall of mud and stone, they found a cheerful company assembled round a glowing fire. An old, old man and woman, with their children and their children's children, and another generation beyond that, all decked out gaily in their holiday attire. The old man, in a voice that seldom rose above the howling of the wind upon the barren waste, was singing them a Christmas song; it had been a very old song when he was a boy; and from time to time they all joined in the chorus. So surely as they raised their voices, the old man got quite blithe and loud; and so surely as they stopped, his vigor sank again.

Again the Ghost sped on, above the black and heaving sea—on, on—until, being far away, as he told Scrooge, from any shore, they lighted on a ship.

It was a great surprise to Scrooge, while listening to the moaning of the wind and thinking what a solemn thing it was to move on through the lonely darkness over an unknown abyss, whose depths were secrets as profound as Death, it was a great surprise to Scrooge, while thus engaged, to hear a hearty laugh. It was a much greater surprise to Scrooge to recognize it as his nephew's, and to find himself in a bright dry, gleaming room, with the Spirit smiling by his side, and looking at the same nephew with approving affability!

"Ha! Ha!" laughed Scrooge's nephew. "Ha, ha, ha!"

If you should happen, by any unlikely chance, to know a man more blessed in a laugh than Scrooge's nephew, all I can say is, I should like to know him too. Introduce him to me, and I'll cultivate his acquaintance.

It is a fair, evenhanded, noble adjustment of things, that while there is infection in disease and sorrow, there is nothing in the world so irresistibly contagious as laughter and good humor. When Scrooge's nephew laughed in this way, holding his sides, rolling his head, and twisting his face into the most extravagant contortions, Scrooge's niece, by marriage, laughed as heartily as he. And their assembled friends being not a bit behindhand, roared out lustily.

"Ha, ha! Ha, ha, ha ha!"

"He said that Christmas was a humbug, as I live!' cried Scrooge's nephew. "He believed it, too!"

"More shame for him, Fred!" said Scrooge's niece, indignantly. Bless these women! They never do anything by halves. They are always in earnest.

She was very pretty, exceedingly pretty. With a dimpled, surprised-looking, capital face, a ripe little mouth that seemed made to be kissed—as no doubt it was; all kinds of good little dots about her chin that melted into one another when she laughed, and

the sunniest pair of eyes you ever saw in any little creature's head. Altogether she was what you would have called provoking, you know, but satisfactory, too. Oh, perfectly satisfactory.

"He's a comical fellow," said Scrooge's nephew, "that's the truth; and not so pleasant as he might be. However, his offenses carry their own punishment and I have nothing to say against him."

"I'm sure he is very rich, Fred," hinted Scrooge's niece. "At least you always tell *me* so."

"What of that, my dear!" said Scrooge's nephew. "His wealth is of no use to him. He don't do any good with it. He don't make himself comfortable with it. He hasn't the satisfaction of thinking—ha, ha, ha!—that he is ever going to benefit Us with it."

"I have no patience with him," observed Scrooge's niece. Scrooge's niece's sisters and all the other ladies expressed the same opinion.

"Oh, I have!" said Scrooge's nephew. "I am sorry for him; I couldn't be angry with him if I tried. Who suffers by his ill whims! Himself, always. Here he takes it into his head to dislike us, and he won't come and dine with us. What's the consequence? He don't lose much of a dinner."

"Indeed, I think he loses a very good dinner," interrupted Scrooge's niece. Everybody else said the same, and they must be allowed to have been competent judges, because they had just had dinner, and with the dessert upon the table, were clustered round the fire, by lamplight.

"Well! I am very glad to hear it," said Scrooge's nephew, "because I haven't any great faith in these young housekeepers. What do *you* say, Topper?"

Topper had clearly got his eyes upon one of Scrooge's niece's sisters, for he answered that a bachelor was a wretched outcast, who had no right to express an opinion on the subject. Whereat Scrooge's niece's sister—the plump one with the lace tucker, not the one with the roses—blushed.

"Do go on, Fred," said Scrooge's niece, clapping her hands. "He never finishes what he begins to say! He is such a ridiculous fellow!"

Scrooge's nephew reveled in another laugh, and as it was impossible to keep the infection off, though the plump sister tried hard to do it with aromatic vinegar, his example was unanimously followed.

"I was only going to say," said Scrooge's nephew, "that the consequence of his taking a dislike to us, and not making merry with us, is, I think, that he loses some pleasant moments which could do him no harm. I am sure he loses pleasanter companions than he can find in his own thoughts, either in his moldy old office or his dusty chambers. I mean to give him the same chance every year, whether he likes it or not, for I pity him. He may rail at Christmas till he dies, but he can't help thinking better of it—I defy him—if he finds me going there, in good temper, year after year, and saying, 'Uncle Scrooge, how are you?' If it only puts him in the vein to leave his poor clerk fifty pounds, that's something; and I think I shook him yesterday."

After a while they played at forfeits, for it is good to be children sometimes, and never better than at Christmas, when its mighty Founder was a child Himself. Stop! There was first a game at blindman's buff. Of course there was. And I no more believe Topper was really blind than I believe he had eyes in his boots. My opinion is that it was a done thing between him and Scrooge's nephew, and that the Ghost of Christmas Present knew it. The way he went after that plump sister in the lace tucker was an outrage on the credulity of human nature. Knocking down the fire irons, tumbling over the chairs, bumping up against the piano, smothering himself among the curtains, wherever she went, there went he! He always knew where the plump sister was. He wouldn't catch anybody else. If you had fallen up against him (as some of them did) on purpose, he would have made a feint of endeavoring to seize you, which would have been an affront to your understanding, and would instantly

have sidled off in the direction of the plump sister. She often cried out that it wasn't fair, and it really was not. But when at last he caught her, when, in spite of all her silken rustlings, and her rapid flutterings past him, he got her into a corner whence there was no escape, then his conduct was the most execrable. For his pretending not to know her, his pretending that it was necessary to touch her headdress, and further to assure himself of her identity by pressing a certain ring upon her finger and a certain chain about her neck, was vile, monstrous! No doubt she told him her opinion of it when, another blindman being in office, they were so confidential together, behind the curtains.

Scrooge's niece was not one of the blindman's buff party, but was made comfortable with a large chair and a footstool, in a snug corner where the Ghost and Scrooge were close behind her. But she joined in the forfeits, and loved her love to admira-

tion with all the letters of the alphabet.

Likewise at the game of How, When, and Where, she was very great, and, to the secret joy of Scrooge's nephew, beat her sisters hollow, though they were sharp girls too, as Topper could have told you. There might have been twenty people there, young and old, but they all played, and so did Scrooge, for, wholly forgetting in the interest he had in what was going on that his voice made no sound in their ears, he sometimes came out with his guess quite loud, and very often guessed right, too; for the sharpest needle, best Whitechapel, warranted not to cut in the eye, was not sharper than Scrooge, blunt as he took it in his head to be.

The Ghost was greatly pleased to find him in this mood, and looked upon him with such favor that he begged like a boy to be allowed to stay until the guests departed. But this the Spirit said could not be done.

"Here is a new game," said Scrooge. "One half-hour, Spirit, only one!"

It was a game called "Yes and No," where Scrooge's nephew had to think of something, and the rest must find out what; he only answering to their questions yes or no, as the case was. The brisk fire of questioning to which he was exposed, elicited from him that he was thinking of an animal, a live animal, rather a disagreeable animal, a savage animal, an animal that growled and grunted sometimes, and talked sometimes, and lived in London, and walked about the streets, and wasn't made a show of, and wasn't led by anybody, and didn't live in a menagerie, and was never killed in a market, and was not a horse, or an ass, or a cow, or a bull, or a tiger, or a dog, or a pig, or a cat, or a bear. At every fresh question that was put to him, this nephew burst into a fresh roar of laughter and was so inexpressibly tickled, that he was obliged to get up off the sofa and stamp.

At last the plump sister, falling into a similar state, cried out, "I have found it out! I know what it is, Fred! I know what it is!"

"What is it?" cried Fred.

"It's your Uncle Scro-o-o-o-oge!"

Which it certainly was. Admiration was the universal sentiment, though some objected that the reply to "Is it a bear?" ought to have been "Yes"; inasmuch as an answer in the negative was sufficient to have diverted their thoughts from Mr. Scrooge, supposing they had ever had any tendency that way.

"He has given us plenty of merriment, I am sure," said Fred, "and it would be ungrateful not to drink his health. Here is a glass of mulled wine ready to our hand at the moment; and I say, 'Uncle Scrooge!'"

"Well! Uncle Scrooge!" they cried.

"A Merry Christmas and a Happy New Year to the old man, wherever he is!" said Scrooge's nephew. "He wouldn't take it from me, but may he have it, nevertheless. Uncle Scrooge!"

Uncle Scrooge had imperceptibly become so gay and light of heart that he would have pledged the unconscious company in return, and thanked them in an inaudible speech if the Ghost had given him time. But the whole scene passed off in the breath of the last word spoken by his nephew; and he and the Spirit were again upon their travels.

Much they saw, and far they went, and many homes they visited, but always with a happy end. The Spirit stood beside sick beds, and they were cheerful; on foreign lands, and they were close at home; by struggling men, and they were patient in their

greater hope; by poverty, and it was rich. In almshouse, hospital and jail, in misery's every refuge, where vain man in his little brief authority had not made fast the door, and barred the Spirit out, he left his blessing, and taught Scrooge his precepts.

It was a long night, if it were only a night; but Scrooge had his doubts of this, because the Christmas holidays appeared to be condensed into the space of time they passed together. It was strange, too, that while Scrooge remained unaltered in his outward form, the Ghost grew older, clearly older. Scrooge had observed this change, but never spoke of it, until they left a children's Twelfth Night party, when, looking at the Spirit as they stood together in an open place, he noticed that his hair was gray.

"Are spirits' lives so short?" asked Scrooge.

"My life upon this globe is very brief," replied the Ghost. "It ends tonight."

"Tonight!" cried Scrooge.

"Tonight at midnight. Hark! The time is drawing near."

The chimes were ringing the three quarters past eleven.

"Forgive me if I am not justified in what I ask," said Scrooge, looking intently at the Spirit's robe, "but I see something strange, and not belonging to yourself, protruding from your skirts. Is it a foot or a claw?"

"It might be a claw, for the flesh there is upon it," was the Spirit's sorrowful reply. "Look here."

From the foldings of its robe it brought two children wretched, abject, frightful, hideous, miserable. They knelt down at its feet and clung upon the outside of its garment.

"Oh, Man! Look here. Look, look, down here!" exclaimed the Ghost.

They were a boy and girl. Yellow, meager, ragged,

scowling, wolfish; but prostrate, too, in their humility.

"Spirit! Are they yours?" Scrooge could say no more.

"They are Man's," said the Spirit, looking down upon them. "And they cling to me, appealing from their fathers. This boy is Ignorance. This girl is Want. Beware of them both, and all of their degree, but most of all beware this boy, for on his brow I see that written which is Doom, unless the writing be erased. Deny it!" cried the Spirit, stretching out its hand toward the city. "Slander those who tell it ye! Admit it for your factious purposes, and make it worse! And bide the end!"

"Have they no refuge or resource?" cried Scrooge.

"Are there no prisons!" said the Spirit, turning on him for the last time with his own words. "Are there no workhouses?"

The bell struck twelve. Scrooge looked about him for the Ghost, and saw it not. As the last stroke ceased to vibrate, he remembered the prediction of old Jacob Marley, and lifting up his eyes, beheld a solemn Phantom, draped and hooded, coming like a mist along the ground toward him.

* * *

The Phantom slowly, gravely, silently approached. When it came near him, Scrooge bent down upon his knee, for in the very air through which this Spirit moved it seemed to scatter gloom and mystery.

It was shrouded in a deep black garment, which concealed its head, its face, its form, and left nothing of it visible save one outstretched hand. But for this it would have been difficult to detach its figure from the night, and separate it from the darkness by which it was surrounded.

He felt that it was tall and stately when it came beside him, and that its mysterious presence filled him with a solemn dread. He knew no more, for the Spirit neither spoke nor moved.

"I am in the presence of the Ghost of Christmas Yet To Come?" said Scrooge.

The Spirit answered not, but pointed onward with its hand.

"You are about to show me shadows of the things that have not happened, but will happen in the time before us," Scrooge pursued. "Is that so, Spirit?"

The upper portion of the garment was contracted for an instant in its folds, as if the Spirit had inclined its head. That was the only answer he received.

It gave him no reply. The hand was pointed straight before them.

"Lead on!" said Scrooge. "Lead on! The night is waning fast, and it is precious time to me, I know. Lead on, Spirit!"

The phantom moved away as it had come toward him. Scrooge followed in the shadow of its dress, which bore him up, he thought, and carried him along.

The Spirit stopped beside one little knot of business men. Observing that the hand was pointed to them, Scrooge advanced to listen to their talk.

"No," said a great fat man with a monstrous chin, "I don't know much about it either way. I only know he's dead."

"When did he die?" inquired another.

"Last night, I believe."

"Why, what was the matter with him?" asked a third, taking a vast quantity of snuff out of a very large snuffbox. "I thought he'd never die."

"God knows," said the first, with a yawn.

"What has he done with his money?" asked a red-faced gentleman with a pendulous excrescence on the end of his nose, that shook like the gills of a turkey cock.

"I haven't heard," said the man with the large chin, yawning again. "Left it to his company, perhaps. He hasn't left it to me. That's all I know."

This pleasantry was received with a general laugh.

"It's likely to be a very cheap funeral," said the same speaker, "for upon my life I don't know of anybody to go to it. Suppose we make up a party and volunteer?"

"I don't mind going if a lunch is provided," observed the gentleman with the excrescence on his nose. "But I must be fed, if I make one."

Another laugh.

"Well, I am the most disinterested among you, after all," said the first speaker, "for I never wear black gloves, and I never eat lunch. But I'll offer to go, if anybody else will. When I come to think of it, I'm not at all sure that I wasn't his most particular friend; for we used to stop and speak whenever we met. By, by!"

Speakers and listeners strolled away and mixed with other groups. Scrooge knew the men, and looked toward the Spirit for an explanation.

The Phantom glided on into a street. Its finger pointed to two persons meeting. Scrooge listened again, thinking that the explanation might lie here.

He knew these men, also, perfectly. They were men of business, very wealthy, and of great importance.

He had made a point always of standing well in their esteem in a business point of view.

"How are you?" said one.

"How are you?" returned the other.

"Well!" said the first. "Old Scratch has got his own at last, hey?"

"So I am told," returned the second. "Cold, isn't it!"

"Seasonable for Christmas time. You are not a skater, I suppose?"

"No. No. Something else to think of. Good morning!"

Not another word. That was their meeting, their conversation, and their parting.

Scrooge was at first inclined to be surprised that the Spirit should attach importance to conversations apparently so trivial, but feeling assured that they must have some hidden purpose, he set himself to consider what it was likely to be. They could scarcely be supposed to have any bearing on the death of Jacob, his old partner, for that was Past, and this Ghost's province was the Future. Nor could he think of any one immediately connected with himself, to whom he could apply them. But nothing doubting that to whomsoever they applied they had some latent moral for his own improvement, he resolved to treasure up every word he heard, and everything he saw, and especially to observe the shadow of himself when it appeared. For he had an expectation that the conduct of his future self would give him the clue he missed, and would render the solution of these riddles easy.

He looked about in that very place for his own  image, but another man stood in his accustomed corner, and though the clock pointed to his usual time of day for being there, he saw no likeness of himself among the multitudes that poured in through the porch. It gave him little surprise, however, for he had been revolving in his mind a change of life, and thought and hoped he saw his newborn resolutions carried out in this.

They left the busy scene and went into an obscure part of the town, where Scrooge had never penetrated before, although he recognized its situation and its bad repute. The ways were foul and narrow, the shops and houses wretched, the people half-naked, drunken, slipshod, ugly. Alleys and archways, like so many cesspools, disgorged their offenses of smell and dirt and life upon the straggling streets; and the whole quarter reeked with crime, with filth, and misery.

Far in this den of infamous resort, there was a low-browed, beetling shop, below a penthouse roof, where iron, old rags, bottles, bones, and greasy offal were brought. Upon the floor within were piled up heaps of rusty keys, nails, chains, hinges, files, scales, weights, and refuse of all kinds.

Secrets that few would like to scrutinize were bred and hidden in mountains of unseemly rags, masses of corrupted fat, and sepulchers of bones. Sitting in among the wares he dealt in, by a charcoal stove made of old bricks, was a gray-haired rascal, nearly seventy-five years of age, who had screened himself from the cold air without, by a frozen curtaining of miscellaneous tatters hung upon a line, and smoked his pipe in all the luxury of calm retirement.

Scrooge and the Phantom came into the presence of this man, just as a woman with a heavy bundle slunk into the shop. But she had scarcely entered, when another woman, similarly laden, came in too; and she closely followed by a man in faded black, who was no less startled by the sight of them, than they had been upon the recognition of each other. After a short period of blank astonishment, in which the old man with the pipe had joined them, they all three burst into a laugh.

"Let the charwoman alone to be the first!" cried she who had entered first. "Let the laundress alone to be the second; and let the undertaker's man alone to be the third. Look here, old Joe, here's a chance! If we haven't all three met here without meaning it!"

"You couldn't have met in a better place," said old Joe, removing his pipe from his mouth. "Come into the parlor. You were made free of it long ago, you know; and the other two ain't strangers. Stop till I shut the door of the shop. Ah! how it skreeks! There ain't such a rusty bit of metal in the place as its own hinges, I believe; and I'm sure there's no such old bones here, as mine. Ha, ha! We're all suitable to our calling, we're well matched. Come into the parlor. Come into the parlor."

The parlor was the space behind the screen of rags. The old man raked the fire together with an old stair rod, and having trimmed his smokey lamp (for it was night) with the stem of his pipe, put it into his mouth again.

While he did this, the woman who had already spoken threw her bundle on the floor and sat down in a flaunting manner on a stool, crossing her elbows on her knees, and looking with a bold defiance at the other two.

"What odds then! What odds, Mrs. Dilber?" said the woman. "Every person has a right to take care of themselves. He always did!"

"That's true, indeed!" said the laundress. "No man more so."

"Why, then, don't stand staring as if you was afraid, woman. Who's the wiser? We're not going to pick holes in each other's coats, I suppose?"

"No, indeed!" said Mrs. Dilber and the man together. "We should hope not."

"Very well, then!" cried the woman. "That's enough. Who's the worse for the loss of a few things like these? Not a dead man, I suppose."

"No, indeed," said Mrs. Dilber, laughing.

"If he wanted to keep 'em after he was dead, a wicked old screw," pursued the woman, "why wasn't he natural in his lifetime? If he had been, he'd have had somebody to look after him when he was struck with Death, instead of lying gasping out his last there, alone by himself."

"It's the truest word that ever was spoke," said Mrs. Dilber. "It's a hard judgment on him."

"I wish it was a little heavier judgment," replied the woman; "and it should have been, you may depend upon it, if I could have laid my hands on anything else. Open that bundle, old Joe, and let me know the value of it. Speak out plain. I'm not afraid to be the first, nor afraid for them to see it. We knew pretty well that we were helping ourselves, before we met here, I believe. It's no sin. Open the bundle, Joe."

But the gallantry of her friends would not allow of this; and the man in faded black, mounting the breach first, produced his plunder. It was not extensive. A seal or two, a pencil case, a pair of sleeve buttons, and a brooch of no great value, were all. They were severally examined and appraised by old Joe, who chalked the sums he was disposed to give for each upon the wall, and added them up into a total when he found that there was nothing more to come.

"That's your account," said Joe, "and I wouldn't give another sixpence, if I was to be boiled for not doing it. Who's next?"

Mrs. Dilber was next. Sheets and towels, a little wearing apparel, two old-fashioned silver teaspoons, a pair of sugar tongs, and a few boots. Her account was stated on the wall in the same manner.

"I always give too much to ladies. It's a weakness of mine, and that's the way I ruin myself," said old Joe. "That's your account. If you ask me for another penny, and made it an open question, I'd repent of being so liberal, and knock off half-a-crown."

"And now undo my bundle, Joe," said the first woman.

Joe went down on his knees for the greater convenience of opening it, and having unfastened a great many knots, dragged out a large heavy roll of some dark stuff.

"What do you call this?" said Joe. "Bed curtains!"

"Ah!" returned the woman, laughing and leaning forward on her crossed arms. "Bed curtains!"

"You don't mean to say you took 'em down, rings

and all, with him lying there?" said Joe.

"Yes, I do," replied the woman. "Why not?"

"You were born to make your fortune," said Joe, "and you'll certainly do it."

"I certainly shan't hold my hand, when I can get anything in it by reaching it out, for the sake of such a man as he was, I promise you, Joe," returned the woman, coolly. "Don't drop that oil upon the blankets, now."

"His blankets?" asked Joe.

"Whose else's do you think?" replied the woman. "He isn't likely to take cold without 'em, I dare say."

"I hope he didn't die of anything catching? Eh?" said old Joe, stopping in his work and looking up.

"Don't you be afraid of that," returned the woman. "I ain't so fond of his company that I'd loiter about him for such things, if he did. Ah! You may look through that shirt till your eyes ache; but you won't find a hole in it, nor a threadbare place. It's the best he had, and a fine one, too. They'd have wasted it, if it hadn't been for me."

"What do you call wasting of it?" asked old Joe.

"Putting it on him to be buried in to be sure," replied the woman with a laugh. "Somebody was fool enough to do it, but I took it off again. If calico ain't good enough for such a purpose, it isn't good enough for anything. It's quite as becoming to the body. He can't look uglier than he did in that one."

Scrooge listened to this dialogue in horror. As they sat grouped about their spoil, in the scanty light afforded by the oldman's lamp, he viewed them with a detestation and disgust which could hardly have been greater, though they had been obscene demons, marketing the corpse itself.

"Ha, ha!" laughed the same woman, when old Joe producing a flannel bag with money in it, told out their several gains upon the ground. "This is the end of it, you see? He frightened every one away from him when he was alive, to profit us when he was dead! Ha, ha, ha!"

"Spirit!" said Scrooge, shuddering from head to foot. "I see, I see. The case of this unhappy man might be my own. My life tends that way, now. Merciful Heaven, what is this!"

He recoiled in terror, for the scene had changed, and now he almost touched a bed, a bare, uncurtained bed, on which, beneath a ragged sheet, there lay something covered up which, though it was dumb, announced itself in awful language.

The room was very dark, too dark to be observed with any accuracy, though Scrooge glanced round it in obedience to a secret impulse, anxious to know what kind of room it was. A pale light rising in the outer air fell straight upon the bed, and on it, plundered and bereft, unwatched, unwept, uncared for, was the body of this man.

He lay, in the dark, empty house, with not a man, a woman, or a child to say, "He was kind to me in this or that, and for the memory of one kind word I will be kind to him." A cat was tearing at the door, and there was a sound of gnawing rats beneath the hearthstone. What they wanted in the room of death, and why they were so restless and disturbed, Scrooge did not dare to think.

"Spirit!" he said. "This is a fearful place. In leaving

it I shall not leave its lesson, trust me. Let us go!"

Still the Ghost pointed with unmoved finger to the head.

"I understand you," Scrooge returned, "and would do it if I could. But I have not the power, Spirit. I have not the power."

Again it seemed to look upon him.

"If there is any person in the town who feels emotion caused by this man's death," said Scrooge, quite agonized, "show that person to me, Spirit, I beseech you!"

The Phantom spread its dark robe before him for a moment, like a wing, and withdrawing it, revealed a room by daylight, where a mother and her children were.

She was expecting someone, and with anxious eagerness, for she walked up and down the room, started at every sound, looked out from the window, glanced at the clock, tried, but in vain, to work with her needle, and could hardly bear the voices of her children in their play.

At length the long-expected knock was heard. She hurried to the door and met her husband, a man whose face was careworn and depressed, though he was young. There was a remarkable expression in it

now, a kind of serious delight of which he felt ashamed, and which he struggled to repress.

He sat down to the dinner that had been hoarding for him by the fire, and when she asked him faintly what news (which was not until after a long silence), he appeared embarrassed how to answer.

"Is it good," she said, "or bad?"—to help him.

"Bad," he answered.

"We are quite ruined?"

"No. There is hope yet, Caroline."

"If he relents," she said, amazed, "there is! Noth-

ing is past hope, if such a miracle has happened."

"He is past relenting," said her husband. "He is dead."

She was a mild and patient creature, if her face spoke truth, but she was thankful in her soul to hear it, and she said so, with clasped hands. She prayed forgiveness the next moment, and was sorry; but the first was the emotion of her heart.

"What the half-drunken woman, whom I told you of last night, said to me when I tried to see him and obtain a week's delay, and what I have thought was a mere excuse to avoid me, turns out to have been quite true. He was not only very ill, but dying then."

"To whom will our debt be transferred?"

"I don't know. But before that time we shall be ready with the money. And even though we were not, it would be bad fortune indeed to find so merciless a creditor in his successor. We may sleep tonight with light hearts, Caroline!"

Yes. Soften it as they would, their hearts were lighter. The children's faces, hushed and clustered round to hear what they so little understood, were brighter; and it was a happier house for this man's death! The only emotion that the Ghost could show him, caused by the event, was one of pleasure.

"Let me see some tenderness connected with a death," said Scrooge; "or that dark chamber, Spirit, which we left just now, will be forever present to me."

The Ghost conducted him through several streets familiar to his feet; and as they went along, Scrooge looked here and there to find himself, but nowhere was he to be seen. They entered poor Bob Cratchit's house; the dwelling he had visited before; and found the mother and the children seated round the fire.

Quiet. Very quiet. The noisy little Cratchits were as still as statues in one corner, and looking up at Peter, who had a book before him. The mother and her daughters were engaged in sewing. But surely they were very quiet!

"'And He took a child, and set him in the midst of them.'"

Where had Scrooge heard these words? He had not dreamed them. The boy must have read them out as he and the Spirit crossed the threshold. Why did he not go on?

The mother laid her work upon the table, and put her hand up to her face.

"The color hurts my eyes," she said.

The color? Ah, poor Tiny Tim!

"They're better now again," said Cratchit's wife. "It makes them weak by candlelight; and I wouldn't show weak eyes to your father when he comes home, for the world. It must be near his time."

"Past it rather," Peter answered, shutting up his book. "But I think he has walked a little slower than he used to, these few last evenings, Mother."

They were very quiet again. At last she said, in a steady, cheerful voice that only faltered once, "I have known him walk with—I have known him walk with Tiny Tim upon his shoulder, very fast, indeed."

"And so have I," cried Peter. "Often."

"And so have I," exclaimed another. So had all.

"But he was very light to carry," she resumed, intent upon her work, "and his father loved him so, that it was no trouble; no trouble. And there is your father at the door!"

She hurried out to meet him; and little Bob in his comforter—he had need of it, poor fellow—came in. His tea was ready for him on the hob, and they all tried who should help him to it most. Then the two young Cratchits got upon his knees and laid, each child, a little cheek against his face, as if they said, "Don't mind it, Father. Don't be grieved!"

Bob was very cheerful with them, and spoke pleasantly to all the family. He looked at the work upon the table, and praised the industry and speed of Mrs. Cratchit and the girls. They would be done long before Sunday, he said.

"Sunday! You went today, then, Robert?" said his wife.

"Yes, my dear," returned Bob. "I wish you could have gone. It would have done you good to see how green a place it is. But you'll see it often. I promised him that I would walk there on a Sunday. My little, little child!" cried Bob. "My little child!"

He broke down all at once. He couldn't help it. If he could have helped it, he and his child would have been farther apart perhaps than they were.

He left the room and went upstairs into the room above, which was lighted cheerfully, and hung with Christmas. There was a chair set close beside the child and there were signs of someone having been there lately. Poor Bob sat down in it, and when he had thought a little and composed himself, he kissed the little face. He was reconciled to what had happened, and went down again quite happy.

They drew about the fire, and talked, the girls and mother working still. Bob told them of the extraordinary kindness of Mr. Scrooge's nephew, whom he had scarcely seen but once, and who, meeting him in the street that day, and seeing that he looked a little—"just a little down, you know," said Bob, inquired what had happened to distress him. "On which," said Bob, "for he is the pleasantest-spoken gentleman you ever heard, I told him. 'I am heartily sorry for it, Mr. Cratchit,' he said, 'and heartily sorry for your good wife.' By the by, how he ever knew that I don't know."

"Knew what, my dear?"

"Why, that you were a good wife," replied Bob.

"Everybody knows that!" said Peter.

"Very well observed, my boy!" cried Bob. "I hope they do. 'Heartily sorry,' he said, 'for your good wife. If I can be of service to you in any way,' he said, giving me his card, 'that's where I live. Pray come to me.' Now, it wasn't," cried Bob, "for the sake of anything he might be able to do for us, so much as for his kind way, that this was quite delightful. It really seemed as if he had known our Tiny Tim, and felt with us."

"I'm sure he's a good soul!" said Mrs. Cratchit.

"You would be sure of it, my dear," returned Bob, "if you saw and spoke to him. I shouldn't be at all surprised—mark what I say!—if he got Peter a better situation."

"Only hear that, Peter," said Mrs. Cratchit.

"And then," cried one of the girls, "Peter will be keeping company with some one, and setting up for himself."

"Get along with you!" retorted Peter, grinning.

"It's just as likely as not," said Bob, "one of these days, though there's plenty of time for that, my dear.

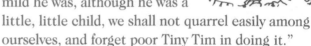

But however and whenever we part from one another, I am sure we shall none of us forget poor Tiny Tim—shall we—or this first parting that there was among us?"

"Never, Father!" cried they all.

"And I know," said Bob, "I know, my dears, that when we recollect how patient and how mild he was, although he was a little, little child, we shall not quarrel easily among ourselves, and forget poor Tiny Tim in doing it."

"No, never, Father!" they all cried again.

"I am very happy," said little Bob; "I am very happy!"

Mrs. Cratchit kissed him, his daughters kissed him, the two young Cratchits kissed him, and Peter and himself shook hands. Spirit of Tiny Tim, thy childish essence was from God!

"Specter," said Scrooge, "something informs me that our parting moment is at hand. I know it, but I know not how. Tell me what man that was whom we saw lying dead?"

The Ghost of Christmas Yet To Come conveyed him, as before—though at a different time, he thought, indeed, there seemed no order in these latter visions, save that they were in the Future—into the resorts of businessmen, but showed him not himself. Indeed, the Spirit did not stay for anything, but went straight on, as to the end just now desired, until besought by Scrooge to tarry for a moment.

"This Court," said Scrooge, "through which we hurry now, is where my place of occupation is, and has been for a length of time. I see the house. Let me behold what I shall be in days to come."

The Spirit stopped. The hand was pointed elsewhere.

"The house is yonder," Scrooge exclaimed. "Why do you point away?"

The inexorable finger underwent no change.

Scrooge hastened to the window of his office and looked in. It was an office still, but not his. The furniture was not the same, and the figure in the chair was not himself. The Phantom pointed as before.

He joined it once again, and wondered why and whither he had gone, accompanied it until they reached an iron gate. He paused to look around before entering.

A churchyard. Here, then, the wretched man whose name he had now to learn, lay underneath the ground. It was a worthy place. Walled in by houses, overrun by grass and weeds, the growth of vegetations' death, not life, choked up with too much burying, fat with repleted appetite. A worthy place!

The Spirit stood among the graves, and pointed down to one. He advanced toward it, trembling. The Phantom was exactly as it had been, but he dreaded that he saw new meaning in its solemn shape.

"Before I draw nearer to that stone to which you point," said Scrooge, "answer me one question. Are these the shadows of the things that Will be, or are they shadows of the things that May be, only?"

Still the Ghost pointed downward to the grave by which it stood.

"Men's courses will foreshadow certain ends, to which, if persevered in, they must lead," said Scrooge. "But if the courses be departed from, the ends will change. Say it is thus with what you show me!"

The Spirit was immovable as ever.

Scrooge crept toward it, trembling as he went, and following the finger, read upon the stone of the neglected grave his own name. *Ebenezer Scrooge*.

"Am I that man who lay upon the bed?" he cried, upon his knees.

The finger pointed from the grave to him, and back again.

"No, Spirit! Oh, no, no!"

The finger still was there.

"Spirit!" he cried, tight clutching at his robe. "Hear me! I am not the man I was. I will not be the man I must have been but for this intercourse. Why show me this, if I am past all hope!"

For the first time the hand appeared to shake.

"Good Spirit," he pursued, as down upon the ground he fell before it. "Your nature intercedes for me, and pities me. Assure me that I yet may change these shadows you have shown me by an altered life?"

The kind hand trembled.

"I will honor Christmas in my heart, and try to keep it all the year. I will live in the Past, the Present, and the Future. The Spirits of all three shall strive within me. I will not shut out the lessons that they teach. Oh, tell me I may sponge away the writing on this stone?"

In his agony he caught the spectral hand. It sought to free itself, but he was strong in his entreaty, and detained it. The Spirit, stronger yet, repulsed him.

Holding up his hands in a last prayer to have his fate reversed, he saw an alteration in the Phantoms's hood and dress. It shrunk, collapsed, and dwindled down into a bedpost.

* * *

Yes! And the bedpost was his own. The bed was his own, the room was his own. Best and happiest of all, the Time before him was his own, to make amends in!

"I will live in the Past, the Present, and the Future!" Scrooge repeated, as he scrambled out of bed. "The Spirits of all three shall strive within me. Oh, Jacob Marley! Heaven, and the Christmas time be praised for this! I say it on my knees, old Jacob, on my knees!"

He was so fluttered and so glowing with his good intentions, that his broken voice would scarcely answer to his call. He had been sobbing violently in his conflict with the Spirit, and his face was wet with tears.

"They are not torn down," cried Scrooge, folding one of his bed curtains in his arms; "they are not torn down, rings and all. They are here—I am here—the shadows of the things that would have been may be dispelled. They will be. I know they will!"

His hands were busy with his garments all this time, turning them inside out, putting them on upside down, tearing them, mislaying them, making them parties to every kind of extravagance.

"I don't know what day of the month it is," said Scrooge. "I don't know how long I have been among the Spirits. I don't know anything. I'm quite a baby. Never mind. I don't care. I'd rather be a baby. Hallo! Whoop! Hallo here!"

He was checked in his transports by the churches ringing out the lustiest peals he had ever heard. Clash, clang, hammer; ding, dong, bell. Bell, dong, ding; hammer, clang, clash! Oh, glorious, glorious!

Running to the window, he opened it and put out his head. No fog, no mist; clear, bright, jovial, stirring, cold; cold, piping for the blood to dance to; golden sunlight; heavenly sky; sweet fresh air; merry bells. Oh, glorious. Glorious!

"What's today?" cried Scrooge, calling downward to a boy in Sunday clothes, who perhaps had loitered in to look about him.

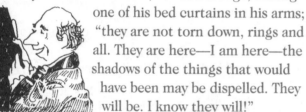

"Eh?" returned the boy, with all his might of wonder.

"What's today, my fine fellow?" said Scrooge.

"Today!" replied the boy. "Why, Christmas Day."

"It's Christmas Day!" said Scrooge to himself. "I haven't missed it. The Spirits have done it all in one night. They can do anything they like. Of course they can. Of course they can. Hallo, my fine fellow!"

"Hallo!" returned the boy.

"Do you know the poulterer's in the next street but one, at the corner?" Scrooge inquired.

"I should hope I did," replied the lad.

"An intelligent boy!" said Scrooge. "A remarkable boy! Do you know whether they've sold the prize turkey that was hanging up there? Not the little prize turkey, the big one?"

"What, the one as big as me?" returned the boy.

"What a delightful boy!" said Scrooge. "It's a pleasure to talk to him. Yes, my buck!"

"It's hanging there now," replied the boy.

"Is it?" said Scrooge. "Go and buy it, and tell 'em to bring it here, that I may give them the direction where to take it. Come back with the man, and I'll give you a shilling. Come back with him in less than five minutes, and I'll give you half a crown!"

The boy was off like a shot. He must have had a steady hand at a trigger who could have got a shot off half so fast.

"I'll send it to Bob Cratchit's," whispered Scrooge, rubbing his hands and splitting with a laugh. "He shan't know who sends it. It's twice the size of Tiny Tim. Joe Miller never made such a joke as sending it to Bob's will be!"

The hand in which he wrote the address was not a steady one, but write it he did, somehow, and went downstairs to open the street door, ready for the coming of the poulterer's man. As he stood there, waiting his arrival, the knocker caught his eye.

"I shall love it as long as I live!" cried Scrooge, patting it with his hand. "I scarcely ever looked at it before. What an honest expression it has in its face! It's a wonderful knocker! Here's the turkey. Hallo! Whoop! How are you! Merry Christmas!"

It was a turkey. He never could have stood upon his legs, that bird. He would have snapped 'em short off in a minute, likesticks of sealing wax.

"Why, it's impossible to carry that to Camden Town," said Scrooge. "You must have a cab."

The chuckle with which he said this, and the chuckle with which he paid for the turkey, and the chuckle with which he paid for the cab, and the chuckle with which he recompensed the boy, were only to be exceeded by the chuckle with which he sat down, breathless, in his chair again, and chuckled till he cried.

Shaving was not an easy task, for his hand continued to shake very much; and shaving requires attention, even when you don't dance while you are at it. But if he had cut the end of his nose off, he would have put a piece of sticking plaster over it and been quite satisfied.

He dressed himself "all in his best," and at last got out into the streets. The people were by this time pouring forth, as he had seen them with the Ghost of Christmas Present; and walking with his hands behind him, Scrooge regarded everyone

with a delighted smile. He looked so irresistibly pleasant, in a word, that three or four good-humored fellows said, "Good morning, sir! A Merry Christmas to you!" And Scrooge said often afterward, that of all the blithe sounds he had ever heard, those were the blithest in his ears.

He had not gone far, when coming on toward him he beheld the portly gentleman who had walked into his countinghouse the day before and said, "Scrooge and Marley's, I believe?" It sent a pang across his heart to think how this old gentleman would look upon him when they met, but he knew what path lay straight before him and he took it.

"My dear sir," said Scrooge, quickening his pace and taking the old gentleman by both hands. "How do you do? I hope you succeeded yesterday. It was very kind of you. A Merry Christmas to you, sir!"

"Mr. Scrooge?"

"Yes," said Scrooge. "That is my name, and I fear it may not be pleasant to you. Allow me to ask your pardon. And will you have the goodness—" Here Scrooge whispered in his ear.

"Lord bless me!" cried the gentleman, as if his breath were

taken away. "My dear Mr. Scrooge, are you serious?"

"If you please," said Scrooge. "Not a far-thing less. A great many back payments are included in it, I assure you. Will you do me that favor?"

"My dear sir," said the other, shaking hands with him. "I don't know what to say to such munifi–"

"Don't say anything, please," retorted Scrooge. "Come and see me. Will you come and see me?"

"I will!" cried the old gentleman. And it was clear he meant to do it.

"Thank'ee," said Scrooge. "I am much obliged to you. I thank you fifty times. Bless you!"

He went to church, and walked about the streets, and watched the people hurrying to and fro, and patted the children on the head, and questioned beggars, and looked down into the kitchens of houses, and up to the windows, and found that everything could yield him pleasure. He had never dreamed that any walk—that anything—could give him so much happiness. In the afternoon he turned his steps toward his nephew's house.

He passed the door a dozen times before he had the courage to go up and knock. But he made a dash, and did it.

"Is your master at home, my dear?" said Scrooge to the girl. Nice girl! Very.

"Yes, sir."

"Where is he, my love?" said Scrooge.

"He's in the dining-room, sir, along with mistress. I'll show you upstairs, if you please."

"Thank'ee. He knows me," said Scrooge, with his hand already on the dining-room lock. "I'll go in here, my dear."

He turned it gently, and sidled his face in round the door. They were looking at the table (which was spread out in great array); for these young housekeepers are always nervous on such points, and like to see that everything is right.

"Fred!" said Scrooge.

Dear heart alive, how his niece by marriage started. Scrooge had forgotten, for the moment, about her sitting in the corner with the footstool, or he wouldn't have done it, on any account.

"Why, bless my soul!" cried Fred. "Who's that?"

"It's I. Your Uncle Scrooge. I have come to dinner. Will you let me in, Fred?"

Let him in! It is a mercy he didn't shake his arm off. He was at home in five minutes. Nothing could be heartier. His niece looked just the same. So did Topper when he came. So did the plump sister when she came. So did every one when they came. Wonderful party, wonderful games, wonderful unanimity, wonderful happiness!

But he was early at the office next morning. Oh, he was early there. If he could only be there first and catch Bob Cratchit coming late! That was the thing he had set his heart upon.

And he did it; yes, he did! The clock struck nine. No Bob. A quarter past. No Bob. He was full eighteen minutes and a half behind his time. Scrooge sat with his door wide open, that he might see him come into the tank.

His hat was off before he opened the door, his comforter too. He was on his stool in a jiffy, driving away with his pen, as if he were trying to overtake nine o'clock.

"Hallo" growled Scrooge, in his accustomed voice as near as he could feign it. "What do you mean by coming here at this time of day?"

"I am very sorry, sir," said Bob. "I am behind my time."

"You are!" repeated Scrooge. "Yes, I think you are. Step this way, sir, if you please."

"It's only once a year, sir," pleaded Bob, appearing from the tank. "It shall not be repeated. I was making rather merry yesterday, sir."

"Now, I'll tell you what, my friend," said Scrooge. "I am not going to stand this sort of thing any longer. And therefore," he continued, leaping from

his stool and giving Bob such a dig in the waistcoat that he staggered back into the tank again, "and therefore I am about to raise your salary!"

Bob trembled, and got a little nearer to the ruler. He had a momentary idea of knocking Scrooge down with it, holding him, and calling to the people in the court for help and a straightwaistcoat.

"A Merry Christmas, Bob!" said Scrooge, with an earnestness that could not be mistaken, as he clapped him on the back. "A merrier Christmas, Bob, my good fellow, than I have given you for many a year! I'll raise your salary and endeavor to assist your struggling family, and we will discuss your affairs this very afternoon, over a Christmas bowl of smoking bishop, Bob! Make up the fires and buy another coal scuttle before you dot another i, Bob Cratchit!"

Scrooge was better than his word. He did it all, and infinitely more; and to Tiny Tim, who did not die, he was a second father. He became as good a friend, as good a master, and as good a man, as the good old city knew, or any other good old city, town,

or borough, in the good old world.

Some people laughed to see the alteration in him, but he let them laugh, and little heeded them, for he was wise enough to know that nothing ever happens on this globe, for good, at which some people did not have their fill of laughter in the outset; and knowing that such as these would be blind anyway, he thought it quite as well that they should wrinkle up their eyes in grins, as have the malady in less attractive forms. His own heart laughed; and that was quite enough for him.

He had no further intercourse with Spirits, but lived upon the Total Abstinence Principle, ever afterward; and it was always said of him, that he knew how to keep Christmas well, if any man alive possessed the knowledge. May that be truly said of us, and all of us! And so, as Tiny Tim observed, God Bless Us, Every One!

THE SEVEN POOR TRAVELLERS
Charles Dickens

After the success of *A Christmas Carol* (featured elsewhere in this section), Charles Dickens spent a good deal of time writing Christmas stories. Every year between 1843 and 1868, with only two exceptions, Dickens wrote a new Christmas tale. "The Seven Poor Travellers," though one of his lesser-known works, aptly captures the underlying spirit of generosity and forgiveness that Dickens himself had helped to revive in the holiday.

CHAPTER I ∽
IN THE OLD CITY OF ROCHESTER

STRICTLY SPEAKING, THERE were only six Poor Travellers; but, being a Traveller myself, though an idle one, and being withal as poor as I hope to be, I brought the number up to seven. This word of explanation is due at once, for what says the inscription over the quaint old door?

RICHARD WATTS, ESQ. by his Will, dated 22 Aug. 1579, founded this Charity for Six poor Travellers, who not being ROGUES, OR PROCTORS, May receive gratis for one Night, Lodging, Entertainment, and Fourpence each.

It was in the ancient little city of Rochester in Kent, of all the good days in the year upon a Christmas-eve, that I stood reading this inscription over the quaint old door in question. I had been wandering about the neighbouring Cathedral, and had seen the tomb of Richard Watts, with the effigy of worthy Master Richard starting out of it like a ship's figurehead; and I had felt that I could do no less, as I give the Verger his fee, than inquire the way to Watts' Charity. The way being very short and very plain, I had come propitiously to the inscription and the quaint old door.

'Now,' said I to myself, as I looked at the knocker, 'I know I am not a Proctor; I wonder whether I am a Rogue!' Upon the whole, though Conscience reproduced two or three pretty faces which might have had smaller attraction for a moral Goliath than they had had for me, who am but a Tom Thumb in that way, I came to the conclusion that I was not a Rogue. So, beginning to regard the establishment as in some sort my property, bequeathed to me divers co-legatees, share and share alike, by the Worshipful Master Richard Watts, I stepped backward into the road to survey my inheritance.

I found it to be a clean white house, of a staid and venerable air, with the quaint old door already three times mentioned (an arched door), choice, little, long, low lattice-windows, and a roof of three gables. The silent High Street of Rochester is full of gables, with old beams and timbers carved into strange faces. It is oddly garnished with a queer old clock that projects over the pavement out of a grave red-brick building, as if Time carried on business there, and hung out his sign. Sooth to say, he did an active stroke of work in Rochester, in the old days of the Romans, and the Saxons, and the Normans; and down to the times of King John, when the rugged castle—I will not undertake to say how many hundreds of years old then—was abandoned to the centuries of weather which have so defaced the dark apertures in its walls, that the ruin looks as if the rooks and daws had pecked its eyes out.

I was very well pleased both with my property and its situation. While I was yet surveying it with growing content, I spied at one of the upper lattices which stood open, a decent body, of a wholesome matronly appearance, whose eyes I caught inquiringly addressed to mine. They said so plainly, 'Do you wish to see the house?' that I answered aloud, 'Yes, if you please.' And within a minute the old door opened, and I bent my head, and went down two steps into the entry.

'This,' said the matronly presence, ushering me into a low room on the right, 'is where the travellers sit by the fire, and cook what bits of suppers they buy with their fourpences.'

'O! Then they have no Entertainment?' said I. For the inscription over the outer door was still running in my head, and I was mentally repeating, in a kind of tune, 'Lodging, entertainment, and fourpence each.'

'They have a fire provided for 'em,' returned the matron—a mighty civil person, not, as I could make out, overpaid; 'and these cooking utensils. And this what's painted on a board is the rules for their behaviour. They have their fourpences when they get their tickets from the steward over the way—for I don't admit 'em myself, they must get their tickets first, and sometimes one buys a rasher of bacon, and another a herring, and another a pound of potatoes, or what not. Sometimes two or three of 'em will club their fourpence together, and make a supper that way. But not much of anything is to be got for fourpence, at present, when provisions is so dear.'

'True indeed,' I remarked. I had been looking about the room, admiring its snug fireside at the

upper end, its glimpse of the street through the low mullioned window, and its beams overhead. 'It is very comfortable,' said I. 'Ill-conwenient,' observed the matronly presence.

I liked to hear her say so; for it showed a commendable anxiety to execute in no niggardly spirit the intentions of Master Richard Watts. But the room was really so well adapted to its purpose that I protested, quite enthusiastically, against her disparagement.

'Nay, ma'am,' said I , 'I am sure it is warm in

winter and cool in summer. It has a look of homely welcome and soothing rest. It has a remarkably cosy fireside, the very blink of which, gleaming out into the street upon a winter night, is enough to warm all Rochester's heart. And as to the convenience of the six Poor Travellers—'

'I don't mean them,' returned the presence. 'I speak of its being an ill-conwenience to myself and my daughter, having no other room to sit in of a night.'

This was true enough, but there was another quaint room of corresponding dimensions on the opposite side of the entry: so I stepped across to it, through the open doors of both rooms, and asked what this chamber was for.

'This,' returned the presence, 'is the Board Room. Where the gentlemen meet when they come here.' Let me see. I had counted from the street six upper windows besides these on the ground-story. Making a perplexed calculation in my mind, I rejoined, 'Then the six Poor Travellers sleep upstairs?'

My new friend shook her head. 'They sleep,' she answered, 'in two little outer galleries at the back, where their beds has always been, ever since the Charity was founded. It being so very ill-conwenient to me as things is at present, the gentlemen are going to take off a bit of the back yard, and make a slip of a room for 'em there, to sit in before they go to bed.'

'And then the six Poor Travellers,' said I, 'will be entirely out of the house?' 'Entirely out of the house,' assented the presence, comfortably smoothing her hands. 'Which is considered much better for all parties, and much more conwenient.'

I had been a little startled, in the Cathedral, by the emphasis with which the effigy of Master Richard Watts was bursting out of his tomb; but I began to think, now, that it might be expected to come across the High Street some stormy night, and make a disturbance here.

Howbeit, I kept my thoughts to myself, and accompanied the presence to the little galleries at the back. I found them on a tiny scale, like the galleries in old inn-yards; and they were very clean. While I was looking at them, the matron gave me to understand that the prescribed number of Poor Travellers were forthcoming every night from year's end to year's end to year's end; and that the beds were always occupied. My questions upon this, and her replies, brought us back to the Board Room so essential to the dignity of the 'gentlemen,' where she showed me the printed accounts of the Charity hanging up by the window. From them I gathered that the greater part of the property bequeathed by the Worshipful Master Richard Watts for the maintenance of this foundation was, at the period of his death, mere marshland; but that, in course of time, it had been reclaimed and built upon, and was very considerably increased in value. I found, too, that about a thirtieth part of the annual revenue was now expended on the purposes commemorated in the inscription over the door; the rest being handsomely laid out in Chancery, law expenses, collectorship, receivership, poundage, and other appendages of management, highly complimentary to the importance of the six Poor Travellers. In short, I made the not entirely new discovery that it may be said of an establishment like this, in dear old England, as of the fat oyster in the American story, that it takes a good many men to swallow it whole.

'And pray, ma'am,' said I, sensible that the blankness of my face began to brighten as the thought occurred to me, 'could one see these Travellers?'

'Well!' she returned dubiously, 'no!' 'Not to-night, for instance!' said I. 'Well!' she returned more positively, 'no. Nobody ever asked to see them, and nobody ever did see them.' As I am not easily

baulked in a design when I am set upon it, I urged to the good lady that this was Christmas-eve; that Christmas comes but once a year—which is unhappily too true, for when it begins to stay with us the whole year round we shall make this earth a very different place; that I was possessed by the desire to treat the Travellers to a supper and a temperate glass of hot Wassail; that the voice of Fame had been heard in that land, declaring my ability to make hot Wassail; that if I were permitted to hold the feast, I should be found comformable to reason, sobriety, and good hours; in a word, that I could be merry and wise myself, and had been even known at a pinch to keep others so, although I was decorated with no badge or medal, and was not a Brother, Orator, Apostle, Saint, or Prophet of any denomination whatever. In the end I prevailed, to my great joy. It was settled that at nine o'clock that night a Turkey and a piece of Roast Beef should smoke upon the board; and that I, faint and unworthy minister for once of Master Richard Watts, should preside as the Christmas-supper host of the six Poor Travellers.

I went back to my inn to give the necessary directions for the Turkey and Roast Beef, and, during the remainder of the day, could settle to nothing for thinking of the Poor Travellers. When the wind blew hard against the windows—it was a cold day, with dark gusts of sleet alternating with periods of wild brightness, as if the year were dying fitfully—I pictured them advancing towards their resting-place along various cold roads, and felt delighted to think how little they foresaw the supper that awaited them.

I painted their portraits in my mind, and indulged in little heightening touches. I made them footsore; I made them weary; I made them carry packs and bundles; I made them stop by finger-posts and milestones, leaning on their bent sticks, and looking wistfully at what was written there; I made them lose their way; and filled their five wits with apprehensions of lying out all night, and being frozen to death. I took up my hat, and went out, climbed to the top of the Old Castle, and looked over the windy hills that slope down to the Medway, almost believing that I could descry some of my Travellers in the distance. After it fell dark, and the Cathedral bell was heard in the invisible steeple—quite a bower of frosty rime when I had last seen it—striking five, six, seven, I became so full of my Travellers that I could eat no dinner, and felt constrained to watch them still in the red coals of my fire. They were all arrived by this time, I thought, had got their tickets, and were gone in. There my leisure was dashed by the reflection that probably some Travellers had come too late and were shut out.

After the Cathedral bell had struck eight, I could smell a delicious savour of Turkey and Roast Beef rising to the window of my adjoining bedroom, which looked down into the inn-yard just where the lights of the kitchen reddened a massive fragment of the Castle Wall. It was high time to make the Wassail now; therefore I had up the materials (which, together with their proportions and combinations, I must decline to impart, as the only secret of my own I was ever known to keep), and made a glorious jorum. Not in a bowl; for a bowl anywhere but on a shelf is a low superstition, fraught with cooling and slopping; but in a brown earthenware pitcher, tenderly suffocated, when full, with a coarse cloth. It being now upon the stroke of nine, I set out for Watts' Charity, carrying my brown beauty in my arms. I would trust Ben, the waiter, with untold gold; but there are strings in the human heart which must never be sounded by another, and drinks that I make myself are those strings in mine.

The Travellers were all assembled, the cloth was laid, and Ben brought a great billet of wood, and had laid it artfully on the top of the fire, so that a touch or two of the poker after supper should make a roaring blaze. Having deposited my brown beauty in a red nook of the hearth, inside the fender, where she soon began to sing like an ethereal cricket, diffusing at the same time odours as of ripe vineyards, spice forests, and orange groves—I say, having stationed my beauty in a place of security and improvement, I introduced myself to my guests by shaking hands all round, and giving them a hearty welcome.

I found the party to be thus composed. Firstly, myself. Secondly, a very decent man indeed, with his right arm in a sling, who had a certain clean, agreeable smell of wood about him, from which I judged him to have something to do with shipbuilding. Thirdly, a little sailor-boy, a mere child, with a profusion of rich dark brown hair, and deep womanly-looking eyes. Fourthly, a shabby-genteel personage in a threadbare black suit, and apparently in very bad circumstances, with a dry, suspicious look; the absent buttons on his waistcoat eked out with red tape; and a bundle of extraordinarily tattered papers sticking out of an inner breast-pocket. Fifthly, a foreigner by birth, but an Englishman in speech, who carried his pipe in the band of his hat, and lost no time in telling me, in an easy, simple, engaging way, that he was a watchmaker from Geneva, and travelled all about the Continent, mostly on foot, working as a journeyman, and seeing new countries—

possibly (I thought) also smuggling a watch or so, now and then. Sixthly, a little widow, who had been very pretty and was still very young, but whose beauty had been wrecked in some great misfortune, and whose manner was remarkably timid, scared, and solitary. Seventhly and lastly, a Traveller of a kind familiar to my boyhood, but now almost obsolete—a Book-Peddler, who had a quantity of Pamphlets

and Numbers with him, and who presently boasted that he could repeat more verses in an evening than he could sell in a twelvemonth.

All these I have mentioned in the order in which they sat at table. I presided, and the matronly presence faced me. We were not long in taking our places, for the supper had arrived with me, in the following procession:

Myself with the pitcher. Ben with Beer. Inattentive Boy with hot plates. THE TURKEY. Female carrying sauces to be heated on the spot. THE BEEF. Man with Tray on his head, containing Vegetables and Sundries. Volunteer Hostler from Hotel, grinning, and rendering no assistance.

As we passed along the High Street, comet-like, we left a long tail of fragrance behind us which caused the public to stop, sniffing in wonder. We had previously left at the corner of the inn-yard a wall-eyed young man connected with the Fly department, and well accustomed to the sound of a railway whistle which Ben always carries in his pocket, whose instructions were, so soon as he should hear the whistle blown, to dash into the kitchen, seize the hot plum-pudding and mince-pies, and speed with

them to Watt's Charity, where they would be received (he was further instructed) by the sauce-female, who would be provided with brandy in a blue state of combustion.

All these arrangements were executed in the most exact and punctual manner. I never saw a finer turkey, finer beef, or greater prodigality of sauce and gravy; and my Travellers did wonderful justice to everything set before them. It made my heart rejoice to observe how their wind and frost hardened faces softened in the clatter of plates and knives and forks, and mellowed in the fire and supper heat. While their hats and caps and wrappers, hanging up, a few small bundles on the ground in a corner, and in another corner three or four old walking-sticks, worn down at the end to mere fringe, linked this snug interior with the bleak outside in a golden chain.

When supper was done, and my brown beauty had been elevated on the table, there was a general requisition to me to 'take the corner;' which suggested to me comfortably enough how much my friends here made of a fire— for when had I ever thought so highly of the corner, since the days when I connected it with Jack Horner? However, as I declined, Ben, whose touch on all convivial instruments is perfect, drew the table apart, and instructing my Travellers to open right and left on either side of me, and form round the fire, closed up the centre with myself and my chair, and preserved the order we had kept at table. He had already, in a tranquil manner, boxed the ears of the inattentive boys until they had been by imperceptible degrees boxed out of the room; and he now rapidly skirmished the sauce-female into the

High Street, disappeared, and softly closed the door.

This was the time for bringing the poker to bear on the billet of wood. I tapped it three times, like an enchanted talisman, and a brilliant host of merry-makers burst out of it, and sported off by the chimney—rushing up the middle in a fiery country dance, and never coming down again. Meanwhile, by their sparkling light, which threw our lamp into the shade, I filled the glasses, and gave my Travellers, CHRISTMAS!—CHRISTMAS-EVE, my friends, when the shepherds, who were Poor Travellers, too, in their way, heard the Angels, 'On earth, peace. Good-will towards men!'

I don't know who was the first among us to think that we ought to take hands as we sat, in deference to the toast, or whether any one of us anticipated the others, but at any rate we all did it. We then drank to the memory of the good Master Richard Watts.

And I wish his Ghost may never have had worse usage under that roof than it had from us.

It was the witching for Story-telling. 'Our whole life, Travellers,' said I, 'is a story more or less intelligible—generally less; but we shall read it by a clearer light when it is ended. I, for one, am so divided this night between fact and fiction, that I scarce know which is which. Shall I beguile the time by telling you a story as we sit here?'

They all answered, yes. I had little to tell them, but I was bound by my own proposal. Therefore, after looking for awhile at the spiral column of smoke wreathing up from my brown beauty, through which I could have almost sworn I saw the effigy of Master Richard Watts less startled than usual, I fired away.

CHAPTER II ~ THE STORY OF RICHARD DOUBLEDICK

IN THE YEAR one thousand seven hundred and ninety-nine, a relative of mine came limping down, on foot, to this town of Chatham. I call it this town, because if anybody present knows to a nicety where Rochester ends and Chatham begins, it is more than I do. He was a poor traveller, with not a farthing in his pocket. He sat by the fire in this very room, and he slept one night in a bed that will be occupied to-night by some one here.

My relative came down to Chatham to enlist in a cavalry regiment, if a cavalry regiment would have him; if not, to take King George's shilling from any corporal or sergeant who would put a bunch of ribbons in his hat. His object was to get shot; but he thought he might as well ride to death as be at the trouble of walking.

My relative's Christian name was Richard, but he was better known as Dick. He dropped his own surname on the road down, and took up that of Doubledick. He was passed as Richard Doubledick; age, twenty-two; height, five foot ten; native place, Exmouth, which he had never been near in his life. There was no cavalry in Chatham when he limped over the bridge here with half a shoe to his dusty feet, so he enlisted into a regiment of the line, and was glad to get drunk and forget all about it.

You are to know that this relative of mine had gone wrong, and run wild. His heart was in the right place, but it was sealed up. He had been betrothed to a good and beautiful girl, whom he had loved better than she—or perhaps even he—believed; but in an evil hour he had given her cause to say to him solemnly, 'Richard, I will never marry another man. I will live single for your sake, but Mary Marshall's lips— her name was Mary Marshall— will never address another word to you on earth. Go, Richard! Heaven forgive you!' This finished him. This brought him down to Chatham. This made him Private Richard Doubledick, with a determination to be shot.

There was not a more dissipated and reckless soldier in Chatham barracks, in the year one thousand seven hundred and ninety-nine, than Private Richard Doubledick. He associated with the dregs of every regiment; he was as seldom sober as he could be, and was constantly under punishment. It became clear to the whole barracks that Private Richard Doubledick would very soon be flogged.

Now the Captain of Richard Doubledick's company was a young gentleman not above five years his senior, whose eyes had an expression in them which affected Private Richard Doubledick in a very remarkable way. They were bright, handsome, dark eyes—what are called laughing eyes generally, and, when serious, rather steady than severe—but they were the only eyes now left in his narrowed world that Private Richard Doubledick could not stand. Unabashed by evil report and punishment, defiant of everything else and everybody else, he had but to know that those eyes looked at him for a moment, and he felt ashamed. He could not so much as salute Captain Taunton in the street like any other officer. He was reproached and confused—troubled by the mere possibility of the captain's looking at him. In his worst moments, he would rather turn back, and go any distance out of his way, than encounter those two handsome, dark, bright eyes.

One day, when Private Richard Doubledick came out of the Black Hole, where he had been passing the last eight-and-forty hours, and in which retreat he spent a good deal of his time, he was ordered to betake himself to Captain Taunton's quarters. In the stale and squalid state of a man just out of the Black Hole, he had less fancy than ever for being seen by the Captain; but he was not so mad yet as to disobey orders, and consequently went up to the terrace over-looking the parade-ground, where the officers' quarters were; twisting and breaking in his hands, as he went along, a bit of the straw that had formed the decorative furniture of the Black Hole.

'Come in!' cried the Captain, when he knocked with his knuckles at the door. Private Richard Doubledick pulled off his cap, took a stride forward, and felt very conscious that he stood in the light of the dark, bright eyes.

There was a silent pause. Private Richard Doubledick had put the straw in his mouth, and was gradually doubling it up into his windpipe and choking himself.

'Doubledick,' said the Captain, 'do you know where you are going to?'

'To the Devil, sir?' faltered Doubledick.

'Yes,' returned the Captain. 'And very fast.' Private Richard Doubledick turned the straw of the Black Hole in his mouth, and made a miserable salute of acquiescence. 'Doubledick,' said the Captain, 'since I entered his Majesty's service, a boy of seventeen, I have been pained to see many men of promise going that road; but I have never been so pained to see a man determined to make the shameful journey as I have been, ever since you joined the regiment, to see you.'

Private Richard Doubledick began to find a film stealing over the floor at which he looked; also to find the legs of the Captain's breakfast-table turning crooked, as if he saw them through water.

'I am only a common soldier, sir,' said he. 'It signifies very little what such a poor brute comes to.'

'You are a man,' returned the Captain, with grave indignation, 'of education and superior advantages; and if you say that, meaning what you say, you have sunk lower than I had believed. How low that must be, I leave you to consider, knowing what I know of your disgrace, and seeing what I see.'

'I hope to get shot soon, sir,' said Private Richard Doubledick; 'and then the regiment and the world together will be rid of me.'

The legs of the table were becoming very crooked. Doubledick, looking up to steady his vision, met the eyes that had so strong an influence over him. He put his hand before his own eyes, and the breast of his disgrace-jacket swelled as if it would fly asunder.

'I would rather,' said the young Captain, 'see this in you, Doubledick, than I would see five thousand guineas counted out upon this table for a gift to my good mother. Have you a mother?'

'I am thankful to say she is dead, sir.'

'If your praises,' returned the Captain, 'were sounded from mouth to mouth through the whole regiment, through the whole army, through the whole country, you would wish she had lived to say, with pride and joy, "He is my son!" '

'Spare me, sir,' said Doubledick. 'She would never have heard any good of me. She would never have had any pride and joy in owning herself my mother. Love and compassion she might have had, and would have always had, I know; but not— Spare me, sir! I am a broken wretch, quite at your mercy!' And he turned his face to the wall, and stretched out his imploring hand.

'My friend—' began the Captain.

'God bless you, sir,' sobbed Private Richard Doubledick.

'You are at the crisis of your fate. Hold your course unchanged a little longer, and you know what must happen. *I* know even better than you can imagine, that, after that has happened, you are lost. No man who could shed those tears could bear those marks.'

'I fully believe it, sir,' in a low, shivering voice said Private Richard Doubledick.

'But a man in any station can do his duty,' said the young Captain, 'and, in doing it, can earn his own respect, even if his case should be so very unfortunate and so very rare that he can earn no other man's. A common soldier, poor brute though you called him just now, has this advantage in the stormy times we live in, that he always does his duty before a host of sympathizing witnesses. Do you doubt that he may so do it as to be extolled through a whole regiment, through a whole army, through a whole country? Turn while you may yet retrieve the past, and try.'

'I will! I ask for only one witness, sir,' cried Richard, with a bursting heart. 'I understand you. I will be a watchful and a faithful one.'

I have heard from Private Richard Doubledick's own lips, that he dropped down upon his knee, kissed that officer's hand, arose, and went out of the light of the dark, bright eyes, an altered man.

In that year, one thousand seven hundred and ninety-nine, the French were in Egypt, in Italy, in Germany—where not? Napoleon Bonaparte had likewise begun to stir against us in India, and most men could read the signs of the great troubles that were coming on. In the very next year, when we formed an alliance with Austria against him, Captain Taunton's regiment was on service in India. And there was not a finer non-commissioned officer in it—no, nor in the whole line—than Corporal Richard Doubledick.

In eighteen hundred and one, the Indian army

were on the coast of Egypt. Next year was the year of the proclamation of the short peace, and they were recalled. It had then become well known to thousands of men, that wherever Captain Taunton, with the dark, bright eyes, led, there, close to him, ever at his side, firm as a rock, true as the sun, and brave as Mars, would be certain to be found, while life beat in their hearts, that famous soldier, Sergeant Richard Doubledick.

Eighteen hundred and five, besides being the great year of Trafalgar, was a year of hard fighting in India. That year saw such wonders done by a Sergeant-Major, who cut his way single-handed though a solid mass of men, recovered the colours

of his regiment, which had been seized from the hand of a poor boy shot through the heart, and rescued his wounded Captain, who was down, and in a very jungle of horses' hoofs and sabres—saw such wonders done, I say, by this brave Sergeant-Major, that he was specially made the bearer of the colours he had won; and Ensign Richard Doubledick had risen from the ranks.

Sorely cut up in every battle, but always reinforced by the bravest of men—for the fame of following the old colours, shot through and through, which Ensign Richard Doubledick had saved, inspired all breasts—this regiment fought its way through the Peninsular War, up to the investment of Badajos in eighteen hundred and twelve. Again and again it had been cheered through the British ranks until the tears had sprung into men's eyes at the mere hearing of the mighty British voice, so exultant in their valour; and there was not a drummer-boy but knew the legend, that wherever the two friends, Major Taunton, with the dark, bright eyes, and Ensign Richard Doubledick, who was devoted to him, were seen to go, there the boldest spirits in the English army became wild to follow.

One day, at Badajos, not in the great storming, but in repelling a hot sally of the besieged upon our men at work in the trenches, who had given way—the two officers found themselves hurrying forward, face to face, against a party of French infantry, who made a stand. There was an officer at their head, encouraging his men—a courageous, handsome, gallant officer of five-and-thirty, whom Doubledick saw hurriedly, almost momentarily, but saw well. He particularly noticed this officer waving his sword, and rallying his men with an eager and excited cry, when they fired in obedience to his gesture, and Major Taunton dropped.

It was over in ten minutes more, and Doubledick returned to the spot where he had laid the best friend man ever had on a coat spread upon the wet clay. Major Taunton's uniform was opened at the breast, and on his shirt were three little spots of blood.

'Dear Doubledick,' said he, 'I am dying.'

'For the love of Heaven, no!' exclaimed the other, kneeling down beside him, and passing his arm round his neck to raise his head. 'Taunton! My preserver, my guardian angel, my witness! Dearest, truest, kindest of human beings! Taunton! For God's sake!'

The bright, dark eyes—so very, very dark now, in the pale face—smiled upon him; and the hand he had kissed thirteen years ago laid itself fondly on his breast.

'Write to my mother. You will see Home again. Tell her how we became friends. It will comfort her, as it comforts me.' He spoke no more, but faintly signed for a moment towards his hair as it fluttered in the wind. The Ensign understood him. He smiled again when he saw that, and, gently turning his face over on the supporting arm as if for rest, died, with his hand upon the breast in which he had revived a soul.

No dry eye look on Ensign Richard Doubledick that melancholy day. He buried his friend on the

field, and became a lone, bereaved man. Beyond his duty he appeared to have but two remaining cares in life—one, to preserve the little packet of hair he was to give to Taunton's mother; the other, to encounter that French officer who had rallied the men under whose fire Taunton fell. A new legend now began to circulate among our troops; and it was, that when he and the French officer came face to face once more, there would be weeping in France.

The war went on—and through it went the exact picture of the French officer on the one side, and the bodily reality upon the other—until the Battle of Toulouse was fought. In the returns sent home appeared these words: 'Severely wounded, but not dangerously, Lieutenant Richard Doubledick.'

At Midsummer-time, in the year eighteen hundred and fourteen, Lieutenant Richard Doubledick, now a browned soldier, seven-and-thirty years of age, came home to England invalided. He brought the hair with him, near his heart. Many a French officer had he seen since that day; many a dreadful night , in searching with men and lanterns for his wounded, had he relieved French officers lying disabled; but the mental picture and the reality had never come together.

Though he was weak and suffered pain, he lost not an hour in getting down to Frome in Somersetshire, where Taunton's mother lived. In the sweet, com-

passionate words that naturally present themselves to the mind tonight, 'he was the only son of his mother, and she was a widow.'

It was a Sunday evening, and the lady sat at her quiet garden-window, reading the Bible; reading to herself, in a trembling voice, that very passage in it, as I have heard him tell. He heard the words: 'Young man, I say unto thee, arise!'

He had to pass the window; and the bright, dark eyes of his debased time seemed to look at him. Her heart told her who he was; she came to the door quickly, and fell upon his neck.

'He saved me from ruin, made me a human creature, won me from infamy and shame. O, God forever bless him! As He will, He will!'

'He will!' the lady answered. 'I know he is in Heaven! Then she piteously cried, 'But O, my darling boy, my darling boy!' Never from the hour when Private Richard Doubledick enlisted at Chatham had the Private, Corporal, Sergeant, Sergeant-Major, Ensign, or Lieutenant breathed his right name, or the name of Mary Marshall, or a word of the story of his life, into any ear except his reclaimer's. That previous scene in his existence was closed. He had firmly resolved that his expiation should be to live unknown; to disturb no more the peace that had long grown over his old offences; to let it be revealed, when he was dead, that he had striven and suffered, and had never forgotten; and then, if they could forgive him and believe him—well, it would be time enough—time enough!

But that night, remembering the words he had cherished for two years, 'Tell her how we became friends. It will comfort her, as it comforts me,' he related everything. It gradually seemed to him as if in his maturity he had recovered a mother; it gradually seemed to her as if in her bereavement she had found a son. During his stay in England, the quiet garden into which he had slowly and painfully crept, a stranger, became the boundary of his home; when he was able to rejoin his regiment in the spring, he left the garden, thinking was this indeed the first time he had ever turned his face towards the old colours with a woman's blessing!

He followed them—so ragged, so scarred and pierced now, that they would scarcely hold together—to Quatre Bras and Ligny. He stood beside them, in an awful stillness of many men, shadowy through the mist and drizzle of a wet June forenoon, on the field of Waterloo. And down to that hour the picture in his mind of the French officer had never been compared with the reality.

The famous regiment was in action early in the battle, and received its first check in many an eventful year, when he was seen to fall. But it swept on to avenge him, and left behind it no such creature in the world of consciousness as Lieutenant Richard Doubledick.

Through pits of mire, and pools of rain; along deep ditches, once roads, that were pounded and ploughed to pieces by artillery, heavy wagons, tramp of men and horses, and the struggle of every wheeled thing that could carry wounded soldiers; jolted among the dying and the dead, so disfigured by blood and mud as to be hardly recognizable for humanity; undisturbed by the moaning of men and the shrieking of horses, which, newly taken from the peaceful pursuits of life, could not endure the sight of the stragglers lying by the wayside, never to resume their toilsome journey; dead, as to any sentient life that was in it, and yet alive—the form that had been Lieutenant Richard Doubledick, with whose praises England rang, was conveyed to Brussels. There it was tenderly laid down in hospital; and there it lay, week after week, through the long, bright

summer days, until the harvest, spared by war, had ripened and was gathered in.

Over and over again the sun rose and set upon the crowded city; over and over again the moonlight nights were quiet on the plains of Waterloo: and all that time was a blank to what had been Lieutenant Richard Doubledick. Rejoicing troops marched into Brussels, and marched out; brothers and fathers, sisters, mothers, and wives, came thronging thither, drew their lots of joy or agony, and departed; so many times a day the bells rang; so many times the shadows of the great buildings changed; so many lights sprang up at dusk; so many feet passed here and there upon the pavements; so many hours of sleep and cooler air of night succeeded: indifferent to all, a marble face lay on a bed, like the face of a recumbent statue on the tomb of Lieutenant Richard Doubledick.

Slowly laboring, at last, through a long, heavy dream of confused time and place, presenting faint glimpses of army surgeons who he knew, and of faces that had been familiar to his youth—dearest and kindest among them, Mary Marshall's, with a solicitude upon it more like reality than anything he could discern—Lieutenant Richard Doubledick came back to life. To the beautiful life of a calm autumn evening sunset, to the peaceful life of a fresh, quiet room with a large window standing open; a balcony beyond, in which were moving leaves and sweet-smelling flowers; beyond, again, the clear sky, with the sun full in his sight, pouring its golden radiance on his bed.

Is was so tranquil and so lovely that he thought he had passed into another world. And he said in a faint voice. 'Taunton, are you near me?'

A face bent over him. Not his, his mother's. 'I came to nurse you. We have nursed you many weeks.

You were moved here long ago. Do you remember nothing?'

'Nothing.' The lady kissed his cheek, and held his hand, soothing him. 'Where is the regiment? What has happened? Let me call you mother. What has happened, mother?'

'A great victory, dear. The war is over, and the regiment was the bravest in the field.' His eyes kindled, his lips trembled, he sobbed, and the tears ran down his face. He was very weak, too weak to move his hand.

'Was it dark just now?' he asked presently.

'No.'

'It was only dark to me? Something passed away, like a black shadow. But as it went, and the sun—O the blessed sun, how beautiful it is!—touched my face, I thought I saw a light white cloud pass out at the door. Was there nothing that went out?'

She shook her head, and in a little while he fell asleep, she still holding his hand, and soothing him. From that time, he recovered. Slowly, for he had been desperately wounded in the head, and had been shot in the body, but making some little advance every day. When he had gained sufficient strength to converse as he lay in bed, he soon began to remark that Mrs. Taunton always brought him back to his own history. Then he recalled his preserver's dying words, and thought, 'It comforts her.'

One day he awoke out of a sleep, refreshed, and asked her to read to him. But the curtain of the bed, softening the light, which she always drew back when he awoke, that she might see him from her table at the bedside where she sat at work, was held undrawn; and a woman's voice spoke, which was not hers.

'Can you bear to see a stranger?' it said softly. 'Will you like to see a stranger?'

'Stranger!' he repeated. The voice awoke old memories, before the days of Private Richard Doubledick.

'A stranger now, but not a stranger once,' it said in tones that thrilled him. 'Richard, dear Richard, lost through so many years, my name—'

He cried out her name, 'Mary,' and she held him in her arms, and his head lay on her bosom.

'I am not breaking a rash vow, Richard. These are not Mary Marshall's lips that speak. I have another name.' She was married. 'I have another name, Richard. Did you ever hear it?'

'Never!' He looked into her face, so pensively beautiful, and wondered at the smile upon it through her tears.

'Think again, Richard. Are you sure you never heard my altered name?'

'Never!'

'Don't move your head to look at me, dear Richard. Let it lie here, while I tell my story. I loved a generous, noble man; loved him with my whole heart; loved him for years and years; loved him faithfully, devotedly; loved him with no hope of return; loved him, knowing nothing of his highest qualities—not even knowing that he was alive. He was a brave soldier. He was honoured and beloved by thousands of thousands, when the mother of his dear friend found me, and showed me that in all his triumphs he had never forgotten me. He was wounded in a great battle. He was brought, dying, here, into Brussels. I came to watch and tend him, as I would have joyfully gone, with such a purpose, to the dreariest ends of the earth. When he knew no one else, he knew me. When he suffered most, he bore his sufferings barely murmuring, content to rest his head where yours rests now. When he lay at the point of death, he married me, that he might call me Wife before he died. And the name, my dear love, that I took on that forgotten night—'

'I know it now!' he sobbed. 'The shadowy remembrance strengthens. It is come back. I thank Heaven that my mind is quite restored! My Mary, kiss me; lull this weary head to rest, or I shall die of gratitude. His parting words were fulfilled. I see Home again!'

Well! They were happy. It was a long recovery, but they were happy through it all. The snow had melted on the ground, and the birds were singing in the leafless thickets of the early spring, when those  three were first able to ride out together, and when people flocked about the open carriage to cheer and congratulate Captain Richard Doubledick.

But even then it became necessary for the Captain, instead of returning to England, to complete his recovery in the climate of Southern France. They found a spot upon the Rhône, within a ride of the old town of Avignon, and within view of its broken bridge, which was all they could desire; they lived there, together, six months; then returned to England. Mrs. Taunton, growing old after three years—though not so old as that her bright, dark eyes were dimmed—and remembering that her strength had been benefited by the change, resolved to go back for a year to those parts. So she went with a faithful servant, who had often carried her son in his arms; and she was to be rejoined and escorted home, at the year's end, by Captain Richard Doubledick.

She wrote regularly to her children (as she called them now), and they to her. She went to the neighborhood of Aix; and there, in their own château near the farmer's house she rented, she grew into intimacy with a family belonging to that part of France. The intimacy began in her often meeting among the vineyards a pretty child, a girl with a most compassionate heart, who was never tired of listening to the solitary English lady's stories of her poor son and the cruel wars. The family were as gentle as the child, and at length she came to know them so well that she accepted their invitation to pass the last month of her residence abroad under their roof. All this intelligence she wrote home, piecemeal as it came about, from time to time; and at last enclosed a polite note, from the head of the château, soliciting, on the occasion of his approaching mission to that neighbourhood, the honour of the company of *cet homme si justement célèbre, Monsieur le Capitaine* Richard Doubledick.

Captain Doubledick, now a hardy, handsome man in the full vigour of life, broader across the chest and shoulders than he had ever been before, despatched a courteous reply, and followed it in person. Travelling through all that extent of country after three years of Peace, he blessed the better days on which the world had fallen. The corn was golden, not drenched in unnatural red; was bound in sheaves for food, not trodden underfoot by men in mortal fight. The smoke rose up from peaceful hearths, not blazing ruins.

The carts were laden with the fair fruits of the earth, not with wounds and death. To him who had so often seen the terrible reverse, these things were beautiful indeed; and they brought him in a softened spirit of the old château near Aix upon a deep blue evening.

It was a large château of the genuine old ghostly kind, with round towers, and extinguishers, and a high leaden roof, and more windows than Aladdin's Palace. The lattice blinds were all thrown open after the heat of the day, and there were glimpses of rambling walls and corridors within. Then there were immense out-buildings fallen into partial decay, masses of dark trees, terrace-gardens, balustrades; tanks of water, too weak to play and too dirty to work; statues, weeds, and thickets of iron railing that seemed to have overgrown themselves like the shrubberies, and to have branched out in all manner of wild shapes. The entrance doors stood open, as doors often do in that country when the heat of the day is past; and the Captain saw no bell or knocker, and walked in.

He walked into a lofty stone hall, refreshingly cool  and gloomy after the glare of a Southern day's travel. Extending along the four sides of this hall was a gallery, leading to suites of rooms; and it was lighted from the top. Still no bell was to be seen. 'Faith,' said the Captain halting, ashamed of the clanking of his boots, 'this is a ghostly beginning!' He started back, and felt his face turn white. In the gallery, looking down at him, stood the French officer—the officer whose picture he had carried in his mind so long and so far. Compared with the original, at last—in every lineament how like it was!

He moved, and disappeared, and Captain Richard Doubledick heard his steps coming quickly down into the hall. He entered through an archway. There was a bright, sudden look upon his face, much such a look as it had worn in that fatal moment.

'*Monsieur le Capitaine Richard Doubledick?* Enchanted to receive him! A thousand apologies! The servants were all out in the air. There was a little fête among them in the garden. In effect, it was the fête day of my daughter, the little cherished and protected of Madame Taunton.'

He was so gracious and so frank that Monsieur le Capitaine Richard Doubledick could not withhold his hand. 'It is the hand of a brave Englishman,' said the French officer, retaining it while he spoke. 'I could respect a brave Englishman, even as my foe, how much more as my friend! I also am a soldier!'

'He has not remembered me, as I have remembered him; he did not take such note of my face, that day, as I took of his,' thought Captain Richard Doubledick. 'How shall I tell him?'

The French officer conducted his guest into a garden and presented him to his wife, an engaging and beautiful woman, sitting with Mrs. Taunton in a whimsical old-fashioned pavilion. His daughter, her fair young face beaming with joy, came running to embrace him; and there was a boy-baby to tumble down among the orange trees on the broad steps, in making for his father's legs. A multitude of children visitors were dancing to sprightly music; and all the servants and peasants about the château were dancing too. It was a scene of innocent happiness that might have been invented for the climax of the scenes of peace which had soothed the Captain's journey.

He looked on, greatly troubled in his mind, until a resounding bell rang, and the French officer begged to show him his rooms. They went upstairs into the gallery from which the officer had looked down; and *Monsieur le Capitaine Richard Doubledick* was cordially welcomed to a grand outer chamber, and a smaller one within, all clocks and draperies, and hearths, and brazen dogs, and tiles, and cool devices, and elegance, and vastness.

'You were at Waterloo,' said the French officer. 'I was,' said Captain Richard Doubledick. 'And at Badajos.' Left alone with the sound of his own stern voice in his ears, he sat down to consider. "What shall I do, and how shall I tell him?" At that time, unhappily, many deplorable duels had been fought between English and French officers, arising out of the recent war; and these duels, and how to avoid

this officer's hospitality were the uppermost thought in Captain Richard Doubledick's mind.

He was thinking, and letting the time run out in which he should have dressed for dinner, when Mrs. Taunton spoke to him outside the door, asking if he could give her the letter he had brought from Mary. 'His mother, above all,' the Captain thought. 'How shall I tell *her*?'

'You will form a friendship with your host, I hope,' said Mrs. Taunton, whom he hurriedly admitted, 'that will last for life. He is so true-hearted and so generous, Richard, that you can hardly fail to esteem one another. If he had been spared,' she kissed (not without tears) the locket in which she wore his hair, 'he would have appreciated him with his own magnanimity, and would have been truly happy that the evil days were past which made such a man his enemy.'

She left the room; and the Captain walked, first to one window, whence he could see the dancing in the garden, then to another, whence he could see the smiling prospect and the peaceful vineyards.

'Spirit of my departed friend,' said he, 'is it through thee these better thoughts are rising in my mind? Is it thou who hast shown me, all the way I have been drawn to meet this man, the blessings of the altered time? Is it thou who has sent thy stricken mother to me, to stay my angry hand? Is it from thee the whisper comes, that this man did his duty as thou didst—and as I did, through thy guidance, which has wholly saved me here on earth—and that he did no more?'

He sat down, with his head buried in his hands, and, when he rose up, made the second strong resolution of his life—that neither to the French officer, nor to the mother of his departed friend, nor to any soul, while either of the two was living, would he breathe what only he knew. And when he touched that French officer's glass with his own, that day at dinner, he secretly forgave him in the name of the Divine Forgiver of injuries.

Here I ended my story as the first Poor Traveller; but, if I had told it now, I could have added that the time has since come when the son of Major Richard Doubledick, and the son of that French officer, friends as their fathers were before them, fought side by side in one cause, with their respective nations, like long-divided brothers whom the better times have brought together, fast united.

CHAPTER III THE ROAD

MY STORY BEING finished, and the Wassail too, we broke up as the Cathedral bell struck twelve. I did not take leave of my travellers that night; for it had come into my head to reappear, in conjunction with some hot coffee, at seven in the morning.

As I passed along the High Street, I heard the Waits a distance, and struck off to find them. They were playing near one of the old gates of the City, at the corner of a wonderfully quaint row of red-brick tenements, which the clarinet obligingly informed me were inhabited by the Minor-Canons. They had odd little porches over the doors, like sounding-boards over old pulpits; and I thought I should like to see one of the Minor-Canons come out upon his top step, and favour us with a little Christmas discourse about the poor scholars of Rochester; taking for his text the words of his Master relative to the devouring of Widows' houses.

The clarinet was so communicative, and my inclinations were (as they generally are) of so vagabond a tendency, that I accompanied the Waits across an open green called the Vines, and assisted—in the French sense—at the performance of two waltzes, two polkas, and three Irish melodies, before I thought of my inn any more. However, I returned to it then, and found a fiddle in the kitchen, and Ben, the wall-eyed young man, and two chambermaids, circling round the great deal table with the utmost animation.

I had a very bad night. It cannot have been owing to the turkey or the beef—and the Wassail is out of the question—but in every endeavor that I made to get to sleep I failed most dismally. I was never asleep; and in whatsoever unreasonable direction my mind rambled, the effigy of Master Richard Watts perpetually embarrassed it.

In a word, I only got out of the Worshipful Master Richard Watts' way by getting out of bed in the dark at six o'clock, and tumbling, as my custom is, into all the cold water that could be accumulated for the purpose. The outer air was dull and cold enough in the street, when I came down there; and the one candle in our supper-room at Watts' Charity looked as pale in the burning as if it had had a bad night too. But my Travellers had all slept soundly, and they took to the hot coffee, and the piles of bread-and-butter, which Ben had arranged like deals in a timber-yard, as kindly as I could desire.

While it was yet scarcely daylight, we all came out into the street together, and there shook hands. The widow took the little sailor towards Chatham, where he was to find a steamboat for Sheerness; the lawyer, with an extremely knowing look, went his own way,  without committing himself by announcing his intentions; two more stuck off by the cathedral and old castle for Maidstone; and the book-peddler accompanied me over the bridge. As for

me, I was going to walk by Cobham Woods, as far upon my way to London as I fancied.

When I came to the stile and footpath by which I was to diverge from the main road, I bade farewell to my last remaining Poor Traveller, and pursued my way alone. And now the mists began to rise in the most beautiful manner, and the sun to shine; and as I went on through the bracing air, seeing the hoar-frost sparkle everywhere, I felt as if all Nature shared in the joy of the great Birthday.

Going through the woods, the softness of my tread upon the mossy ground and among the brown leaves enhanced the Christmas sacredness by which I felt surrounded. As the whitened stems environed me, I thought how the Founder of the time had never raised his benignant hand, save to bless and heal, except in the case of one unconscious tree. By Cobham Hall, I came to the village, and the church-yard where the dead had been quietly buried, 'in the sure and certain hope' which Christmas-time inspired. What children could I see at play, and not be loving of, recalling who had loved them! No garden that I passed was out of unison with the day, for I remembered that the tomb was in a garden, and that 'she supposing him to be the gardener,' had said, 'Sir, if thou have borne him hence, tell me where thou hast laid him, and I will take him away.' In time, the distant river with the ships came full in view, and with it pictures of the poor fishermen, mending their nets, who arose and followed him—of the teaching of the people from a ship pushed off a little way from shore, by reason of the multitude—of a majestic figure walking on the water, in the loneliness of night. My very shadow on the ground was eloquent of Christmas; for did not the people lay their sick where the mere shadows of the men who had heard and seen him might fall as they passed along?

Thus Christmas begirt me, far and near, until I had

come to Blackheath, and had walked down the long vista of gnarled old trees in Greenwich Park, and was being steam-rattled through the mists now closing in once more, towards the lights of London. Brightly they shone, but not so brightly as my own fire, and the brighter faces around it, when we came together to celebrate the day. And there I told of worthy Master Richard Watts, and of my supper with the Six Poor Travellers who were neither Rogues nor Proctors, and from that hour to this, I have never seen one of them again.

THE ADVENTURE OF THE BLUE CARBUNCLE
Sir Arthur Conan Doyle

How does Sherlock Holmes celebrate the holiday season? By getting to the bottom of a mysterious misdeed, of course! Here is one of the classic Holmes stories—with a Christmas setting, no less. The goose that figures prominently in this tale was, of course, a staple of the late nineteenth-century Christmas celebration in many households.

I HAD CALLED upon my friend Sherlock Holmes upon the second morning after Christmas, with the intention of wishing him the compliments of the season. He was lounging upon the sofa in a purple dressing gown, a pipe-rack within his reach upon the right, and a pile of crumpled morning papers, evidently newly studied, near at hand. Beside the couch was a wooden chair, and on the angle on the back hung a very seedy and disreputable felt hat, much the worse for the wear, and cracked in several places. A lens and forceps lying upon the seat of the chair suggested that the hat had been suspended in this manner for the purpose of examination.

"You are engaged," said I; "perhaps I interrupt you."

"Not at all. I am glad to have a friend with whom I can discuss my results. The matter is a perfectly trivial one"—he jerked his thumb in the direction of the old hat—"but there are points in connection with it which are not entirely devoid of interest and even of instruction."

I seated myself in his armchair and warmed my hands before his crackling fire, for a sharp frost had set in, and the windows were thick with the ice crystals. "I suppose," I remarked, "that, homely as it looks, this thing has some deadly story linked on to it—that it is the clue which will guide you in the solution of some mystery and the punishment of some crime."

"No, no. No crime," said Sherlock Holmes, laughing. "Only one of those whimsical little incidents which will happen when you have four million human beings all jostling each other within the space of a few square miles. Amid the action and reaction of so dense a swarm of humanity, every possible combination of events may be expected to take place, and many a little problem will be presented which may be striking and bizarre without being criminal. We have already had experience of such."

"So much so," I remarked, "that of the last six cases which I have added to my notes, three have been entirely free of any legal crime."

"Precisely. You allude to my attempt to recover the Irene Adler papers, to the singular case of Miss. Mary Sutherland, and to the adventure of the man with the twisted lip. Well, I have no doubt that this small matter will fall into the same innocent category. You know Peterson, the commissionaire?"

"Yes."

"It is to him that this trophy belongs."

"It is his hat?"

"No, no; he found it. Its owner is unknown. I beg that you will look upon it not as a battered billycock but as an intellectual problem. And, first, as to how it came here. It arrived upon Christmas morning, in company with a good fat goose, which is, I have no doubt, roasting at this moment in front of Peterson's fire. The facts are these: about four o'clock on Christmas morning, Peterson, who as you know, is a very honest fellow, was returning from some small jollification and was making his way homeward down Tottenham Court Road. In front of him he saw, in the gaslight, a tallish man, walking with a slight stagger, and carrying a white goose hung over his shoulder. As he reached the corner of Goodge Street, a row broke out between this stranger and a little knot of roughs. One of the latter knocked off the man's hat, on which he raised his stick to defend himself and, swinging it over his head, smashed the shop window behind him. Peterson had rushed forward to protect the stranger from his assailants; but the man, shocked at having broke the window, and seeing an official-looking person in uniform rushing towards him, dropped his goose, took to his heels, and vanished amid the labyrinth of small streets which lie at the back of Tottenham Court Road. The roughs had also fled at the appearance of Peterson, so that he was left in possession of the field of battle, and also of the spoils of victory in the shape of this battered hat and a most unimpeachable Christmas goose."

"Which surely he restored to their owner?"

"My dear fellow, there lies the problem. It is true that 'For Mrs. Henry Baker' was printed upon a small card which was tied to the bird's left leg, and it is true that the initials 'H.B.' are legible upon the lining of this hat; but as there are some thousands of Bakers, and some hundreds of Henry Bakers in this city of ours, it is not easy to restore lost property to any one of them."

"What, then, did Peterson do?"

"He brought round both hat and goose to me on Christmas morning, knowing that even the smallest problems are of interest to me. The goose we retained until this morning, when there were signs that, in spite of the slight frost, it would be well that it should be eaten without unnecessary delay. Its finder has carried it off, therefore, to fulfill the ultimate destiny of a goose, while I continue to retain the hat of the unknown gentleman who lost his Christmas dinner."

"Did he not advertise?"

"No."

"Then, what clue could you have as to his identity?"

"Only as much as we can deduce."

"From his hat?"

"Precisely."

"But you are joking. What can you gather from this old battered felt?"

"Here is my lens. You know my methods. What can you gather yourself as to the individuality of the man who has worn this article?"

I took the tattered object in my hands and turned it over rather ruefully. It was a very ordinary black hat of the usual round shape, hard and much the worse for wear. The lining had been of red silk, but was a good deal discolored. There was a maker's name; but, as Holmes had remarked, the initials "H.B." were scrawled upon one side. It was pierced in the brim for a hat-securer, but the elastic was missing. For the rest, it was cracked, exceedingly dusty, and spotted in several places, although there seemed to have been some attempt to hide the discolored patches by smearing them with ink.

"I can see nothing," said I, handing it back to my friend.

"On the contrary, Watson, you can see everything. You fail, however, to reason from what you see. You are too timid in drawing your inferences."

"Then pray tell me what it is that you can infer from this hat?"

He picked it up and gazed at it in the peculiar introspective fashion which was characteristic of him. "It is perhaps less suggestive than it might have been," he remarked, "and yet there are a few inferences which are very distinct, and a few others which represent at least a strong balance of probability. That the man was highly intellectual is of course obvious upon the face of it, and also that he was fairly well-to-do within the last three years, although he has now fallen upon evil days. He had foresight, but has less now than formerly, pointing to a moral regression, which, when taken with the decline of his fortunes, seems to indicate some evil influence, probably drink, at work upon him. This may account also for the obvious fact that his wife has ceased to love him."

"My dear Holmes!"

"He has, however, retained some degree of self respect," he continued, disregarding my remonstrance. "He is a man who leads a sedentary life, goes out little, is out of training entirely, is middle-aged, has grizzled hair which he has had cut within the last few days, and which he anoints with lime cream. These are the more patent facts which are to be deduced from his hat. Also, by the way, that it is extremely improbable that he has gas laid on in his house."

"You are certainly joking, Holmes."

"Not in the least. Is it possible that even now, when I give you these results, you are unable to see how they are attained?"

"I have no doubt that I am very stupid, but I must confess that I am unable to follow you. For example, how did you deduce that this man was intellectual?"

For answer Holmes clapped the hat upon his head. It came right over the forehead and settled upon the bridge of his nose. "It is a question of cubic capacity," said he; "a man with so large a brain must have something in it."

"The decline of his fortunes, then?"

"This hat is three years old. These flat brims curled at the edge came in then. It is a hat of the very best quality. Look at the band of ribbed silk and the excellent lining. If this man could afford to buy so expensive a hat three years ago, and has had no hat since, then he has assuredly gone down in the world."

"Well, that is clear enough, certainly. But how about the foresight and the moral regression?"

Sherlock Holmes laughed. "Here is the foresight," said he, putting his finger upon the little disc and loop of the hat-securer. "They are never sold upon hats. If this man ordered one, it is a sign of a certain amount of foresight, since he went out of his way to take this precaution against the wind. But since we see that he has broken the elastic and has not troubled to replace it, it is obvious that he has less foresight now than formerly, which is a distinct proof of a weakening nature. On the other hand, he has endeavored to conceal some of these stains upon the felt by daubing them with ink, which is a sign that he has not entirely lost his self-respect."

"Your reasoning is certainly plausible."

"The further points, that he is middle-aged, that his hair is grizzled, that it has been recently cut, and that he uses lime-cream, are all to be gathered from a close examination of the lower part of the lining. The lens discloses a large number of hair-ends, clean cut by the scissors of the barber. They all appear to be adhesive, and there is a distinct odour of lime-cream. This dust, you will observe, is not the gritty, gray dust of the street but the fluffy brown dust of the house, showing that it has been hung up indoors most of the time; while the marks of moisture upon the inside are proof positive that the wearer perspired very freely, and could, therefore, hardly be in the best of training."

"But his wife—You said that she had ceased to love him."

"This hat has not been brushed for weeks. When I see you, my dear Watson, with a week's accumulation of dust upon your hat, and when your wife allows you to go out in such a state, I shall fear that you have also been unfortunate enough to lose your wife's affection."

"But he might be a bachelor."

"Nay, he was bringing home the goose as a peace-offering to his wife. Remember the card upon the bird's leg."

"You have an answer to everything. But how on earth do you deduce that the gas is not laid on in his house?"

"One tallow stain, or even two, might come by chance; but when I see no less than five, I think that there can be little doubt that the individual must be brought into frequent contact with burning tallow-walks upstairs at night probably with his hat in one hand and a guttering candle in the other. Anyhow, he never got tallow-stains from a gas-jet. Are you satisfied?"

"Well, it is very ingenious," said I, laughing; "but since, as you said just now, there has been no crime committed, and no harm done save the loss of a goose, all this seems to be rather a waste of energy."

Sherlock Holmes had opened his mouth to reply, when the door flew open, and Peterson, the commissionaire, rushed into the apartment with flushed cheeks and the face of a man who is dazed with astonishment.

"The goose, Mr. Holmes! The goose, sir!" he gasped.

"Eh? What of it, then? Has it returned to life and flapped off through the kitchen window?" Holmes twisted himself round upon the sofa to get a fairer view of the man's excited face.

"See here, sir! See what my wife found in its crop!" He held out his hand and displayed upon the centre of the palm a brilliantly scintillating blue stone, rather smaller than a bean in size, but of such purity and radiance that it twinkled like an electric point in the dark hollow of his hand.

Sherlock Holmes sat up with a whistle. "By Jove, Peterson!" said he, "this is treasure trove indeed. I suppose you know what you have got?"

"A diamond, sir? A precious stone. It cuts into glass as though it were putty."

"It's more than a precious stone. It is *the* precious stone."

"Not the Countess of Morcar's blue carbuncle!" I ejaculated.

"Precisely so. I ought to know its size and shape, seeing that I have read the advertisement about it in the *Times* every day lately. It is absolutely unique, and its value can only be conjectured, but the reward offered of a thousand pounds is certainly not within a twentieth part of the market price."

"A thousand pounds! Great Lord of mercy!" The commissionaire plumped down into the chair and stared from one to the other of us.

"That is the reward, and I have reason to know that there are sentimental considerations in the background which would induce the Countess to part with half her fortune if she could but recover the gem."

"It was lost, if I remember aright, at the Hotel Cosmopolitan," I remarked.

"Precisely so, on December 22nd, just five days ago. John Horner, a plumber, was accused of having abstracted it from the lady's jewel case. The evidence against him was so strong that the case has been referred to the Assizes. I have some account of this matter here, I believe." He rummaged amid his newspaper, glancing over the dates, until at last he smoothed one out, doubled it over, and read the following paragraph:

Hotel Cosmopolitan Jewel Robbery. John Horner, 26, plumber, was brought up upon the charge of having upon the 22nd inst., abstracted from the jewel-case of the Countess of Morcar the valuable gem known as the blue carbuncle. James Ryder, upper-attendant at the hotel, gave his evidence to the effect that he had shown Horner up to the dressing-room of the

Countess of Morcar upon the day of the robbery in order that he might solder the second bar of the grate, which was loose. He had remained with Horner some little time, but had finally been called away. On returning, he found that Horner had disappeared, that the bureau had been forced open, and that the small morocco casket in which, as it afterwards transpired, the Countess was accustomed to keep her jewel, was lying empty upon the dressing-table. Ryder instantly gave the alarm, and Horner was arrested the same evening; but the stone could not be found either upon his person or in his rooms. Catherine Cusack, maid to the Countess, deposed to having heard Ryder's cry of dismay on discovering the robbery, and to have rushed into the room, where she found matters as described by the last witness. Inspector Bradstreet, B division, gave evidence as to the arrest of Horner, who struggled frantically, and protested his innocence in the strongest terms. Evidence of a previous conviction for robbery having been given against the prisoner, the magistrate refused to deal summarily with the offence, but referred it to the Assizes. Horner, who had shown signs of intense emotion during the proceedings, fainted away at the conclusion and was carried out of the court.

"Hum! So much for the police-court," said Holmes thoughtfully, tossing aside the paper. "The question for us now to solve is the sequence of events leading from a rifled jewel-case at one end to the crop of a goose in Tottenham Court Road at the other. You see, Watson, our little deductions have suddenly assumed a much more important and less innocent aspect. Here is the stone; the stone came from the goose, and the goose came from Mr. Henry Baker, the gentleman with the bad hat and all the other characteristics with which I have bored you. So now we must set ourselves very seriously to finding this gentleman and ascertaining what part he has played in this little mystery. To do this, we must try the simplest means first, and these lie undoubtedly in an advertisement in all the evening papers. If this

fails, I shall have recourse to other methods."

"What will you say?"

"Give me a pencil and that slip of paper. Now then:

Found at the corner of Goodge Street, a goose and a black felt hat. Mr. Henry Baker can have the same by applying at 6:30 this evening at 221B Baker Street.

"That is clear and concise."

"Very. But will he see it?"

"Well, he is sure to keep an eye on the papers, since, to a poor man, the loss was a heavy one. He was clearly so scared by his mischance in breaking the window and by the approach of Peterson that he thought nothing but flight, but since then he must have bitterly regretted the impulse which caused him to drop his bird. Then, again, the introduction of his name will cause him to see it, for everyone who knows him will direct his attention to it. Here you are, Peterson, run down to the advertising agency and have this put in the evening papers."

"In which, sir?"

"Oh, in the *Globe, Star, Pall Mall, St. James, Evening News Standard, Echo,* and any others that occur to you."

"Very well, sir. And this stone?"

"Ah, yes, I shall keep the stone. Thank you. And, I say, Peterson, just buy a goose on your way back and leave it here with me, for we must have one to give to this gentlemen in place of the one which your family is now devouring."

When the commissionaire had gone, Holmes took up the stone and held it against the light. "It's a bonny thing," said he. "Just see how it glints and sparkles. Of course it is a nucleus and focus of crime. Every good stone is. They are the devil's pet baits. In the larger and older jewels every facet may stand for a bloody deed. This stone is not yet twenty years old. It was found in the banks of the Amoy River in southern China and is remarkable in having every characteristic of the carbuncle, save that it is blue in shade instead of ruby red. In spite of its youth, it has already a sinister history. There have been two murders, a vitriol-throwing, a suicide, and several robberies brought about for the sake of this forty-grain weight of crystallized charcoal. Who would think that so pretty a toy would be a purveyor to the gallows and the prison? I'll lock it up in my strong box now and drop a line to the Countess to say that we have it."

"Do you think that this man Horner is innocent?"

"I cannot tell."

"Well, then, do you imagine that this other one, Henry Baker, had anything to do with the matter?"

"It is, I think, much more likely that Henry Baker is an absolutely innocent man, who had no idea that the bird which he was carrying was of considerably more value than if it were made of solid gold. That, however, I shall determine by a very simple test if we have an answer to our advertisement."

"And you can do nothing until then?"

"Nothing."

"In that case I shall continue my professional round. But I shall come back in the evening at the hour you have mentioned, for I should like to see the solution of so tangled a business."

"Very glad to see you. I dine at seven. There is a woodcock, I believe. By the way, in view of recent occurrences, perhaps I ought to ask Mrs. Hudson to examine its crop."

I had been delayed at a case, and it was a little after half-past six when I found myself in Baker Street once more. As I approached the house I saw a tall man in a Scotch bonnet with coat which was buttoned up to his chin waiting outside in the bright semicircle which was thrown from the fanlight. Just

as I arrived the door opened, and we were shown up together to Holmes's room.

"Mr. Henry Baker, I believe," said he, rising from his armchair and greeting his visitor with the easy air of geniality which he could so readily assume. "Pray take this chair by the fire, Mr. Baker. It is a cold night, and I observe that your circulation is more adapted for summer than for winter. Ah, Watson, you have just come at the right time. Is that your hat, Mr. Baker?"

"Yes sir, that is undoubtedly my hat."

He was a large man with rounded shoulders, a massive head, and a broad, intelligent face, sloping down to a pointed beard of grizzled brown. A touch of red in nose and cheeks, with a slight tremor of his extended hand, recalled Holmes's surmise  as to his habits. His rusty black frock-coat was buttoned right up in front, with the collar turned up, and his lank wrists protruded from his sleeves without a sign of cuff or shirt. He spoke in a slow staccato fashion, choosing words with care, and gave the impression generally of a man of learning and letters who had ill-usage at the hands of fortune.

"We have retained these things for some days," said Holmes, "because we expected to see an advertisement from you giving your address. I am at a loss to know now why you did not advertise."

Our visitor gave a rather shamefaced laugh. "Shillings have not been so plentiful with me as they once were," he remarked. "I had no doubt that the gang of roughs who assaulted me had carried off both my hat and the bird. I did not care to spend more money in a hopeless attempt at recovering them."

"Very naturally. By the way, about the bird, we were compelled to eat it."

"To eat it!" Our visitor half rose from his chair in his excitement.

"Yes, it would have been of no use to anyone had we not done so. But I presume that this other goose upon the sideboard, which is about the same weight and perfectly fresh, will answer your purpose equally well?"

"Oh, certainly, certainly," answered Mr. Baker with a sigh of relief.

"Of course, we still have the feathers, legs, crop, and so on of your own bird, so if you wish—"

The man burst into a hearty laugh. "They might be useful to me as relics of my adventure," said he, "but beyond that I can hardly see what use the *disjecta membra* of my late acquaintance are going to be to me. No, sir, I think that, with your permission, I will confine my attentions to the excellent bird which I perceive upon the sideboard."

Sherlock Holmes glanced sharply across at me with a slight shrug of his shoulders.

"There is your hat, then, and there is your bird," said he. "By the way, would it bore you to tell me where you got the other one from? I am somewhat of a fowl fancier, and I have seldom seen a better grown goose."

"Certainly sir," said Baker, who had risen and tucked his newly gained property under his arm. "There are a few of us who frequent the Alpha Inn, near the Museum—we are to be found in the Museum itself during the day, you understand. This year our good host, Windigate by name, instituted a goose club, by which, on consideration of some few pence every week, we were each to receive a bird at Christmas. My pence were duly paid, and the rest is familiar to you. I am much indebted to you, sir, for a Scotch bonnet is fitted neither to my years nor my gravity." With a comical pomposity of manner he bowed solemnly to both of us and strode off upon his way.

"So much for Mr. Henry Baker," said Holmes when he had closed the door behind him. "It is quite certain that he knows nothing whatsoever about the matter. Are you hungry, Watson?"

"Not particularly."

"Then I suggest that we turn our dinner into a supper and follow up this clue while it is till hot."

"By all means." It was a bitter night, so we drew on our ulsters and wrapped cravats about our throats. Outside, the stars were shining coldly in a cloudless sky, and the breath of the passers-by blew out into smoke like so many pistol shots. Our footfalls rang out crisply and loudly as we swung through the doctors' quarter, Wimpole Street, Harley Street, and so through Wigmore Street into Oxford Street. In a quarter of an hour we were in Bloomsbury at the Alpha Inn, which is a small public-house at the corner of one of the streets which runs down into Holborn. Holmes pushed open the door of the private bar and ordered two glasses of beer from the ruddy-faced, white-aproned landlord.

"Your beer should be excellent if it is as good as your geese," said he.

"My geese!" The man seemed surprised.

"Yes. I was speaking only half an hour ago to Mr. Henry Baker, who was a member of your goose club."

"Ah! yes, I see. But you see, sir, them's not *our* geese."

"Indeed! Whose, then?"

"Well, I got the two dozen from a salesman in Covent Garden."

"Indeed? I know some of them. Which was it?"

"Breckinridge is his name."

"Ah! I don't know him. Well, here's your good health, landlord, and prosperity to your house. Goodnight."

Now for Mr. Breckinridge," he continued, buttoning up his coat as we came out into the frosty air. "Remember, Watson, that though we have so homely a thing as a goose at one end of this chain, we have at the other a man who will certainly get seven years' penal servitude unless we can establish his innocence. It is possible that our inquiry may but confirm his guilt; but, in any case, we have a line of investigation which has been missed by the police, and which a singular chance has placed in our hands. Let us follow it out to the bitter end. Faces to the south, then, and quick march!"

We passed across Holborn, down Endell Street, and so through a zigzag of slums to Covent Garden Market. One of the largest stalls bore the name of Breckinridge upon it, and the proprietor, a horsy-looking man, with a sharp face and trim side-whiskers, was helping a boy to put up the shutters.

"Good-evening. It's a cold night," said Holmes.

The salesman nodded and shot a questioning glance at my companion.

"Sold out of geese, I see," continued Holmes, pointing at the bare slabs of marble.

"Let you have five hundred to-morrow morning."

"That's no good."

"Well, there are some on the stall with the gas-flare."

"Ah, but I was recommended to you."

"Who by?"

"The landlord of the Alpha."

"Oh, yes; I sent him a couple of dozen."

"Fine birds they were, too. Now where did you get them from?"

To my surprise the question provoked a burst of anger from the salesman.

"Now, then, mister," said he, with his head cocked and his arms akimbo, "what are you driving at? Let's have it straight, now."

"It is straight enough. I should like to know who sold you the geese which you supplied to the Alpha."

"Well, then, I shan't tell you. So now!"

"Oh, it is a matter of no importance; but I don't know why you should be so warm over such a trifle."

"Warm! You'd be as warm, maybe, if you were as pestered as I am. When I pay good money for a good article there should be an end of the business; but it's 'Where are the geese?' and 'Who did you sell the geese to?' and 'What will you take for the geese?' One would think they were the only geese in the world, to hear the fuss that is made over them."

"Well, I have no connection with any other people who have been making inquiries," said Holmes carelessly. "If you won't tell us the bet is off, that is all. But I'm always ready to back my opinion on a matter of fowls, and I have a fiver on it that the bird I ate is a country bred."

"Well, then, you've lost your fiver, for it's town bred," snapped the salesman. "It's nothing of the kind."

"I say it is."

"I don't believe it."

"D'you think you know more about fowls than I, who have handled them ever since I was a nipper? I tell you, all those birds that went to the Alpha were town bred."

"You'll never persuade me to believe that."

"Will you bet, then?"

"It's merely taking your money, for I know that I am right. But I'll have a sovereign on with you, just to teach you not to be so obstinate."

The salesman chuckled grimly. "Bring me the books, Bill," said he.

The small boy brought round a small thin volume and a great greasy-backed one, laying them out together beneath the hanging lamp.

"Now, then, Mr. Cocksure," said the salesman, "I thought that I was out of geese, but before I finish you'll find that there is still one left in my shop. You see this little book?"

"Well?"

"That's the list of the folk from whom I buy. D'you

see? Well, then, here on this page are the country folk, and the numbers after their names are where their accounts are in the big ledger. Now, then! You see this other page in red ink? Well, that is a list of my town suppliers. Now, look at that third name. Just read it out to me."

"Mrs. Oakshott, 117, Brixton Road—249," read Holmes.

"Quite so. Now turn that up in the ledger."

Holmes turned to the page indicated. "Here you are, 'Mrs. Oakshott, 117, Brixton Road, egg and poultry supplier.'"

"Now, then, what's the last entry?"

"'December 22nd. Twenty-four geese at 7s. 6.'"

"Quite so. There you are. And underneath?"

"'Sold to Mr. Windigate of the Alpha, at 12s.'"

"What have you to say now?"

Sherlock Holmes looked deeply chagrined. He drew a sovercign from his pocket and threw it down upon the slab, turning away with the air of a man whose disgust is too deep for words. A few yards off he stopped under a lamp-post and laughed in the hearty, noiseless fashion which was peculiar to him.

"When you see a man with whiskers of that cut and the 'Pink 'un' protruding out of his pocket, you can always draw him out of a bet," said he. "I dare say that if I had put a hundred pounds down in front of him, that man would not have given me such complete information as was drawn from him by the idea that he was doing me on a wager. Well, Watson, we are, I fancy, nearing the end of our quest, and the only point which remains to be determined is whether we should go on to this Mrs. Oakshott to-night, or whether we should reserve it for to-morrow. It is clear from what that surly fellow said that there are others besides ourselves who are anxious about the matter, and I should—"

His remarks were suddenly cut short by a loud hubbub which broke out from the stall which we had just left. Turning round we saw a little rat-faced fellow standing in the center of the circle of yellow light which was thrown by the swinging lamp, while Breckinridge, the salesman, framed in the door of his stall, was shaking his fists fiercely at the cringing figure.

"I've had enough of you and you're geese," he shouted. "I wish you were all at the devil together. If you come pestering me any more with your silly talk I'll set the dog at you. You bring Mrs. Oakshott here and I'll answer her, but what have you to do with it? Did I buy the geese off you?"

"No; but one of them was mine all the same," whined the little man.

"Well, then, ask Mrs. Oakshott for it."

"She told me to ask you."

"Well, you can ask the King of Proosia, for all I care. I've had enough of it. Get out of this!" He rushed fiercely forward, and the inquirer flitted away into the darkness.

"Ha! this may save us a visit to Brixton Road," whispered Holmes. "Come with me, and we will see what is to be made of this fellow." Striding through the scattered knots of people who lounged round the flaring stalls, my companion speedily overtook the little man and touched him upon the shoulder. He sprang round, and I could see in the gas-light that every vestige of color had been driven from his face.

"Who are you, then? What do you want?" he asked in a quavering voice.

"You will excuse me," said Holmes blandly, "but I could not help overhearing the questions which you put to the salesman just now. I think that I could be of assistance to you."

"You? Who are you? How could you know anything of this matter?"

"My name is Sherlock Holmes. It is my business to

know what other people don't know."

"But you can know nothing of this?"

"Excuse me, I know everything of it. You are endeavoring to trace some geese which were sold by Mrs. Oakshott, of Brixton Road, to a salesman named Breckinridge, by him in turn to Mr. Windigate, of the Alpha, and by him to his club, of which Mr. Henry Baker is a member."

"Oh, sir, you are the very man whom I have longed to meet," cried the little fellow with outstretched hands and quivering fingers. "I can hardly explain to you how interested I am in this matter."

Sherlock Holmes hailed a four-wheeler which was passing. "In that case we had better discuss it in a cosy room rather than in this wind-swept marketplace," said he. "But pray tell me, before we go farther, who it is that I have the pleasure of assisting."

The man hesitated for an instant. "My name is John Robinson," he answered with a sidelong glance.

"No, no; the real name," said Holmes sweetly. "It is always awkward doing business with an alias."

A flush sprang to the white cheeks of the stranger. "Well, then," said he, "my real name is James Ryder."

"Precisely so. Head attendant at the Hotel Cosmopolitan. Pray step into the cab, and I shall soon be able to tell you everything which you wish to know."

The little man stood glancing from one to the other of us with half-frightened, half-hopeful eyes, as one who is not sure whether he is on the verge of a windfall or of a catastrophe. Then he stepped into the cab, and in half an hour we were back in the sitting-room at Baker Street. Nothing had been said during our drive, but the high, thin breathing of our new companion, and the claspings and unclaspings of his hands, spoke of the nervous tension within him.

"Here we are!" said Holmes cheerily as we filed into the room. "The fire looks very seasonable in this weather. You look cold, Mr. Ryder. Pray take the basket-chair. I will just put on my slippers before we settle this little matter of yours. Now, then! You want to know what became of those geese?"

"Yes, sir."

"Or rather, I fancy, of that goose. It was one bird, I imagine, in which you were interested—white, with a black bar across the tail."

Ryder quivered with emotion. "Oh, sir," he cried, "can you tell me where it went to?"

"It came here."

"Here?"

"Yes, and a most remarkable bird it proved. I don't wonder that you should take an interest in it. It laid an egg after it was dead—the bonniest, brightest little blue egg that ever was seen. I have it here in my museum."

Our visitor staggered to his feet and clutched the mantelpiece with his right hand. Holmes unlocked the strong-box and held up the blue carbuncle, which shone out like a star, with a cold, brilliant, many-pointed radiance. Ryder stood glaring with a drawn face, uncertain whether to claim or disown it.

"The game's up, Ryder," said Holmes quietly. "Hold up, man, or you'll be into the fire! Give him an arm back into his chair, Watson. He's not got blood enough to go in for felony with impunity. Give him a dash of brandy. So! Now he looks a little more human. What a shrimp it is, to be sure!"

For a moment he had staggered and nearly fallen, but the brandy brought a tinge of colour into his cheeks, and he sat staring with frightened eyes at his accuser.

"I have almost every link in my hands, and all the proofs which I could possibly need, so there is little which you need tell me. Still, that little may as well be cleared up to make the case complete. You had heard, Ryder, of this blue stone of the Countess of Morcar's?"

"It was Catherine Cusack who told me of it," said he in a crackling voice.

"I see—her ladyship's waiting-maid. Well, the temptation of sudden wealth so easily acquired was too much for you, as it has been for better men before you; but you were not very scrupulous in the means you used. It seems to me, Ryder, that there is the making of a very pretty villain in you. You knew that this man Horner, the plumber, had been concerned in some such matter before, and that suspicion would rest the more readily upon him. What did you do, then? You made some small job in my lady's room—you and your confederate Cusack—and you managed that he should be the man sent for. Then, when he had left, you rifled the jewel-case, raised the alarm, and had this unfortunate man arrested. You then—"

Ryder threw himself down suddenly upon the rug and clutched at my companion's knees. "For God's sake, have mercy!" he shrieked. "Think of my father! of my mother! It would break their hearts. I never went wrong before! I never will again. I swear it. I'll swear it on a Bible. Oh, don't bring it into court! For Christ's sake, don't!"

"Get back into your chair!" said Holmes sternly. "It is very well to cringe and crawl now, but you thought little enough of this poor Horner in the dock for a crime of which he knew nothing."

"I will fly, Mr. Holmes. I will leave the country, sir. Then the charges against him will break down."

"Hum! We will talk about that. And now let us hear a true account of the next act. How came the stone into the goose, and how came the goose into the open market? Tell us the truth, for there lies your only hope of safety."

Ryder passed his tongue over his parched lips. "I will tell you just as it happened, sir," he said. "When Horner had been arrested, it seemed to me that it would be best for me to get away with the stone at once, for I did not know at what moment the police might take it into their heads to search me and my room. There was no place about the hotel where it would be safe. I went out, as if on some commission, and I made for my sister's house. She had married a man named Oakshott, and lived on Brixton Road, where she fattened fowls for the market. All the way there every man I met seemed to me to be a policeman or a detective; and, for all that it was a cold night, the sweat was pouring down my face before I came to the Brixton Road. My sister asked me what was the matter, and why I was so pale; but I told her that I had been upset by the jewel robbery at the hotel. Then I went into the backyard and smoked a pipe, and wondered what it would be best to do.

"I had a friend once called Maudsley, who went to the bad, and has just been serving his time in Pentonville. One day he had met me, and fell into talk about the ways of thieves, and how they could get rid of what they stole. I knew that he would be true to me, for I knew one or two things about him; so I made up my mind to go right on to Kilburn, where he lived, and take him into my confidence. He would show me how to turn the stone into money. But how to get to him in safety? I thought of the agonies I had gone through in coming from the hotel. I might at any moment be seized and searched, and there would be the stone in my waistcoat pocket. I was leaning against the wall at the time and looking at the geese which were waddling round my feet, and suddenly an idea came into my head which showed me how I could beat the best detective that ever lived.

"My sister had told me some weeks before that I

might have the pick of her geese for a Christmas present, and I knew that she was always as good as her word. I would take my goose now, and in it I would carry the stone to Kilburn. There was a little shed in the yard, and behind this I drove one of the birds—a fine big one, white, with a barred tail. I caught it, and, prying its bill open, I thrust the stone down its throat, as far as my finger could reach. The bird gave a gulp, and I felt the stone pass along its gullet and down into its crop. But the creature flapped and struggled, and out came my sister to know what was the matter. As I turned to speak to her the brute broke loose and fluttered among the others.

"'Whatever were you doing with that bird, Jem?' says she.

"'Well,' said I, 'you said you'd give me one for Christmas, and I was feeling which was the fattest.'

"'Oh,' says she, 'we've set yours aside for you—Jem's bird, we call it. It's the big white one over yonder. There's twenty-six of them, which makes one for you, and one for us, and two dozen for the market.'

"'Thank you, Maggie,' says I; 'but if it is all the same to you, I'd rather have that one I was handling just now.'

"'The other is a good three pound heavier,' said she, 'and we fattened it expressly for you.'

"'Never mind. I'll have the other, and I'll take it now,' said I.

"'Oh, just as you like' said she, a little huffed. 'Which is it you want, then?'

"'That white one with the barred tail, right in the middle of the flock.'

"'Oh, very well. Kill it and take it with you.'

"Well, I did what she said, Mr. Holmes, and I carried the bird all the way to Kilburn. I told my pal what I had done, for he was a man that it was easy to tell a thing like that to. He laughed until he choked, and we got a knife and opened the goose. My heart turned to water, for there was no sign of the stone, and I knew that some terrible mistake had occurred. I left the bird, rushed back to my sister's, and hurried into the back yard. There was not a bird to be seen there.

"'Where are they all, Maggie?' I cried.

"'Gone to the dealer's, Jem.'

"'Which dealer's?'

"'Breckinridge, of Covent Garden.'

"'But was there another with a barred tail?' I asked, 'the same as the one I chose?'

"'Yes, Jem; there were two barred-tailed ones, and I could never tell them apart.'

"Well, then, of course I saw it all, and I ran off as hard as my feet would carry me to this man Breckinridge; but he had sold the lot at once, and not one word would he tell me as to where they had gone. You heard him yourselves to-night. Well, he has always answered me like that. My sister thinks that I am going mad. Sometimes I think that I am myself. And now—and now I am myself a branded thief, without ever having touched the wealth for which I sold my character. God help me! God help me!" He burst into convulsive sobbing, with his face buried in his hands.

There was a long silence, broken only by his heavy breathing, and by the measured tapping of Sherlock Holmes' finger-tips upon the edge of the table. Then my friend rose and threw open the door.

"Get out!" said he.

"What, sir! Oh, Heaven bless you!"

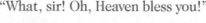

"No more words. Get out!"

And no more words were needed. There was a rush, a clatter upon the stairs, the bang of a door, and the crisp rattle of running footfalls from the street.

"After all, Watson," said Holmes, reaching up his hands for his clay pipe, "I am not retained by the police to supply their deficiencies. If Horner were in danger it would be another thing; but this fellow will not appear against him, and the case must collapse. I suppose that I am committing a felony, but it is just possible that I am saving a soul. This fellow will not go wrong again; he is too terribly frightened. Send him to jail now, and you make him a jail-bird for life. Besides, it is the season for forgiveness. Chance has put in our way a most singular and whimsical problem, and its solution is its own reward. If you will have the goodness to touch the bell, Doctor, we will begin another investigation, in which, also, a bird will be the chief feature."

THE CROWDED INN
John McGaw Foster

"The Crowded Inn" is an extended account of Mary and Joseph's search for lodging in the days before Jesus' birth. But the story is unique in its focus on the innkeeper and his tenants, each of whom personifies one of man's worst qualities. Perhaps the most pathetic figure is the innkeeper, too self-absorbed to see the miracle that has come his way.

THE KEEPER OF THE INN stood in his doorway as the winter sun was declining towards the west. He looked out from the hilltop on which the village stood, over the slopes where shepherds tended their flocks amid the stretches of vineyard intersected by winding paths. There had been much stir along those pathways all day, and the innkeeper had profited by it. Many strangers had traveled over the narrow roads, on foot or on donkey-back, and had crowded the khan or inn of the village to overflowing. It was needful for them to come—all who were of the ancient and royal lineage which had its seat in that little town—to have their names enrolled there in obedience to the mandate of the Emperor. Those who had no friends or kindred in the town, went to the inn. For many days the innkeeper had welcomed these guests with the elaborate salutations of Oriental hospitality, and many nights, with like formalities of courtesy, he had told the late comers that all his guest chambers were full and the only place where they could find shelter for the night was in the open court where the travelers' animals were stabled. This afternoon there had been a larger number than usual of those seeking lodging, and already the rooms which were reserved for the use of travelers were occupied.

As the innkeeper stood there, slowly up the narrow village street came a man walking by the side of a donkey on which sat a young woman. The man was approaching middle-age, tall, with firm muscles and bronzed hands, and heavy dark-brown hair and beard. The woman was much younger, and as she sat wearily on her saddle, the innkeeper looked at her with something of regret that he must say to these newcomers that he could not provide them with hospitality. And as he looked, his gaze rested on her face. There was something about it which seemed to distinguish it from the faces of the women whom he knew. Not its beauty alone or the pathetic expression of weariness held him, but an indefinable radiance which made him instinctively bow his head in reverence. He wished indeed that he might shelter this strong man and her whose countenance so affected him. But the inn was full.

They stopped before the door, and the man helped his companion to dismount and seat herself upon a bench. She moved wearily. Then he spoke to the innkeeper.

"Peace be to thee and thine house."

"And peace to thee."

"May we lodge here tonight with you?"

"Good friend, alas, there is no room in the inn."

The stranger's face showed deep disappointment and anxiety.

"No room?" he said. "What can I do? We had thought to lodge with acquaintances in the town; but their guest-chamber is already taken, so we have come here as the final resort. Can you do nothing for me?"

"In the stable, good friend, you can find shelter."

"The stable—but, my wife…"

"Many women have had worse lodging."

"But you do not understand, good innkeeper. You know not whom you turn away."

The innkeeper began a spirited retort. But as he was about to speak, his glance turned again to the woman's face, and he checked himself.

"I know not who you may be," said he; "but as for

her, he who looks can perceive that she is not as most wayfarers whom I greet here. I can but regret that my inn is full—else I might have the privilege of harboring a saintly woman."

"You have spoken well, friend innkeeper; though she is my espoused wife, God gives me the right to say that your words tell not half the truth. Receive her, I beg of you; she is weary and ill."

"I see," replied the innkeeper. "You have been faring far. Necessity brings you here, as many another pilgrim in these days. As to your request for lodging, if I knew of any of my guests whom I could ask to depart that you might be accommodated, I would gladly do so. Here is my porter; I will consult him."

The porter, a large, burly man, came out of the  door. But to his master's question he replied that he could not think of any of the occupants of the inn who would be likely to be willing to go to the stable for shelter.

"Good friend," said the stranger, "you say this is your porter. Cannot we occupy his room? Surely he might better lodge with the beasts than to ask this weary woman to go there."

"Ah, traveler, I could not carry on my business were he not in the house. His name is Self-Interest. He has always been with me. He has a wonderful faculty of divining whether any would-be guest is likely to prove profitable or troublesome. I never receive anybody of whom Self-Interest does not approve, and many a one who gives trouble or does not pay me his charges he casts out. No; I could not ask him to go, even for a night."

"Is there not some such unprofitable guest then, whom he can make depart?"

The innkeeper thought a moment.

"Why, yes," he said and, opening, showed the figure of a man sleeping on the floor. "Here is one; his name is Indolence. He has occupied a room for a long time, and I really ought to get rid of him." And turning to the porter, he bade him cast him out.

The porter made an effort to rouse the man.

"It is no use, master," he said; he will not go. After all he is harmless. Why should we put him out?"

"True," said the innkeeper, "he does no real harm. Let Indolence remain. He is a comfortable companion."

"Is there no other?" said the traveler anxiously.

"There is one," replied the innkeeper; "but I know it is no use to try to cast him out. I have done it many times, and he always returns. I have given up trying to get rid of him, and I have learned to like him now. His name is Habit."

"So all your rooms are full?"

"Yes, and I will tell you who occupies them. In the first are two ladies. One is very fair and beautiful. I love to look at her, and my wife is not jealous, for she, too, admires her. Her name is Vanity. The other lady is not beautiful, but she has wondrous dignity of bearing, and keeps aloof from all but her friend Vanity. They call her Pride. I could not disturb these ladies, even for you. The next room is occupied by a man and his wife. They are not a gracious pair, but they pay me, and I could never suggest their leaving. The man is large and strong and of terrible countenance. His wife is ill-favored, and speaks bitterly.

They are called Anger and Hatred. They have children, Envy and Malice, who occupy the next apartment with their nurse, Jealousy. Sometimes I think I should like to have them all leave me; and yet what would my house be if Anger and Hatred, Envy, Malice and Jealousy were not in it? They are a part of my own family, as much as Indolence and Habit, or my good porter, Self-Interest. No, I cannot ask them to go."

"Are these all your guests?" said the stranger, a gleam of hope lighting his face. "Surely you have more rooms than those."

"Yes; but I said truth when I told you that all were occupied. Some of the guests are now in the court. Perhaps you will tell them your story and they may consent to oblige you. There are two of them now, seated on the floor over there. They are engaged in their favorite occupations. When they are not eating and drinking they are gambling. Sometimes I feel disgusted with them, and then I forget them for a time. But ever and again I have a longing for their company, and then I am glad that they have not departed. But if you told them to go, perhaps they would do so to oblige you, and then they might not come back, and my house would be better off."

"What are their names, that I may speak to them?"

"Appetite and Avarice."

The traveler approached the pair. They looked indifferently at him, and turned again to their feasting.

"Peace to you, good friends," he said. "The host has given me permission to address you, if perchance it might please you to take for the night your lodging in the courtyard, that my wife, who is weary and ill from her long journey, may find shelter within."

"And, pray, who are you?"

"It matters not. We are humble folk, but worthy; and the innkeeper would be glad to receive us, if he had room in the inn."

"But we are well content here, good sir. Why should we go?"

"That you may give comfort to a weary woman, and afford opportunity to our friend, the host, to entertain one whose presence will be a blessing to him."

They laughed. "That is very fine, my friend, but we are old acquaintances and the innkeeper would be a fool to let us go, that he may entertain some unknown yokel and his wife. You are from Galilee. We know your speech."

Discouraged, the traveler was about to turn back to the doorway when his glance fell on the figure of a small man sitting shrinkingly by himself in a corner of the courtyard. "Perhaps here is one who will grant my request," he said to himself. "He does not seem like one who would rudely repel me." He approached the man and told his story. "I ask this of you but for the night," he said. But the man shrank back farther into the dusk of his corner.

"Oh," he said, "I should not dare. I cannot leave my room, and pass the night out here. Be sure I would gladly oblige you if I could."

"Well," said the traveler. "Be it so. I know not your name that I may thank you for your kind intentions."

"I am Cowardice," replied the man.

At that moment a man came hurriedly across the court. As he approached he smiled benevolently and held out his hand. "You seem to be in trouble, good sir. Can I serve you?"

"Oh, if you could leave your room for this night, that a woman weary from a long journey may find rest there."

"Gladly, sir, gladly. I go to make ready to leave at

once."
He turned
away without
waiting to receive
the thanks of the
grateful stranger.
The porter was
standing near by,
and to him the
traveler told of the kindly offer.

"Trust him not, sir," was the porter's answer. "He
will never go out for you. His name is Hypocrisy. I
know too well what his words mean. Even if he
should really think of obliging you his companion,
Deceit, who shares his room with him, would not
permit it. Do not count upon his promises, for he
will not keep them, nor will he take the trouble even

to come back to tell you. You will not see
him again."

Sadly the traveler returned to
the doorway. As he passed out, a
woman with a sweet face turned
from the bench where his companion sat, and spoke to the innkeeper.

"I beg you," she said, "give these people lodging."

"I should be glad to do so, friend Charity," he
answered; "but I have no room."

Just then a man hurried through the doorway. He

seemed to be setting forth on a journey. His figure was tall and lithe, his
whole bearing full of eager alertness.
The innkeeper looked troubled as he
spoke to him; "You are not leaving
me, friend Ambition?"

"I have a plan which I wish to carry through," the
man answered. "I had thought to come back tonight. But," he said, as he looked at the travelers, "if
these good people need my room I will stay away."

"No, no," said the innkeeper, hastily. "I cannot

part with you. Others may give up to these
newcomers—not you. Come back."

The man passed out, and the stranger turned
to his companion. "I fear it is no use, Mary," he said.
"There is no room for us."

Slowly the woman rose, and lifted her face to his
with a smile of heavenly patience.

"Let us go," she said.

The innkeeper stepped forward. "I am sorry," he
said. "Just around the turn of the road you will find a
stable in a cave. It is empty, and you will be quieter
there. There is straw, too, on which you can rest, and
you may have it without charge."

The woman he had called Charity moved to their
side. "I will show you the way," she whispered.

A shepherd on his way to watch his flock passed by
them as they left the inn. He
paused a moment and then
followed them slowly down the
slope of the street. It was nearly
night now. As the keeper of the
inn watched them till they were

out of sight, there passed across his face a shadow
which seemed to tell of his feeling that some great
opportunity had slipped away from him.

Early in the morning the innkeeper was again at
his door. There was bustle then, for some of the tran-
sient guests were departing, and men were bringing
animals out of the courtyard and loading their
packs. The innkeeper had bowed his low gesture of
farewell to one of the
parting guests, and
turned to place in his bag
the coins which he had left
with him. As he turned
he saw the shepherd who
had passed his door the
evening before.

"Peace to thee," he said.

"And peace to this house. Ah, friend innkeeper, I am sorry for you."

"And wherefore?"

"That you felt constrained to turn away those travelers yesterday afternoon."

"You mean the Galilean with the saintly-faced wife?"

"Yes."

"I was indeed sorry to let them go. But it was a question of room. I even tried to persuade some of the guests to make place for them. But I cannot see why I deserve your sympathy. My inn is full, and I need no extra guests." And he shook the bag in his hand, for the last one to depart had been bountiful.

"Listen," said the shepherd. "Wondrous things have come to Israel. Last night, as some of us watched in the field, we saw a heavenly light and heard the song of angels. It told us that the Saviour of Israel, the Messiah, is born. And we hastened to  the spot the angels told us of, and there, in the manger in the cave, was the holy babe, new-born of the woman whom you sent forth last night from this inn. Oh, if you had only kept them—if you had only listened to the voice of Charity as she begged you to take them in—the Christ-child might have been here, under your roof, today."

"'Tis a strange tale, shepherd. But why should I regret? The unearthly light might have frightened my guests. The presence of a new-born babe might cause some of them to leave."

"Yes, my friend, the presence of the Christ-Child drives out such guests as yours. Pride and Anger, Avarice and Self-Interest and all the rest live not where He dwells. He is the richest and the fairest guest the world will ever know, and His presence brings peace and salvation and Eternal Life to whom- soever bids Him enter."

"But, after all," the innkeeper muttered, "there was no room in the inn."

THE ELVES AND THE SHOEMAKER
The Brothers Grimm

Though Jacob and Wilhelm Grimm devoted their lives to the study of literature, they never wrote any of the stories that won them world renown. The tales that made them famous, *Der Kinder-und Hausmärchen (The Children and the House of Fairy Tales)* were collected from the European folklore and legends of the time. While "The Elves and the Shoemaker" stands on its own as a fairy tale, it is also an example of how an act of selfless giving has the power to change lives for the better.

NCE UPON A TIME there was a poor shoemaker. He made excellent shoes and worked quite diligently, but even so he could not earn enough to support himself and his family. He became so poor that he could not even afford to buy the leather he needed to make shoes; finally he had only enough to make one last pair. He cut them out with great care and put the pieces on his workbench, so that he could sew them together the following morning.

"Now, I wonder," he sighed, "will I ever make another pair of shoes? Once I've sold this pair I shall need all the money to buy food for my family. I will not be able to buy any new leather."

That night, the shoemaker went to bed a sad and distraught man.

The next morning, he awoke early and went down to his workshop. On his bench he found an exquisite pair of shoes! They had small and even stitches,

formed so perfectly that he knew he couldn't have produced a better pair himself.

Upon close examination, the shoes proved to be made from the very pieces of leather he had set out the night before. He immediately put the fine pair of shoes in the window of his shop and drew back the blinds.

"Who in the world could have done this service for me?" he asked himself. Even before he could make up an answer, a rich man strode into his shop and bought the shoes—and for a fancy price.

The shoemaker was ecstatic; he immediately went out and purchased plenty of food for his family—and some more leather. That afternoon he cut out two pairs of shoes and, just as before, laid all the pieces on his bench so that he could sew them the next day. Then he went upstairs to enjoy a good meal with his family.

"My goodness!" he cried the next morning when he found two pairs of beautifully finished shoes on his workbench. "Who could make such fine shoes— and so quickly?" He put them in his shop window, and before long some wealthy people came in and paid a great deal of money for them. The happy shoemaker went right out and bought even more leather.

For weeks, and then months, this continued. Whether the shoemaker cut two pairs or four pairs, the fine new shoes were always ready the next morning. Soon his small shop was crowded with customers. He cut out many types of shoes: stiff boots lined with fur, delicate slippers for dancers, walking shoes for ladies, tiny shoes for children. Soon his shoes had bows and laces and buckles of fine silver. The little shop prospered as never before, and its proprietor was soon a rich man himself. His family wanted for nothing.

As the shoemaker and his wife sat by the fire one night, he said, "One of these days, I shall learn who has been helping us."

"We could hide behind the cupboard in your workroom," she said. "That way, we would find out just who your helpers are." And that is just what they did. That evening, when the clock struck twelve, the shoemaker and his wife heard a noise. Two tiny men, each with a bag of tools, were squeezing beneath a crack under the door. Oddest of all, the two elves were stark naked!

The two men clambered onto the workbench and

began working. Their little hands stitched and their little hammers tapped ceaselessly the whole night through.

"They are so small! And they make such beautiful shoes in no time at all!" the shoemaker whispered to his wife as dawn rose. (Indeed, the elves were about the size of his own needles.)

"Quiet!" his wife answered. "See how they are cleaning up now." And in an instant, the two elves had disappeared beneath the door.

The next day, the shoemaker's wife said, "Those little elves have done so much good for us. Since it is nearly Christmas, we should make some gifts for them."

"Yes!" cried the shoemaker. "I'll make some boots that will fit them, and you make some clothes." They worked until dawn. On Christmas Eve the presents were laid out upon the workbench: two tiny jackets, two pairs of trousers, and two little woolen caps. They also left out a plate of good things to eat and drink. Then they hid once again behind the cupboard and waited to see what would happen.

Just as before, the elves appeared at the stroke of midnight. They jumped onto the bench to begin their work, but when they saw all the presents they began to laugh and shout with joy. They tried on all the clothes, then helped themselves to the food and drink. Then they jumped down, danced excitedly around the workroom, and disappeared beneath the door.

After Christmas, the shoemaker cut out his leather as he always had—but the two elves never returned. "I believe they may have heard us whispering," his wife said. "Elves are so very shy when it comes to people, you know."

"I know I will miss their help," the shoemaker said, "but we will manage. The shop is always so busy now. But my stitches will never be as tight and small as theirs!"

That shoemaker did indeed continue to prosper, but he and his family always remembered the good elves who had helped them during the hard times. And each and every Christmas Eve from that year onward, they gathered around the fire to drink a toast their tiny friends.

THE GIFT OF
THE MAGI
O. Henry

"The Gift of the Magi" is probably the best known of all O. Henry's works, and it's not hard to see why. The story, which features a classic example of the ironic endings that made the author famous, captures the essence of the spirit of Christmas. The poor young couple in the story, like their Biblical counterparts, leave an unforgettable impression, thanks to the pureness of their intent, the selflessness of their giving, and the power of their love.

ONE DOLLAR AND eighty-seven cents. That was all. And sixty cents of it was in pennies. Pennies saved one and two at a time by bulldozing the grocer and the vegetable man and the butcher until one's cheeks burned with the silent imputation of parsimony that such close dealing implied. Three times Della counted it. One dollar and eighty-seven cents. And the next day would be Christmas.

There was clearly nothing to do but flop down on the shabby little couch and howl. So Della did it. Which instigates the moral reflection that life is made up of sobs, sniffles, and smiles, with sniffles predominating.

While the mistress of the home is gradually subsiding from the first stage to the second, take a look at the home. A furnished flat at eight dollars per week. It did not exactly beggar description, but it certainly had that word on the lookout for the mendicancy squad.

In the vestibule below was a letter-box into which no letter would go, and an electric button from which no mortal finger could coax a ring. Also appertaining thereunto was a card bearing the name "Mr. James Dillingham Young."

The "Dillingham" had been flung to the breeze during a former period of prosperity when its possessor was being paid thirty dollars per week. Now, when the income was shrunk to twenty dollars, the letters of "Dillingham" looked blurred, as though they were thinking seriously of contracting to a modest and unassuming D. But whenever Mr. James Dillingham Young came home and reached his flat above he was called "Jim" and greatly hugged by Mrs. James Dillingham Young, already introduced to you as Della. Which is all very good.

Della finished her cry and attended to her cheeks with a powder puff. She stood by the window and looked out dully at a gray cat walking a gray fence in a gray back yard. Tomorrow would be Christmas Day, and she had only $1.87 to buy Jim a present. She had been saving every penny she could for months, with this result. Twenty dollars a week doesn't go far. Expenses had been greater than she had calculated. They always are. Only $1.87 to buy a present for Jim. Her Jim. Many a happy hour she had spent planning for something nice for him. Something fine and rare and sterling—something just a little bit near to being worthy of the honor of being owned by Jim.

There was a pier glass between the windows of the room. Perhaps you have seen a pier glass in an eight-dollar flat. A very thin and very agile person may, by observing his reflection in a rapid sequence of longitudinal strips, obtain a fairly accurate conception of his looks. Della, being slender, had mastered the art.

Suddenly she whirled from the window and stood before the glass. Her eyes were shining brilliantly, but her face had lost its color within twenty seconds. Rapidly she pulled down her hair and let it fall to its full length.

Now, there were two possessions of the James Dillingham Youngs in which they both took a mighty pride. One was Jim's gold watch that had been his father's and his grandfather's. The other was Della's hair. Had the Queen of Sheba lived in the flat across the airshaft, Della would have let her hair hang out the window some day to dry just to depreciate Her Majesty's jewels and gifts. Had King Solomon been the janitor, with all his treasures piled up in the basement, Jim would have pulled out his watch every time he passed, just to see him pluck at his beard from envy.

So now Della's beautiful hair fell about her, rippling and shining like a cascade of brown waters. She did it up again nervously and quickly. Once she faltered for a minute while a tear splashed on the worn red carpet.

On went her old brown jacket; on went her old brown hat. With a whirl of skirts and with the brilliant sparkle still in her eyes, she fluttered out the door and down the stairs to the street.

Where she stopped the sign read: "Mme. Sofronie. Hair Goods of All Kinds." One flight up Della ran, and collected herself, panting. Madame, large, too white, chilly, hardly looked the "Sofronie."

"Will you buy my hair?" asked Della. "I buy hair," said Madame. "Take yer hat off and let's have a sight at the looks of it." Down rippled the brown cascade. "Twenty dollars," said Madame, lifting the mass with a practiced hand. "Give it to me quick," said Della. Oh, and the next two hours tripped on rosy wings. Forget the hashed metaphor. She was ransacking the stores for Jim's present.

She found it at last. It surely had been made for Jim and no one else. There was no other like it in any of the stores, and she had turned all of them inside out. It was a platinum watch-chain, simple and chaste in design, properly proclaiming its value by substance alone and not by meretricious ornamentation—as all good things should do. It was even worthy of The Watch. As soon as she saw it she knew that it must be Jim's. It was like him. Quietness and value—the description applied to both. Twenty-one dollars they took from her for it, and she hurried home with the eighty-seven cents. With that chain on his watch Jim might be properly anxious about the time in any company. Grand as the watch was, he sometimes looked at it on the sly on account of

the shabby old leather strap that he used in place of a proper gold chain.

When Della reached home her intoxication gave way a little to prudence and reason. She got out her curling-irons and lighted the gas and went to work repairing the ravages made by generosity added to love. Which is always a tremendous task, dear friends—a mammoth task.

Within forty minutes her head was covered with tiny close-lying curls that made her look wonderfully like a truant schoolboy. She looked at her reflection in the mirror long, carefully, and critically.

"If Jim doesn't kill me," she said to herself, "before he takes a second look at me, he'll say I look like a Coney Island chorus girl. But what could I do—oh! what could I do with a dollar and eighty-seven cents?"

At seven o'clock the coffee was made and the frying pan was on the back of the stove, hot and ready to cook the chops. Jim was never late, Della doubled the watch chain in her hand and sat on the corner of the table near the door that he always entered. Then she heard his step on the stair away down on the first flight, and she turned white for just a moment. She had a habit of saying little silent prayers about the simplest everyday things, and now she whispered: "Please, God, make him think I am still pretty."

The door opened and Jim stepped in and closed it. He looked thin and very serious. Poor fellow, he was only twenty-two—and to be burdened with a family! He needed a new overcoat and he was without gloves.

Jim stepped inside the door, as immovable as a setter at the scent of quail. His eyes were fixed upon Della, and there was an expression in them that she could not read, and it terrified her. It was not anger, nor surprise, nor disapproval, nor horror, nor any of the sentiments that she had been prepared for. He simply stared at her fixedly with that peculiar expression on his face.

Della wriggled off the table and went for him. "Jim, darling," she cried, "don't look at me that way. I had my hair cut off and sold it because I couldn't have lived through Christmas without giving you a present. It'll grow out again—you won't mind, will you? I just had to do it. My hair grows awfully fast. Say 'Merry Christmas!' Jim, and let's be happy. You don't know what a nice—what a beautiful gift I've got for you."

"You've cut off your hair?" asked Jim, laboriously, as if he had not arrived at that patent fact yet even after the hardest mental labor.

"Cut if off and sold it," said Della. "Don't you like me just as well, anyhow? I'm me without my hair, ain't I?" Jim looked about the room curiously. "You say your hair is gone?" he said, with an air almost of idiocy. "You needn't look for it," said Della. "It's sold, I tell you—sold and gone, too. It's Christmas Eve, boy. Be good to me, for it went for you. Maybe the hairs of my head were numbered," she went on with a sudden serious sweetness, "but nobody could ever count my love for you. Shall I put the chops on, Jim?"

Out of his trance Jim seemed to quickly wake. He enfolded his Della. For ten seconds let us regard with discreet scrutiny some inconsequential object in the other direction. Eight dollars a week or a million a year—what is the difference? A mathematician or a wit would give you the wrong answer. The Magi brought valuable gifts, but that was not among them. This dark assertion will be illuminated later on.

Jim drew a package from his overcoat pocket and threw it upon the table. "Don't make any mistake, Dell," he said, "about me. I don't think there's anything in the way of a haircut or a shave or a shampoo that could make me like my girl any less. But if you'll unwrap that package you may see why you had me going awhile at first."

White fingers and nimble tore at the string and paper. And then an ecstatic scream of joy; and then, alas! a quick feminine change to hysterical tears and wails, necessitating the immediate employment of all the comforting powers of the lord of the flat.

For there lay The Combs—the set of combs that Della had worshiped for long in a Broadway window. Beautiful combs, pure tortoise shell, with jeweled rims—just the shade to wear in the beautiful vanished hair. They were expensive combs, she knew, and her heart had simply craved and yearned over them without the least hope of possession. And now they were hers, but the tresses that should have adorned the coveted adornments were gone.

But she hugged them to her bosom, and at length she was able to look up with dim eyes and a smile and say: "My hair grows so fast, Jim!"

And then Della leaped up like a little singed cat and cried, "Oh, oh!" Jim had not yet seen his beautiful present. She held it out to him eagerly upon her open palm. The dull precious metal seemed to flash with a reflection of her bright and ardent spirit.

"Isn't is a dandy, Jim? I hunted all over town to find it. You'll have to look at the time a hundred times a day now. Give me your watch. I want to see how it looks on it."

Instead of obeying, Jim tumbled down on the couch and put his hands under the back of his head and smiled. "Dell," said he, "let's put our Christmas presents away and keep 'em awhile. They're too nice to use just at present. I sold the watch to get the money to buy your combs. And now suppose you put the chops on."

The Magi, as you know, were wise men—wonderfully wise men—who brought gifts to the Babe in the manger. They invented the art of giving Christmas presents. Being wise, their gifts were no doubt wise ones, possibly bearing the privilege of exchange in case of duplication. And here I have lamely related to you the uneventful chronicle of two foolish children in a flat who most unwisely sacrificed for each other the greatest treasures of their house. But in a last word to the wise of these days let it be said that of all who give gifts these two were the wisest. Of all who give and receive gifts, such as they are the wisest. Everywhere they are the wisest. They are the Magi.

THE LEGEND OF THE CHRISTMAS ROSE
Selma Lagerlof

Although there are a number of versions of this tale, Selma Lagerlof's is one of the most popular. With its emphasis on the exiled thieves, her story demonstrates that the spirit of Christmas can bring even the darkest souls to light.

ROBBER MOTHER, who lived in Robbers' Cave up in Goinge forest, went down to the village one day on a begging tour. Robber Father, who was an outlawed man, did not dare to leave the forest. She took with her five youngsters, and each youngster bore a sack on his back as long as himself. When Robber Mother stepped inside the door of a cabin, no one dared refuse to give her whatever she demanded; for she was not above coming back the following night and setting fire to the house if she had not been well received. Robber Mother and her brood were worse than a pack of wolves, and many a man felt like running a spear through them; but it was never done, because they all knew that the man stayed up in the forest, and he would have known how to wreak vengeance if anything had happened to the children or the old woman.

Now that Robber Mother went from house to house and begged, she came to Ovid, which at that  time was a cloister. She rang the bell of the cloister gate and asked for food. The watchman let down a small wicket in the gate and handed her six round bread cakes— one for herself and one for each of the five children.

While the mother was standing quietly at the gate, her youngsters were running about. And now one of them came and pulled at her skirt, as a signal that he had discovered something which she ought to come and see, and Robber Mother followed him promptly.

The entire cloister was surrounded by a high and strong wall, but the youngster had managed to find a little back gate which stood ajar. When Robber Mother got there, she pushed the gate open and walked inside without asking leave, as it was her custom to do.

Ovid Cloister was managed at that time by Abbot Hans, who knew all about herbs. Just within the cloister wall he had planted a little herb garden, and it was into this that the old woman had forced her way.

At first glance Robber Mother was so astonished that she paused at the gate. It was high summertide, and Abbot Hans' garden was so full of flowers that the eyes were fairly dazzled by the blues, reds, and yellows, as one looked into it. But presently an indulgent smile spread over her features, and she started to walk up a narrow path that lay between many flowerbeds.

In the garden a lay brother walked about, pulling up weeds. It was he who had left the door in the wall open, that he might throw the weeds and tares on the rubbish heap outside.

When he saw Robber Mother coming in, with all five youngsters in tow, he ran toward her at once and ordered them away. But the beggar woman walked right on as before. The lay brother knew of no other remedy than to run into the cloister and call for help.

He returned with two stalwart monks, and Robber Mother saw that now it meant business! She let out a perfect volley of shrieks, and, throwing herself upon the monks, clawed and bit at them; so did all the youngsters. The men soon learned that she could overpower them, and all they could do was to go back into the cloister for reinforcements.

As they ran through the passage-way which led to the cloister, they met Abbot Hans, who came rushing out to learn what all this noise was about.

He upbraided them for using force and forbade their calling for help. He sent both monks back to their work, and although he was an old and fragile man, he took with him only the lay brother.

He came up to the woman and asked in a mild tone if the garden pleased her.

Robber Mother turned defiantly toward Abbot Hans, for she expected only to be trapped and over-powered. But when she noticed his white hair and bent form, she answered peaceably, "First, when I saw this, I thought I had never seen a prettier garden; but now I see that it can't be compared with one I know of. If you could see the garden of which I am thinking you would uproot all the flowers planted here and cast them away like weeds."

The Abbot's assistant was hardly less proud of the flowers than the Abbot himself, and after hearing her remarks he laughed derisively.

Robber Mother grew crimson with rage to think that her word was doubted, and she cried out: "You monks, who are holy men, certainly must know that on every Christmas Eve the great Goinge forest is transformed into a beautiful garden, to commemo-rate the hour of our Lord's birth. We who live in the forest have seen this happen every year. And in that garden I have seen flowers so lovely that I dared not lift my hand to pluck them."

Ever since his childhood, Abbot Hans had heard it said that on every Christmas Eve the forest was dressed in holiday glory. He had often longed to see it, but he had never had the good fortune. Eagerly he begged and implored Robber Mother that he might come up to the Robbers' Cave on Christmas Eve. If she would only send one of her children to show him the way, he could ride up there alone, and he would never betray them—on the contrary, he would reward them insofar as it lay in his power.

Robber Mother said no at first, for she was thinking of Robber Father and of the peril which might befall him should she permit Abbot Hans to ride up to their cave. At the same time the desire to prove to the monk that the garden which she knew was more beautiful than his got the better of her, and she gave in.

"But more than one follower you cannot take with you," said she, "and you are not to waylay us or trap us, as sure as you are a holy man."

This Abbot Hans promised, and then Robber Mother went her way.

It happened that Archbishop Absalon from Lund came to Ovid and remained through the night. The lay brother heard Abbot Hans telling the Bishop about Robber Father and asking him for a letter of ransom for the man, that he might lead an honest life among respectable folk.

But the Archbishop replied that he did not care to let the robber loose among honest folk in the vill-ages. It would be best for all that he remain in the forest.

Then Abbot Hans grew zealous and told the Bishop all about Goinge forest, which, every year at Yuletide, clothed itself in summer bloom around the Robbers' Cave. "If these bandits are not so bad but that God's glories can be made manifest to them, surely we cannot be too wicked to experience the same blessing."

The Archbishop knew how to answer Abbot Hans. "This much I will promise you, Abbot Hans," he said, smiling, "that any day you send me a blossom from the garden in Goinge forest, I will give you letters of ransom for all the outlaws you may choose to plead for."

The following Christmas Eve Abbot Hans was on his way to the forest. One of the Robber Mother's wild youngsters ran ahead of him, and close behind him was the lay brother.

It turned out to be a long and hazardous ride. They climbed steep and slippery side paths, crawled over swamp and marsh, and pushed through windfall and bramble. Just as daylight was waning, the robber boy guided them across a forest meadow, skirted by tall, naked leaf trees and green fir trees. Back of the meadow loomed a mountain wall, and in this wall they saw a door of thick boards. Now Abbot Hans understood that they had arrived, and dismounted. The child opened the heavy door for him, and he looked into a poor mountain grotto, with bare stone walls. Robber Mother was seated before a log fire that burned in the middle of the floor. Alongside the walls were beds of virgin pine and moss, and on one of these beds lay Robber Father asleep.

"Come in, you out there!" shouted Robber Mother without rising, "and fetch the horses in with you, so they won't be destroyed by the night cold."

Abbot Hans walked boldly into the cave, and the lay brother followed. Here were wretchedness and poverty! and nothing was done to celebrate Christmas.

Robber Mother spoke in a tone as haughty and dictatorial as any well-to-do peasant woman. "Sit down by the fire and warm yourself, Abbot Hans," said she; "and if you have food with you, eat, for the food which we in the forest prepare you wouldn't care to taste. And if you are tired after the long journey, you can lie down on one of these beds to sleep. You needn't be afraid of oversleeping, for I'm sitting here by the fire keeping watch. I shall awaken you in time to see that which you have come up here to see."

Abbot Hans obeyed Robber Mother and brought forth his food sack; but he was so fatigued after the journey he was hardly able to eat, and as soon as he could stretch himself on the bed, he fell asleep.

The lay brother was also assigned a bed to rest in, and he dropped into a doze.

When he woke up, he saw that Abbot Hans had left his bed and was sitting by the fire talking with Robber Mother. The outlawed robber sat also by the fire. He was a tall, raw-boned man with a dull, sluggish appearance. His back was turned to Abbot Hans, as though he would have it appear that he was not listening to the conversation.

Abbot Hans was telling Robber Mother all about the Christmas preparations he had seen on the journey, reminding her of Christmas feasts and games which she must have known in her youth, when she lived at peace with mankind.

At first Robber Mother answered in short, gruff sentences, but by degrees she became more subdued and listened more intently. Suddenly Robber Father turned toward Abbot Hans and shook his clenched fist in his face. "You miserable monk! Did you come here to coax from me my wife and children? Don't you know that I am an outlaw and may not leave the forest?"

Abbot Hans looked him fearlessly in the eyes. "It is my purpose to get a letter of ransom for you from Archbishop Absalon," said he. He had hardly finished speaking when the robber and his wife burst out laughing. They knew well enough the kind of mercy a forest robber could expect from Bishop Absalon!

"Oh, if I get a letter of ransom from Absalon," said Robber Father, "then I'll promise you that never again will I steal so much as a goose."

Suddenly Robber Mother rose. "You sit here and talk, Abbot Hans," she said, "so that we are forgetting to look at the forest. Now I can hear, even in this cave, how the Christmas bells are ringing."

The words were barely uttered when they all sprang up and rushed out. But in the forest it was still dark night and bleak winter. The only thing they marked was a distant clang borne on a light south wind.

When the bells had been ringing a few moments, a sudden illumination penetrated the forest; the next moment it was dark again, and then light came back. It pushed its way forward between the stark trees, like a shimmering mist. The darkness merged into a faint daybreak. Then Abbot Hans saw that the snow had vanished from the ground, as if someone had removed a carpet, and the earth began to take on a green covering. The moss-tufts thickened and raised themselves, and the spring blossoms shot upward their swelling buds, which already had a touch of color.

Again it grew hazy; but almost immediately there came a new wave of light. Then the leaves of the trees burst into bloom, crossbeaks hopped from branch to branch, and the woodpeckers hammered on the limbs until the splinters fairly flew around them. A flock of starlings from up country lighted in a fir top to rest.

When the next warm wind came along, the blueberries ripened and the baby squirrels began playing on the branches of the trees.

The next light wave that came rushing in brought with it the scent of newly ploughed acres. Pine and spruce trees were so thickly clothed with red cones that they shone like crimson mantles and forest flowers covered the ground till it was all red, blue, and yellow.

Abbot Hans bent down to the earth and broke off a wild strawberry blossom, and, as he straightened up, the berry ripened in his hand.

The mother fox came out of her lair with a big litter of black-legged young. She went up to Robber Mother and scratched at her skirt, and Robber Mother bent down to her and praised her young.

Robber Mother's youngsters let out perfect shrieks of delight. They stuffed themselves with wild strawberries that hung on the bushes. One of them played with a litter of young hares; another ran a race with some young crows, which had hopped from their nest before they were really ready.

Robber Father was standing out on a marsh eating raspberries. When he glanced up, a big black bear stood beside him. Robber Father broke off a twig and struck the bear on the nose. "Keep to your own ground, you!" he said; "this is my turf." The huge bear turned around and lumbered off in another direction.

Then all the flowers whose seeds had been brought from foreign lands began to blossom. The loveliest roses climbed up the mountain wall in a race with the blackberry vines, and from the forest meadow sprang flowers as large as human faces.

Abbot Hans thought of the flower he was to pluck for Bishop Absalon; but each new flower that appeared was more beautiful than the others, and he wanted to choose the most beautiful of all.

Then Abbot Hans marked how all grew still; the birds hushed their songs, the flowers ceased growing, and the young foxes played no more. From far in the distance faint harp tones were heard, and celestial song, like a soft murmur, reached him.

He clasped his hands and dropped to his knees. His face was radiant with bliss.

But beside Abbot Hans stood the lay brother who had accompanied him. In his mind there were dark thoughts. "This cannot be a true miracle," he thought, "since it is revealed to malefactors. This does not come from God, but is sent hither by Satan. It is the Evil One's power that is tempting us and compelling us to see that which has no real existence."

The angel throng was so near now that Abbot Hans saw their bright forms through the forest branches. The lay brother saw them, too; but back of all this wondrous beauty he saw only some dread evil.

All the while the birds had been circling around the head of Abbot Hans, and they let him take them in his hands. But all the animals were afraid of the lay brother; no bird perched on his shoulder, no snake played at his feet. Then there came a little forest dove. When she marked that the angels were nearing, she plucked up courage and flew down on the lay brother's shoulder and laid her head against his cheek.

Then it appeared to him as if sorcery were come right upon him, to tempt and corrupt him. He struck with his hand at the forest dove and cried in such a loud voice that it rang throughout the forest, "Go thou back to hell, whence thou art come!"

Just then the angels were so near that Abbot Hans felt the feathery touch of their great wings, and he bowed down to earth in reverent greeting.

But when the lay brother's words sounded, their song was hushed and the holy guests turned in flight. At the same time the light and the mild warmth vanished in unspeakable terror for the darkness and cold in a human heart. Darkness sank over the earth, like a coverlet; frost came, all the growths shrivelled up; the animals and birds hastened away; the leaves dropped from the trees, rustling like rain.

Abbot Hans felt how his heart, which had but late-ly swelled with bliss, was now contracting with insufferable agony. "I can never outlive this," thought he, "that the angels from heaven had been so close to me and were driven away; that they wanted to sing Christmas carols for me and were driven to flight."

Then he remembered the flower he had promised Bishop Absalon, and at the last moment he fumbled among the leaves and moss to try and find a blossom. But he sensed how the ground under his fingers froze and how the white snow came gliding over the ground. Then his heart caused him even greater anguish. He could not rise, but fell prostrate on the ground and lay there.

When the robber folk and the lay brother had groped their way back to the cave, they missed Abbot Hans. They took brands with them and went out to search for him. They found him dead upon the coverlet of snow.

When Abbot Hans had been carried down to Ovid, those who took charge of the dead saw that he held his right hand locked tight around something which he must have grasped at the moment of death. When they finally got his hand open, they found that the thing which he had held in such an iron grip was a pair of white root bulbs, which he had torn from among the moss and leaves.

When the lay brother who had accompanied Abbot Hans saw the bulbs, he took them and planted them in Abbot Hans' herb garden.

He guarded them the whole year to see if any flower would spring from them. But in vain he waited through the spring, the summer, and the autumn. Finally, when winter had set in and all the leaves and the flowers were dead, he ceased caring for them.

But when Christmas Eve came again, he was so

strongly reminded of Abbot Hans that he wandered out into the garden to think of him. And look! as he came to the spot where he had planted the bare root bulbs, he saw that from them had sprung flourishing green stalks, which bore beautiful flowers with silver white leaves.

He called out all the monks at Ovid, and when they saw that this plant bloomed on Christmas Eve, when all the other growths were as if dead, they understood that this flower had in truth been plucked by Abbot Hans from the Christmas garden in Goinge forest. Then the lay brother asked the monks if he might take a few blossoms to Bishop Absalon.

When Bishop Absalon beheld the flowers, which had sprung from the earth in darkest winter, he turned as pale as if he had met a ghost. He sat in silence a moment; thereupon he said, "Abbot Hans has faithfully kept his word and I shall also keep mine."

He handed the letter of ransom to the lay brother, who departed at once for the Robbers' Cave. When he stepped in there on Christmas Day, the robber came toward him with axe uplifted. "I'd like to hack you monks into bits, as many as you are!" said he. "It must be your fault that Goinge forest did not last night dress itself in Christmas bloom."

"The fault is mine alone," said the lay brother, "and I will gladly die for it; but first I must deliver a message from Abbot Hans." And he drew forth the Bishop's letter and told the man that he was free.

Robber Father stood there pale and speechless, but Robber Mother said in his name, "Abbot Hans has indeed kept his word, and Robber Father will keep his."

When the robber and his wife left the cave, the lay brother moved in and lived all alone in the forest, in constant meditation and prayer that his hard-heartedness might be forgiven him.

But Goinge forest never again celebrated the hour of our Saviour's birth; and of all its glory, there lives today only the plant which Abbot Hans had plucked. It has been named CHRISTMAS ROSE. And each year at Christmastide she sends forth from the earth her green stalks and white blossoms, as if she never could forget that she had once grown in the great Christmas garden at Goinge forest.

THE WORST CHRISTMAS STORY
Christopher Morley

"The Worst Christmas Story" is actually a rather nice piece of work. Although its plot revolves around the artist's choice between accepting commercialism and succumbing to starvation, the story is actually a subtle reminder that there is plenty of room for humor at Christmas.

WE HAD BEEN DOWN to an East Side settlement house on Christmas afternoon. I had watched my friend Dove Dulcet, in moth-riddled scarlet and cotton wool trimmings, play Santa Claus for several hundred adoring urchins and their parents. He had done this for many years, but I had never before seen him insist on the amiable eccentricity of returning uptown still wearing the regalia of the genial saint. But Dove is always unusual, and I thought—as did the others who saw him, in the subway and elsewhere—it was a rather kindly and innocent concession to the hilarity of the day.

When we had got back to his snug apartment he beamed at me through his snowy fringes of false whisker, and began rummaging in the tall leather boots of his costume. From each one he drew a bottle of chianti. "From a grateful parent on Mulberry Street," he said. "My favorite bootlegger lives down that way, and I've been playing Santa to his innumerable children for a number of years. The garb attributed—quite inaccurately, I expect—to Saint Nicholas of Bari, has its uses. Even the keenest revenue agent would hardly think of holding up poor old Santa."

He threw off his trappings, piled some logs on the fire, and we sat down for our annual celebration. Dove and I have got into the habit of spending Christmas together. We are both old bachelors, with no close family ties, and we greatly enjoy the occasion. It isn't wholly selfish, either, for we usually manage to spice our fun with a little unexpected charity in some of the less fortunate quarters of town.

As my friend uncorked the wicker-bound bottles I noticed a great pile of Christmas mail on his table.

"Dove, you odd fish," I said. "Why don't you open your letters? I should have thought that part of the fun of Christmas is hurrying to look through the greetings from friends. Or do you leave them to the last, to give them greater savor?"

He glanced at the heap, with a curious expression on his face.

"The Christmas cards?" he said. "I postpone them as long as I possibly can. It's part of my penance."

"What on earth do you mean?"

He filled two glasses, passed one to me, and sat down beside the cheerful blaze.

"Here's luck, old man!" he said. "Merry Christmas."

I drank with him, but something evasive in his manner impelled me to repeat my question.

"What a ferret you are, Ben!" he said. "Yes, I put off looking at the Christmas cards as long as I dare. I suppose I'll have to tell you. It's one of the few skeletons in my anatomy of melancholy that you haven't exhumed. It's a queer kind of Christmas story."

He reached over to the table, took up a number of the envelopes, and studied their handwritings. He tore them open one after another, and read the enclosed cards.

"As I expected," he said. "Look here, it's no use your trying to make copy out of this yarn. No editor would look at it. It runs counter to all the good old Christmas tradition."

"My dear Dove," I said, "if you've got a Christmas story that's 'different,' you've got something that editors will pay double for."

"Judge for yourself," he said. From the cards in his lap he chose four and gave them to me. "Begin by reading those."

Completely mystified, I did so.

The first showed a blue bird perched on a spray of holly. The verse read:

Our greeting is "Merry Christmas!"
None better could we find,
And tho' you are now out of sight,
You're ever in our mind.

The second card said, below a snow scene of mid-Victorian characters alighting from a stage coach at the hospitable door of a country mansion:

Should you or your folk ever call at our door
You'll be welcome, we promise you—nobody more;
We wish you the best of the Joy and Cheer
That can come with Christmas and last through
    the year!

The third, with a bright picture of three stout old gentlemen in scarlet waistcoats, tippling before an open fire:

Jolly old Yule, Oh the jolly old Yule
Blesses rich man and poor man and wise man
    and fool—
Be merry, old friend, in this bright winter weather
And you'll Yule and I'll Yule, we'll all Yule together!

The fourth—an extremely ornate vellum leaflet, gilded with Oriental designs and magi on camels—ran thus:

I pray the prayer the Easterners do;
May the Peace of Allah abide with you—
Through days of labor and nights of rest
May the love of Allah make you blest.

"Well," I said, "of course I wouldn't call them great poetry, but the sentiments are generous enough. Surely it's the spirit in which they're sent that counts. It doesn't seem like you to make fun—"

Dulcet leaned forward. "Make fun?" he said. "Heavens, I'm not making fun of them. The ghastly thing is, I wrote those myself."

There was nothing to say, so I held my peace.

"You didn't know, I trust, that at one time I was regarded as the snappiest writer of greeting sentiments (so the trade calls them) in the business? That was long ago, but the sentiments themselves, and innumerable imitations of them, go merrily on. You see, out of the first ten cards that I picked up, four are my own composition. Can you imagine the horror of receiving, every Christmas, every New Year, every Easter, every birthday, every Halloween, every Thanksgiving, cards most of which were written by yourself? And when I think of the honest affection with which those cards were chosen for me by my unsuspecting friends, and contrast their loving simplicity with—"

He broke off, and refilled the glasses.

"I told you," he said, "that this was the worst Christmas story in the world! But I must try to tell it a little better, at any rate. Well, it has some of the traditional ingredients.

"You remember the winter of the Great Panic—1906, wasn't it? I had a job in an office downtown, and was laid off. I applied everywhere for work—nothing doing. I had been writing a little on the side, verses and skits for the newspapers, but I couldn't make enough that way to live on. I had an attic in an old lodging house on Gay Street. (The Village was still genuine then, no hokum about it.) I used to reflect on the irony of that name, Gay Street, when I was walking about trying not to see the restaurants, they made me feel so hungry. I still get a queer feeling in the pit of my stomach when I pass by Gonfarone's—there was a fine thick savor of spaghetti and lentil soup that used to float out from the basement as I went along Eighth Street.

"There was a girl in it too, of course. You'll smile when I tell you who she was. Peggy Cassell, who does the magazine covers. Yes, she's prosperous enough now—so are we all. But those were the days.

"It's the old bachelors who are the real sentimentalists, hey? But by Jove, how I adored that girl! She was fresh from upstate somewhere, studying at the League, and doing small illustrating jobs to make ends approach. I was as green and tender as she. I was only twenty-five, you know. To go up to what Peggy called her studio—which was only a bleak bedroom she shared with another girl—and smoke cigarettes and see her wearing a smock and watch

her daub away at a thing she intended to be a 'portrait' of me, was my idea of high tide on the seacoast of Bohemia. Peggy would brew cocoa in a chafing dish and then the other girl would tactfully think of some errand, and we'd sit, timidly and uncomfortably, with our arms around each other, and talk about getting married some day, and prove by Cupid's grand old logarithms that two can live cheaper than one. I used to recite to her that ripping old song 'My Peggy is a young thing, And I'm not very auld,' and it would knock us both cold.

"The worst of it was poor Peggy was almost as

hard up as I was. In fact, we were both so hard up that I'm amazed we didn't get married, which is what people usually do when they have absolutely no prospects. But with all her sweet sentiment Peggy had a streak of sound caution. And as a matter of fact, I think she was better off than I was, because she did get a small allowance from home. Anyway, I was nearly desperate, tearing my heart out over the thought of this brave little creature facing the world for the sake of her art, and so on. She complained of the cold, and I remember taking her my steamer rug off my own bed, telling her I was too warm. After that I used to shingle myself over with newspapers when I went to bed. It was bitter on Gay Street that winter.

"But I said this was a Christmas story. So it is. It began like this. About Hallowe'en I had a little poem in *Life*—nothing of any account, but a great event to me, my first appearance in Big Time journalism. Well, one day I got a letter from a publisher in Chicago asking permission to reprint it on a card. He said also that my verses had just the right touch which was needed in such things, and that I could probably do some 'holiday greetings' for him. He would be glad to see some Christmas 'sentiments,' he said, and would pay one dollar each for any he could use.

"You can imagine that it didn't take me long to begin tearing off sentiments though I stipulated, as a last concession to my honor, that my name should not be used. There was no time to lose: it was now along in November, and these things—to be sold to the public for Christmas a year later—must be submitted as soon as possible so that they could be illustrated and ready for the salesmen to take on the road in January.

"Picture, then, the young author of genial greeting cards, sitting ironically in the chilliest attic on Gay Street—a dim and draughty little elbow of the city—and attempting to ignite his wits with praise of the glowing hearth and the brandied pudding. The room was heated only by a small gas stove, one burner of which had been scientifically sealed by the landlady; and apparatus, moreover, in which asphyxia was the partner of warmth. When that sickly sweetish gust became too overpotent, see the author throw up the window and retire to bed, meditating under a mountain of news-print further applause of wintry joy and fellowship. I remember one sentiment—very likely it is among the pile on the table here, it is a great favorite—which went:

> *May blazing log and steaming bowl*
> *And wreaths of mistletoe and holly*
> *Remind you of a kindred soul*
> *Whose love for you is warm and jolly!*

My, how cold it was the night I wrote that."

Dove paused, prodded the logs to a brighter flame, and leaned closer to the chimney as though feeling a reminiscent chill.

"Well, as Christmas itself drew nearer, I became more and more agitated. I had sent in dozens of these compositions; each batch was duly acknowledged, and highly praised. The publisher was pleased to say that I had a remarkable aptitude for 'greetings;' my Christmas line, particularly, he applauded as being full of the robust and hearty spirit of the old-fashioned Yule. My Easter touch, he felt, was a little thin and tepid by comparison. So I redoubled my metrical cheer. I piled the logs higher and higher upon my imaginary hearth; I bore in cups of steaming wassail; blizzards drummed at my baronial window panes; stage coaches were halted by drifts axle-deep; but within the circle of my mid-Victorian halloo, all was mirth: beauty crowded beneath the pale mistletoe; candles threw a tawny shine; the goose was carved and the port wine sparkled. And all the while, if you please, it was December of the panic winter; no check had yet arrived from the delighted publisher; I had laid aside other projects to pursue this golden phantom; I ate once a day, and sometimes kept warm by writing my mellow outbursts of gladness in the steam-heated lobbies of hotels.

"I had said nothing to Peggy about this professional assumption of Christmas heartiness. For one thing, I had talked to her so much, and with such youthful ardor, of my literary ambitions and ideals, that I feared her ridicule; for another, my most eager hope was to surprise her with an opulent Christmas present. She, poor dear, was growing a trifle threadbare too; she had spoken, now and then, of some sort of fur neckpiece she had seen in shop windows; this, no less, was my secret ambition. And so, as the streets grew brighter with the approach of the day, and still the publisher delayed his remittance, I wrote him a masterly letter. It was couched in the form of a Christmas greeting from me to him; it acknowledged the validity of his contention that he had postponed a settlement because I was still submitting more and more masterpieces and he planned to settle *en bloc*; but it pointed out the supreme and tragic irony of my having to pass a Christmas in starvation and misery because I had spent so much time dispersing altruistic and factitious good will.

"As I waited anxiously for a reply, I was further disquieted by distressing behavior on Peggy's part. She had been rather strange with me for some time, which I attributed partly to my own shabby appearance and wretched preoccupation with my gruesome task. She had rallied me—some time before—on my mysterious mien, and I may have been clumsy in my retorts. Who can always know just the right accent with which to chaff a woman? At any rate, she had—with some suddenly assumed excuse of propriety—forbidden me the hospitality of her bedroom studio; even my portrait (which we had so blithely imagined as a national triumph in future years when we both stood at the crest of our arts) had been discontinued. We wandered the streets together, quarrelsome and unhappy; we could agree about nothing. In spite of this, I nourished my hopeful secret, still believing that when my check came, and enabled me to mark the Day of Days with the coveted fur, all would be happier than ever.

"It was two days before Christmas, and you may elaborate the picture with all the traditional tints of Dickens pathos. It was cold and snowy and I was hungry, worried, and forlorn. I was walking along Eighth Street wondering whether I could borrow enough money to telegraph to Chicago. Just by the Brevoort I met Peggy, and to my chagrin and despair she was wearing a beautiful new fur neckpiece—a tippet, I think they used to call them in those days. She looked a different girl: her face was pink, her small chin nestled adorably into the fur collar, her eyes were bright and merry. Well, I was only human, and I guess I must have shown my wretched disappointment. Of course she hadn't known that I hoped to surprise her in just that way, and when I blurted out something to that effect, she spoke tartly.

"'You!' she cried. "How could you buy me anything like that? I suppose you'd like me to tramp around in the snow all winter and catch my death of cold!"

"In spite of all the Christmas homilies I had written about good will and charity and what not, I lost my temper.

"'Ah,' I said bitterly, 'I see it all now! I wasn't prosperous enough, so you've found someone else who can afford to buy furs for you. That's why you've kept me away from the studio, eh? You've got some other chap on the string.'

"I can still see her little flushed face, rosy with wind and snow, looking ridiculously stricken as she stood on that wintry corner. She began to say something, but I was hot with the absurd rage of youth. All my weeks of degradation on Gay Street suddenly boiled up in my mind. I was grotesquely melodramatic and absurd.

"'A rich lover!' I sneered. 'Go ahead and take him! I'll stick to poverty and my ideals. You can have the furs and fleshpots!'

"Well, you never know how a woman will take things. To my utter amazement, instead of flaming up with anger, she burst into tears. But I was too proud and troubled to comfort her.

"'Yes, you're right,' she sobbed. 'I had such fine dreams, but I couldn't stick it out. I'm not worthy of your ideals. I guess I've sold myself.' She turned and ran away down the slippery street, leaving me flabbergasted.

"I walked around and around Washington Square, not knowing what to do. She had as good as admitted that she had thrown me over for some richer man. And yet I didn't feel like giving her up without a struggle. Perhaps it all sounds silly now, but it was terribly real then.

"At last I went back to Gay Street. On the hall table was a letter from the publisher, with a check for fifty dollars. He had accepted fifty of the hundred or so pieces I had sent, and said if I would consider going to Chicago he would give me a position on his staff as Assistant Greeting Editor. 'Get into a good sound business,' he wrote. 'There will never be a panic in the Greeting line.'

"When I read that letter I was too elated to worry about anything. I would be able to fix things with

Peggy somehow. I would say to her, in a melting voice, 'My Peggy is a young thing,' and she would tumble. She must love me still, or she wouldn't have cried. I rushed round to her lodging house, and went right upstairs without giving her a chance to deny me. I knocked, and when she came to the door she looked frightened and ill. She tried to stop me, but I burst in and waved the letter in front of her.

"'Look at this, Peggy darling!' I shouted. 'We're going to be rich and infamous. I didn't tell you what I was doing, because I was afraid you'd be ashamed of me, after all my talk about high ideals. But anything is better than starving and freezing on Gay Street, or doing without the furs that pretty girls need.'

"She read the letter, and looked up at me with the queerest face.

"'Now no more nonsense about the other man,' I said. 'I'll buy you a fur for Christmas that'll put his among camphor balls. Who is he, anyway?'

"She surprised me again, for this time she began to laugh.

"'It's the same one,' she said. 'I mean, the same publisher—your friend in Chicago. Oh Dove, I've been doing drawings for Christmas cards, and I think they must be yours.'

"It was true. Her poor little cold studio was littered with sketches for Christmas drawings—blazing fires and ruddy Georgian squires with tankards of hissing ale and girls in sprigged muslin being coy under the mistletoe. And when she showed me the typewritten verses the publisher had sent her to illustrate, they were mine, sure enough. She had had her check a day sooner than I, and had rushed off to buy herself the fur her heart yearned for.

"'I was so ashamed of doing the work,' she said—with her head on my waistcoat—'that I didn't dare tell you.'"

Dove sighed, and leaned back in his chair. A drizzle of rain and sleet tinkled on the window pane, but the fire was a core of rosy light.

"Not much of a Christmas story, eh?" he said. "Do you wonder, now, that I hesitate to look back at the cards I wrote and Peggy illustrated?"

"But what happened?" I asked. "It seems a nice enough story as far as you've gone."

"Peggy was a naughty little hypocrite," he said. "I found out that she wasn't really ashamed of illustrating my greetings at all. She thought they were lovely. She honestly did. And presently she told me she simply couldn't marry a man who would capitalize Christmas. She said it was too sacred."

ONE YOUNG LADDIE'S CHRISTMAS
Kate Whiting Patch

Patch's story—set in the Boston of nearly a century ago—is a particularly touching portrayal of the power of a child's unshakable faith. It is an unapologetically sentimental look at the man who may be the world's most lovable figure — Santa Claus.

IT WAS THE DAY BEFORE Christmas, and the hurrying, busy crowd of happy people filled the Boston streets and shops. A very small atom in that crowd was Sandy Martin, but he carried a large share of the Christmas happiness, although his hands were mittenless and his pockets full of holes. How could one help being light-hearted and glad in the midst of all that joyous bustle and flurry? It made Sandy feel as if he were going to have a glorious big Christmas himself, and he quite forgot to

sigh because he was not. He stood by the big toy-shop window, flattening his little purple nose against the glass, and watching the people go in and out. He wondered what they were buying and what boy or girl was to be made glad with the contents of those mysterious parcels.

But by and by he began to grow cold, and the coldness set him to thinking; and as he walked along, up past the Common, he began to wonder, just a little, why it was that Santa Claus should have so much to do with all these people and so little to do with him. The puzzled look had not disappeared from his small, freckled face, when he looked across the street and could hardly believe his own eyes—for there was Santa Claus himself, walking through the Common!

Sandy stopped short, and stared and stared until his eyes couldn't open any wider. Yes, that was surely Santa Claus. He did not have his reindeer and sleigh, to be sure, for there was no snow; but nobody but Santa could own such a jolly face and long white beard and nice furry clothes and big boots. Then he had a good many toys about him, too; and he carried a great sign, with something in big letters on it, which told people that the rarest treasures for Christmas stockings were to be found at a certain big store on Washington Street.

But Sandy could not read and he did not bother with the letters. He just stared and stared.

Santa was evidently tired; for while Sandy was looking at him, the old saint paused in his walk and sat down on one of the benches.

"It *is* Santa Claus," said Sandy to himself. "I'm going over to talk with him, and I'll ask him why he doesn't come down our chimney, too."

No sooner said than done. Across the street Sandy hurried, and marching up to the old man, he said, in a friendly way, "How do you do, Mr. Santa Claus?"

Santa looked up, a little surprised, but smiled good-naturedly at the ragged urchin before him, and remarked affably, "Well, young man, how do you do? And what may be your name?"

"I'm Sandy Martin," was the prompt answer. And with that, Sandy Martin, waiting for no further invitation, proceeded to pull himself up on the seat beside Mr. Santa Claus. "I've come over here to ask you a question," he began at once. "I want to know why you don't come to our house Chris'mus; we've got jus' as good a chimney as any one, and there's an ole lightning rod beside it fer you to tie your reindeer to."

Santa seemed immensely pleased, and chuckled to himself.

"You see," said he to Sandy, "I have so many places to go to, it is very hard to find 'em all. Where do you live, any way?"

"Up in Gower Street, No. 65. I thought you might have forgotten.

"At this point Sandy became conscious that a third person was listening to the conversation. A tall, dark lady in deep mourning had come up to where the two were sitting, and stood near, waiting for a street-car. Her face was very pale and sad, and it quite surprised Sandy to think that any one could look so at Christmas-time, and before the very eyes of Santa Claus, too. As he stared up at her, the sadness was chased away for an instant by an amused smile. Sandy, who stood in awe of no one, smiled back at her, and said cheerfully, "Merry Christmas, ma'am."

The lady smiled, but sighed too.

"Thank you, my dear," she said, in a sweet, sad voice. "I hope that you may have a merry Christmas, but the day cannot be a merry one for me."

Sandy was surprised again, and gazed in bewilderment from Santa to the lady.

"Why? Don't grown-up people have merry Christmases?" he asked.

"Sometimes," answered the lady sadly. "I thought," continued Sandy, "that it was even more fun for the grown-up people than for the children; 'cause I thought you all knew Santa Claus and had secrets with him. All the other people I've seen looked jolly and glad, an' I thought every one was happy 'cause they was all thinkin' how they'd surprise some other one."

A shadow fell across Sandy's little face, and the lady saw it.

"My dear little boy," she said, with something like tears in her voice, although her eyes were smiling again, "don't let me spoil your thought of Christmas happiness. You are right, and I have been wrong; every one should be happy at this blessed season, and I am going to have a secret with Santa Claus, and a merry Christmas, too."

Sandy looked happy again, and began to slide off the seat.

"I've got to go home now, for it's getting dark," he said; "but I'm ever so glad I met you, Mr. Santa Claus, and I hope you'll find your way tonight all right. If you can, I wish you'd bring Maggie a doll with blue eyes, and Benny a sled, and mother a new shawl; and, Mr. Santa Claus," he added in a loud whisper, "I hope you'll give that lady there something she likes and make her have a good time."

Then Sandy trudged away, and when he looked back he was delighted to see the sad lady and Santa talking earnestly together.

While they ate their supper that night, Sandy excited the whole family with his story of meeting Santa Claus. His mother, tired out with her day's work, sighed, and tried to persuade him that it was not really Santa Claus he had seen—in vain; before they went to bed, each child hung up a ragged stocking back of the kitchen stove.

Mrs. Martin looked at them, and then sank down in her chair and had a good cry. She had been sewing hard all day, poor soul; but the money she had earned was no more than enough to keep a roof over their heads and procure food for the hungry little mouths—there was nothing to spare for Christmas stockings.

"Oh, what will they say in the morning," she wept, "when they find them empty! I can't bear it; no, I can't."

She looked about the room, and finally rose and took her shawl down from the peg.

"It's no use," she said, "I can't have them disappointed; I'll go out and pawn this and get a few things to put in them stockings."

She walked across the room and opened the door,

but she did not go out, for someone was standing there.

"How do you do, ma'am?" he said, walking into the room. "I am Santa Claus, and as I couldn't very well get down the chimney I took the liberty of coming in at the door. I've a few things here for the little folks, and I promised your boy I'd come; I see he is ready for me."

With that, Santa Claus went to work, and Mrs. Martin dropped into her chair and uttered never a word; she felt as if she were dreaming. Had the myths of her childhood come back again? Was there really a Santa Claus, and had Sandy met him that afternoon? Surely it could be no one else who stood there before her; and had not this bluff, kindly old man with his own lips declared his identity?

Mrs. Martin sat perfectly dazed, and watched him 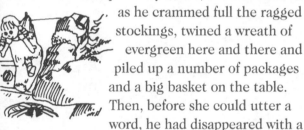 as he crammed full the ragged stockings, twined a wreath of evergreen here and there and piled up a number of packages and a big basket on the table. Then, before she could utter a word, he had disappeared with a "Merry Christmas," leaving her to wonder if she had not indeed awakened from a dream.

Before light, next morning, great was the joyful excitement and noise at 65 Gower Street; and this only settled into momentary awe when mother told the children, that she herself had seen Santa Claus fill the stockings!

"But I thought you said there wasn't a Santa Claus," said Sandy, reproachfully.

"Well, I didn't believe there was," answered his mother helplessly; "but if that wasn't Santa Claus I don't know who it was."

"Course it was Santa Claus!" exclaimed Maggie; "didn't Sandy tell him to bring me a doll with blue eyes?" (Sandy nodded solemnly.) "Well, and he did

bring her, didn't he?—the pretty darling! See, ma, she's got lace-edged clothes clear through, and buttoned boots."

"And didn't Sandy tell him to bring me a sled?" broke in Benny. (Sandy nodded solemnly again.) "And ain't the sled right here? And didn't the snow come, too, last night? And ain't I going coasting on the Common this very day?" Saying which Benny flung himself upon the shiny sled and tried to coast across the kitchen floor.

As if these arguments were not enough, Sandy turned to his mother again.

"And didn't I ask him to bring you a new shawl?" he said.

Mrs. Martin laid her hand on the soft thick shawl which Maggie had spread across the rocking-chair, and then she patted Sandy's shoulder gently.

"What did you tell him to bring to *you*?" she asked.

Sandy looked up in sudden surprise.

"Why, I never told him about me!" he exclaimed. "It was getting late, and I just remembered about the doll and the sled and the shawl. I forgot all about me; but now I'm sure it was Santa Claus, for he brought just the things I wanted."

"So he did!" said Maggie wonderingly. "There is the tool-chest, and the harmonica, and the big picture-book."

Benny had been peeping into the market-basket. "Whew!" he cried. "There's nuts and oranges and 'nanas and grapes; and there's red jelly and a turkey!"

"I see crackers and bread and 'taters," exclaimed Maggie from the other side of the basket. "Oh, ma! ma! we can have a regular dinner, can't we!"

It is needless to tell of all the comfort and joy that happy Christmas brought to Sandy and his home.

But his faith in Santa Claus is firm and sure and even Mrs. Martin half believes that the good old saint does somewhere exist, and was drawn down to their humble home by little Sandy's Christmas spirit.

MARKHEIM
Robert Louis Stevenson

Although its dark tone and brief violent passages may render "Markheim" best suited to preteens and older members of the family, Robert Louis Stevenson's Christmas story is a remarkable examination of sin and redemption fully in keeping with the spirit of the season. It can be said to represent a darker, briefer, version of Dickens' *A Christmas Carol*. The tale substitutes a relatively young man's epiphany for the one old Scrooge undergoes, and focuses our attention not so much on the sweep of an entire misspent life as on a single harrowing crime.

"YES," SAID THE DEALER, "our windfalls are of various kinds. Some customers are ignorant, and then I touch a dividend on my superior knowledge. Some are dishonest," and here he held up the candle, so that the light fell strongly on his visitor, "and in that case," he continued, "I profit by my virtue."

Markheim had but just entered from the daylight streets, and his eyes had not yet grown familiar with the mingled shine and darkness in the shop. At these pointed words, and before the near presence of the flame, he blinked painfully and looked aside.

The dealer chuckled. "You come to see me on Christmas Day," he resumed, "when you know that I am alone in my house, put up my shutters, and make a point of refusing business. Well, you will have to pay for that; you will have to pay for my loss of time, when I should be balancing my books; you will have to pay, besides, for a kind of manner that I remark in you today very strongly. I am the essence of discretion, and ask no awkward questions; but when a customer cannot look me in the eye, he has to pay for it." The dealer once more chuckled; and then, changing to his usual business voice, though still with a note of irony, "You can give, as usual, a clear account of how you came into the possession of the object?" he continued. "Still your uncle's cabinet? A remarkable collector, sir!"

And the little pale, round-shouldered dealer stood almost on tip-toe, looking over the top of his gold spectacles, and nodding his head with every mark of disbelief. Markheim returned his gaze with one of infinite pity, and a touch of horror.

"This time," said he, "you are in error. I have not come to sell, but to buy. I have no curios to dispose of; my uncle's cabinet is bare to the wainscot; even were it still intact, I have done well on the Stock Exchange, and should more likely add to it than otherwise, and my errand today is simplicity itself. I seek a Christmas present for a lady," he continued, waxing more fluent as he struck into the speech he had prepared; "and certainly I owe you every excuse for thus disturbing you on so small a matter. But the thing was neglected yesterday; I must produce my little compliment at dinner; and, as you very well know, a rich marriage is not a thing to be neglected."

There followed a pause, during which the dealer seemed to weigh this statement incredulously. The ticking of many clocks among the curious lumber of the shop, and the faint rushing of the cabs in a near thoroughfare, filled up the interval of silence.

"Well, sir," said the dealer, "be it so. You are an old customer after all; and if, as you say, you have the chance of a good marriage, far be it from me to be an obstacle. Here is a nice thing for a lady now," he went on, "this hand-glass—fifteenth century, warranted; comes from a good collection, too; but I reserve the name, in the interests of my customer, who was just like yourself, my dear sir, the nephew and sole heir of a remarkable collector."

The dealer, while he thus ran on in his dry and biting voice, had stooped to take the object from its place; and, as he had done so, a shock had passed through Markheim, a start both of hand and foot, a sudden leap of many tumultuous passions to the face. It passed as swiftly as it came, and left no trace beyond a certain trembling of the hand that now received the glass.

"A glass," he said hoarsely, and then paused, and repeated it more clearly. "A glass? For Christmas? Surely not?"

"And why not?" cried the dealer. "Why not a glass?"

Markheim was looking upon him with an indefinable expression. "You ask me why not?" he said. "Why, look here—look in it—look at yourself! Do you like to see it? No! Nor I—nor any man."

The little man had jumped back when Markheim had so suddenly confronted him with the mirror; but now, perceiving there was nothing worse on hand, he chuckled. "Your future lady, sir, must be pretty hard favoured," said he.

"I ask you," said Markheim, "for a Christmas present, and you give me this—this damned reminder of years, and sins and follies—this hand-conscience! Did you mean it? Had you a thought in your mind? Tell me. It will be better for you if you do. Come, tell me about yourself. I hazard a guess now, that you are in secret a very charitable man?"

The dealer looked closely at his companion. It was very odd. Markheim did not appear to be laughing; there was something in his face like an eager sparkle of hope, but nothing of mirth.

"What are you driving at?" the dealer said.

"Not charitable?" returned the other gloomily. "Not charitable; not pious; not scrupulous; unloving, unbeloved; a hand to get money, a safe to keep it. Is that all? Dear God, man, is that all?"

"I will tell you what it is," began the dealer, with some sharpness, and then broke off again into a chuckle. "But I see this is a love-match of yours, and you have been drinking the lady's health."

"Ah!" cried Markheim, with a strange curiosity. "Ah, have you been in love? Tell me about that."

"I," cried the dealer, "I in love! I never had the time, nor have I the time today for all this nonsense. Will you take the glass?"

"Where is the hurry?" returned Markheim. "It is very pleasant to stand here talking; and life is so short and insecure that I would not hurry away from any pleasure—no, not even from so mild a one as this. We should rather cling, cling, to what little we can get, like a man at a cliff's edge. Every second is a cliff, if you think upon it—a cliff a mile high—high enough, if we fall, to dash us out of every feature of humanity. Hence it is best to talk pleasantly. Let us talk of each other: why should we wear this mask? Let us be confidential. Who knows, we might become friends."

"I have just one word to say to you," said the dealer. "Either make your purchase, or walk out of my shop!"

"True, true," said Markheim. "Enough fooling. To business. Show me something else."

The dealer stooped once more, this time to replace the glass upon the shelf, his thin, blond hair falling over his eyes as he did so. Markheim moved a little nearer, with one hand in the pocket of his greatcoat; he drew himself up and filled his lungs; at the same time many different emotions were depicted together on his face—terror, horror and resolve, fascination and a physical repulsion; and through a haggard lift of his upper lip, his teeth looked out.

"This, perhaps, may suit," observed the dealer; and then, as he began to re-arise, Markheim bounded from behind upon his victim. The long skewerlike dagger flashed and fell. The dealer struggled like a hen, striking his temple on the shelf, and then tumbled on the floor in a heap.

Time had some score of small voices in that shop, some stately and slow as was becoming to their great age; others garrulous and hurried. All these told out the seconds in an intricate chorus of tickings. Then the passage of a lad's feet, heavily running on the pavement, broke in upon these smaller voices and startled Markheim into the consciousness of his surroundings. He looked about him awfully. The candle stood on the counter, its flame solemnly wagging in a draft; and by that inconsiderable movement, the whole room was filled with noiseless bustle and kept heaving like a sea; the tall shadows nodding, the gross blots of darkness swelling and dwindling as with respiration, the faces of the portraits and the china gods changing and wavering like images in water. The inner door stood ajar, and peered into that leaguer of shadows with a long slit of daylight like a pointing finger.

From these fear-stricken rovings, Markheim's eye returned to the body of his victim, where it lay both humped and sprawling, incredibly small and strangely meaner than in life. In these poor, miserly clothes, in that ungainly attitude, the dealer lay like so much sawdust. Markheim had feared to see it, and lo! It was nothing. And yet, as he gazed, this bundle of old clothes and pool of blood began to find eloquent voices. There it must lie; there was none to work the cunning hinges or direct the miracle of locomotion—there it must lie till it was found. Found! Ay, and then? Then would his dead flesh lift up a cry that would ring over England, and fill the world with the echoes of pursuit. Ay, dead or not, this was still the enemy. "Time was that when the brains were out," he thought; and the first word struck into his mind. Time, now that the deed was accomplished—time, which had closed for the victim, had become instant and momentous for the slayer.

The thought was yet in his mind, when, first one and then another, with every variety of pace and voice—one deep as the bell from a cathedral turret, another ringing on its treble notes the prelude of a waltz—the clocks began to strike the hour of three in the afternoon.

The sudden outbreak of so many tongues in that dumb chamber staggered him. He began to bestir himself, going to and fro with the candle, beleaguered by moving shadows, and startled to the soul by chance reflections. In many rich mirrors, some of home design, some from Venice or Amsterdam, he saw his own face repeated and repeated, as if it were an army of spies; his own eyes met and detected him; and the sound of his own steps, lightly as they fell, vexed the surrounding quiet. And still, as he continued to fill his pockets, his mind accused him with a sickening iteration of the thousand faults of his design. He should have chosen a more quiet hour; he should not have used a knife; he should have been more cautious and only bound and gagged the dealer, and not killed him; he should have been more bold and killed the servant also; he should have done all things otherwise; poignant regrets, weary, incessant toiling of the mind to change what was unchangeable, to plan what was now useless, to be the architect of the irrevocable past. Meanwhile, and behind all this activity, brute terrors, like the scurrying of rats in a deserted attic, filled the more remote chambers of his brain with riot; the hand of the constable would fall heavy on his shoulder, and his nerves would jerk like a hooked fish; or he beheld, in galloping defile, the dock, the prison, the gallows, and the black coffin.

Terror of the people in the street sat down before his mind like a besieging army. It was impossible, he thought, but that some rumour of the struggle must have reached their ears and set on edge their curiosity; and now, in all the neighboring houses, he divined them sitting motionless and with uplifted ear—solitary people, condemned to spend Christmas dwelling alone on memories of the past, and now startlingly recalled from that tender exercise; happy family parties, struck into silence round the table, the mother still with raised finger: every degree and age and humour, but all, by their own hearths, prying and hearkening and weaving the rope that was to hang him. Sometimes it seemed to him he could not move too softly; the clink of the tall Bohemian goblets rang out loudly like a bell; and alarmed by the bigness of the ticking, he was tempted to stop the clocks. And then, again, with a swift transition of his terrors, the very silence of the place appeared a source of peril, and a thing to strike and freeze the passer-by; and he would step more boldly, and bustle aloud among the contents of the shop and imitate, with elaborate bravado, the movements of a busy man at ease in his own house.

But he was now so pulled about by different alarms that, while one portion of his mind was still alert and cunning, another trembled on the brink of lunacy. One hallucination in particular took a strong hold on his credulity. The neighbour hearkening with white face beside his window, the passer-by arrested by a horrible surmise on the pavement—these could at worst suspect, they could not know; through the brick walls and shuttered windows only sounds could penetrate. But here, within the house, was he alone? He knew he was; he had watched the servant set forth sweethearting, in her poor best, "out for the day" written in every ribbon and smile. Yes, he was alone, of course; and yet, in the bulk of an empty house above him, he could surely hear a stir of delicate footing—he was surely conscious, inexplicably conscious of some presence. Ay, surely; to every room and corner of the house his imagination followed it; and now it was a faceless thing, and yet had eyes to see with; and again it was a shadow of himself; and yet again behold the image of the dead dealer, reinspired with cunning and hatred.

At times, with a strong effort, he would glance at the open door which still seemed to repel his eyes. The house was tall, the skylight small and dirty, the day blind with fog; and the light that filtered down to the ground story was exceedingly faint, and showed dimly on the threshold of the shop. And yet, in that strip of doubtful brightness, did there not hang wavering a shadow?

Suddenly, from the street outside, a very jovial gentleman began to beat with a staff on the shop door, accompanying his blows with shouts and railleries in which the dealer was continually called upon by name. Markheim, smitten into ice, glanced at the dead man. But no! He lay quite still; he was fled away far beyond earshot of these blows and shoutings; he was sunk beneath the seas of silence; and his name, which would once have caught his notice above the howling of a storm, had become an empty sound. And presently the jovial gentleman desisted from his knocking and departed.

Here was a broad hint to hurry what remained to be done, to get forth from this accusing neighbourhood, to plunge into a bath of London multitudes, and to reach, on the other side of day, that haven of safety and apparent innocence—his bed. One visitor had come: at any moment another might follow and be more obstinate. To have done the deed, and yet not reap the profit, would be too abhorrent a failure. The money, that was now Markheim's concern; and as a means to that, the keys.

He glanced over his shoulder at the open door, where the shadow was still lingering and shivering; and with no conscious repugnance of the mind, yet with a tremor of the belly, he drew near the body of his victim. The human character had quite departed. Like a suit half-stuffed with bran, the limbs lay scattered, the trunk doubled, on the

floor; and yet the thing repelled him. Although so dingy and inconsiderable to the eye, he feared it might have more significance to the touch. He took the body by the shoulders and turned it on its back. It was strangely light and supple, and the limbs, as if they had been broken, fell into the oddest postures. The face was robbed of all expression; but it was as pale as wax, and shockingly smeared with blood about one temple. That was, for Markheim, the one displeasing circumstance. It carried him back, upon the instant, to a certain fair-day in a fishers' village; a grey day, a piping wind, a crowd upon the street, the blare of brasses, the booming of drums, the nasal voice of a ballad singer; and a boy going to and fro, buried over head in the crowd and divided between interest and fear, until, coming out on the chief place of concourse, he beheld a booth and a great screen with pictures, dismally designed, garishly coloured: Brownrigg with her apprentice, the Mannings with their murdered guest; Weare in the death-grip of Thurtell; and a score besides of famous crimes. The thing was as clear as an illusion; he was once again that little boy; he was looking once again, and with the same sense of physical revolt, at these vile pictures; he was still stunned by the thumping of the drums. A bar of that day's music returned upon his memory; and at that, for the first time, a qualm came over him, a breath of nausea, a sudden weakness of the joints, which he must instantly resist and conquer.

He judged it more prudent to confront than to flee from these considerations; looking the more hardily in the dead face, bending his mind to realise the nature and greatness of his crime. So little a while ago that face had moved with every change of sentiment, that pale mouth had spoken, that body had been all on fire with governable energies; and now, and by his act, that piece of life had been arrested, as the horologist, with interjected finger, arrests the beating of the clock. So he reasoned in vain; he could rise to no more remorseful consciousness; the same heart which had shuddered before the painted effigies of crime, looked on its reality unmoved. At best, he felt a gleam of pity for one who had been endowed in vain with all those faculties that can make the world a garden of enchantment, one who had never lived and who was now dead. But of penitence, no, not a tremor.

With that, shaking himself clear of these considerations, he found the keys and advanced towards the open door of the shop. Outside, it had begun to rain smartly; and the sound of the shower upon the roof had banished silence. Like some dripping cavern, the chambers of the house were haunted by an incessant echoing, which filled the ear and mingled with the ticking of the clocks. And, as Markheim approached the door, he seemed to hear, in answer to his own cautious tread, the steps of another foot withdrawing up the stair. The shadow still palpitated loosely on the threshold. He threw a ton's weight of resolve upon his muscles, and drew back the door.

The faint, foggy daylight glimmered dimly on the bare floor and stairs; on the bright suit of armour posted, halbert in hand, upon the landing; and on the dark wood-carvings and framed pictures that hung against the yellow panels of the wainscot. So loud was the beating of the rain through all the house, that, in Markheim's ears, it began to be distinguished into many sounds. Footsteps and sighs, the tread of regiments marching in the distance, the chink of money in the counting, and the creaking of doors held stealthily ajar, appeared to mingle with the patter of drops upon the cupola and the gushing of the water in the pipes. The sense that he was not alone grew upon him to the verge of madness. On every side he was haunted and begirt by presences.

He heard them moving in the upper chambers; from the shop, he heard the dead man getting to his legs; and as he began with a great effort to mount the stairs, feet fled quietly before him and followed stealthily behind. If he were but deaf, he thought, how tranquilly he would possess his soul! And then again, and hearkening with ever fresh attention, he blessed himself for that unresting sense which held the outposts and stood a trusty sentinel upon his life. His head turned continually on his neck; his eyes, which seemed starting from their orbits, scouted on every side, and on every side were half-rewarded as with the tail of something nameless vanishing. The four-and-twenty steps to the first floor were four-and-twenty agonies.

On that first story the doors stood ajar, three of them like three ambushes, shaking his nerves like the throats of cannon. He could never again, he felt, be sufficiently immured and fortified from men's observing eyes; he longed to be home, girt in by walls, buried among bedclothes, and invisible to all but God. And at that thought he wondered a little, recollecting tales of other murderers and the fear they were said to entertain of heavenly avengers. It was not so, at least, with him. He feared the laws of nature, lest in their callous and immutable procedure they should preserve some damning evidence of his crime. He feared tenfold more, with a slavish, superstitious terror, some scission in the continuity of man's experience, some willful illegality of nature. He played a game of skill, depending on the rules, calculating consequence from cause; and what if nature, as the defeated tyrant overthrew the chessboard, should break the mould of their succession? The like had befallen Napoleon (so writers said) when the winter chanted the time of its appearance. The like might befall Markheim; the solid walls might become transparent and reveal his doings like those of bees in a glass hive; the stout planks might yield under his foot like quicksands and detain him in their clutch; ay, and there were soberer accidents that might destroy him; if, for instance, the house should fall and imprison him beside the body of his victim; or the house next door should fly on fire, and the firemen invade him from all sides. These things he feared; and, in a sense, these things might be called the hands of God reached forth against sin. But about God Himself he was at ease; his act was doubtless exceptional, but so were his excuses, which God knew; it was there, and not among men, that he felt sure of justice.

When he had got safe into the drawing-room and shut the door behind him, he was aware of a respite from alarms. The room was quite dismantled, uncarpeted besides, and strewn with packing-cases and incongruous furniture; several great pier glasses, in which he beheld himself at various angles, like an actor on a stage; many pictures, framed and unframed, standing, with their faces to the wall; a fine Sheraton sideboard, a cabinet of marquetry, and a great old bed, with tapestry hangings. The windows opened to the floor; but by great good fortune the lower part of the shutters had been closed, and this concealed him from the neighbours. Here, then, Markheim drew in a packing-case before the cabinet and began to search among the keys. It was a long business, for there were many, and it was irksome, besides; for, after all, there might be nothing in the cabinet, and time was on the wing. But the closeness of the occupation sobered him. With the tail of his eye he saw the door—even glanced at it from time to time directly, like a besieged commander pleased to verify the good estate of his defences. But in truth he was at peace. The rain falling in the street sounded natural and pleasant. Presently, on the other side, the notes of a piano were wakened to the music of a hymn, and the voices of many children took up the air and words. How stately, how comfortable was the melody! How fresh the youthful voices! Markheim gave ear to it smilingly, as he sorted out the keys; and his mind was thronged with answerable ideas and images; church-going children and the pealing of the high organ; children afield, bathers by the brook-side, ramblers on the brambly common, kite-fliers in the windy and cloud-navigated sky; and then, at another cadence of the hymn, back again to church, and the somnolence of summer Sundays, and the high genteel voice of the parson (which he smiled a little to recall), and the painted Jacobean tombs, and the dim lettering of the Ten Commandments in the chancel.

And as he sat thus, at once busy and absent, he was startled to his feet. A flash of ice, a flash of fire, a bursting gush of blood, went over him, and then he stood transfixed and thrilling. A step mounted the stair slowly and steadily, and presently a hand was laid upon the knob, the lock clicked, and the door opened.

Fear held Markheim in a vise. What to expect he knew not, whether the dead man walking, or the official ministers of human justice, or some chance witness blindly stumbling in to consign him to the gallows. But when a face was thrust into the aperture, glanced around the room, looked at him, nodded and smiled as if in friendly recognition, and then withdrew again, and the door closed behind it, his fear broke loose from his control in a hoarse cry. At the sound of this the visitant returned.

"Did you call me?" he asked pleasantly, and with that he entered the room and closed the door behind him.

Markheim stood and gazed at him with all his eyes. Perhaps there was a film upon his sight, but the outlines of the newcomer seemed to change and waver like those of the idols in the wavering candlelight of the shop; and at times he thought he knew him; at times he thought he bore a likeness to himself; and always, like a lump of living terror, there lay in his bosom the conviction that this thing was not of the earth and not of God.

And yet the creature had a strange air of the commonplace, as he stood looking on Markheim with a smile; and when he added: "You are looking for the money, I believe?" it was in a tone of everyday politeness.

Markheim made no answer.

"I should warn you," resumed the other, "that the maid has left her sweetheart earlier than usual and will soon be here. If Mr. Markheim is to be found in this house, I need not describe to him the consequences."

"You know me?" cried the murderer.

The visitor smiled. "You have long been a favourite of mine," he said; "and I have long observed and often sought to help you."

"What are you?" cried Markheim: "the Devil?"

"What I many be," returned the other, "cannot affect the service I propose to render you."

"It can," cried Markheim; "it does! Be helped by you? No, never; not by you! You do not know me yet; thank God, you do not know me!"

"I know you," replied the visitant, with a sort of kind severity or rather firmness. "I know you to the soul."

"Know me!" cried Markheim. "What can do so? My life is but a travesty and slander on myself. I have lived to belie my nature. All men do; all men are better than this disguise that grows about and stifles them. You see each dragged away by life, like one whom bravos have seized and muffled in a cloak. If they had their own control—if you could see their faces, they would be altogether different, they would shine out for heroes and saints! I am worse than most; myself is more overlaid; my excuse is known to me and God. But, had I the time, I could disclose myself."

"To me?" inquired the visitant.

"To you before all," returned the murderer. "I supposed you were intelligent. I thought—since you exist—you would prove a reader of the heart. And you would propose to judge me by my acts! Think of it; my acts! I was born and I have lived in a land of giants; giants have dragged me by the wrists since I was born out of my mother—the giants of circumstance. And you would judge me by my acts! But can you not look within? Can you not understand that evil is hateful to me? Can you not see within me the clear writing of conscience, never blurred by any willful sophistry, although too often disregarded? Can you not read me for a thing that surely must be as common as humanity—the unwilling sinner?"

"All this is very feelingly expressed," was the reply, "but it regards me not. These points of consistency are beyond my province, and I care not in the least by what compulsion you may have been dragged away, so as you are but carried in the right direction. But time flies; the servant delays, looking in the faces of the crowd and at the pictures on the hoardings, but still she keeps moving nearer; and remember, it is as if the gallows itself was striding towards you though the Christmas streets! Shall I help you; I, who know all? Shall I tell you where to find the money?"

"For what price?" asked Markheim.

"I offer you the service as a Christmas gift," returned the other.

Markheim could not refrain from smiling with a kind of bitter triumph. "No," said he, "I will take nothing at your hands; if I were dying of thirst, and it was your hand that put the pitcher to my lips, I should find the courage to refuse. I may be credu-

lous, but I will do nothing to commit myself to evil."

"I have no objection to a death-bed repentance," observed the visitant.

"Because you disbelieve their efficacy!" Markheim cried.

"I do not say so," returned the other; "but I look on these things from a different side, and when the life is done my interest falls. The man has lived to serve me, to spread black looks under the cover of religion, or to sow tares in the wheatfield, as you do, in a course of weak compliance with desire. Now that he draws so near to his deliverance, he can add but one act of service—to repent, to die smiling, and thus to build up in confidence and hope the more timorous of my surviving followers. I am not so hard a master. Try me. Accept my help. Please yourself in life as you have done hitherto; please yourself more amply, spread your elbows at the board; and when the night begins to fall and the curtains to be drawn, I tell you, for your greater comfort, that you will find it even easy to compound your quarrel with your conscience, and to make a truckling peace with God. I came but now from such a death-bed, and the room was full of sincere mourners, listening to the man's last words: and when I looked into that face, which had been set as a flint against mercy, I found it smiling with hope."

"And do you, then, suppose me such a creature?" asked Markheim. "Do you think I have no more generous aspirations than to sin, and sin, and sin, and at the last sneak into heaven? My heart rises at the thought. Is this, then, your experience of mankind? Or is it because you find me with red hands that you presume such baseness? And is this crime of murder indeed so impious as to dry up the very springs of good?"

"Murder is to me no special category," replied the other. "All sins are murder, even as all life is war. I behold your race, like starving mariners on a raft, plucking crusts out of the hands of famine and feeding on each other's lives. I follow sins beyond the moment of their acting; I find in all that the last consequence is death; and to my eyes, the pretty maid who thwarts her mother with such taking graces on a question of a ball, drips no less visibly with human gore than such a murderer as yourself. Do I say that I follow sins? I follow virtues also; they differ not by the thickness of a nail, they are both scythes for the reaping angel of Death. Evil, for which I live, consists not in action but in character. The bad man is dear to me; not the bad act, whose fruits, if we could follow them far enough down the hurtling cataract of the ages, might yet be found more blessed than those of the rarest virtues. And it is not because you have killed a dealer, but because you are Markheim, that I offer to forward your escape."

"I will lay my heart open to you," answered Markheim. "This crime on which you find me is my last. On my way to it I have learned many lessons; itself is a lesson, a momentous lesson. Hitherto I have been driven with revolt to what I would not; I was a bond-slave to poverty, driven and scourged. There are robust virtues that can stand in these temptations; mine was not so: I had a thirst of pleasure. But today, and out of this deed, I pluck both warning and riches—both the power and a fresh resolve to be myself. I become in all things a free actor in the world; I begin to see myself all changed, these hands the agents of good, this heart at peace. Something comes over me out of the past; something of what I have dreamed on Sabbath evenings to the sound of the church organ, of what I forecast when I shed tears over noble books, or talked, an innocent child, with my mother. There lies my life; I have wandered a few years, but now I see once more my city of destination."

"You are to use this money on the Stock Exchange, I think?" remarked the visitor; "and there, if I mistake not, you have already lost some thousands?"

"Ah," said Markheim, "but this time I have a sure thing."

"This time, again, you will lose," replied the visitor quietly.

"Ah, but I keep back the half!" cried Markheim.

"That also you will lose," said the other.

The sweat started upon Markheim's brow. "Well, then, what matter?" he exclaimed. "Say it be lost, say I am plunged again in poverty, shall one part of me, and that the worse, continue until the end to override the better? Evil and good run strong in me, haling me both ways. I do not love the one thing, I love all. I can conceive great deeds, renunciations, martyrdoms; and though I be fallen to such a crime as murder, pity is no stranger to my thoughts. I pity the poor; who knows their trials better than myself? I pity and help them; I prize love, I love honest laughter; there is no good thing nor true thing on earth but I love it from my heart. And are my vices only to direct my life, and my virtues to lie without effect, like some passive lumber of the mind? Not so; good, also, is a spring of acts."

But the visitant raised his finger. "For six-and-thirty years that you have been in this world," said he, "through many changes of fortune and varieties of humor, I have  watched you steadily fall. Fifteen years ago you would have started at a theft. Three years ago you would have blenched at the name of murder. Is there any crime, is there any cruelty or meanness, from which you still recoil? Five years from now I shall detect you in the fact! Downward, downward, lies your way; nor can anything but death avail to stop you."

"It is true," Markheim said huskily, "I have in some degree complied with evil. But it is so with all; the very saints, in the mere exercise of living, grow less dainty, and take on the tone of their surroundings."

"I will propound to you one simple question," said the other; "and as you answer, I shall read to you your moral horoscope. You have grown in many things more lax; possibly you do right to be so; and at any account it is the same with all men. But granting that, are you in any one particular, however trifling, more difficult to please with your own conduct, or do you go in all things with a looser rein?"

"In any one?" repeated Markheim, with an anguish of consideration. "No," he added with despair, "in none! I have gone down in all!"

"Then," said the visitor, "content yourself with what you are, for you will never change; and the words of your part on this stage are irrevocably written down."

Markheim stood for a long while silent, and indeed it was the visitor who first broke the silence. "That being so," he said, "shall I show you the money?"

"And grace?" cried Markheim.

"Have you not tried it?" returned the other. "Two or three years ago, did I not see you on the platform of revival meetings, and was not your voice the loudest in the hymn?"

"It is true," said Markheim, "and I see clearly what remains for me by way of duty. I thank you for these lessons from my soul; my eyes are opened, and I behold myself at last for what I am."

At this moment the sharp note of the doorbell rang through the house; and the visitant, as though this were some concerted signal for which he had been waiting, changed at once in his demeanor.

"The maid!" he cried. "She has returned, as I forewarned you, and there is before you one more difficult passage. Her master, you must say, is ill; you must let her in, with an assured but rather serious countenance—no smiles, no overacting—and I promise you success! Once the girl is within, and the door closed, the same dexterity that has already rid you of the dealer will relieve you of this last danger in your path. Thenceforward you have the whole evening—the whole night, if needed—to ransack the treasures of the house and to make good your safety. This is help that comes to you with the mask of danger. Up!" he cried; "up, friend; your life hangs trembling in the scales; up, and act!"

Markheim steadily regarded his counsellor. "If I be condemned to evil acts," he said, "there is still one door of freedom open—I can cease action. If my life be an ill thing, I can lay it down. Though I be, as you say truly, at the beck of every small temptation, I can yet, by one decisive gesture, place myself beyond the reach of all. My love of good is damned to barrenness; it may, and let it be! But I have still my hatred of evil; and from that, to your galling disappointment, you shall see that I can draw both energy and courage."

The features of the visitor began to undergo a wonderful and lovely change: they brightened and softened with a tender triumph, and, even as they brightened, faded and dislimned. But Markheim did not pause to watch or understand this transformation. He opened the door and went downstairs very slowly, thinking to himself. His past went soberly before him; he beheld it as it was, ugly and strenuous like a dream, random as a chance-medley—a scene of defeat. Life, as he thus reviewed it, tempted him no longer; but on the farther side her perceived a quiet haven for his bark. He paused in the passage and looked into the shop, where the candle still burned by the dead body. It was strangely silent. Thoughts of the dealer swarmed into his mind as he stood gazing. And then the bell once more broke out

into impatient clamour.

He confronted the maid upon the threshold with something like a smile.

"You had better go for the police," said he: "I have killed your master."

A LETTER FROM SANTA CLAUS
Mark Twain

Clement Moore was not the only father who dabbled in Christmas writings to please his children. The father of young Susie Clemens, Samuel Langhorne Clemens (a.k.a. Mark Twain), once took pen in hand to craft an unforgettable Christmas offering.

Palace of St. Nicholas In the Moon
Christmas Morning

MY DEAR SUSIE CLEMENS:

I have received and read all the letters which you and your little sister have written me by the hand of your mother and your nurses; I have also read those which you little people have written me with your own hands—for although you did not use any characters that are in grown people's alphabet, you used the characters that all children in all lands on earth and in the twinkling stars use; and as all my subjects in the moon are children and use no character but that, you will easily understand that I can read your and your baby sister's jagged and fantastic marks without any trouble at all. But I had trouble with those letters which you dictated through your mother and the nurses, for I am a foreigner and cannot read English writing well. You will find that I made no mistakes about the things which you and the baby ordered in your own letters—I went down your chimney at midnight when you were asleep and delivered them all myself—and kissed both of you, too, because you are good children, well trained, nice mannered, and about the most obedient little people I ever saw. But in the letter which you dictated there were some words which I could not make out for certain, and one or two small orders which I could not fill because we ran out of stock. Our last lot of kitchen furniture for dolls has just gone to a very poor little child in the North Star away up in the cold country above the Big Dipper. Your mama can show you that star and you will say: "Little Snow Flake" (for that is the child's name), "I'm glad you got that furniture, for you need it more than I." That is, you must *write* that, with your own hand, and Snow Flake will write you an answer. If you only spoke it she wouldn't hear you. Make your letter light and thin, for the distance is great and the postage very heavy.

There was a word or two in your mama's letter which I couldn't be certain of. I took it to be "a trunk full of doll's clothes." Is that it? I will call at your kitchen door about nine o'clock to inquire. But I must not see anybody and I must not speak to anybody but you. When the kitchen doorbell rings, George must be blindfolded and sent to open the door. Then he must go back to the dining room or the china closet and take the cook with him. You must tell George he must walk on tiptoe and not speak—otherwise he will die someday. Then you must go up to the nursery and stand on a chair or the nurse's bed and put your ear to the speaking tube that leads down to the kitchen and when I whistle through it you must speak in the tube and say, "Welcome, Santa Claus!" Then I will ask whether it was a trunk you ordered or not. If you say it was, I shall ask you what *color* you want the trunk to be.

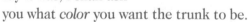

Your mama will help you to name a nice color and then you must tell me every single thing in detail which you want the trunk to contain. Then when I say "Good-by and a merry Christmas to my little Susie Clemens," you must say "Good-by, good old Santa Claus, I thank you very much and please tell that little Snow Flake I will look at her star tonight and she must look down here—I will be right in the west bay window; and every fine night I will look at her star and say, 'I know somebody up there and *like*

her, too.'" Then you must go down into the library and make George close all the doors that open into the main hall, and everybody must keep still for a little while. I will go to the moon and get those things and in a few minutes I will come down the chimney that belongs to the fireplace that is in the hall—if it is a trunk you want—because I couldn't get such a thing as a trunk down the nursery chimney, you know.

People may talk if they want, until they hear my footsteps in the hall. Then you tell them to keep quiet a little while till I go back up the chimney. Maybe you will not hear my footsteps at all—so you may go now and then and peep through the dining-room doors, and by and by you will see that thing which you want, right under the piano in the drawing room—for I shall put it there.

If I should leave any snow in the hall, you must tell George to sweep it into the fireplace, for I haven't time to do such things. George must not use a broom, but a rag—else he will die someday. You must watch George and not let him run into danger. If my boot should leave a stain on the marble, George must not holystone it away. Leave it there always in memory of my visit; and whenever you look at it or show it to anybody you must let it remind you to be a good little girl. Whenever you are naughty and somebody points to that mark which your good old Santa Claus's boot made on the marble, what will you say, little sweetheart?

Good-by for a few minutes, till I come down to the world and ring the kitchen doorbell.

Your loving SANTA CLAUS
Whom people sometimes call "The Man in the Moon"

FROM
THE GOSPEL ACCORDING TO ST. LUKE

The four Gospels can be divided into various categories. There are Matthew, Mark, and Luke, which are known collectively as the Synoptics (from the Greek for "same eye," meaning that the essential source material is an oral tradition distinct from that of John). Of the three Synoptic gospels, only Matthew and Luke include Nativity stories. And of these two, it is Luke's account that is perhaps most beloved, with its focus on the humble manger birth, the gathering of shepherds and angels, and the enduring message of peace on earth.

AND IT CAME TO PASS in those days, that there went out a decree from Caesar Augustus, that all the world should be taxed. (And this taxing was first made when Cyre'-ni-us was governor of Syria.)

And all went to be taxed, every one into his own city. And Joseph also went up from Galilee, out of the city of Nazareth, into Judea, unto the city of David, which is called Beth-lehem; (because he was of the house and lineage of David:) to be taxed with Mary his espoused wife, being great with child.

And so it was, that, while they were there, the days  were accomplished that she should be delivered. And she brought forth her first-born son, and wrapped him in swaddling clothes, and laid him in a manger; because there was no room for them in the inn.

And there were in the same country shepherds abiding in the field, keeping watch over their flock at night. And, lo, the angel of the Lord came upon them, and the glory of the Lord shone round about them: and they were sore afraid.

And the angel said unto them, "Fear not: for, behold, I bring you good tidings of great joy, which shall be to all people. For unto you is born this day in the city of David a Saviour, which is Christ the Lord. And this shall be a sign unto you; Ye shall find the babe wrapped in swaddling clothes, lying in a manger."

And suddenly there was with the angel a multitude of the heavenly host praising God, and saying, "Glory to God in the highest, and on earth peace, good will toward men."

And it came to pass, as the angels were gone away from them into heaven, the shepherds said one to another, "Let us now go even unto Beth-lehem, and see this thing which is come to pass, which the Lord hath made known unto us."

And they came with haste, and found Mary, and Joseph, and the babe lying in a manger. And when they had seen it they made known abroad the saying which was told them concerning this child. And all they that heard it wondered at those things which were told them by the shepherds.

But Mary kept all these things, and pondered them in her heart. And the shepherds returned, glorifying and praising God for all the things that they had heard and seen, as it was told unto them.

FROM
THE GOSPEL ACCORDING TO ST. MATTHEW

Often, what is most surprising about the Gospel accounts of Christ's birth is what they do not contain. The Gospel of Matthew, for instance, is the undeniable source for the "Three Kings of Orient" long celebrated in song—and yet it makes no mention of any king other than Herod, and it does not specify any particular number of men following the "star in the east." The reverence and devotion of these figures, however, is what probably what leaves the most indelible impression in this story of the birth of Christ.

Now when Jesus was born in Bethlehem of Judea in the days of Herod the king, behold, there came Wise Men from the east to Jerusalem, saying, "Where is he that is born King of the Jews? For we have seen his star in the east, and are come to worship him."

When Herod the king had heard these things, he was troubled, and all Jerusalem with him. And when he had gathered all the chief priests and scribes of the people together, he demanded of them where Christ should be born. And they said unto him, "In Bethlehem of Judea: for thus it is written by the prophet, 'And thou Beth-lehem, in the land of Judah, art not the least among the princes of Judah: for out of thee shall come a Governor, that shall rule my people Israel.'"

Then Herod, when he had privily called the Wise Men, inquired of them diligently what time the star appeared. And he sent them to Bethlehem, and said, "Go and search diligently for the young child; and when ye have found him, bring me word again, that I may come and worship him also."

When they had heard the king, they departed; and, lo, the star, which they saw in the east, went before them, till it came and stood over where the young child was. When they saw the star, they rejoiced with exceeding great joy. And when they were come into the house, they saw the young child with

Mary his mother, and fell down, and worshiped him: and when they had opened their treasures, they presented unto him gifts: gold, and frankincense, and myrrh. And being warned of God in a dream that they should not return to Herod, they departed into their own country another way.

And when they were departed, behold, the angel of the Lord appeareth to Joseph in a dream, saying, "Arise, and take the young child and his mother, and flee into Egypt, and be thou there until I bring thee word: for Herod will seek the young child to destroy him." When he arose, he took the young child and his mother by night, and departed into Egypt.

CHAPTER FOUR

CHRISTMAS POETRY

From William Shakespeare to Robert Frost, some of the most important poets in history have written about Christmas. In this chapter you'll find some of the most unforgettable verse ever written in the holiday spirit. Whether you choose to read the selections aloud or enjoy them privately, you're sure to get a big dose of the spirit of the season!

THE HOLLY AND THE IVY

Traditional

In English lore, holly and ivy were often personified as male and female, which made them popular topics for carols. In the words to this carol, however, the holly represents the Virgin Mary, while the berry stands for the infant Jesus.

The holly and the ivy,
When they are both full grown,
Of all the trees that are in the wood,
The holly bears the crown.

The rising of the sun,
And the running of the deer,
The playing of the merry organ,
Sweet singing in the choir.

The holly bears a blossom
As white as the lily flower,
And Mary bore sweet Jesus Christ
To be our sweet savior.

The holly bears a berry
As red as any blood,
And Mary bore sweet Jesus Christ
To do poor sinners good.

The holly bears a prickle
As sharp as any thorn
And Mary bore sweet Jesus Christ
On Christmas day in the morn.

The holly bears a bark
As bitter as any gall,
And Mary bore sweet Jesus Christ
For to redeem us all.

The holly and the ivy,
When they are both full grown,
Of all the trees that are in the wood
The holly bears the crown.

MERRY CHRISTMAS, EVERYONE! ❧
Anonymous

The author of this poem is, alas, unknown. Simple and beautiful, "Merry Christmas, Everyone!" provides a memorable picture of childhood innocence and anticipation at Christmas time.

In the rush of the merry morning,
When the red burns through the gray,
And the wintry world lies waiting
For the glory of the day,
Then we hear a fitful rushing
Just without, upon the stair,
See two white phantoms coming,
Catch the gleam of sunny hair.

Rosy feet upon the threshold,
Eager faces peeping through,
With the first red ray of sunshine
Chanting cherubs come in view;
Mistletoe and gleaming holly,
Symbols of a blessed day,
In their chubby hands they carry,
Streaming all along the way.

Well we know them, never weary
Of their innocent surprise;
Waiting, watching, listening always
With full hearts and tender eyes,
While our little household angels,
White and golden in the Sun.
Greet us with the sweet old welcome—
"Merry Christmas, everyone!"

MISTLETOE ❧
Walter De La Mare

In years past, mistletoe was not just an excuse for kissing—it was also considered to bring good luck. While mistletoe can be found adorning the doorways of many a would-be lover, it has historically been prohibited from church premises because of its status as an old world "charm."

Sitting under the mistletoe
(Pale-green, fairy mistletoe),
One last candle burning low,
All the sleepy dancers gone,
Just one candle burning on,
Shadows lurking everywhere:
Some one came, and kissed me there.

Tired I was; my head would go
Nodding under the mistletoe
(Pale-green, fairy mistletoe),
No footsteps came, no voice, but only,
Just as I sat there, sleepy, lonely,
Stooped in the still and shadowy air
Lips unseen—and kissed me there.

CHRISTMAS TREES

Robert Frost

*R*obert Frost, perhaps the single most popular American poet, gained a worldwide audience by writing about nature and life in the country. It seems inevitable that he would choose to write a poem about the Christmas tree. His offering is a subtle exploration of the tension between commercialism and the natural way of life.

The city had withdrawn into itself
And left at last the country to the country;
When between whirls of snow not come to lie
And whirls of foliage not yet laid, there drove
A stranger to our yard, who looked the city,
Yet did in country fashion in that there
He sat and waited till he drew us out,
A-buttoning coats, to ask him who he was.
He proved to be the city come again
To look for something it had left behind
And could not do without and keep its Christmas.
He asked if I would sell my Christmas trees;
My woods—the young fir balsams like a place
Where houses all are churches and have spires.
I hadn't thought of them as Christmas trees.
I doubt if I was tempted for a moment
To sell them off their feet to go in cars
And leave the slope behind the house all bare,
Where the sun shines now no warmer than the
    moon.
I'd hate to have them know it if I was.
Yet more I'd hate to hold my trees except
As others hold theirs or refuse for them,

Beyond the time of profitable
    growth,
The trial by market everything must come to.
I dallied so much with the thought of selling.
Then whether from mistaken courtesy
And fear of seeming short of speech, or whether
From hope of hearing good of what was mine,
I said, "There aren't enough to be worth while."
"I could soon tell how many they would cut,
You let me look them over."

                        "You could look.
But don't expect I'm going to let you have them."
Pasture they spring in, some in clumps too close
That lop each other of boughs, but not a few
Quite solitary and having equal boughs
All round and round. The latter he nodded "Yes" to,
Or paused to say beneath some lovelier one,
With a buyer's moderation, "That would do."
I thought so, too, but wasn't there to say so.
We climbed the pasture on the south, crossed
    over,
And came down on the north.

                        He said, "A thousand."

"A thousand Christmas trees!—at what apiece?"

He felt some need of softening that to me:
"A thousand trees would come to thirty dollars."

Then I was certain I had never meant
To let him have them. Never show surprise!
But thirty dollars seemed so small beside
The extent of pasture I should strip, three cents
(For that was all they figured out apiece),
Three cents so small beside the dollar friends
I should be writing to within the hour
Would pay in cities for good trees like those,

Regular vestry trees whole Sunday
    Schools
Could hang enough on to pick off enough.

A thousand Christmas trees I didn't know I had!
Worth three cents more to give away than sell
As may be shown by a simple calculation.
Too bad I couldn't lay one in a letter.
I can't help wishing I could send you one,
In wishing you herewith a Merry Christmas.

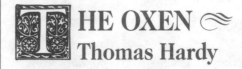

THE OXEN
Thomas Hardy

Though most of his work focuses on the doings of characters in the fictitious Wessex county, Thomas Hardy also wrote on the subject of Christmas. In "The Oxen," Hardy puts to verse a centuries-old legend: that at midnight on the eve of Christ's birth, and every Christmas Eve thereafter, the oxen fall to their knees in honor of the Lord.

Christmas Eve, and twelve of the clock.
    "Now they are all on their knees,"
An elder said as we sat in a flock
    By the embers in hearthside ease.

We pictured the meek mild creatures where
    They dwelt in their strawy pen,
Nor did it occur to one of us there
    To doubt they were kneeling then.

So fair a fancy few would weave
    In these years! Yet, I feel,
If someone said on Christmas Eve,
    "Come; see the oxen kneel

"In the lonely barton by yonder coomb
        Our childhood used to know,"
I should go with him in the gloom,
        Hoping it might be so.

CEREMONIES FOR CHRISTMAS 〜

Robert Herrick

Robert Herrick was part of a popular group of seventeenth-century English writers that came to be known as "The Cavalier Poets," but his early career lay with the clergy. The ceremonies he describes in this poem are part of the older, more robust English Christmas that was commonplace before the Puritan rule. The line "With last year's brand light the new block" refers to the custom of saving a piece of the Yule log to use in lighting the next year's log. Though not widely practiced today, the customs Herrick recalls remain a cherished part of a classic Old English Christmas.

Come, bring with a noise,
My merry, merry boys,
The Christmas log to the firing;
While my good dame, she
Bids ye all be free;
And drink to your heart's desiring.

With the last year's brand
Light the new block, and
For good success in his spending,
On your psalteries play,
That sweet luck may
Come while the log is a-tending.

Drink now the strong beer,
Cut the white loaf here,
The while the meat is shredding;
For the rare mince-pie
And the plums stand by
To fill the paste that's a-kneading.

POEMS FOR CHRISTMAS

Marie Irish

Marie Irish specialized in poems, songs, and plays for children to perform at Christmas time. Here are a few examples of her delightful work.

Christmas Lights

Bright Christmas stars shine on high,
Golden stars in the wint'ry sky;
Christmas candles in windows bright
Send a greeting into the night;
While in our hearts the Christmas flame,
Glows with a love like His who came,
The infant Christ of lowly birth,
To bring good will and peace to earth.

Merry Christmas

I like Christmas day,
With its wreaths of holly,
I like Santa Claus
With his smile so jolly;
I like the Christmas tree,
Shining straight and tall,
And my pretty presents,
I surely like them all.
I like the smiles and cheer,
And how I like to hear
The happy people say
"Merry Christmas" in such a pleasant way.

The Merry Day

Mother Nature robes herself
In her snowy gown of white,
Father Winter scatters frost
That glistens with a sparkling light.

Old December lags along
With reluctant footsteps slow,
Until Miss Christmas comes at last,
With the jolliest hours we know.

Santa Claus, the bountiful,
Helps her in his lavish way—
December, Christmas, Santa Claus,
O, what a merry, merry day!

Christmas Secrets

Think of the thousands of secrets
That are tucked securely away,
All sorts of wonderful secrets
To be revealed on Christmas day.

Secrets large and secrets small,
Secrets short and secrets tall,
Secrets thick and secrets thin—
Won't the folks who get them grin?

There are secrets flat on their backs.
There are others hanging up high,
Some are standing smack on their heads,
Some in pitchy-black corners lie.

Secrets round and secrets square,
Secrets dark and secrets fair,
Secrets sour and secrets sweet,
Secrets to wear and secrets to eat.

And if all these secrets were one,
And laid out on a long, long shelf,
I think it would surely surprise
Dear old jolly Santa himself.

CHRISTMAS— 1863

Henry Wadsworth Longfellow

Although describing a specific Christmas during the Civil War, Longfellow stresses in this poem a theme that is pertinent to every era: Even though life is full of hardship, the goodness of God will always prevail.

I hear the bells on Christmas day
The old familiar carols play,
And wild and sweet,
The words repeat
Of peace on earth, good-will to men.

Then from each black, accursed mouth
The cannon thundered in the South;
And with that sound
The carols drowned
Of peace on earth, good-will to men.

It was as if an earthquake rent
The hearthstones of a continent,
And made forlorn
The household born
Of peace on earth, good-will to men.

And in despair I bowed my head,
"There is no peace on earth," I said,
"For hate is strong
And mocks the song
Of peace on earth, good-will to men."

Then pealed the bells more loud and deep;
"God is not dead, nor doth He sleep;
The Wrong shall fail,
The Right prevail,
With peace on earth, good-will to men."

A VISIT FROM ST. NICHOLAS ('TWAS THE NIGHT BEFORE CHRISTMAS) ∽
Clement C. Moore

On Christmas Eve, 1822, Dr. Clement Clarke Moore unveiled what is arguably the most popular Christmas poem of all time, "A Visit from Saint Nicholas." Also known as "The Night Before Christmas," the poem was written strictly for the enjoyment of Moore's children, but a listener present at the reading was impressed enough to send the poem to The Troy Sentinel, where it was published the following December. Moore, a professor of Biblical Learning at the New York General Theological Seminary, liked to dabble in rhymes and poetry, but was too embarrassed by "A Visit" to take public credit for it. The poem was published anonymously until 1844 when Moore, presumably encouraged by the poem's success, included it in a collection of his other works.

'Twas the night before Christmas, when all
    through the house
Not a creature was stirring, not even a mouse;
The stockings were hung by the chimney with
    care,
In hopes that Saint Nicholas soon would be there;

The children were nestled all snug in their beds,
While visions of sugarplums danced in their heads;
And Mama in her kerchief, and I in my cap,
Had just settled our brains for a long winter's
    nap—

When out on the lawn there arose
    such a clatter,
I sprang from my bed to see what was the matter.
Away to the window I flew like a flash,

Tore open the shutters and threw up the sash.

The moon on the breast of the new-fallen snow
Gave a lustre of midday to objects below;
When what to my wondering eyes should appear,
But a miniature sleigh and eight tiny reindeer,

With a little old driver, so lively and quick
I knew in a moment it must be Saint Nick!
More rapid than eagles his coursers they came,
And he whistled and shouted and called them by
    name:

"Now, Dasher! now, Dancer! now, Prancer and
    Vixen!
On, Comet! on, Cupid! on, Donder and Blitzen!
To the top of the porch, to the top of the wall!
Now dash away, dash away, dash away all!"

As dry leaves that before the wild
    hurricane fly,
When they meet with an obstacle, mount
    to the sky,
So up to the housetops the coursers they flew,
With a sleigh full of toys—and Saint Nicholas, too.

And then in a twinkling I heard on the roof
The prancing and pawing of each little hoof.
As I drew in my head, and was turning around,
Down the chimney Saint Nicholas came with a
    bound.

He was dressed all in fur from his head to his foot,
And his clothes were all tarnished with ashes and
    soot;
A bundle of toys he had flung on his back,
And he looked like a peddler just opening his
    pack.

His eyes, how they twinkled! his dimples, how
    merry!
His cheeks were like roses, his nose like a cherry;
His droll little mouth was drawn up like a bow,
And the beard on his chin was as white as the
    snow.

The stump of a pipe he held tight in
    his teeth,
And the smoke it encircled his head like a
    wreath.
He had a broad face and a little round belly
That shook, when he laughed, like a bowl full of
    jelly.

He was chubby and plump—a right jolly old elf;
And I laughed, when I saw him, in spite of myself.
A wink of his eye and a twist of his head
Soon gave me to know I had nothing to dread.

He spoke not a word, but went straight to his
    work,
And filled all the stockings; then turned with a
    jerk,
And laying his finger aside of his nose,
And giving a nod, up the chimney he rose.

He sprang in his sleigh, to his team gave a whistle,
And away they all flew like the down of a thistle;
But I heard him exclaim, ere he drove out of sight:
"Happy Christmas to all, and to all a good-night!"

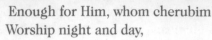

A CHRISTMAS CAROL

Christina Rossetti

Christina Rossetti is one of only a very few popular female poets of the nineteenth century. Her poem and the Dickens classic share not only a title, but also a reverence for Christmas and the spirit that surrounds it. The last stanza of this poem is often published alone under the title "My Gift." Whether excerpted or whole, the poem reminds us that it is the desire to give, and not the gift itself, that is the essence of the Christmas spirit.

In the bleak mid-winter
Frosty wind made moan,
Earth stood hard as iron,
Water like a stone;
Snow had fallen, snow on snow,
Snow on snow,
In the bleak mid-winter
Long ago.

Our God, Heaven cannot hold Him
Nor earth sustain;
Heaven and earth shall flee away
When He comes to reign;
In the bleak mid-winter
A stable-place sufficed
The Lord God Almighty
Jesus Christ.

Enough for Him, whom cherubim
Worship night and day,
A breastful of milk
And a mangerful of hay;
Enough for Him, whom angels
Fall down before,
The ox and ass and camel
Which adore.

Angels and archangels
May have gathered there,
Cherubim and seraphim
Thronged the air;
But only His mother
In her maiden bliss
Worshipped the Beloved
With a kiss.

What can I give Him
Poor as I am?
If I were a shepherd
I would bring a lamb,
If I were a Wise Man
I would do my part,—
Yet what I can I give Him,
Give my heart.

BIRD OF DAWNING ∾

William Shakespeare

What would a collection of Christmas literature be without a contribution from the Bard himself? This extract, from Act One, Scene One of Hamlet, conveys in a few brief lines the essential sacredness of the season.

Some say that ever 'gainst that season comes
Wherein our Saviour's birth is celebrated,
The bird of dawning singeth all
    night long;
And then, they say, no spirit
    dare stir abroad;
The nights are wholesome;
    then no planets strike,
No fairy takes, nor witch hath
    power to charm,
So hallow'd and so gracious is that time.

CHRISTMAS AT SEA ≈

Robert Louis Stevenson

Anyone who's ever had to spend a Christmas away from loved ones will be able to identify with the speaker in Stevenson's sea poem. Rich in atmosphere and powerful in its evocation of a sense of longing, "Christmas at Sea" reminds us not to take for granted the presence of those closest to us.

The sheets were frozen hard, and they cut the
    naked hand;
The decks were like a slide, where a seaman
    scarce could stand;
The wind was a nor'wester, blowing squally off the
    sea;
And cliffs and spouting breakers were the only
    things a-lee.

They heard the surf a-roaring before
    the break of day;
But 'twas only with the peep of light we saw how
    ill we lay.
We tumbled every hand on deck instanter, with a
    shout,
And we gave her the maintops'l, and stood by to
    go about.

All day we tacked and tacked between the South
    Head and the North;
All day we hauled the frozen sheets, and got no
    further forth;
All day as cold as charity, in bitter pain and dread,
For very life and nature we tacked from head to
    head.

We gave the South a wider berth, for there the
    tide race roared;
But every tack we made we brought the North
    Head close aboard:
So's we saw the cliffs and houses, and the breakers
    running high,
And the coastguard in his garden, with his glass
    against his eye.

The frost was on the village roofs as white as
    ocean foam;
The good red fires were burning in ev'ry longshore
    home;
The windows sparkled clear, and the chimneys
    volleyed out;
And I vow we sniffed the victuals as the vessel
    went about.

The bells upon the church were rung
with a mighty jovial cheer;
For it's just that I should tell you how (of
all the days in the year)
This day of our adversity was blessed Christmas
morn,
And the house above the coastguard's was the
house where I was born.

O well I saw the pleasant room, the pleasant faces
there,
My mother's silver spectacles, my father's silver
hair;
And well I saw the firelight, like a flight of homely
elves,
Go dancing round the china-plates that stand
upon the shelves.

And well I knew the talk they had, the talk that
was of me,
Of the shadow on the household and the son that
went to sea;
And O the wicked fool I seemed, in every kind of
way,
To be here and hauling frozen ropes on blessed
Christmas Day.

They lit the high sea-light, and the dark began to
fall.
"All hands to loose the topgallant sails," I heard
the captain call.
"By the Lord, she'll never stand it," our first mate,
Jackson, cried.
"It's the one way or the other, Mr. Jackson," he
replied.

She staggered to her bearings, but
the sails were new and good,
And the ship smelt up to windward just as
though she understood.
As the winter's day was ending, in the entry of the
night,
We cleared the weary headland, and passed below
the light.

And they heaved a mighty breath, every soul on
board but me,
As they saw her nose again pointing handsome
out to sea.
But all that I could think of, in the darkness and
the cold,
Was just that I was leaving home, and my folks
were getting old.

CHRISTMAS AND NEW YEAR BELLS ≈
Alfred, Lord Tennyson

Alfred, Lord Tennyson held the esteemed post of Poet Laureate of England from 1850 until his death in 1892. "Christmas and New Year Bells" recalls the importance bells hold to the celebration of the Yule: ringing out the old, and ringing in the new.

The time draws near the birth of Christ:
The moon is hid; the night is still;
The Christmas bells from hill to hill
Answer each other in the mist.

Four voices of four hamlets round,
From far and near, on mead and moor,
Swell out and fail, as if a door
Were shut between me and the sound:

Each voice four changes on the wind,
That now dilate, and now decrease,
Peace and goodwill, goodwill and peace,
Peace and goodwill, to all mankind.

This year I slept and woke with pain,
I almost wish'd no more to wake,
And that my hold on life would break
Before I heard those bells again.

But they my troubled spirit rule,
For they controll'd me when a boy;
They bring me sorrow touch'd with joy,
The merry, merry bells of Yule.

Ring out, wild bells, to the wild sky,
The flying cloud, the frosty light:
The year is dying in the night;
Ring out, wild bells, and let him die.

Ring out the old, ring in the new,
Ring, happy bells, across the snow:
The year is going, let him go;
Ring out the false, ring in the true.

Ring out the grief that saps the mind,
For those that hear we see no more;
Ring out the feud of rich and poor,
Ring in redress to all mankind.

Ring out a slowly dying cause,
And ancient forms of party strife;
Ring in the nobler modes of life,
With sweeter manners, purer laws.

Ring out the want, the care, the sin,
The faithless coldness of the times;
Ring out, ring out my mournful rhymes,
But ring the fuller minstrel in.

Ring out false pride in place and
   blood,
The civic slander and the spite;
Ring in the love of truth and right,
Ring in the common love of good.

Ring out old shapes of foul disease,
Ring out the narrowing lust of gold;
Ring out the thousand wars of old,
Ring in the thousand years of peace.

Ring in the valiant man and free,
The larger heart, the kindlier hand;
Ring out the darkness of the land,
Ring in the Christ that is to be.

CHAPTER FIVE

CAROLS

Perhaps no other holiday on the calendar is as closely associated with music and singing as Christmas is. In this chapter, you'll find lyrics for the most important carols of the season—as well as a little information on the background of each immortal composition. Why not gather some friends, plan your route around the neighborhood, and start singing?

THE ANGEL GABRIEL

Traditional English   Traditional English

1. The An – gel Ga – bri – el from God was sent to Gal – i – lee, Un-

to a vir – gin fair and free, whose name was called Ma – ry. And

when the An – gel thith – er came, he fell down on his knee, And

look – ing up in the vir – gin's face, he said, — "All — hail, Ma – ry": Then

sing we all, both great and small, Now – ell, Now – ell Now – ell; We

may re – joice to hear the voice of the An – gel — Ga – bri – el.

1. The Angel Gabriel from God was sent to Galilee,
   Unto a virgin fair and free, whose name was called Mary.
   And when the angel thither came, he fell down on his knee,
   And looking up in the virgin's face, he said, "All hail, Mary."
   Refrain: Then sing we all, both great and small,
   Nowell, Nowell, Nowell;
   We may rejoice to hear the voice
   Of the Angel Gabriel.

2. Mary anon looked him upon, and said, "Sir, what are ye?
   I marvel much at these tidings which thou hast brought to me.
   Married I am unto an old man as the lot fell unto me;
   Therefore, I pray, depart away, for I stand in doubt of thee."
   (Refrain)

3. "Mary," he said, "be not afraid, but do believe in me:
   The power of the Holy Ghost shall overshadow thee;
   Thou shalt conceive without any grief, as the Lord told unto me;
   God's own dear Son from Heaven shall come, and shall be born of thee."
   (Refrain)

4. This came to pass as God's will was even as the angel told,
   About midnight an angel bright came to the shepherd's fold
   And told them then both where and when born was the Child our Lord,
   And all along this was their song, "All glory be given to God."
   (Refrain)

5. Good people all, both great and small, the which do hear my voice,
   With one accord let's praise the Lord, and in our hearts rejoice;
   Like sister and brother, let's love one another whilst we our lives do
       spend,
   Whilst we have space let's pray for grace, and so let my carol end.
   (Refrain)

ANGELS WE HAVE HEARD ON HIGH

Traditional French   *Traditional French*

1. Angels we have heard on high,
   Sweetly singing o'er the plains,
   And the mountains in reply,
   Echoing their joyous strains.
   Refrain: Gloria in excelsis Deo!
   Gloria in excelsis Deo!

2. Shepherds, why this jubilee?
   Why your joyous strains prolong?
   What the gladsome tidings be
   Which inspire your heav'nly song?
   (Refrain)

3. Come to Bethlehem and see
   Him whose birth the angels sing;
   Come, adore on bended knee,
   Christ the Lord, the newborn King.
   (Refrain)

AS JOSEPH WAS A-WALKING

Appalachian Spiritual

Appalachian Spiritual

As Jo-seph was-a walk-ing, he heard an an-gel—
sing: "This— night shall be the birth-night of— Christ, the heav'n-ly
King; This— night shall be the birth-night of—— Christ, the heav'n-ly King."

1. As Joseph was a-walking, he heard an angel sing:
"This night shall be the birthnight of Christ, the
    heav'nly King." (repeat)

2. "He neither shall be bornéd in house nor in the hall,
Nor in a king's palace, but in an oxen's stall."
    (repeat)

3. "He neither shall be washen in white wine nor in red,
But in the clear spring water with which we were
    christenéd." (repeat)

4. "He neither shall be clothéd in purple nor in pall,
But in the fair white linen that usen babies all."
    (repeat)

5. "He neither shall be rockéd in silver nor in gold,
But in a wooden cradle that rocks upon the mold."
    (repeat)

6. "On the sixth day of January His birthday shall be,
When the stars and the elements shall tremble with
    glee." (repeat)

7. As Joseph was a-walking, thus did the angel sing,
And Mary's Son at midnight was born to be our King.
    (repeat)

AWAY IN A MANGER

Anonymous

(?) James R. Murray (1841–1904)

1. A – way in a man – ger no crib for His bed, The lit – tle Lord

Je – sus laid down His sweet head. The stars in the sky — looked

down where He lay, The lit – tle Lord Je – sus a – sleep on the hay.

1. Away in a manger, no crib for His bed,
   The little Lord Jesus laid down His sweet head.
   The stars in the sky looked down where He lay,
   The little Lord Jesus asleep on the hay.

2. The cattle are lowing, the Baby awakes,
   But little Lord Jesus, no crying He makes.
   I love thee, Lord Jesus, look down from the sky,
   And stay by my cradle till morning is nigh.

A BABE IS BORN

Traditional English   Traditional English

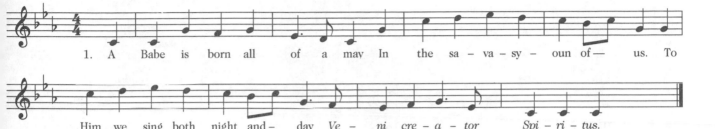

1. A Babe is born all of a may In the sa - va - sy - oun of— us. To
Him we sing both night and— day Ve - ni cre - a - tor Spi - ri - tus.

1. A Babe is born all of a may
   In the savasyoun of us
   To Him we sing both night and day
   Veni creator Spiritus.

2. At Bethlehem, that blessed place,
   The Child of bliss now born He was;
   And Him to serve God give us grace,
   O lux beata Trinitas.

3. There came three kings out of the east,
   To worship the King that is so free,
   With gold and myrrh and frankincense,
   A solis ortus cardine.

4. The shepherd's heard and angel's cry,
   A merye song then sungyn he:
   Why are ye so sore aghast?
   Iam ortus solis cardine.

5. The angels came down with one cry:
   A fair song that night sungyn they
   In the worship of that Child:
   Gloria tibi Domine.

Translations

may: maid
savasyoun: salvation
Veni creator Spiritus: Come, creator Spirit
O lux beata Trinitas: O Trinity, blessed light
A solis ortus cardine: Risen from the quarter of the sun
   (east)
merye: merry
sungyn: sang
Iam ortus solis cardine: Now risen from the east
Gloria tibi Domine: Glory to thee, O Lord

BALOO, LAMMY

Traditional Scottish

Traditional Scottish

1. This day — to — you — is born — a — Child Of Ma - ry — meek, – the Vir – gin – mild. That bless – ed bairn, ——— So lov – ing and — kind, Shall now — re – joice ——— both heart — and — mind. Ba - loo, — Lam – my.

This day to you is born a child
Of Mary meek, the Virgin mild.
That blessed bairn, so loving and kind,
Shall now rejoice both heart and mind.
Baloo, Lammy.

THE BOAR'S HEAD CAROL
Perhaps by a student at Queen's College, Oxford

Traditional English

1. The boar's head in hand bear I, Be-decked with bays and rose-ma-ry; And I pray you my mas-ters be mer-ry, Quot es-tis in con-vi-vi-o: Ca-put a-pri de-fe-ro, Re-dens lau-des Do-mi-no.

1. The boar's head in hand bear I,
   Bedecked with bays and rosemary;
   And I pray you my masters, be merry,
   Quot estis in convivio:
   Refrain: Caput apri defero
   Redens laudes Domino!

2. The boar's head, as I understand,
   Is the rarest dish in all this land,
   When thus bedecked with a gay garland;
   Let us *servire cantico:*
   (Refrain)

3. Our steward hath provided this,
   In honor of the King of bliss,
   Which on this day to be served is,
   In Reginensi atrio:
   (Refrain)

Translations

Quot estis is convivio: (Lat.) As many as are dining together.

Caput apri defero, Redens laudes Domino: I bring in the boar's head, singing the praises of the Lord.

servire cantico: To serve with a song.

In Reginensi atrio: In the hall of the Queen (i.e., Queen's College, Oxford)

A CHILD THIS DAY IS BORN

Traditional English   Traditional English

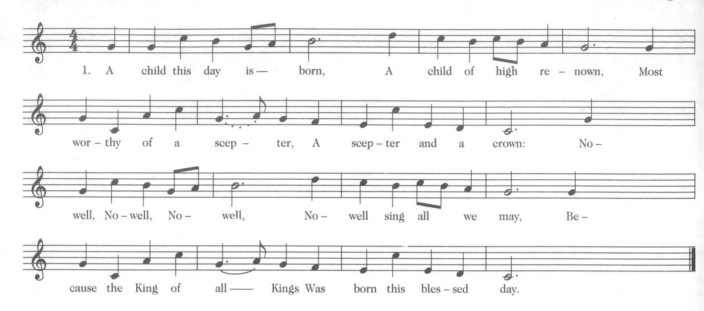

1. A child this day is born, / A child of high re-nown, / Most wor-thy of a scep-ter, / A scep-ter and a crown: / No-well, No-well, No-well, / No-well sing all we may, / Be-cause the King of all — Kings Was born this bles-sed day.

1. A child this day is born,
   A child of high renown,
   Most worthy of a scepter,
   A scepter and a crown:
   Refrain: Nowell, Nowell, Nowell,
   Nowell sing all we may,
   Because the King of all kings
   Was born this blessed day.

2. These tiding shepherds heard,
   In field watching their fold,
   Were by an angel unto them
   That night revealed and told:
   (Refrain)

3. To whom the angel spoke,
   Saying, "Be not afraid;
   Be glad, poor silly shepherds —
   Why are you so dismayed?
   (Refrain)

4. "For lo! I bring you tidings
   Of gladness and of mirth,
   Which cometh to all people by
   This Holy Infant's birth."
   (Refrain)

5. Then was there with the angel
   An host incontinent
   Of heavenly bright soldiers
   Which from the Highest was sent:
   (Refrain)

6. Lauding the Lord of God,
   And His celestial King;
   All glory be in Paradise,
   This heavenly host did sing:
   (Refrain)

7. And as the angel told them,
   So to them did appear;
   They found the young Child, Jesus Christ
   With Mary, his mother dear:
   (Refrain)

CHRIST WAS BORN ON CHRISTMAS DAY

Traditional German   Traditional German

1. Christ was born on Christmas Day,
   Wreathe the holly, twine the bay;
   Christus natus hodie;
   The Babe, the Son, the Holy One of Mary.

2. He is born to set us free,
   He is born our Lord to be,
   Ex Maria Virgine,
   The God, the Lord, by all adored forever.

3. Let the bright red berries glow,
   Ev'rywhere in goodly show,
   Christus natus hodie;
   The Babe, the Son, the Holy One of Mary.

4. Christian folk, rejoice and sing,
   'Tis the birthday of a King,
   Ex Maria Virgine;
   The God, the Lord, by all adored forever.

Translations

Christus natus hodie: Christ this day is born
Ex Maria Virgine: Of the Virgin Mary

A DAY OF JOY AND FEASTING

A group of high-school children

Traditional English

1. A day of joy and feast - ing, Of hap - pi - ness and mirth; And ev - ery year it com - eth here To glad - den all the earth. Sing No - well! Sing No - well! And — mer - ry be al - way; —— Join in the song, the sound pro - long All on a Christ - mas day.

1. A day of joy and feasting,
   Of happiness and mirth;
   And every year it cometh here
   To gladden all the earth.
   Refrain: Sing Nowell! Sing Nowell!
   And merry be alway;
   Join in the song, the sound prolong
   All on a Christmas day.

2. All hail the shining holly,
   All hail the mistletoe!
   With carol gay, all hail the day
   That cometh o'er the snow!
   (Refrain)

3. Long may the Christmas spirit
   Of kindness and good will
   Through joy and pain with us remain
   Our hearts with warmth to fill!
   (Refrain)

DECK THE HALLS WITH BOUGHS OF HOLLY

Traditional Welsh   Traditional Welsh

1. Deck the halls with boughs of hol – ly, Fa – la – la – la – la, la – la – la – la;

'Tis the sea – son to be jol – ly, Fa – la – la – la – la, la – la – la – la.

Don we now our gay ap – par – el, Fa – la – la, fa – la – la, la – la – la.

Troll the an – cient Yule – tide car – ol, Fa – la – la – la – la, la – la – la – la!

1. Deck the halls with boughs of holly,
   Falalalala, lalalala;
   'Tis the season to be jolly,
   Falalalala, lalalala.
   Don we now our gay apparel,
   Falala, falala, lalala.
   Troll the ancient Yuletide carol,
   Falalalala, lalalala.

2. See the blazing yule before us,
   Falalalala, lalalala;
   Strike the harp and join the chorus
   Falalalala, lalalala.
   Follow me in merry measure,
   Falala, falala, lalala.
   While I sing of Christmas treasure,
   Falalalala, lalalala.

3. Fast away the old year passes,
   Falalalala, lalalala;
   Hail the new, ye lads and lasses,
   Falalalala, lalalala.
   Sing we joyous songs together,
   Falala, falala, lalala.
   Heedless of the wind and weather,
   Falalalala, lalalala.

THE FIRST NOWELL

Traditional

Traditional

1. The — first — Now – ell The — an – gel did say was to cer – tain poor shep - herds in fields where they lay; In — fields —— where – they lay — keep - ing their sheep, on a cold win – ter's night — that was — so deep. Now —— ell, —— Now — ell Now — ell, Now – ell, Born is the King — of Is – ra – el.

1. The first Nowell, the angel did say,
   Was to certain poor shepherds in fields as they lay,
   In fields where they lay keeping their sheep
   On a cold winter's night that was so deep.
   Refrain: Nowell, nowell, nowell, nowell,
   Born is the King of Israel

2. They looked up and saw a star
   Shining in the east, beyond them far,
   And to the earth it gave great light,
   And so it continued both day and night.
   (Refrain)

3. And by the light of that same star
   Three wise men came from country far;
   To see the King was their intent,
   And to follow the star where e'er it went.
   (Refrain)

4. This star drew nigh to the northwest,
   O'er Bethlehem it took its rest;
   And there it did both stop and stay,
   Right over the place where Jesus lay.
   (Refrain)

5. Then entered in those wise men three,
   Full reverently upon the knee,
   And offered there, in His presence
   Their gold and myrrh and frankincense.
   (Refrain)

6. Then let us all with one accord
   Sing praises to our heav'nly Lord;
   That hath made heaven and earth of naught
   And with His blood mankind hath bought.
   (Refrain)

GLOUCESTERSHIRE WASSAIL

Traditional English   Traditional English

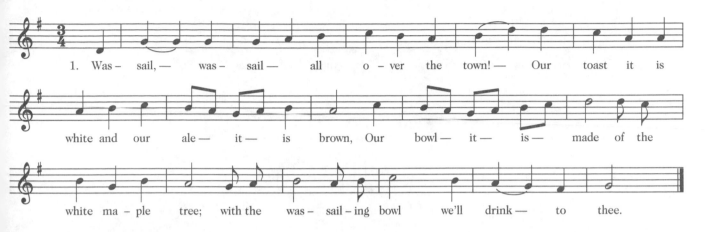

1. Was- sail, — was- sail — all o - ver the town! — Our toast it is
white and our ale — it — is brown, Our bowl — it — is — made of the
white ma - ple tree; with the was - sail – ing bowl we'll drink — to thee.

1. Wassail, wassail, all over the town!
    Our toast it is white, and our ale it is brown,
    Our bowl it is made of the white maple tree;
    With the wassailing bowl we'll drink to thee.

2. So here is to Cherry and to his right cheek,
    Pray God send our master a good piece of beef,
    And a good piece of beef, that may we all see;
    With the wassailing bowl we'll drink to thee.

3. And here is to Dobbin and to his right eye,
    Pray God send our master a good Christmas pie,
    And a good Christmas pie, that may we all see;
    With our wassailing bowl we'll drink to thee.

4. And here is to Broad May and to her broad horn,
    May God send our master a good crop of corn,
    And a good crop of corn, that may we all see;
    With the wassailing bowl we'll drink to thee.

5. And here is to Fillpail and to her left ear,
    Pray God send our master a happy New Year,
    And a happy New Year as e'er he did see;
    With our wassailing bowl we'll drink to thee.

6. And here is to Colly and to her long tail,
    Pray God send our master he never may fail,
    A bowl of strong beer; I pray you draw near,
    And our jolly wassail it's then you shall hear.

7. Come, butler, come fill us a bowl of the best,
    And pray that your soul in heaven may rest;
    But if you do draw us a bowl of the small,
    May the devil take butler, bowl, and all!

8. Then here's to the maid in the lily-white smock,
    Who tripped to the door and slipped back the lock!
    Who tripped to the door and pulled back the pin,
    For to let these jolly wassailers come in.

GOD REST YOU MERRY, GENTLEMEN

Traditional English   Traditional English

1. God rest you merry, gentlemen, Let nothing you dis-may, Remember Christ our Sav-iour was born on Christ-mas Day; To
save us all from Sa-tan's pow'r When we were gone a-stray O——
ti-dings of com——fort and joy com-fort and joy; O—— ti-dings of
com——fort and joy.

1. God rest you merry, gentlemen,
   Let nothing you dismay
   Remember Christ our Saviour
   Was born on Christmas Day;
   To save us all from Satan's pow'r
   When we were gone astray.
   Refrain: *O tidings of comfort and joy, comfort and joy;*
   O tidings of comfort and joy

2. From God our heav'nly Father
   The blessed angel came
   And unto certain shepherds
   Brought tidings of the same
   How that in Bethlehem was born
   The Son of God by name.   *(Refrain)*

3. "Fear not, then," said the angel
   "Let nothing you affright,
   This day is born a Saviour
   Of a pure Virgin bright,
   To free all those who trust in Him
   From Satan's pow'r and might."   *(Refrain)*

4. The shepherds at those tidings
   Rejoiced much in mind,
   And left their flocks a-feeding
   In tempest, storm, and wind,
   And went to Bethlehem straightway
   This blessed Babe to find.   *(Refrain)*

5. But when to Bethlehem they came,
   Whereat this Infant lay,
   They found Him in a manger,
   Where oxen feed on hay;
   His mother Mary kneeling
   Unto the Lord did pray.   *(Refrain)*

6. Now to the Lord sing praises,
   All you within this place,
   And with true love and brotherhood
   Each other now embrace;
   This holy tide of Christmas
   All others doth deface.   *(Refrain)*

GOOD KING WENCESLAS

John Mason Neale (1818–1866)

Piae Cantiones, 1582

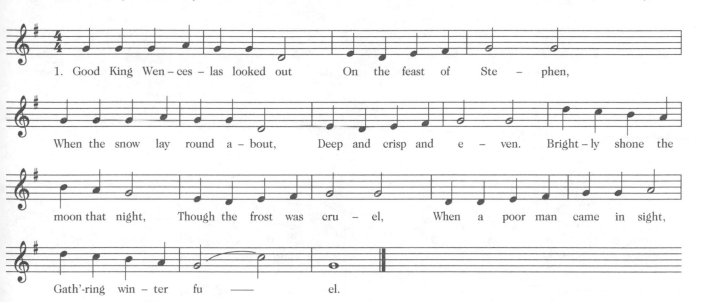

1. Good King Wen – ces – las looked out On the feast of Ste – phen,
When the snow lay round a – bout, Deep and crisp and e – ven. Bright – ly shone the
moon that night, Though the frost was cru – el, When a poor man came in sight,
Gath'ring win – ter fu —— el.

1. Good King Wenceslas looked out
On the feast of Stephen,
When the snow lay all about,
Deep and crisp and even.
Brightly shone the moon that night,
Though the frost was cruel,
When a poor man came in sight,
Gath'ring winter fuel.

2. "Hither, page, and stand by me,
If thou know'st it telling,
Yonder peasant, who is he?
Where and what his dwelling?"
"Sire, he lives a good league hence,
Underneath the mountains,
Right against the forest fence,
By Saint Agnes' fountain."

3. "Bring me flesh, and bring me wine,
Bring me pine logs hither
Thou and I shall see him dine,
When we bear them thither."
Page and monarch, forth they went,
Forth they went together;
Through the rude wind's wild lament
And the bitter weather.

4. "Sire the night is darker now,
And the wind grows stronger,
Fails my heart, I know not how;
I can go lo longer."
"Mark my footsteps, my good page,
Tread thou in them boldly;
Thou shalt find the winter's rage
Freeze thy blood less coldly."

5. In his master's steps he trod,
Where the snow lay dinted;
Heat was in the very sod
Which the Saint had printed.
Therefore Christian men, be sure,
Wealth or rank possessing,
Ye who now will bless the poor
Shall yourselves find blessing.

GREEN GROW'TH THE HOLLY

Attributed to King Henry VIII

16th-century English

1. Green grow'th the hol – ly, So doth the i – vy; Though win – ter blasts blow

ne'er so high, Green grow'th the hol – ly.

1. Green grow'th the holly,
    So doth the ivy;
      Though winter blasts blow ne'er so high,
    Green grow'th the holly.

2. Gay are the flowers,
    Hedgerows and ploughlands;
      The days grow longer in the sun,
    Soft fall the showers.

3. Full gold the harvest,
    Grain for thy labor;
      With God must work for daily bread,
    Else, man, thou starvest.

4. Fast fall the shed leaves,
    Russet and yellow;
      But resting buds are snug and safe
    Where swung the dead leaves.

5. Green grow'th the holly,
    So doth the ivy;
      The God of life can never die,
    Hope! saith the holly.

HARK! THE HERALD ANGELS SING

Charles Wesley (1707–1788)   Felix Mendelssohn-Bartholdy (1809–1847)

1. Hark! the herald angels sing, — "Glory to the newborn King;
Peace on earth, and mercy mild, — God and sinners reconciled!"
Joyful, all ye nations, rise, — Join the triumph of the skies, —
With angelic host proclaim, "Christ is — born in Bethlehem!"
Hark, the herald angels sing, "Glory — to the newborn King."

1. Hark! the herald angels sing,
    "Glory to the newborn King;
    Peace on earth, and mercy mild,
    God and sinners reconciled!"
    Joyful, all ye nations, rise,
    Join the triumph of the skies;
    With th'angelic hosts proclaim,
    "Christ is born in Bethlehem!"
    Refrain: Hark! the herald angels sing,
            "Glory to the newborn King."

2. Christ by highest heav'n adored;
    Christ the everlasting Lord;
    Come, desire of nations, come,
    Fix in us thy humble home.
    Veiled in flesh the Godhead see;
    Hail th'Incarnate Deity,
    Pleased as man with man to dwell;
    Jesus, our Emmanuel.
    (Refrain)

3. Hail, the heav'n-born Prince of Peace!
    Hail, the Sun of Righteousness!
    Light and life to us He us brings,
    Ris'n with healing in His wings;
    Mild He lays his glory by,
    Born that man no more may die,
    Born to raise the sons of earth,
    Born to give them second birth;
    (Refrain)

THE HOLLY AND THE IVY

Traditional English

Traditional English

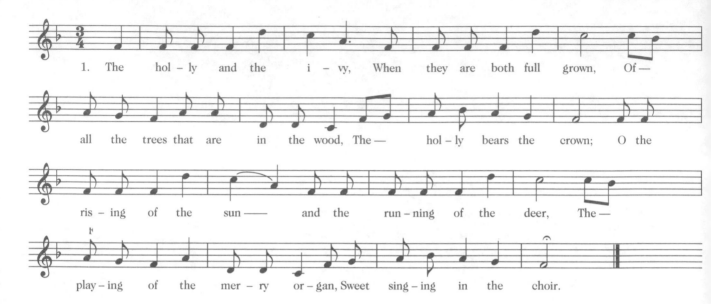

1. The hol-ly and the i-vy, When they are both full grown, Of— all the trees that are in the wood, The— hol-ly bears the crown; O the ris-ing of the sun— and the run-ning of the deer, The— play-ing of the mer-ry or-gan, Sweet sing-ing in the choir.

1. The holly and the ivy,
   When they are both full grown,
   Of all the trees that are in the wood
   The holly bears the crown.
   Refrain: O the rising of the sun,
   And the running of the deer,
   The playing of the merry organ,
   Sweet singing in the choir.

2. The holly bears a blossom,
   As white as the lily flower,
   And Mary bore sweet Jesus Christ
   To be our sweet Saviour.
   (Refrain)

3. The holly bears a berry,
   As red as any blood,
   And Mary bore sweet Jesus Christ
   To do poor sinners good.
   (Refrain)

4. The holly bears a prickle,
   As sharp as any thorn,
   And Mary bore sweet Jesus Christ
   On Christmas Day in the morn.
   (Refrain)

5. The holly bears a bark,
   As bitter as any gall,
   And Mary bore sweet Jesus Christ
   For to redeem us all.
   (Refrain)

6. The holly and the ivy,
   When they are both full grown,
   Of all the trees that are in the wood
   The holly bears the crown.
   (Refrain)

I SAW THREE SHIPS

Traditional English   Traditional English

1. I saw three ships come sail – ing in, On Christ – mas Day, on

Christ – mas Day, I saw three ships come sail – ing in, on Christ – mas Day in the

morn –   ing.

1. I saw three ships come sailing in,
    On Christmas Day, on Christmas Day,
    I saw three ships come sailing in,
    On Christmas Day in the morning.

2. And what was in those ships all three?
    On Christmas Day, on Christmas Day,
    And what was in those ships all three?
    On Christmas Day in the morning.

3. Our Saviour Christ and His lady,
    On Christmas Day, on Christmas Day,
    Our Saviour Christ and His lady,
    On Christmas Day in the morning.

4. Pray, whither sailed those ships all three?
    On Christmas Day, on Christmas Day,
    Pray, whither sailed those ships all three?
    On Christmas Day in the morning.

5. O, they sailed into Bethlehem
    On Christmas Day, on Christmas Day,
    O, they sailed into Bethlehem
    On Christmas Day in the morning.

6. And all the bells on earth shall ring,
    On Christmas Day, on Christmas Day,
    And all the bells on earth shall ring,
    On Christmas Day in the morning.

7. And all the angels in heaven shall sing,
    On Christmas Day, on Christmas Day,
    And all the angels in heaven shall sing,
    On Christmas Day in the morning.

8. And all the souls on earth shall sing,
    On Christmas Day, on Christmas Day,
    And all the souls on earth shall sing,
    On Christmas Day in the morning.

9. Then let us all rejoice amain!
    On Christmas Day, on Christmas Day,
    Then let us all rejoice amain!
    On Christmas Day in the morning.

IT CAME UPON A MIDNIGHT CLEAR

Edmund Sears (1810–1876)   Richard S. Willis (1819–1900)

1. It came upon a midnight clear, That glorious song of Old, From angels bending near the earth To touch their harps of gold; "Peace on the earth, — good will to men, From heav'n's all-gracious King." — The world in solemn stillness lay To hear the angels sing.

1. It came upon a midnight clear,
   That glorious song of old,
   From angels bending near the earth
   To touch their harps of gold;
   "Peace on the earth, good will to men,
   From heav'n's all-gracious King."
   The world in solemn stillness lay
   To hear the angels sing.

2. Still through the cloven skies they came,
   With peaceful wings unfurled,
   And still their heav'nly music floats
   O'er all the weary world.
   Above its sad and lowly plains
   They bend on hov'ring wing,
   And ever o'er its Babel sounds
   The blessed angels sing.

3. O ye, beneath life's crushing load
   Whose forms are bending low,
   Who toil along the climbing way
   With painful steps and slow,
   Look now, for glad and golden hours
   Come swiftly on the wing:
   O rest beside the weary road,
   And hear the angels sing!

4. For lo, the days are hast'ning on,
   By prophets seen of old,
   When with the ever circling years,
   Shall come the time foretold,
   When the new heav'n and earth shall own
   The Prince of Peace their King,
   And the whole world send back the song
   Which now the angels sing.

JINGLE BELLS

John Pierpont (1785–1866)   John Pierpont

Dash – ing through the snow, In a one – horse o – pen sleigh, O'er the fields we go, Laugh – ing all the way; Bells on bob – tail ring, Mak – ing spir – its bright, What fun it is to ride and sing a sleigh – ing song to – night! Jin – gle bells, jin – gle bells, Jin – gle all the way! Oh, what fun it is to ride In a one – horse o – pen sleigh! Jin – gle bells, jin – gle bells, Jin – gle all the way! Oh what fun it is to ride In a one-horse o – pen sleigh!

Dashing through the snow,
In a one-horse open sleigh,
O'er the fields we go,
Laughing all the way;
Bells on bobtail ring,
Making spirits bright,
What fun it is to laugh and sing
A sleighing song tonight!

Jingle bells, jingle bells,
Jingle all the way!
Oh, what fun it is to ride
In a one-horse open sleigh!

Jingle bells, jingle bells,
Jingle all the way!
Oh, what fun it is to ride
In a one-horse open sleigh!

JOY TO THE WORLD

Isaac Watts (1674–1748)

Unknown

1. Joy to the world! the Lord is come; Let earth re - ceive her King; Let ev — 'ry — heart — pre – pare – Him — room, —— And heav'n and na – ture – sing, And – heav'n and na – ture – sing, And heav'n, — And heav'n and na – ture sing.

1. Joy to the world! the Lord is come;
   Let earth receive her King;
   Let ev'ry heart prepare Him room,
   And heav'n and nature sing,
   And heav'n and nature sing,
   And heav'n, and heav'n and nature sing.

2. Joy to the world! the Saviour reigns;
   Let men their songs employ;
   While fields and floods, rocks, hills, and plains
   Repeat the sounding joy,
   Repeat the sounding joy,
   Repeat, repeat the sounding joy.

3. He rules the world with truth and grace,
   And makes the nations prove
   The glories of His righteousness,
   And wonders of His love,
   And wonders of His love,
   And wonders, and wonders of His love.

LO, HOW A ROSE E'ER BLOOMING

German: anon., 15th century; Translation by Theodore Baker (1851–1934)

Traditional German

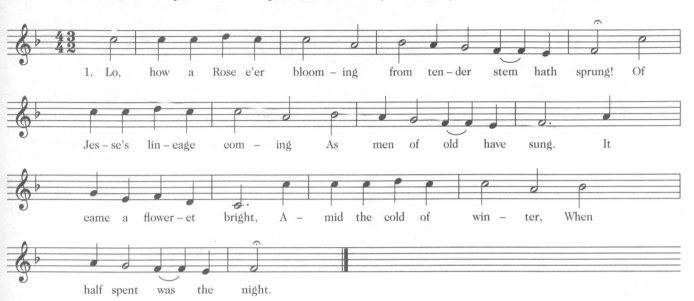

1. Lo, how a Rose e'er bloom – ing from ten – der stem hath sprung! Of

Jes – se's lin – eage com – ing As men of old have sung. It

came a flower – et bright, A – mid the cold of win – ter, When

half spent was the night.

1. Lo, how a Rose e'er blooming
   From tender stem hath sprung!
   From Jesse's lineage coming
   As men of old have sung.
   It came, a floweret bright,
   Amid the cold of winter,
   When half spent was the night.

2. Isaiah 'twas foretold it,
   The rose I have in mind.
   With Mary we behold it,
   The Virgin Mother kind.
   To show God's love aright
   She bore to us a Saviour,
   When half spent was the night.

LULLY, LULLAY

Robert Croo (16th century)

Traditional English

Lul – ly, lul – lay, thou lit – tle ti – ny Child, By, by, lul –

ly, lul – lay; Lul – lay, thou lit – tle

ti – ny Child, By, by, lul – ly, lul – lay.

1. Lully, lullay, thou little tiny Child,
   By, by, lully, lullay:
   Lullay, thou little tiny Child,
   By, by, lully, lullay.

2. O sisters too, how may we do,
   For to preserve this day
   This poor Youngling for whom we do sing
   By, by, lully, lullay.

3. Herod the king in his raging,
   Chargéd he hath this day
   His men of might, in his own sight
   All young children to slay.

4. Then woe is me, poor Child, for Thee,
   And ever mourn and say,
   For Thy parting nor say nor sing
   By, by, lully, lullay.

NO ROOM IN THE INN

Traditional English   Traditional English

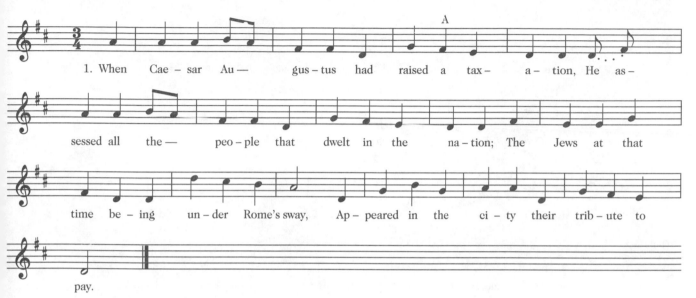

1. When Cae – sar Au — gus – tus had raised a tax – a – tion, He as –
sessed all the — peo – ple that dwelt in the na – tion; The Jews at that
time be – ing un – der Rome's sway, Ap – peared in the ci – ty their trib – ute to
pay.

1. When Caesar Augustus had raised a taxation,
   He assessed all the people that dwelt in the nation;
   The Jews at that time being under Rome's sway,
   Appeared in the city their tribute to pay.

2. Then Joseph and Mary, who from David did spring,
   Went up the city of David, their king;
   And there, being entered, cold welcome they find:
   From the rich to the poor, they are mostly unkind.

3. Good Joseph was troubled, but most for his dear,
   For her blessed burden whose time now drew near;
   His heart with true sorrow was sorely afflicted
   That his virgin spouse was so rudely neglected.

4. He could get no houseroom who houses did frame,
   But Joseph and Mary must go as they came.
   For little is the favor the poor man can find:
   From the rich to the poor they are mostly unkind.

5. While the great and the wealthy do frolic in hall,
   Possess all the groundrooms and chambers and all,
   Poor Joseph and Mary are thrust from the table
   In Bethlehem City, ground inhospitáble.

6. And with their mean lodging, contented they be,
   For the minds of the just with their fortunes agree;
   They bear all affronts with their meekness of mind,
   And be not offended though the rich be unkind.

7. O Bethlehem, Bethlehem, welcome this stranger
   That was born in a stable and laid in a manger;
   For he is a physician to heal all our smarts:
   Come welcome, sweet Jesus, and lodge in our hearts.

O COME, ALL YE FAITHFUL (*Adeste Fidelis*)

(?)John Francis Wade (1712–1786)

(?) John Reading (d. 1692)

1. O come, all ye faithful, joyful and triumphant,
   O come ye, o come ye to Bethlehem;
   Come and behold Him, born the King of angels;
   Refrain: O come, let us adore Him,
   O come, let us adore Him,
   O come, let us adore Him, Christ the Lord!

2. Sing, choirs of angels, sing in exultation,
   O sing, all ye citizens of heaven above!
   Glory to God, all glory in the highest;
   (Refrain)

3. Yea, Lord, we greet Thee, born this happy morning,
   Jesus, to Thee be all glory giv'n;
   Word of the Father, now in flesh appearing;
   (Refrain)

O COME, O COME, EMMANUEL

Latin, 12th century

Plain Song, 12th century

Translated by John M. Neale (1818–1866)

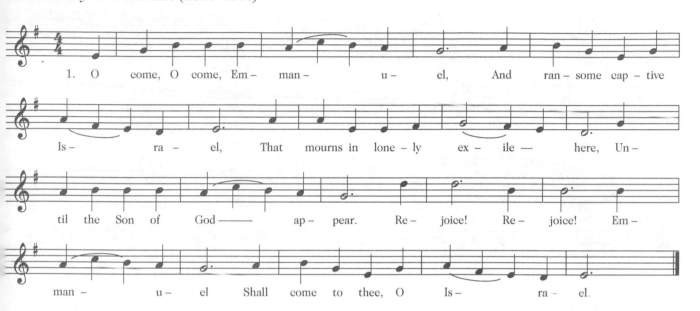

1. O Come, O Come, Emmanuel
   And ransom captive Israel,
   That mourns in lonely exile here,
   Until the Son of God appear.
   Refrain: Rejoice! Rejoice! Emmanuel
       Shall come to thee, O Israel!

2. O come, Thou Dayspring, come and cheer
   Our spirits by Thine advent here;
   Disperse the gloomy clouds of night,
   And death's dark shadows put to flight.
   (Refrain)

O HOLY NIGHT

Cappeau de Roquemaure

Adolph Charles Adam (1803–1856)

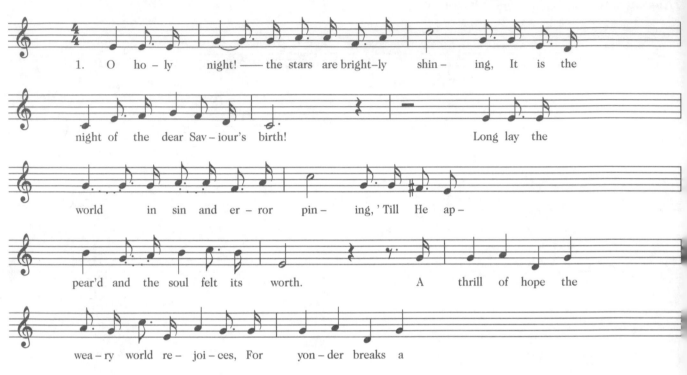

1. O ho – ly night! —— the stars are bright–ly shin – ing, It is the night of the dear Sav – iour's birth! Long lay the world in sin and er – ror pin – ing, 'Till He ap – pear'd and the soul felt its worth. A thrill of hope the wea – ry world re – joi – ces, For yon – der breaks a

1. O holy night! the stars are brightly shining,
   It is the night of our dear Saviour's birth!
   Long lay the world, in sin and error pining,
   'Til He appear'd, and the soul felt its worth.
   A thrill of hope the weary world rejoices,
   For yonder breaks a new and glorious morn!
   Fall on your knees! O hear the angel voices!
   O night divine, O night when Christ was born!
   O night divine, O night, O night divine!

2. Led by the light of faith serenely beaming,
   With glowing hearts by His cradle we stand.
   So, led by light of a star sweetly gleaming,
   Here came the wise men from the Orient land.
   The King of Kings lay thus in lowly manger,
   In all our trials born to be our friend;
   He knows our need, to our weakness no stranger;
   Behold your King! Before the Lowly bend!
   Behold your King! your King! before Him bend!

O HOLY NIGHT

Continued

new and glo – rious morn!   Fall   on your   knees!   O

hear   the an – gel   voi –   ces!   O   night   di –

vine!   O   night   when Christ was   born   O

night   di –   vine!   O   night,   O   night   di –

vine!

O LITTLE TOWN OF BETHLEHEM

Phillips Brooks (1835–1893)   Lewis H. Redner (1831–1908)

1. O little town of Bethlehem,
   How still we see thee lie
   Above thy deep and dreamless sleep
   The silent stars go by;
   Yet in thy dark streets shineth
   The everlasting Light;
   The hopes and fears of all the years
   Are met in thee tonight.

2. For Christ is born of Mary,
   And gathered all above,
   While mortals sleep, the angels keep
   Their watch of wond'ring love.
   O morning stars, together
   Proclaim the holy birth,
   And praises sing to God the King,
   And peace to all the earth.

3. How silently, how silently,
   The wondrous gift is giv'n!
   So God imparts to human hearts
   The blessings of His heav'n.
   No ear may hear His coming,
   But in this world of sin,
   Where meek souls will receive Him still,
   The Dear Christ enters in.

4. O holy Child of Bethlehem,
   Descend to us, we pray,
   Cast out our sin and enter in;
   Be born in us today!
   We hear the Christmas angels
   The great glad tidings tell;
   O come to us, abide with us
   Our Lord Emmanuel!

RISE UP, SHEPHERD AND FOLLOW

Negro Spiritual

There's a star in the East on Christmas morn,
Rise up, shepherd, and follow!
It will lead to the place where the Saviour's born;
Rise up, shepherd, and follow!
Leave your sheep and leave your lambs;
Rise up, shepherd, and follow!
Leave your ewes and leave your rams;
Rise up, shepherd, and follow!
Follow, follow!
Rise up, shepherd, and follow!
Follow the star of Bethlehem;
Rise up, shepherd, and follow!

SILENT NIGHT

Joseph Mohr (1792–1848)

Franz Xavier Gruber (1787–1863)

1. Si — lent night, ho — ly night! All is calm, all is bright
Round yon Vir — gin Mo — ther and Child. Ho — ly In — fant so ten — der and mild,
Sleep in heav — en — ly peace, —— Sleep in hea — ven — ly peace.

1. Silent night, holy night!
    All is calm, all is bright
    Round yon Virgin Mother and Child
    Holy Infant, so tender and mild,
    Sleep in heavenly peace,
    Sleep in heavenly peace.

2. Silent night, holy night!
    Shepherds quake at the sight,
    Glories stream from heaven afar,
    Heav'nly hosts sing alleluia!
    Christ the Saviour is born!
    Christ the Saviour is born!

3. Silent night, holy night!
    Wondrous star, lend thy light!
    With the angels, let us sing
    Alleluia to our King!
    Christ the Saviour is here,
    Jesus the Saviour is here.

THE TRUTH FROM ABOVE

Traditional English   Traditional English

1. This is the tru–th sent from a–bove, The truth of God,— the
God of love, There–fore don't turn me — from your door, But —
heark-en all — both — rich — and poor.

1. This is the truth sent from above,
   The truth of God, the God of love,
   Therefore don't turn me from your door,
   But hearken all both rich and poor.

2. The first thing which I do relate
   Is that God did man create;
   The next thing which to you I'll tell
   Woman was made with man to dwell.

3. Thus we were heirs to endless woes
   Till God the Lord did interpose;
   And so a promise soon did run
   That He would redeem us by His Son.

4. And at that season of the year
   Our blest Redeemer did appear;
   He here did live, and here did preach,
   And many thousands He did teach.

5. Thus He in love to us behaved,
   To show us how we must be saved;
   And if you want to know the way,
   Be pleas'd to hear what He did say.

THE TWELVE DAYS OF CHRISTMAS

Traditional English   Traditional English

THE TWELVE DAYS OF CHRISTMAS

Continued

On the sixth
sev – enth
eighth   day of Christ – mas my   true love sent to me
ninth
tenth
elev – enth
twelfth

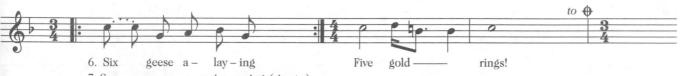

6. Six   geese a – lay – ing   Five   gold —— rings!
7. Sev – en swans   a – swim – ming (six *etc.*)
8. Eight   maids   a – milk – ing (seven *etc.*)
9. Nine   la – dies   danc – ing (eight *etc.*)
10. Ten   lords   a – leap – ing (nine *etc.*)
11. Elev – en pi – pers   pi – ping (ten *etc.*)
12. Twelve drum – mers drum – ming (eleven *etc.*)

1. On the first day of Christmas my true love sent to me
   A partridge in a pear tree.

2. On the second day of Christmas my true love sent to me
   Two turtle doves and a partridge in a pear tree.

3. On the third day of Christmas my true love sent to me
   Three French hens, two turtle doves, and a partridge in
   a pear tree.

4. On the fourth day of Christmas my true love sent to me
   Four calling birds, three French hens, two turtle doves,
   and a partridge in a pear tree.

5. On the fifth day of Christmas my true love sent to me
   Five gold rings, four calling birds, three French hens,
   two turtle doves, and a partridge in a pear tree.

6. On the sixth day of Christmas my true love sent to me
   Six geese a-laying, five gold rings, four calling birds. . .

7. On the seventh day of Christmas my true love sent to
   me
   Seven swans a-swimming, six geese a laying. . .

8. On the eighth day of Christmas my true love sent to me
   Eight maids a-milking. . .

9. On the ninth day of Christmas my true love sent to me
   Nine ladies dancing. . .

10. On the tenth day of Christmas my true love sent to me
    Ten lords a-leaping. . .

11. On the eleventh day of Christmas my true love sent
    to me
    Eleven pipers piping. . .

12. On the twelfth day of Christmas my true love sent to me
    Twelve drummers drumming. . .

WE THREE KINGS OF ORIENT ARE

John Henry Hopkins, Jr. (1820–1891)   John Henry Hopkins, Jr.

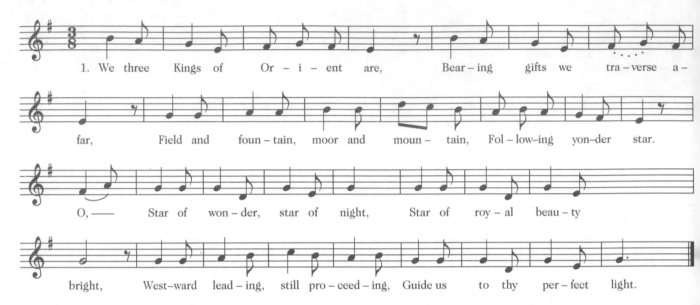

1. We three Kings of Or – i – ent are, Bear – ing gifts we tra – verse a –
far, Field and foun – tain, moor and moun – tain, Fol – low – ing yon – der star.
O, —— Star of won – der, star of night, Star of roy – al beau – ty
bright, West – ward lead – ing, still pro – ceed – ing, Guide us to thy per – fect light.

1. We three kings of Orient are,
   Bearing gifts we traverse afar,
   Field and fountain, moor and mountain,
   Following yonder star.
   Refrain: O, star of wonder, star of night,
   Star of royal beauty bright,
   Westward leading, still proceeding,
   Guide us to thy perfect light.

2. Born a King on Bethlehem's plain,
   Gold I bring to crown Him again,
   King forever, ceasing never
   Over us all to reign.
   (Refrain)

3. Frankincense to offer have I,
   Incense owns a Deity nigh:
   Prayer and praising
   All men raising,
   Worship Him, God on high.
   (Refrain)

4. Myrrh is mine; its bitter perfume
   Breathes a life of gathering gloom;
   Sorrow, sighing, bleeding, dying,
   Sealed in the stone-cold tomb.
   (Refrain)

5. Glorious now, behold Him arise,
   King, and God, and sacrifice;
   Heaven sings alleluia:
   Alleluia the earth replies.
   (Refrain)

WE WISH YOU A MERRY CHRISTMAS

Traditional English

Traditional English

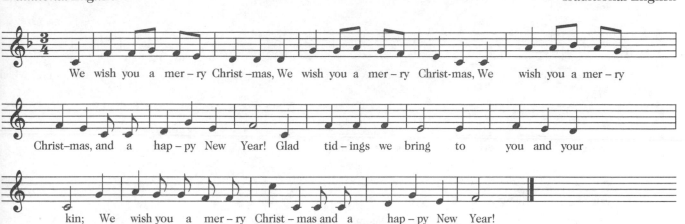

We wish you a mer–ry Christ–mas, We wish you a mer–ry Christ-mas, We wish you a mer–ry Christ–mas, and a hap–py New Year! Glad tid–ings we bring to you and your kin; We wish you a mer–ry Christ–mas and a hap–py New Year!

We wish you a Merry Christmas,
We wish you a Merry Christmas,
We wish you a Merry Christmas
And a Happy New Year!
Glad tiding we bring,
To you and your kin
We wish you a Merry Christmas
And a Happy New Year!

WHAT CHILD IS THIS?

William Chatterton Dix (1837–1898)

16th-century English

1. What Child is this, — Who laid to rest — on Ma – ry's lap — is sleep – ing? Whom
an – gels greet — with an–thems sweet, — While shep — herds watch — are keep – ing?
This, this — is Christ the King, — Whom shep–herds guard — and an – gels sing:
This, this — is Christ the King, — The Babe, – the Son — of Ma – ry.

1. What child is this, Who, laid to rest,
   On Mary's lap is sleeping?
   Whom angels greet with anthems sweet,
   While shepherds watch are keeping?
   Refrain: This, this is Christ the King,
   Whom shepherds guard and angels sing:
   This, this is Christ the King,
   The Babe, the Son of Mary.

2. Why lies He in such mean estate,
   Where ox and ass are feeding?
   Good Christian, fear: for sinners here
   The silent Word is pleading.
   (Refrain)

3. So bring Him incense, gold, and myrrh,
   Come, peasant, king, to own Him;
   The King of Kings salvation brings,
   Let loving hearts enthrone Him.
   (Refrain)

CHAPTER SIX

The LIFE And TIMES of SANTA CLAUS

Who is the man who bellows "Ho, ho, ho"? The modern-day Santa we all know and love is an engaging combination of myth, reality, and mispronunciation. What follows is a brief account of the great man's evolution through the years.

ALTHOUGH HIS ROOTS reach back into antiquity, the man we think of when we think of Christmas has been refined and popularized largely through the media of the nineteenth and twentieth centuries. Two written accounts—Clement C. Moore's 1822 poem "A Visit from St. Nicholas" and the *New York Sun's* famous response to young Virginia O'Hanlon's 1897 query about him—probably did the most to establish Santa as a figure in the popular imagination. (Both of those pieces appear in this book.) Even though his most memorable features are relatively recent, however, our Santa Claus evolved from many sources over many years—most notably from the life and deeds ascribed to St. Nicholas, an early Christian Bishop in the land of Asia Minor, now western Turkey.

These days, the Vatican has its doubts about St. Nicholas. A special report penned in 1969 by senior Church officials and approved by Pope Paul VI concluded that many of the recorded deeds of some of the early saints—including the forerunner of Santa—may well be those of legendary heroes rather than historical personages.

The records of Nicholas's life certainly appear to be, at best, a mixture of fact and fantastic myth, but there is no denying the impact this revered figure had on the development of the Santa Claus tradition. He remains quite popular in Europe, where there are more churches named for him than for any apostle.

Leaving aside for the moment the most extraordinary aspects of the Nicholas legend, we are left with a very few basic facts. A young man became the Bishop of Myra while still in his teens, earning the nickname of Boy Bishop. Through his courage and generosity, this bishop, Nicholas, is said to have touched the lives of many people, saving any number from famine and despair. He founded an orphanage and was known for his love of and wonderful relationship with children. Nicholas also spent some time in captivity, imprisoned by the Roman Empire during a time of religious persecution. He and others were finally reprieved by the emperor Constantine, whose attitude towards Christianity was softening. Nicholas died on December 6 in approximately A.D. 343; the day is celebrated as St. Nicholas's Day in many European countries.

Inspiring tales about Nicholas made him extremely popular throughout Christendom; he was named the patron saint of children, sailors, thieves, hobos, pawnbrokers, and bankers—as well as Russia, Greece, and Sicily. It is not surprising, then, that Nicholas was so revered even in death. In later years his body was stolen from its crypt in Myra by sailors from Bari, Italy, who were seeking to protect his remains from Muslim invaders. The sailors brought the remains to Bari and buried them in a basilica there; to this day, St. Nicholas's Day is celebrated by the people of Bari on May 9, the date of the sailors' arrival. The theft brought Nicholas the distinction of patron saint of thieves, and added to his already sizeable legend.

THE LEGEND OF ST. NICHOLAS

Beyond evidence that Nicholas was a very good man, there are the rumors and legends that suggest he was nothing short of otherworldly. His birth is said to have been a miraculous one, as his parents, according to legend, had been married thirty years and had long since given up hope of ever conceiving a child. It is said that shortly after his birth he was able to stand up in his crib, as if praying.

The tradition of stuffing gifts in Christmas stockings is probably rooted in a gift of gold coins attributed to St. Nicholas.

Nicholas appears to have had no doubt about his vocation; he prepared to enter the monastery at a young age. Before devoting his life to his faith, however, he was required to rid himself of all his worldly possessions. The way in which he is said to have accomplished this has helped to establish his identification as a gift giver. As the story goes, there was a family in town with three daughters of marriageable

age, but they were so poor that they had no dowry; no dowry meant no marriage. Nicholas, hearing of their plight, disguised himself and went at night to their house, where he threw three bags of gold coins down their chimney, saving the daughters from a life of prostitution. The gold is said to have landed in the girls' stockings, which were hanging in the fireplace to dry. As legend has it, the father of the family caught Nicholas in the act, and though Nicholas tried to swear him to secrecy, the story spread through the town quickly.

Shortly after entering the monastery, Nicholas became the Bishop of Myra. The church in Myra had been having great trouble replacing the former bishop, and the people were at their wits' end as to how to solve the dilemma. One night it came to a church official in a dream that the first one to enter the church for mass the next day should be the new bishop; his name would be Nicholas. It happened that Nicholas had been traveling on a ship that encountered rough weather. He prayed for safety, and when he arrived on land he headed immediately for the church in Myra to give thanks; the rest is history.

During his lifetime St. Nicholas would undergo another rough voyage on a ship, a journey that would result in his being named patron saint of sailors. While returning from a pilgrimage to the Holy Land, the vessel that carried him ran into a terrible storm. Nicholas began to pray for help; witnesses said the sea calmed the instant Nicholas dropped to his knees. So important did he become to sailors that Greek and Russian seamen always sailed with an icon of St. Nicholas.

There are many more legends surrounding St. Nicholas; though the details may vary from place to place, the essence of the stories and their popular impact remain the same. One of the more famous legends has Nicholas stopping for rest at an inn during his travels. The innkeeper offered him meat, which turned out to be the flesh of three little boys the innkeeper had killed. Though the stories differ concerning who the boys were, how they were killed, and whether they were stuck in salt or pickle barrels, the result remains the same: Nicholas figured out what the innkeeper was up to and brought the boys back to life. (This act is commemorated in current St. Nicholas's Day celebrations, particularly in Lorraine, France, a town said to have been entrusted to St. Nicholas by the Virgin Mary herself.)

Nicholas's status as the patron saint of sailors helped to make him known in other lands. Italian and Dutch sailors introduced St. Nicholas to the

West, and by the Middle Ages he was as popular in Europe as he was in his homeland. He was soon an important part of the Christmas holiday season—and so, not coincidentally, was the idea of giving gifts to children.

Vladimir of Russia discovered Nicholas in Constantinople in 1003 and brought his legend home to Russia, where Nicholas later became the patron saint.

The day of the saint's death (December 6) is still observed in Europe as St. Nicholas's Day; it marks the beginning of the Christmas season in many countries, where children receive gifts said to be from the kindly saint.

Though popular throughout Europe, nowhere is the saint more celebrated than in Holland, where his name was transformed to Sinter Klaas. Like any respectable Dutchman, he wears breeches, a long Dutch pipe, and a broad-rimmed hat; the bearded man rides a white horse with a basket of treats for good children, and birch rods for naughty ones. (This is but one of the many instances of a "carrot-and-stick" approach to the St. Nicholas tradition; in Germany, children were terrified into obedience by the prospect of an encounter with a dirty, rather sinister figure known as "furred Nicholas," who invariably doled out good things to eat before leaving the house.)

St. Nick may be a jolly old fellow today, but his legend has had its dark side. He has often been depicted as a rather ominous wandering visitor who carried not only gifts for good boys and girls but also long switches for naughty children. German children of the last century were taught to fear the menacing Pelznicken ("furred Nicholas"). Eventually an ogre-like companion joined the saint, the side-kick's task typically being the meting out of justice to errant little ones.

According to the Dutch, Sinter Klaas spends the majority of the year in Spain with his servant Black Peter (a Moor), who keeps scrupulous records of the behavior of girls and boys. A few weeks before St. Nicholas's Eve, Sinter Klaas packs up for the Netherlands. Dressed in full bishop regalia, he arrives by steamer on the last Saturday in November; the whole city turns out to greet him, and there is a ceremony featuring all the area officials. St. Nicholas spends the time before St. Nicholas's Eve visiting hospitals, schools, and markets, giving little gifts to good kids while Black Peter gives switches to the bad ones. The biggest presents are left for St. Nicholas's Eve; children leave their shoes out at night filled with hay for Sinter Klaas's horse and are given gifts in return—not wrapped, but disguised or cleverly hidden. Each present comes with a note that

must be read aloud and often contains a line or two that will embarrass the recipient.

Many of these customs, incidentally, are carry-overs from old Norse mythology and ritual. The god Wodin (whom the American St. Nicholas often resembled in the late eighteenth century) was said to ride around on his horse checking up on little children.

Our Santa Claus appears to have been influenced not only by St. Nicholas, the patron saint of children, but also by the Norse gods Thor and Wodin.

Beginning in the sixteenth century, the Protestant Reformation led many parts of Europe to reject the cult of saints and anything associated with it. The legend of St. Nicholas might have died then and there, but it seems his popularity was simply too great. Most countries did change his name slightly, while leaving his background and other characteristics fully intact. To the English he became Father Christmas; to the French, Pere Noel. Though many people incorrectly assign the German name for the Christ Child—Christkindle or Kris Kringle—to St. Nicholas, the true German equivalent is Weihnactsmann, meaning "Christmas man." In Holland, too, the man and events surrounding him have been made more secular.

St. Nicholas-inspired gift givers, differing from St. Nicholas only in name and in a few particulars, can be found elsewhere in Europe. Russia's Nikolai Chudovorits evolved into Father Frost, who lives beyond the Arctic Circle and comes to Russia on New Year's Day on a reindeer-pulled sleigh with his daughter, the Snow Maiden, to place presents under trees. The Scandinavian gift givers are much more impish and mischievous. The Norwegian Julesvenn, the Danish Julenisse, and the Swedish Jultomten, are left treats on St. Nicholas's Eve in an effort to get them to do the same, as well as dissuade them from trickery and, in the case of farmers, ensure they'll protect the livestock.

In some parts of Europe, the legend of St. Nicholas was incorporated into the winter solstice festivals, which later became part of our Christmas celebration. St. Nicholas's Day had long opened the Christmas season, and as we have seen, the saint's selfless gift giving and love of children was in keeping with the themes of the Nativity. Because of the closeness in time, some places eventually merged the two days. Germany and France, for example, transferred most of the activities surrounding St. Nicholas's Eve to Christmas Eve. The majority of European countries still keep the two separate, however; St. Nicholas brings goodies on his day, and the Christ Child or the Three Wise Men deliver on Christmas or Epiphany Eve.

In some places, St. Nicholas is also celebrated as the Boy Bishop. In England, a Boy Bishop was chosen to preside over the solstice festival, along with St. Nick's older incarnation, Father Christmas.

SANTA IN THE NEW WORLD

St. Nicholas came to America by way of the Dutch in the 1600s. Sinter Claes, as the name was rendered, was obviously an important figure to the Dutch settlers: They named their first church in the New World the St. Nicholas Collegiate Church, even though it was Protestant.

In the Dutch settlement of New Amsterdam— later New York City— St. Nicholas Day and Christmas were celebrated in a merry fashion unknown to the rest of the colonies. Because of the strictly Puritan background of most of the New World settlers, any celebration of saints or Christmas was unheard of.

Illegal in New England until 1681, Christmas was later observed in the strictly religious sense—but it would be wrong to say that it was actually *celebrated* there in any meaningful way before the American Revolution. Certainly any impious foolery involving St. Nicholas was considered beyond the pale in the region for decades after independence was won.

It was only in the years after the war that Christmas began to win slow acceptance as a cause for revelry in various regions of the United States, and only at the dawn of the nineteenth century that any meaningful references to the man we would come to call Santa Claus began to appear. The change in the national attitude can probably be traced to two main factors: the intermarriage of the Pennsylvania Dutch with other settlers, and the influx of German immigrants to the new country. (German immigrants were perhaps the most enthusiastic celebrants of Christmas in northern cities during this period.)

Although Washington Irving's nostalgic turn-of-the century satires of New Amsterdam society feature some of the earliest American literary treatments of the St. Nicholas legend, the evolution from St. Nicholas to the American Santa we are familiar with today appears to have begun in earnest at least two or three decades later. Clement C. Moore's enormously influential poem "A Visit from St. Nicholas" was *written* in 1822, but it did not become widely popular until several years after that. It was published anonymously, and to increasingly enthusiastic public response, until 1837, when Moore finally acknowledged authorship. Although his lines are perhaps the most influential in forming an image of the modern Santa Claus, it is interesting to note that that name does not appear in the poem, and nor do any of its variants. Presumably the other formulations were passed over by the poet in favor of the less foreign-sounding St. Nicholas.

Much of what we now consider as essential to Santa—such as his plumpness—first appeared in Clement C. Moore's poem "A Visit from St. Nicholas." Moore apparently based his St. Nick on a rotund gardener who worked for him.

He wrote the verses for his own children, reciting it before his family for the first time on Christmas Eve. Although Santa has grown over the years from the elflike stature Moore assigned to him, it is from his lines that we get the first (and by far the most influential) concrete physical description of Santa.

He was dressed all in fur from his head to his foot,
And his clothes were all tarnished with ashes and
*   soot;*
A bundles of toys he had flung on his back,
And he looked like a peddler just opening his pack.

His eyes, how they twinkled! his dimples, how
*   merry!*
His cheeks were like roses, his
*   nose like a cherry;*
His droll little mouth was
*   drawn up like a bow,*
And the beard on his chin
*   was as white as the snow.*

The stump of a pipe he held tight in his teeth,
And the smoke it encircled his head like a wreath.
He had a broad face and a little round belly
That shook, when he laughed, like a bowl full of
*   jelly.*

Moore's portrayal of St. Nicholas as a generous gift-giver and friend to children was, of course, an outgrowth of the legends surrounding St. Nicholas. The influence of Irving's (often imaginative) accounts of the Dutch legend is also apparent throughout the poem.

The poem's emphasis on snowy winter weather may be due to earlier traditions linking St. Nicholas with winter cold—or to the fact that Moore himself enjoyed a white Christmas season in the year he composed the poem.

Moore was not the first to assign a reindeer to St. Nicholas, but he was the first to set the total at

eight, and the first to popularize the names we now associate with the animals. They are, for the record, Dasher, Dancer, Prancer, Vixen, Comet, Cupid, Donder, and Blitzen. (Rudolph would come along much later, in a 1939 story by Robert L. May.)

Thomas Nast's 1863 illustrations for the poem "A Visit from St. Nicholas," which went a long way toward standardizing the jolly one's physical appearance, were the turning point in Nast's career. Although his later political cartoons also won him national acclaim, he made a tradition of supplying fresh drawings of Santa for the Christmas issue of Harper's Weekly *each year.*

In 1842, a popular children's book featured illustrations of a stout, bearded gift-giving character it referred to as Kriss Kringle. Although uniform depictions of this figure would not surface for another twenty years, the book's drawings were in fact the first modern representations of the St. Nicholas we think of today.

The name by which we more commonly know him would not gain currency until the middle of the century, when the pronunciation of Sinter Claes had either evolved or been corrupted, depending on your outlook, to Santa Claus.

Although it had far less influence on our vision of Santa than Moore's poem, the *New York Sun's* editorial response to young Virginia O'Hanlon's query about his existence has probably had a greater effect on the way we think about him. The piece, which ran first in 1897 and has resurfaced seemingly every holiday season thereafter, captured for both adults and children the essential innocence and trust of the Santa Claus tradition. The *Sun* piece also supplied the nation with a catch-phrase that helped to unify the (previously disparate) role Santa had played in various ethnic traditions. It is probably no coincidence that the phrase "Yes, Virginia, there is a Santa Claus" entered the national lexicon at about the same time the mass media in general—and advertisers in particular—began in earnest to capitalize on the bearded one's popularity. The nation finally had a single perception of Santa to which publishers and marketers alike could appeal.

Francis Church, the writer for the New York Sun *who penned the famous response to Virginia O'Hanlon's 1897 query about the existence of Santa Claus, never received credit for the work during his lifetime.*

Although Thomas Nast's drawings had the greatest impact as far as standardizing the various images of St. Nicholas into a single chubby, smiling figure, the final touches were added (or at least formalized) in the 1920s by artist Haddon Sundblom in a series of Coca-Cola ads. Sundblom's Santa had red cheeks, wore a red gown with white fur trim, and radiated a rotund good cheer. Not surprisingly, he also liked Coca-Cola. The ad campaign ran for thirty-five years, and has even been revived in the 1990s.

DO YOU KNOW THE WAY TO SANTA CLAUS? ❧

Proof of Santa's early popularity in the United States can be found in the Indiana town of Santa Claus, named by Swiss colonists all the way back in 1852. Legend has it that this naming occurred on Christmas Eve. As the townspeople sat in their new church contemplating names, children began to yell "Santa Claus," and the name took. By the 1940s, the Santa Claus post office was flooded with mail addressed to Santa, the person. Far from being dismayed by this daunting flow of correspondence, the town welcomed the attention, although volunteers often had to be recruited to help handle the large volume. The town is a nice place to visit during the Christmas season, with its Kris Kringle street, a twenty-three-foot-high statue of Santa, and a Santa Claus park.

In 1949, the first of many Santa theme parks was set up. The North Pole Village, located in Wilmington, New York, opened for business complete with reindeer, toy workshop, and post office. It is still in operation, a popular tourist spot during its June 1 to November 1 season.

There is actually a University of Santa Claus; it trains department store Santas. Graduates receive a Bs.C., Bachelor of Santa Clausery. Similar, though not quite as catchy, is the one-day training school for store Santas run by Western Temporary Services in California. Potential Santas must meet physical and performance requirements, and pass a strict background check. After graduating, Santas must abide by a code of conduct to ensure the safety of the children and protect the sanctity of the figure they portray. Some of the more interesting guidelines are as follows:

- *Bathe daily, using a strong deodorant and mouthwash.*
- *Clean the beard and gloves nightly to keep them white.*
- *Don't leave the Santa seat, even if a child vomits or has "an accident."*
- *Do not say "ho, ho, ho!"; it may frighten children.*
- *Do not flirt with the elves.*
- *Rather than informing the crowd of a bathroom break, say "Santa is going to feed the reindeer."*

And so St. Nicholas has made his way from Asia Minor to American department stores—undergoing a few alterations on the way. Indeed, it is extremely doubtful whether St. Nicholas would recognize himself in Santa Claus today if the two were to come face to face. Still, perhaps somewhere, somehow, St. Nicholas is aware of the joy his existence has brought to children and children at heart everywhere. After all, if it were not for this quietly devout and generous man, there would be no Santa Claus. And who could imagine Christmas without Santa?

CHAPTER SEVEN

DECK The HALLS

Perhaps it is possible to get through Valentine's Day without taping up cardboard hearts and little Cupids, through Easter without coloring eggs, or even through Halloween without dressing up. Who among us, however, can imagine letting Christmas pass by without some kind of decoration? Such decorations can and do go beyond the traditional lighted Christmas tree and store-bought Santa picture on the front door. When the season to be jolly comes around, let your surroundings show it!

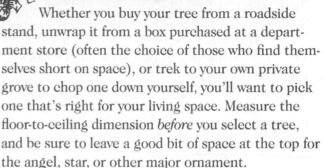

ANY ROOM—KITCHEN, bathroom, sundeck—is fair game for Christmas decorating, not just the room where the tree is. And don't forget the outside of the house! Couldn't the porch, windows, mailboxes, bushes, and even the shrubs benefit from a bit of colorful holiday decorating? Between nature and your own ingenuity, you should discover ample means of decking those halls.

NATURAL TRIMMINGS

"Shopping" in your own backyard is one opportunity for great Christmas decorations. Some simple suggestions:

Collect pine or other branches and pine cones from the woods or a nearby park and bring them inside to decorate windowsills, fireplace mantels, or other appropriate places in your home.

Decorate the house with extra branches from the Christmas tree. Find some mistletoe to hang not so discreetly in the arch of a doorway.

Stock up on that traditional Christmas plant, the  poinsettia. Place them anywhere or everywhere! (We know of one household that makes it a point to place poinsettias on just about every unoccupied surface in the house during the holidays. You may not want to go that far.)

Use holly boughs to create a large arch over your front door. Begin by standing large branches at each side of the door and build up the branches with greenery using tacks.

Make a natural garland for your Christmas tree with pine cones, berries or other natural and colorful ingredients.

THE TREE

Whether you buy your tree from a roadside stand, unwrap it from a box purchased at a department store (often the choice of those who find themselves short on space), or trek to your own private grove to chop one down yourself, you'll want to pick one that's right for your living space. Measure the floor-to-ceiling dimension *before* you select a tree, and be sure to leave a good bit of space at the top for the angel, star, or other major ornament.

Assuming yours is a live tree, you should mount the base of the tree in a little water to reduce the risk of fire. (Most good stands have a watering indentation that will not leak.) Before you set up the Christmas tree stand, however, place a layer of newspaper underneath it, and then some red or green tissue paper on which to place the gifts.

We'll leave the selection of tree decorations up to your own tastes and family tradition. Note, though, that there are a number of good ideas later in this chapter for specific homemade holiday crafts projects; many are suitable for the tree.

WREATHS

The most popular wreaths are those made from pine branches and holly berries. Wreaths are easy to make and present virtually limitless possibilities when it comes to decorating.

To make a wreath, you need a frame. This can be either two untwisted coat hangers or, if you can find them, switches of willow. Make a circular frame of about one foot in diameter. For an evergreen wreath, tie small branches of evergreen to the frame with wire, building around the wreath until it's as full as desired. Decorate with berries, pine cones, or a simple ribbon.

You might also want to try wreaths that feature dried and polished (lacquered) fruit and nuts; just fruit; just nuts; pine cones and greenery; candy; cotton balls; dried flowers; or any combination of the foregoing.

HOME CRAFT IDEAS

Opening up your home supply closet is a great way to get started with your holiday decorating. You can do a whole lot on a low budget using wrapping paper, ribbons, tape, yarn, and other odds and ends around the house. Following are some ideas.

There's a lot more around the house to wrap than presents!

"Wrap" doors, pictures, and mailboxes with ribbons, bows, and wrapping paper—so that they look like gifts. You may want to do the mailbox wrapping a day or so before Christmas at the earliest; you may also want to check the weather forecast, as there's no point securing your gaily colored paper to the mailbox an hour before a major snowstorm is due to hit! Of course, you should be sure your decorations are applied in such a way as to allow the mailbox to open and close normally.

With red tissue paper, make big mock poinsettia leaves; affix them to lamp shades, window shades, and curtain rods.

Glue a picture of a favorite Christmas scene (or perhaps a family portrait) on a cardboard base, leaving six inches of cardboard around the sides. Then glue pine branches or other greenery to the outside edges. This can be a very attractive centerpiece for a coffee table at holiday time. (Be sure, as you decorate, that the base of the box can lay flat; you don't want the centerpiece wobbling!)

Why not decorate glass balls to hang on your tree or elsewhere in your home? No, you don't have to blow the glass yourself; clear glass ornaments can be bought in any craft store and leave lots of room for personal touches. For example, you can remove the top from the ball and fill it with potpourri, sparkles, dried flowers, or a mixture of all three. Put the top back on and tie with a colored ribbon or lace. Another idea is to draw Christmas symbols on the glass with acrylic paint. Use glue to write a name in fancy script; add some glitter. Or, to make the ball even more special, put a small, favorite memento or a picture of a loved one inside. Making homemade personalized glass balls for a child's first Christmas—and/or successive ones—is also a nice idea.

Puff-ball trees are another great idea. Take a sheet of Styrofoam about a foot and a half long and cut out the shape of a tree, complete with trunk. Cover it with green cotton or felt, then cover the trunk with another color (for example, dotted Swiss). Then, using cotton and fabric scraps, stuff and sew material of various colors into little balls about two and a half inches in diameter. Cover the tree with the balls, using glue; the quilt-like effect is quite lovely, and makes for a striking holiday wall hanging.

Clothespin decorations are always a hit on Christmas trees, and can be great fun for kids who want to make something for the holidays. Using pipe cleaners, red and green felt, cotton balls, paint, glue, and glitter, you can let your imagination run wild. Can you make a reindeer? A toy soldier? A man with very long legs?

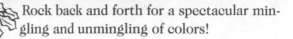

DECORATIONS FROM THE KITCHEN

Kitchen materials can help you come up with some unique Christmas decorations—some of them edible! Here are some ideas.

Tie up some cinnamon sticks with a holiday bow; place this on the stove or on the mantel. The fragrance is lovely, and the look is one of old-fashioned charm.

Holiday garlands add a festive air to your tree.

Looking for an easy, fun way to spruce up your tree? Make a garland. All you need is a long piece of string, yarn, or twine, a needle, a kitchen, and your imagination. The classic, of course, is the popcorn and cranberry version, but garlands can be made out of anything: candy, raisins, or dried dates, alternated with, say, buttons or colored squares of construction paper. Kids love to help, but watch those needles! Best to select large, dull ones, and to monitor children closely during this activity.

Try making a holiday wave bottle. You'll need white olive oil, white vinegar, green and red food coloring, and an large old *clear* wine bottle, complete with cork, that's had the label scrubbed off. Measure a third of a cup of each liquid. (Increase by equal proportions if your bottle seems to warrant it.) Add the red food coloring to the oil; add the green food coloring to the vinegar. Then pour both liquids into the wine bottle and secure tightly with the cork.

Rock back and forth for a spectacular mingling and unmingling of colors!

CHRISTMAS CRAFTS FOR CHILDREN

Children remember Christmas as a time filled with special activities and unexpected treats. Working on holiday craft projects will give kids something to remember—and make your house look bright and festive.

Safety reminder: Always carefully monitor crafts activities involving children and scissors. We strongly suggest safety scissors for all of the following activities.

Here are some simple craft ideas to bring out the artist (and the Christmas spirit) in young ones. *Construction paper stockings* are a timeless classic. You will need: red construction paper; green felt; cotton balls; gold and silver glitter; glue; and scissors. Cut a stocking shape out of red construction paper. Brush some glue on the top portion of the stocking and paste down cotton balls, to give the impression of the fur trim. Spread glue elsewhere on the stocking and decorate with glitter and felt as desired. Use a paper punch to poke a hole in the top of the ornament. Children can cut out names from different-colored paper or write them on with markers. String with yarn to hang.

The *paper-plate Santa* is another holiday favorite.

You will need: red construction paper; a paper plate; cotton balls; colored markers or crayons; glue; and scissors. On the paper plate, draw Santa's eyes, nose, and mouth using markers or crayons. Brush some glue above his eyes and around his mouth, and paste down cotton balls to make bushy eyebrows and a beard. Cut a triangle out of red construction paper for Santa's head. Glue the hat to the top of the drawing. Then glue one cotton ball to the tip of the hat. Let dry.

Or how about a *paper-plate wreath*? You will need: a paper plate; crayons; other decorating goodies of your choice, such as small pieces of felt, buttons, glitter, confetti, or fabric scraps, and scissors. Cut out the center of the paper plate. Color with crayons. (Green is recommended, but if your kids feel like getting creative, we certainly won't stand in their way.) Then glue bits of holiday magic to the wreath.

Many families go in for *pine cone ornaments*—and save the glittering mementos of Christmas for years and years. Here'show to make them. Pour a small amount of glue onto a paper plate. Roll the pine cone around in the glue, then sprinkle the cone with colored glitter and let dry. Use a pipe cleaner to create a loop or hook at the top for hanging.

Another favorite: *egg ornaments*. Get an uncooked white egg; poke a small hole in each end with a needle. (Parents will need to supervise this step.) *Carefully* blow into one hole; this will cause the white and yolk to come out the other. When all the material is removed, decorate the egg with glitter, paint, felt, or whatever other materials strike your fancy. One popular option is to decorate the egg with different colors of melted wax, carefully applying the wax with a toothpick.

Speaking of eggs, why not make some *egg carton ornaments*? They're simple and fun. Cut each individual compartment out of an egg carton, making a small hole at the top. (You'll thread this hole with string later on when it's time to hang the ornament.) Using markers, color the compartments. Some popular themes: faces, snowflakes, and stars. It's also fun to hang a little bell inside with ribbon or thread.

Cup ornaments are just about as easy to make. You will need: Styrofoam or paper cups; string or ribbon; crayons or markers; pictures cut out of old Christmas cards or magazines; and scissors. Turn a cup upside down and poke two *small* holes on either side just above the bottom. String ribbon through the holes and tie a big loop so the ornament can be hung. Then decorate the cup by coloring it, gluing down pictures from cards and magazines, or both. Feeling creative? Use glue to add glitter or pieces of colored fabric!

Cupcake holder ornaments are lots of fun, too. Just get hold of some cupcake papers—foil or paper, plain or decorated. Flatten them out. Decorate foil ones by drawing on the plain side with crayons or markers. Decorate the plain ones with stickers or glitter. Tape a yarn loop to the top of the ornament to hang.

Don't throw out that Styrofoam tray— turn it into a holiday decoration!

Think twice before jettisoning that Styrofoam meat tray! Wash it clean, dry it thoroughly, and make *star ornaments*. Cut out star shapes; brush on glue and sprinkle with silver or gold glitter. Using a paper punch, make a hole at the top big enough for yarn to pass through; make a loop for hanging.

The *construction-paper snowflake* has a long and distinguished history in many families. It's colorful and very easy to make. Just fold colored construction paper in quarters (or more times, depending on how intricate you want the snowflake) and cut little designs in the paper. Loop a string through one of the holes and hang. (You can also tape the flakes to a poster or wall; they're beautiful on their own, too.)

If you're willing to help with the kitchen work, *clay ornaments* can be a lot of fun, too. But the cooking part is just for grownups. You will need to mix together in a big pan three cups of cornstarch and six cups of baking soda. Mix well; add three and three-quarters cups of water. Cook over low heat, stirring constantly, until the mixture is the consistency of mashed potatoes. Remove it from the heat and cover it with a damp dish towel. When cool, remove the clay from the pan and knead it until smooth. Cover a tabletop with waxed paper taped securely to the underside of the table. Roll the clay to a quarter-inch thickness. Cut out shapes with Christmas-theme cookie cutters. When the shapes are completed, use a knitting needle or unsharpened pencil to poke a small hole in the top of the ornament; it should be big enough to fit yarn through. Mix acrylic paint with a little water and let the children paint their ornaments. Be sure to let them dry thoroughly! Once the ornaments are hard enough, you may want to date each one and write the name of the artist on the back. These pieces tend to become heirlooms.

Macaroni ornaments are another classic, and like the clay figures, they tend to stick around for years. You will need: various types of macaroni; heavy paper or a clean, dry Styrofoam meat tray (cardboard will also do); glue; and gold spray paint (adult use only). Cut a wreath shape out of heavy paper or a Styrofoam meat tray. Decorate with different pieces of uncooked macaroni, gluing them down in desired spots. For variety, use a number of different kinds of macaroni. When the glue is completely dry, spray the ornament with gold paint (a grownup job). Use a paper punch to poke a hole in the top of the ornament and string with yarn to hang. We've suggested a wreath here, but of course you can customize this approach to make macaroni stockings, candy canes, trees, or whatever else you desire.

Holiday placemats can be great fun. All you need are large square pieces of white, red, or green construction paper, markers or crayons, and any other decorating goodies. Have children draw a large circle in the center of the paper to mark where the plate should go. Draw a smaller circle for a glass, and outlines of forks, spoons, and knives. Decorate the paper until you have a set of festive placemats for your table.

Homemade Christmas cards lessen the pressure on the purse strings for parents and add a personal touch to the traditional exchange of cards. Depending on whether the card is from the family, or from the child only, you will need: white, red, or green construction paper, crayons or markers, pictures cut from magazines or old Christmas cards, family photos, and all the regular decorating goodies. Fold the paper in half. Decorate the outside and inside, leaving enough space to write a Christmas message. Homemade envelopes can be made by using larger pieces of construction paper, folded and stapled together on the sides. Decorate the envelopes with glitter, or use markers to make some Christmas designs.

Older children can make a *Santa Mobile* to help younger siblings join in on the Christmas spirit. You will need: small Styrofoam balls; paper plates; black, yellow, and red construction paper; dental floss or yarn, cotton, glue, markers, and silver paper. Cut Santa's boots and hat out of construction paper and then cut a strip of black paper for the belt and a small square of yellow for the buckle. Draw or paint his eyes, nose, and mouth on a Styrofoam ball, then glue on his hat. Glue cotton to the tip and brim of the hat. Paint or color the paper plate red, and glue on the paper belt and buckle. Thread a large needle with dental floss (an adult job); poke it through the top of the Styrofoam head and out the neck, tying a loop at the top of Santa's head. Tape the other end of the dental floss to the back of the paper plate to join the head and body, then connect the boots to the plate by taping floss to the back of each boot and the back of the plate. Hang from the loop at the top. (You can also substitute a smaller paper plate for Santa's head if necessary.)

To add to the snowflakes on the wall, many children like to make *paper Christmas trees*. You will need: green construction paper; glue; markers; felt; small decorative cake balls; and assorted decorating goodies. To make the shape, cut a green tree shape of the desired size from the construction paper. (Or cut three triangles—big, bigger, biggest—and show the child how to glue them, overlappping each to make a tree.) Decorate using cake balls, felt, and any other goodies you have handy.

OTHER IDEAS

It takes a little work—and some cleanup time—but we think your children will enjoy taking whacks at a real piñata for the holidays. Warning: Start early; the papier-maché piñata must dry for several days! Combine one-third of a cup of flour with one-quarter of a cup of water; transfer the mixture to a plastic bag and knead it to make paste. Transfer the paste to a large bowl. Now blow up a balloon. Dip strips of newspaper into the paste and use them to cover the balloon. Let it dry. Meanwhile, roll some newspaper into a tight ball to form the donkey's head, and tape it to balloon. Cover the head with paper dipped in paste. For ears, use cardboard from an egg carton or a box. Tape them on the head and cover them with paper dipped in paste. For legs, use four toilet paper rolls, again wrapped with paper dipped in paste. Tape them to the body. Let the donkey dry for two days. With poster paints, paint with bright colors, adding eyes, mouth, and other elements to the head; let dry. Once it's dry, *gently* cut a small hole in the top of the body section (you'll pop the balloon in the process) and then drop in candy, gum, party favors, and other treats. Use string or yarn to hang the piñata from the ceiling.

For variety, instead of a donkey, use your poster paints to create a reindeer piñata, complete with red nose.

For a yummy decoration, expand your Christmas decoration list to include the makings of a *candy sled*, complete with all the fixings: two candy canes, one candy roll (Lifesavers, for instance), one large pack of gum (a big pack with at least fifteen sticks), and chocolate kisses. Take the pack of gum and lie it flat so that the widest part is facing up. Tape or glue one candy cane to each side of the pack, making the runners for the sled. For the riders: tape or glue the roll of Lifesavers to the pack of gum; tape or glue chocolate kisses

to the Lifesavers roll (the kisses are the head, arms, and legs) and you've got yourself a sled that will slide its way to the tummy.

Making *homemade wrapping paper* is another fun—and inexpensive—decorating activity. You will need: one large roll of paper; crayons; markers; paint; pictures cut from magazines; glue; glitter; lace; ribbons; and anything else you think might look good as a wrapping! Roll out some paper, then cut in appropriate-size sheets to wrap specific gifts. Try to personalize your sheets; if the person who is to receive the gift is a sports enthusiast, adorn the wrapping paper with images clipped from *Sports Illustrated*. It's best to carefully glue the decorations and let the paper dry, rather than use transparent tape. Customized wrapping, when prepared carefully, adds an unforgettable personal touch to gift giving.

CHAPTER EIGHT

The 20th-Century American Christmas

Americans sometimes forget that the Christmas they are familiar with is a relatively recent development. Take the question of Santa's appearance. For some time, the Bearded One's attire and physique had any number of variations from artist to artist and region to region. The famous man's look was not really finalized until a nationwide ad campaign for Coca-Cola broke in the 1920s. And Christmas itself, the celebration that for most of us towers over all others, was not an official holiday in every corner of the Union until 1890. Even at that time, New Year's Day was a strong competitor for the honor of prime gift-giving holiday.

Although its roots extend back for centuries, the Christmas Americans know and love is fundamentally a twentieth-century phenomenon. The following surveys and excerpts from published accounts of Christmases past offer a glimpse of the evolution of the holiday—and the nation that fell in love with it.

YOUR CHRISTMAS BUDGET: THE 1900s ≈

Representative prices for items popular at various times during the decade, culled from newspaper and magazine ads of the period:

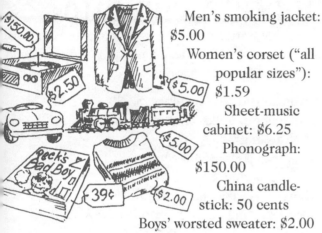

Men's smoking jacket: $5.00

Women's corset ("all popular sizes"): $1.59

Sheet-music cabinet: $6.25

Phonograph: $150.00

China candlestick: 50 cents

Boys' worsted sweater: $2.00

Toy sewing machine: $1.00

Toy automobile "with rubber tire wheels": $2.50

Elevated railroad set: $5.00

Clothbound copy of *Peck's Bad Boy*: 39 cents

ITEM: MORGAN CELEBRATES THE SEASON ≈

NEW YORK, December 23—Ten clerks employed by J. Pierpont Morgan are reported to have each received from the banker a present of a $5,000 gold certificate. A messenger for Mr. Morgan drew the bills from the subtreasury.

For the benefit of those who are not on intimate terms with $5,000 gold certificates, it may be explained that they are among the most beautiful examples of the printer's art. In color they are a most effective blending of orange, black, and green.

(1901 *Boston Globe* account)

ITEM: AN ACT OF BENEVOLENCE ≈

Pay the Boy a Nickel!

To the Editor:

Every person purchasing a paper [on Christmas Eve] should pay the newsboy therefor five cents [instead of the customary two]. The amount will not be missed by the giver and a great good will result.

(Letter appearing in the *Boston Globe*)

A POEM SUITABLE FOR THE SEASON ≈

The merry halls may jingle in the good, old-fashioned way;
In merriment we mingle, with the music holding sway.
The "Gloria in Excelsis" is sounding everywhere,
But, really, 'tisn't Christmas, if Mother isn't there.

She hangs a newer halo round the mistletoe on high;
A spirit of bravado drew away the weary sigh—
For sorrow is no mistress, and life lets go its fear
Amid the joys of Christmas, when Mother, dear, is here.

The fire upon the hearthstone lights up with
ruddier glow;
The laughter is more mirthsome, bubbling
forth in frolic flow;
The Christ Child truly comes to us, in all His
heavenly cheer,
If the advent of old Christmas finds mother, also,
here.

(William Hopkins)

ITEM: A THOUGHT FOR THE HOLIDAY SEASON ∾

On the seamy side there comes at Christmas a
feeling that the word is, to those who are not of the
elect, most unkind; and it is the experience of police
that most of the injudicious, unlimited drinking . . .
is not caused so much by the exuberance of people
wanting to celebrate Christmas, as by the efforts of
those who would forget.

(*Boston Globe* editorial in support of the growing
movement toward prohibition of liquor)

CHRISTMAS ADVERTISING: THE 1900s ∾

Dependable Goods, Fair Prices, and Your Goodwill
are responsible for the throngs which have filled our
stores and the marked enthusiasm displayed during
these Xmas holidays. Although the buying has been
beyond expectation and our assortments are yet
complete, still each day makes a large hole in the
stock. In order not to carry over Xmas Goods, from

now on goods will be marked at prices that
will be simply irresistible. Come and profit during
these last two days.

(Gilchrist Department Store advertisement)

YOUR CHRISTMAS BUDGET: THE 1910s ∾

Representative prices for items popular at various
times during the decade, culled from newspaper and
magazine ads of the period:

Women's leather handbag: $3.50
Folding umbrella ("indispensable when
traveling"): $4.00
Opera glasses: $5.00
French plume: $1.95
Singer "sewmachine": $24.50
"Self-starting" Everett automobile: $1,250.00
Girls' wool dress: $2.95

ITEM: A PLEA ∾

Dear Santa, I've got to go
To bed—it's late, you see—
So listen, please, for you must know
Just what to bring to me.
I want a pair of skates, a knife,
A pony that can trot;
I want a nice big drum and fife
And all the books you've got.
I want a kite with miles of string
And several Christmas trees
But when you come this year, don't bring
Another baby, please.

(Anonymous poem, circa 1915)

ITEM: BETTER LATE THAN NEVER ≈

It occurred to a Pittsfield man yesterday that Christmas was coming. In that merry relation, a

thought struck him. Glancing up at a shelf in the office where he is employed, he saw thereon a package [addressed to a friend], which just one year ago his wife had given him to mail . . . He sent the package along . . .

(From the *Berkshire Evening Eagle*, 1911)

CHRISTMAS ADVERTISING: THE 1910s ≈

Churchill's Wonderful Christmas Review, "Cornell's Follies"

For the entertainment of our many guests, and in keeping with the Christmas Spirit of Gladness and Good-will, we present this extraordinary review headed by the "Cornells" and assisted by a chorus of *twenty beautiful girls* . . . . We promise an evening of delightful entertainment, bewildering in the variety of its enjoyment.

Churchill's: More than a restaurant—a Broadway institution. Broadway at 49th St.

YOUR CHRISTMAS BUDGET: THE 1920s ≈

Representative prices for items popular at various times during the decade, culled from newspaper and magazine ads of the period:

Men's winter overcoat: $18.50
Fountain pen: $2.50
Silk hat: $7.50
Victrola brand phonograph: $99.80
RCA Radiola ("musical quality unsurpassed"): $115
With loudspeaker: $150
Persian rug: $38.75
One-pound box of chocolates: $6.50
Ladies' silk umbrella: $10.00
Toy tool chest: $1.55
"Juvenile model" bicycle: $48.75
Girls' ice skates: $5.00
"Beautiful stately jointed doll" with wig, dress, shoes, and stockings: $1.95

ITEM: WOULD THAT IT WERE SO ≈

"Peace on Earth" Near Fulfillment

(*Boston Globe* headline, December 25, 1921; the lead story referred to progress in a Washington peace conference of major international powers.)

ITEM: PROHIBITION MAKES ITS PRESENCE FELT ∾

(Shortly after the Volstead Act went into effect, Federal authorities issued an announcement, apparently meant for inclusion in Christmas Eve editions of the nation's newspapers, that the use of "fermented wines for sacramental purposes" during religious services would be forbidden. The substitution of a "specially prepared fruit juice" was said to be under consideration by major religious leaders. At about the same time, at an elite Christmas party attended by Channing H. Cox, the Governor of Massachusetts, prohibition agent Harold Wilson seized four bottles of "White Horse Cellar" whiskey. A major scandal ensued. The bottles disappeared under mysterious circumstances.)

ITEM: THOSE INCONSIDERATE LAST-MINUTE SHOPPERS ∾

Way of Women at Christmas Puzzles a Woman

Why Not Start List Now (December 5) and Do Your Christmas Giving Sensibly, with Regard to Feelings of Others, as well as for Time, Strength, and Money? Leaving Everything until Last Minute Makes Season Harder for Clerks and Spoils Holiday!

(Headline of an article in the December 5, 1926, *Providence Journal* urging procrastinating wives to show a little more thought during the holiday season. The article is accompanied by an illustration of an unnamed acquaintance of the author's who "used to dread Christmas and spent the whole holiday in bed, utterly spent, and with ice-bags at her head and feet.")

ITEM: A "CHRISTMAS CARD SUGGESTION" OF THE ERA ∾

To a Stout Lady in a Short Skirt

May your silk hose be filled to overflowing
With all the gifts that Santa's shops comprise
And may you have the joy that comes of knowing
It takes so much to fill a hose your size.

(Anonymous poem, circa 1925)

CHRISTMAS ADVERTISING: THE 1920s ∾

With the approach of the world's greatest holiday, the question of Seasonable Clothing and Suitable Gifts for family and friends absorbs the attention of the majority of the people. How to satisfy this very laudable ambition is the question. Let us help you. Go to the JOYCE STORE nearest you . . . You don't need to pay cash for your Xmas clothing! We will gladly charge your purchases and you may pay for them in easy partial payments—next year!

(Joyce Store advertisement)

YOUR CHRISTMAS BUDGET: THE 1930s ∽

Representative prices for items popular at various times during the decade, culled from newspaper and magazine ads of the period:

"Satin or metallic" men's pajamas: $10.95
Pullman men's slippers: $4.00
Quart bottle of Monopole champagne: $5.00
Westinghouse radio: $21.00
Boys' knickers: $1.49
Child's wagon (red): $3.49
Doll, layette, and basket: $4.94
Dollhouse: $5.00
Toy airplane: 65 cents
Toy typewriter: $1.95

ITEM: THE PRESIDENT APPARENTLY FINDS THE IDEA OF A LONG WEEKEND REPUGNANT ∽

(In 1931, back in the days of the six-day work week, President Hoover granted Federal workers the day off for December 26, a Saturday, but denied them the day after New Year's Day. In less than a year, weary Depression-era voters would grant Hoover some time off.)

ITEM: LITTLE ORPHAN ANNIE ON CHRISTMAS DURING THE GREAT DEPRESSION ∽

ANNIE (after hearing two society ladies complain elaborately about the hectic holiday shopping season): Well, I haven't but two or three folks to give to, and only a buck or so to spend—I guess in some ways it's a cinch to be poor! Anyway, it's lots simpler . . .

(From the December 24, 1936 syndicated comic strip by Harold Gray)

ITEM: A BREAD LINE CHRISTMAS ∽

(In 1931, roughly 5,000 unemployed men showed up to eat a free Christmas dinner of turkey and mulligan stew at one site in Manhattan. The total number of New York City families recieving charity food baskets or free meals that year is not known, but it was clearly in the tens of thousands. An unspecified number of men took part in a Christmas dinner for "the city's hoboes" at the Hobo College on East Fourth Street. Nationwide, six million people—perhaps eight percent of the adult population of the country—were looking for work.)

ITEM: MAIL EARLY— POSTAL WORKERS NEED THE HOURS ⮑

A plea to "mail early" during the Xmas season, in order to aid the local unemployed, was issued last night over station WBZ by Postmaster William E. Hurley, who urged that Xmas cards and packages be sent this week.

"During the Xmas season," said Postmaster Hurley, "the mail increases about 300%, and the handling of this enormous quantity of mail taxes the facilities of the Postal Service to the limit. It has been necessary to augment our regular force with a large number who are unskilled in Post Office work, but we cannot give them more than two days unless you give us your Christmas mail at once."

(Boston Globe, December 20, 1931)

ITEM: SANTA LIVES ⮑

(Brooklyn salesman Sam Coplon, a Spanish Civil War veteran who recuperated from his wounds at a hospital in North Creek, New York, was eager to find a way to express his gratitude. For twenty years— most notably in the early 1930s, at the height of the Great Depression—he delivered toys to the impoverished children of the Adirondacks at Christmastime. In one year alone, Coplon delivered over 12,000 toys with the help of local clergy and charitable organizations.)

CHRISTMAS ADVERTISING: THE 1930s ⮑

Christmas Greetings That Are Spoken Ring True

Spreading over far horizons, Xmas voices will soon be bringing joy into millions of hearts and homes throughout the land.

Somewhere there is someone who would like to hear you say, "Merry Christmas"; someone whose happily surprised answer "The same to you and many of them" will brighten the day for you.

Although miles apart, the telephone will quickly bridge the gap, sending and bringing back holiday greetings with all the warmth and sincerity that only voices can give.

(A New York Telephone Company ad from the early 1930s)

YOUR CHRISTMAS BUDGET: THE 1940s ⮑

Representative prices for items popular at various times during the decade. (Note, however, that many prices fluctuated wildly during the war.) Culled from newspaper and magazine ads of the period:

Metal cigarette case: $9.95
Zippered rayon ladies' robe: $6.98
Upright vacuum cleaner: $49.90
Electric iron: $2.49
Electric coffee maker: $6.98
Roller skates: $9.95
Magnetized soldier doll with American flag: $4.00
Tiddlywinks game: 39 cents

ITEM: PEARL HARBOR BRINGS A DIFFERENT KIND OF CHRISTMAS ❧

While preparations are going on here, in a mild way to be sure, due to wartime conditions, our little British cousins across the seas have not been overlooked. Old Santa, that kindly bewhiskered man, will pay them a visit through the thoughtfulness of the relief agencies here . . . Of the many thousands (of) toys of various types and descriptions sent across the  seas by Bundles for Britain, most of them are soft dolls and animals made from scraps of materials in the sewing looms . . .

(The *New York Times*, December 21, 1941)

CHRISTMAS ADVERTISING: THE 1940s ❧

More than 3 million faces testify!

The Schick Shaver is a gift men really use! *Swell* for service men! Soldiers, sailors, or marines . . . because they can be plugged in at camp or on a boat—and work!

(Ad appearing shortly after the Japanese attack on Pearl Harbor)

ITEM: THE POWER OF CHRISTMAS ACROSS THE CENTURIES ❧

From the centuries between [the first Christmas] and now, come stories of holy men, of bishops and peasant-saints, and of brave men who preached the White Christ to the Vikings of the north or on Iona's isle. As in popular belief, with each returning eve of the Nativity the miracles of the first Christmas happen again, so in these tales the thorn-tree blossoms anew and wonderful roses bloom in the bleak forest.

(From the foreword for *The Christmas Book of Legends and Stories*, a popular 1944 release)

ITEM: ENTER BING CROSBY, SINGING ❧

There's a lot to be said against a White Christmas. It is awkward, trying to fit an old-fashioned Christmas on a new-fashioned, hard-surfaced world, obliterating its familiar signposts, cunningly disguising its modern dangers, hiding its unpleasantness under a soft veil.

But here it is, the enchanted world you looked out on as a kid, white, mystic, beautiful, through which a jovial creature half fat man, half spirit came riding, a transformed world in which anything could happen. All you had to do was believe hard enough that it could.

Listen! Sleigh bells? Do you suppose there is such a spirit, after all?

(From the *Providence Journal*, December 24, 1947)

YOUR CHRISTMAS BUDGET: THE 1950s ∾

Representative prices for items popular at various times during the decade, culled from newspaper and magazine ads of the period:

Slide projector: $43.95
Men's topcoat: $18.00
Quilted rayon and taffeta robe: $8.95
Pipe and lighter set: $1.94
Television set with "livesize seventeen-inch screen": $229.95
Donald Duck xylophone: $2.65
Mickey Mouse train set: $1.59
Musical milk mug: $6.95

ITEM: A MESSAGE FROM INDEPENDENCE ∾

"Our hearts are saddened on this Christmas Eve by the suffering and the sacrifice of our brave men and women in Korea. We miss our boys and girls who are out there . . . they are trying to prevent another world war. We pray to the Prince of Peace for their success and safety."

(President Harry Truman in Independence, Missouri, December 24, 1951)

ITEM: DWIGHT AND MAMIE SEND THEIR BEST ∾

(Forsaking the White House tradition of sending solemn, formal Christmas cards, President and Mrs. Eisenhower commission cards that feature drawings of them in caricature, wearing bright red suits with white trimming and wishing the recipient a merry Christmas. Clearly, observers note, this is a First Couple that does not mind letting down its guard now and then.)

ITEM: THE CHOICE ∾

If Western civilization dies in a rain of nuclear explosions, it will be written in a later day that the tragedy of our century was the inability of man to apply to the problems of peace the genius that loosed a most fearful Armageddon. "Peace on earth," the angels sang 2,000 years ago, but peace today is as tremulous as thin fog at dawn along the shore . . . Today is a day for happiness . . . but we shall end by trading that happiness for horror if we cannot recapture the humility, the simplicity, the understanding, the faith, the affection, and the lack of fear that marked the shepherds who saw His tiny fists wave in the lamplight of a stable at Bethlehem.

(From an editorial in the *Providence Journal* December 25, 1957)

CHRISTMAS ADVERTISING: THE 1950s ⤳

Hectic Xmas Shopping Give You Gas, Indigestion, "Hurry-Worry Stomach"?

You shop too fast, eat on the run, worry. No wonder your stomach gets upset! But you can now get *immediate long-lasting relief*—with AMITONE! Only AMITONE contains GLYCINE, that automatically regulates excess stomach acids. Minty tablets melt on your tongue. At drugstores.

(An ad from the early 1950s)

YOUR CHRISTMAS BUDGET: THE 1960s ⤳

Representative prices for items popular at various times during the decade, culled from newspaper and magazine ads of the period:

Lazy Susan: $4.76
Electric can opener: $7.77
Ladies' stretch slacks: $3.97
Aluminum Christmas tree and stand: $2.99
Monaural copy of Ray Coniff's LP *Memories are Made of This*: $2.40
Stereophonic copy of Ray Coniff's LP *Memories are Made of This*: $2.90
"Your kiddie's Polaroid picture taken with Santa himself": 49 cents

Viewmaster stereo viewer in "rugged, shock-resistant plastic": $1.75
Sled: $3.00
"Poor Pitiful Pearl" doll and "change of clothes that makes her a princess": $8.00

ITEM: TRADING STAMPS TO THE RESCUE ⤳

Mrs. Phyllis Stephens, 20, of Scotia, New York, said she faced a gloomy holiday when she learned that neither she nor her husband, Corporal Luther C. Stephens, could afford the $146 round-trip fare from his station at the U.S. Marine Training School at Memphis, Tenn. Then she remembered that she had collected 80 books of trading stamps. The young wife knew the stamps were redeemable for gifts and in desperation sent a telegram to the Triple S Blue Stamps company in Hackensack, New Jersey. The firm decided to play Santa Claus. It told Mrs. Stephens it would supply a plane ticket to bring her Marine home Friday and return him to Memphis Christmas night.

(United Press International report, December 21, 1961)

ITEM: THE PEANUTS GANG WEIGHS IN ⤳

(The animated television special "A Charlie Brown Christmas" premieres in December, 1965. Remember that pathetic little tree? Reviews and ratings are both excellent; the show becomes a staple holiday broadcast in every following year.)

ITEM: A CHRISTMAS GREETING WITH AN INTERESTING PERSPECTIVE

. . . And God called the dry land Earth; and the gathering together of the waters called He seas; and God saw that it was good. And from the crew of Apollo 8, we close with good night, good luck, a merry Christmas, and God bless all of you—all of you on the good Earth.

> (Message from Apollo 8 astronauts, Christmas Eve, 1968)

CHRISTMAS ADVERTISING: THE 1960s

If He Has Everything: Bottled Portable Radio, $35.00

Would you ever guess that there is an eight-transistor radio tucked inside this bottle of "Ballantine's Whisky"? Its quality components give it a fine full sound and selectivity. Runs on penlight batteries!

> (From a 1966 ad for a Rhode Island department store)

YOUR CHRISTMAS BUDGET: THE 1970s

Representative prices for items popular at various times during the decade, culled from newspaper and magazine ads of the period:

Stereo set with turntable and 8-track player: $199.95
AM radio mounted in headphones: $14.95
Lava lamp: $45.00
"25-function" calculator: $49.95
CB radio: $89.95
Bionic Man action figure: $6.66
Baby Thataway: $8.88
Ten-speed bicycle: $99.50
Evel Knievel stunt cycle: $9.96

ITEM: PINING FOR THE PRE-WATERGATE CHRISTMAS

(*New York Times* columnist Russell Baker, writing in December, 1974—the first Christmas of the Ford administration—recorded his wistful observations of the gray holidays of his immediate Washington past. Back then white Christmases, Baker wrote solemnly, were out; gray ones were much more fashionable, because that was the color that could get you past security. "Several days before Christmas," Baker recalled, "everyone in the Government seemed to leave town, and we would be left alone in the great empty city with only the wiretap police, the undercover CIA agents, and the holdup men . . .")

ITEM: THE IMMIGRANT'S PUZZLEMENT ≋

Understanding Santa Is Troublesome for Laotians on Their First American Yule

Khamchanh Chantharangsy was preparing about a dozen of his fellow Laotians for their first American Christmas . . . They had never heard of Santa Claus . . . Now that the refugees are in America, he said, "We try to do everything like American. . . ."

Khamchanh interpreted [for his friend Xiong Tong]: "He says it is quite strange, quite interesting but quite impossible for this man to penetrate the roof of his house with such a large sack of toys."

(From the *Providence Journal*, December 24, 1976)

CHRISTMAS ADVERTISING: THE 1970s ≋

Santa, Conserve Your Energy!

No need to shop around . . . just one stop at Azuma—thousands of gift ideas for everyone on your list—their huge selection will "sleigh" you!

(Ad for a New York store during the height of the oil crisis)

YOUR CHRISTMAS BUDGET: THE 1980s ≋

Representative prices for items popular at various times during the decade, culled from newspaper and magazine ads of the period:

Microwave oven: $227.00
Videocassette recorder (1980): $1,395
Videocassette recorder (1989): $299
Garfield telephone: $44.70
Space Invaders video game cassette: $24.88
Your favorite Care Bear: $13.99
Castle Greyskull, from the Masters of the Universe Collection: $23.99
Lazer tag game kit: $29.99
Rambo Rocket water launcher: $14.96

ITEM: AND THEN WHAT? ≋

(Highlights from columnist Ellen Goodman's tongue-in-cheek 1981 *Boston Globe* column "Ways to Lose Weight During the Holidays" included giving birth, "the only surefire way to drop seven pounds overnight between Christmas and New Year's"; joining a cult that consumes only food of a certain shade; hiring a food stylist to assemble beautiful, but inedible, meals; and getting a divorce.)

ITEM: CHRISTMAS, USA

Bethlehem: 838
Holly: 542
Joy: 145
Holiday: 110
Christmas: 89
Noel: 30
Carol: 17
Mistletoe: 12
Santa Claus: 7

(From a 1985 U.S. Geological Survey report
of places, including local landmarks, bearing
names reminiscent of Christmas themes)

ITEM: A YUPPIFIED CHRISTMAS

"Ghost," said Jeremy, "tell me, please, what do I
have to do to become president—or at least managing director?"

(From Michael Lewis's 1989 *New York Times*
column *A Christmas Bonus*, a parody of
A Christmas Carol in which a Wall Streeter
ponders his awful fate in years to come: a door
bearing the words "Jeremy Gaunt, Vice President.")

ITEM: THE BRADY BUNCH, REVISITED

Debuting on Sunday, December 18, 1988, *A Very
Brady Christmas* was CBS's highest-rated TV movie
of that year . . . Following its premiere broadcast,
the telepicture elevated CBS's third-place ranking to
the number-two spot for the first time that season in

the weekly ratings . . .

Says (producer) Sherwood (Schwartz), "The
success of it was a combination of two things.
One was the fact that it was Christmas time,
which is family time, so it was a perfect opportunity
to bring them back. And number two, many people
wanted to know what they looked like. There was a
great longing to see what happens. It's like with any
family reunion."

(From Elizabeth Moran's book *Bradymania*.)

YOUR CHRISTMAS BUDGET: THE 1990s

Based on current price estimates.

Men's sport jacket (smoking optional): $79.95
Gift certificate from Victoria's Secret (corsets in
    short supply): $50.00
Sheet-music cabinet: $450.00
Portable CD player: $269.95
China candlestick: $25.00
Boys' worsted sweater: $25.00
Big Point sewing kit: $5.00
Toy automobile:
    $4.99
Railroad set:
    $29.99
Paperbound
    copy of
    *Peck's Bad
    Boy*: $4.50

CHAPTER NINE

'TIS MORE BLESSED *to* GIVE *than to* RECIEVE

The most obvious feature of the modern American Christmas is the giving and receiving of gifts. Gifts have become almost synonymous with December 25, so much so that some fear they have overshadowed the true meaning of the holiday. What follows is a brief history of the Christmas giving tradition. It may surprise you!

There's no disputing that Christmas giving has become very big business indeed; a strong holiday selling season often means the difference between a good and a bad year for a retailer. In the shopping frenzy that lasts from the opening of the Christmas buying season to the closing hours of Christmas Eve, it's easy to forget what all the fuss is for.

It wasn't always like that. There was, not so long ago, a time when Christmas involved no gift exchange whatsoever, and in some countries things remain that way. The union of Christmas and gift giving was a gradual one; actually, the full story of the bright packages beneath the tree begins in the days *before* the birth of Christ.

GIFTS AND CELEBRATIONS, OLD AND NEW

In ancient Rome, gifts were exchanged during the Saturnalia and the New Year's celebrations. At first these gifts were very simple—a few twigs from a sacred grove, statues of gods, food, and the like. Many gifts were in the form of vegetation in honor of the fertility goddess Strenia. During the Northern European Yule, fertility was celebrated with gifts made of wheat products, such as bread and alcohol.

As time went on, gifts became more elaborate and less edible. While most of this giving was done on a voluntary basis, history has had its share of leaders who did their level best to ensure they'd have plenty of gifts to open. One year Emperor Caligula of Rome declared to all that he would be receiving presents on New Year's Day; gifts he deemed inadequate or inappropriate were ridiculed.

(As readers of Robert Graves's works will remember, displeasing Caligula could be a dangerous undertaking.) Then there was Henry III, who closed down the merchants of England one December because he was not impressed with the amount of their monetary gifts.

Ho, ho, ho: If you'd been a merchant whose end-of-year cash gift was too small to suit England's King Henry III, you might have found yourself out of business.

Although we may question his Christmas spirit, Henry was only following long-established tradition in focusing on end-of-year gifts. Like many old customs, gift exchange was difficult to get rid of even as Christianity spread and gained official status. Early church leaders tried to outlaw the custom, but the people cherished it too much to let it go. So instead, as was beginning to be the pattern, church leaders sought a Christian justification for the practice. The justification was found in the Magi's act of bearing gifts to the infant Jesus, and in the concept that Christ was a gift from God to the world, bringing in turn the gift of redemption and everlasting life.

After Christianity had established itself throughout Europe, Christmas celebrations were quite common; gift giving as a component of Christmas Day, however, was not. The concept of a gift exchange on the holiday itself remained more the exception than the rule, and much of the gift giving at that time was confined to New Year's, as in the days of the ancient Romans. Some countries, particularly those

under Spanish cultural influence, saved gift giving for Epiphany (January 6), the day marking the visit of the Magi to Jesus.

ENGLAND LEADS THE WAY

Even though the roots of the Christmas present extend to ancient times, the gift-giving tradition we are familiar with today owes perhaps the most to Victorian England. The Victorians, who brought a renewed warmth and spirit to Christmas after it had experienced a long period of decline, made the idea of family (and particularly children) an integral part of the celebration. Also important to them was the act of helping the less fortunate in society. Friendliness and charity filled many hearts during their Christmas season, so giving gifts was a natural.

In gift giving as in so many other things related to Christmas, the Victorians had a tremendous impact.

If the Victorians didn't invent the motto "it's the thought that counts," they may as well have. To them the *act* of giving was far more important than the present, and a great deal of thought and creativity went into each gift. The ultimate reason for giving a gift, they felt, was as an expression of kindness, a sentiment that tied in nicely with the historical tradition of the holiday.

Accordingly, Victorians surrounded the act of gift giving with a great deal of ingenuity and merriment; simply tearing into a cache of wrapped boxes would have been to miss the point. Far more thought and preparation than that were in order during the holiday season.

Cobweb parties, for instance, were lots of messy fun. Each family member was assigned a color, then shown to a room crisscrossed with yarn of various colors. Each person was to follow an assigned color through the web of yarn until he or she reached the present tied to the end. Yarn was also used to wrap small gifts: the ball was unwound, then rewound to conceal the present.

The Christmas pie was another favorite diversion, although it was not exactly edible. Small gifts were concealed in a large bowl of grain; after Christmas dinner, everyone gathered around the pie and took turns taking a spoonful. Whatever treat was in your spoonful was yours to keep.

Though Victorian gift giving was filled with the spirit of Christmas, much of the actual exchange was still done on New Year's Day. It was only in the late 1800s that the custom was finally transferred to Christmas.

Across the pond, Christmas was taking a similar shape in America. Of course, the American Christmas was greatly influenced by the Victorians, gift-giving tradition and all. America expanded on the concept with the addition of Santa Claus, whose forerunner St. Nicholas was legendary for his generosity. The association with gifts was a natural one. Soon Santa or one of his earlier incarnations became responsible for the presents left in an ever-increasing number of stockings.

THE ECONOMICS OF CHRISTMAS

By the late nineteenth century the simple and essentially nonmaterialistic gift-giving tradition had begun to wither away. Christmas had come face to face with commercialism, and the new message was: buy.

It wasn't long before shopping and the idea of gifts had woven itself into the fabric of Christmas. This transition was encouraged by merchants (and everyone else in the developing economies of Europe and America) who stood to benefit from a year-end buying binge. It was—and is—an open question whether this development did more harm than good to the holiday. Skeptics wonder whether the emphasis on buying, shopping, and getting ultimately brings more happiness or disappointment—especially to those who can afford little. Others have found a new and robust variation on the holiday spirit in the shopping-related hustle and bustle around Christmastime. Perhaps, they argue, it is too much to expect that Christmas, having adapted itself to so many civilizations over the years, *wouldn't* be affected by the modern consumer culture in which we live.

In the end, it's likely that the best way to approach Christmas gift-giving is with both viewpoints in mind. Most parents of young children are unwilling or unable to mount the sustained battle necessary to do away entirely with what might be called the "gimme" Christmas—but there's no reason some of the laudable spirit of past holidays can't be incorporated as well.

WHAT WAS BEING GIVEN?

Back in the days of Ancient Rome, a citizen might have received the makings of a nice salad for Saturnalia; a Victorian chap might have the pleasure of a new pipe or a snuff box. But what about the United States, the country that put the "C" (for commercialism) in Christmas giving and receiving? What were the popular gifts as the giving tradition unfolded?

In the early part of the century, the crayon and the teddy bear took their place among children's classic toys.

In the first part of the twentieth century, gifts were a great deal simpler than they are today. Clothing was a staple for adults and children, with the latter getting a toy or two for enjoyment. The first decade of the twentieth century gave us two childhood classics: the crayon and the teddy bear.

The Crayola crayon was born in 1903, bringing out the artist in children everywhere. The teddy bear, which came along four years later, was created by Morris and Rosie Michtom. The Michtoms got the idea from a  cartoon of the day that detailed a hunting trip taken by President Teddy Roosevelt. Apparently the president had refused to shoot a bear that had been tied up for him; in the cartoon, the bear was portrayed as tiny and helpless. Rosie Michtom made a stuffed bear cub, which her husband displayed in the window of his store along with the inspirational cartoon. The bear was very popular, and eventually the Michtoms received permission from the president himself to mass-market the stuffed cubs as "Teddy Bears."

For youngsters who liked to tinker, Tinker Toys came along in 1914. Raggedy Ann dolls were mass produced in 1918, becoming one of the more popular dolls of that time. In general, dolls and games were popular during this period, as they are today, notwithstanding countless changes in toy trends. Other highlights of this time were the rideable toys: sleds, rocking horses, and red wagons.

The yo-yo and the BB gun helped to tide youngsters through the Great Depression.

Despite the Depression of the 1930s, toy manufacturers continued to come up with occasional classics that people somehow managed to scrape enough money together to buy. Yo-yos were quite popular. Those who have seen *A Christmas Story*, a delightful 1983 movie about one boy's Christmas wish during this era, will doubtless recall the Red Ryder BB gun, a big seller in real life. The gun got its name from a comic book character, one of the first of a very long (and ever-growing) list of toys based on comic, TV, or movie characters.

Guns as a whole were popular at this time, along with other cowboy and cops-and-robbers paraphernalia. War toys were also big sellers, especially toy

soldiers. A fascination with science and science fiction also seems to have begun in this period, as witnessed by the popularity of chemistry sets and fantasy stories.

After America made it through the Depression and World War II, the country began to prosper as never before. Industry and technology were in high gear; more and better jobs meant Americans had more discretionary income to spend on things like Christmas gifts. It was the beginning of a glorious time for toys.

THE POSTWAR TOY BOOM ~

The number of American children exploded in the years after the war, and so, not surprisingly, did the national appetite for toys. Some of the most enduring playthings of today—such as the Etch-A-Sketch, Play Doh modeling clay, and the Barbie doll—were introduced in the decade and a half following the end of World War II.

TV left its mark on the gift-giving tradition in the 1950s.

In the late 1940s and early 1950s, science fiction toys remained popular, while toys connected with comic characters and other media-driven figures began to loom large in the market. Toys associated with TV characters benefited by being seen by a steadily larger television audience. For a time, Howdy Doody presents were all the rage.

Dolls of Howdy, Clarabell, Princess Summer-Fall-Winter-Spring, puzzles, sewing kits, stuffed animals, comic books, paint sets, and more made their way under a lot of Christmas trees in the early 1950s.

Not all the big gifts were connected to Howdy and his gang, of course. A Jackie Robinson doll was quite popular in 1950. (This may have been the first mainstream doll portraying an African-American that did not parody racial characteristics.) The best-selling toy of 1953 was an update of that 1930s classic, the Red Ryder No. 960 Noisemaker BB gun. It did everything a real BB gun did—except shoot. Perhaps the most popular toy for boys in the early 1950s was the electric train. These were times to remember for Lionel, American Flyer, and Marx.

1954 was a very big year for adventurer Buck Rogers, but Buck was outdone the following year, which saw Davy Crockett coonskin hats and guns on the top of many a boy's Christmas list.

Crockett merchandise was incredibly popular; one story has it that a tent manufacturer, stuck with thousands of unsold units, stenciled the words "Davy Crockett" on each—and got rid of them all in a matter of days. Total 1955 retail sales of Crockett-related items was estimated at a cool $100 million.

What else did the initial wave of Baby Boomers want for Christmas? The list from the decade of the 1950s includes: Silly Putty; Frisbees (originally, they were called Pluto Platters); hula hoops; Mr. Potato Head sets; slot cars; Betsy Wetsy dolls; Lego blocks; The Game of Life; pogo sticks; matchbox cars; and, for the younger set, the classic Chatter telephone from Fisher-Price.

The good people at Mattel, who keep track of such things, report that more Barbie dolls have been manufactured since her introduction than there have been people born in the United States during the same period.

Although she made her debut in the 1950s, it was in the following decade that Barbie hit the big time. Although it's hard to fix a single event that marks Barbie's emergence as a perennial favorite, she appeared in the Sears Christmas catalogue for the first time in 1961. From that day to this, Barbie, Skipper, Ken, and their many companions and accessories (sold, as ever, separately) have brightened many a young girl's Christmas morning.

Barbie's male counterpart, G.I. Joe, enjoyed a similar robust popularity during the 1960s. In 1978, G.I. Joe was put to rest, reportedly because of the high price of petroleum products. (It may have been no coincidence, however, that Joe, who was a huge hit during the nation's hawkish early- and mid-sixties period, was withdrawn at a time when national misgivings about our past involvement in Southeast Asia were at their height. He made a major comeback during the Reagan administration.)

Other popular 1960s Christmas gifts included: Beatles records, coloring books, toy guitars, lunchboxes, and related merchandise; "Hot Wheels" miniature cars; the Super Ball; Instant Insanity, a colored cube game akin to the later Rubik's cube; Tonka trucks; and the Twister game. ("Right foot green!") Board games were also a very popular gift category. Strong sellers from the decade include: Clue, Risk, Candyland, Go to the Head of the Class, Cooties, Scrabble, Yahtzee, Operation!, Parcheesi, and Jeopardy (the Art Fleming, rather than Alex Trebek, incarnation). The Mousetrap game sold 1.2 million copies in 1963.

After about 1966, spy-related toys and dolls (or, to use the preferred terminology, "action figures") were brisk-selling Christmas gifts. Products based on the James Bond movies and the television series *The Man from U.N.C.L.E.* were the favorites in this category. Kids could go undercover with briefcases, cigarette cases, and fake lighters that concealed toy cameras and the like. Also available were lunch boxes, cars, puzzles, bubblegum cards, costumes, books, and records, all specially designed for the preteen espionage crowd.

The supercharged economy of the middle 1960s yielded some extravagant Christmas gifts.

By the middle 1960s, the American middle class, against which many young people had begun to rebel, was buying for Christmas at a fevered pitch—and children weren't the only ones on the receiving end. Adults were indulging in some "toys" of their own, and not all of them were cheap.

There were home steam baths and saunas, jewelry, and, for quiet (or not-so-quiet) evenings at home, newfangled color television sets. As one Chicago retailer put it, Americans were "loaded."

And it seems that some retailers priced their merchandise based on that belief. For one Christmas buying season, Tiffany's in New York offered their upscale patrons the opportunity to purchase a $550 sterling-silver watering can. Neiman-Marcus's offerings ranged from $300 lace hankies to $10,000 wristwatches to $20,000 teapots to $125,000 diamond rings. Not to be outdone, San Francisco's Joseph Magnin sold three-liter flacons of Shalimar perfume for $2,500, to be delivered to the lucky recipient via Rolls-Royce. (Presumably the driver picked a route that discreetly avoided the Haight-Ashbury district of The City; his vehicle would have been woefully out of place in the counterculture encampment that had begun to spring up there.)

THE 1970s-1990s

The unparalleled prosperity of the middle 1960s yielded to social division, inflation, and an energy crisis. Despite all that, America still found the stamina to purchase Big Wheels, Inchworms, Huffy bikes, Mrs. Beasely Dolls, and Pitchback baseball. For adults, Christmas 1973 brought novelty "I Am

Not a Crook" watches bearing an image of President Nixon, his eyes shifting back and forth with each movement of the second hand. Other memorable Christmas gifts of the era included eight-track cartridges and players, trolls with tufts of incandescent hair, and Super Spirographs. The merchandising/ mass entertainment link reached new heights of commercial success as George Lucas's *Star Wars* movies spawned scores of lucrative toys, books, and related paraphernalia. In a foreshadowing of the video boom to come, the first basic home arcade games appeared at the end of the decade. A television-friendly version of the arcade hit Pong (which seems quaint and simple by today's gaming standards) was a huge hit.

 Christmas giving in the '70s was also affected by fads (CB radios and pet rocks) and fashion diversions (puka shell necklaces and mood rings), about which the less said, the better.

What parent of the early 1980s who stood in line for hours could forget the Cabbage Patch doll?

In the 1980s America entered the consumer electronics age in earnest. Along with the usual stereo, photographic, and appliance electronics, there were now compact disc players, video cassette recorders, and sophisticated video games. It was during this decade, after a brief incursion by the ubiquitous Cabbage Patch Kids, that the word video began to

figure prominently in just about anything that found its way to the top of the average kid's Christmas list.

In one year, the Nintendo company was responsible for three of the top ten toys sold at retail, including the number-one item, the Nintendo Action Set. Coming years would bring Nintendo NES, Nintendo Super Mario Bros., Nintendo Game Boy, and Nintendo Game Genie, among countless other offerings. For a time, blinking, beeping, video games of one brand or another (but usually Nintendos) were poised to take over every living room and young, unoccupied palm in the country. And then, it seemed, they did.

Similarly mind-boggling in popularity were the Teenage Mutant Ninja Turtles, whose reign would extend well into the next decade. Radioactive turtles may have seemed an implausible idea for a toy, game, film, and video juggernaut, but young boys had an insatiable appetite for the heroes. Other popular toys from the decade of the 1980s included the talking Pee-Wee Herman doll, assorted Smurf paraphernalia, the Li'l Miss Makeup doll, and, for younger kids, the Fisher-Price tape recorder. For adults, top gifts of the era included exercise bikes, ice cream makers, Trivial Pursuit games, Pictionary games, camcorders, VCRs, and, toward the end of the decade, laptop computers.

Bart Simpson weighed in with an attitude in the 1990s.

As the 1990s began, yet another television-spawned merchandising bonanza enjoyed remarkable popularity, but this time the innocence of Howdy Doody was nowhere to be found. Bart Simpson, who would probably have done something quite rude to Howdy on principle if he had gotten within a yard of him, became one of the biggest television stars in the country. Bart and his demented, anti-utopian world, complete with odd relatives, served as a weekly vehicle for biting social satire and remarks likely to embarrass teachers when repeated

in class. Kids couldn't get enough of him, and cash registers rang up huge sales for his books, clothes, and other products during the holidays. The more squeamish parents grudgingly complied with Christmas requests and comforted themselves by observing that things probably couldn't get much worse. (They would be in for a surprise with the advent of Beavis and Butt-Head.)

The 1980s success of high-tech toys carried over into the 1990s. Yet ironically, and despite white-hot sales of things like Power Rangers sets, the toys that have remained popular through decades of trends are the ones that don't require batteries, plugs, headphones, or TV tie-ins—just imagination, the desire for fun, and maybe a few friends. The chances are good that children will, for the foreseeable future, wake up Christmas morning and find that Santa has left them one or two things that he left for their parents many years ago. And as we head into the next century, dolls, board games, building blocks, stuffed animals, Play Doh, Legos, toy guns, crayons, and bicycles are sure to make that journey, too.

OOPS!

Have you put things off until the last minute? Here are ten good last-minute gifts to consider:

- *Perfume or cologne*
- *Page-a-day calendar (available in bookstores)*
- *Videocassette of* Citizen Kane *(considered by many the greatest American film of all time) and/or* Plan Nine from Outer Space *(considered by many the worst American film of all time).*
- *Slippers*
- *Recipe file*
- *Chocolates*
- *Blank book for entering family recipes (or with family recipes already entered)*
- *Art from the children in your family (best if you can buy a frame in which to place it).*
- *Alarm clock*
- *Personal stereo*

You say you're in even worse trouble? You say it's Christmas Eve and you've forgotten someone? Don't panic. Get in the car and find a gas station; many offer snazzy premiums with a fill-up at this time of year: toys, games, or videos.

CHAPTER TEN

A MASS MEDIA CHRISTMAS

Frank Capra's
It's A
Wonderful Life
An RKO Radio Release

W hen we think of Christmas these days, we often think of television, music, and the movies. Whether this is a good or a bad state of affairs is not our concern here; the fact is that, for most of the people reading this book, the Grinch, George Bailey, Rudolph the Red-Nosed Reindeer, and a host of other figures who came to prominence after World War II now play an important part in our celebration of the holiday. Their popularity is fundamentally different than the popularity enjoyed by, say, a classic Christmas carol; we learned about these characters not over centuries, but suddenly, and with bewildering speed, thanks to modern means of communication.

Rather than pretend that the mass-media aspect of Christmas is somehow heretical, we prefer to think of it as a lot of fun—and we celebrate it here. Dig in!

THE ULTIMATE MASS-MEDIA CHRISTMAS TRIVIA QUIZ ≈

HEREWITH THE MOST COMPREHENSIVE trivia quiz on Christmas songs, films, television programs, and videos you're likely to come across anywhere. Grab a separate sheet of paper and jot down your answers. (Note: this is a particularly good group activity for a Christmas party!)

How do you or your group rate?

20 or fewer correct: As a general rule, you've been doing something other than watching television at Christmas time over the past thirty or forty years. Congratulations on that, but don't pick "Holiday Films" as a *Jeopardy* category.

21 to 40 correct: Okay. You got the easy ones. You've been rocking to "Jingle Bell Rock," but you could probably stand to rent "It's a Wonderful Life" a time or two.

41 to 60 correct: You've definitely got the holiday spirit, but Andy Williams still thinks you can do better.

61 to 80 correct: Nice work. You can probably recite the lyrics to "White Christmas" without batting an eye. Spread the good cheer!

81 to 100 correct: Ho, ho, ho! Somewhere in heaven, Nat King Cole is crooning "The Christmas Song" just for you.

101 to 106 correct: You can probably recite the entire script of *The Grinch Who Stole Christmas* verbatim—from deep sleep. Take a bow.

1. What role does Cary Grant play in 1947's *The Bishop's Wife*?

   (a) A hard-boiled newsroom editor
   (b) A befuddled collector of dinosaur bones
   (c) A dashing, sophisticated man about town who is being pursued by a sinister international espionage ring
   (d) A debonair angel

2. What is it that the little girl wants for Christmas in the 1991 film *All I Want for Christmas*?

   (a) Her two front teeth
   (b) A life-size poster of Keanu Reeves
   (c) For her divorced parents to get back together
   (d) An end to the blood feud that has set her town against itself for seven years

3. In what year was the Gian-Carlo Menotti operetta *Amahl and the Night Visitors*, in which a young boy encounters the Three Wise Men on the eve of Christ's birth, first broadcast on network television?

   (a) 1950
   (b) 1951
   (c) 1955
   (d) 1968

4. In the movie *A Christmas Story,* why is the boy's mother afraid to let him have a B.B. gun?

   (a) She's afraid he'll forget all about his other Christmas toys
   (b) She's afraid he'll shoot his eyes out
   (c) She's afraid he'll run away from home, secure in his newfound power
   (d) She's afraid he'll have an accident while cleaning the gun

5. How did *Amahl and the Night Visitors* come to be written?

(a) It was composed by a medieval monk who left the score behind a stone wall in a monastery, where it would rest undisturbed for two and a half centuries
(b) It was written at the request of His Royal Highness King Edward II
(c) It was commissioned for a special Christmas television broadcast
(d) It was composed for the London stage in the early 1930s

6. Who plays Bob Cratchit in 1992's *The Muppet Christmas Carol*?

(a) Michael Caine
(b) John Denver
(c) Bob Denver
(d) Kermit the Frog

7. Charles Dickens himself makes an appearance in *The Muppet Christmas Carol*. Who plays him?

(a) Hunter S. Thompson
(b) Michael J. Fox
(c) George C. Scott
(d) The Great Gonzo

8. In the 1949 classic *Holiday Affair*, what two actors played suitors to Janet Leigh?

(a) Robert Mitchum and Wendell Corey
(b) Dean Martin and Jerry Lewis
(c) Bud Abbott and Lou Costello
(d) Bob Hope and Bing Crosby

9. Why does Ernest want to find a replacement for Santa in 1988's *Ernest Saves Christmas*?

(a) Ernest has it on good authority that Santa's best days are behind him, although the old man refuses to face it
(b) Santa has decided that it's time to retire
(c) The reindeer won't work on Christmas Eve anymore because Santa refuses to pay them time and a half
(d) Santa is missing

10. Who plays the handyman in 1984's *Christmas Lilies of the Field*?

(a) Billy Dee Williams
(b) Sidney Poitier
(c) Clarence Williams III
(d) Caroll O'Connor

11. For which of the following films did Irving Berlin compose the song "White Christmas"?

(a) *White Christmas*
(b) *Holiday Inn*
(c) *It's a Wonderful Life*
(d) *Last Tango in Paris*

12. What is the request made to Heaven by a recently-dead police officer (played by Mickey Rooney) in 1984's *It Came Upon a Midnight Clear*?

(a) That he be allowed to put on one last show in the barn
(b) That peace on earth and goodwill among men be made manifest
(c) That Santa be allowed to make his annual trip despite the evil designs of the Anti-Christmas League
(d) That he be allowed to spend one final Christmas with his grandson

13. Who played the hapless slogan composer in 1940's *Christmas in July*?

(a) Ronald Reagan
(b) Jimmy Stewart
(c) Preston Sturges
(d) Dick Powell

14. Of the following, which was a slogan that was actually used in *Christmas in July*?

(a) "If you can't sleep, it's not the coffee, it must be the bunk."
(b) "Make it a special Christmas. Make it a regular Christmas. Chew Simulax tablets."
(c) "Coffee the way it was meant to be."
(d) "Good to the last drop."

15. In what year was "A Charlie Brown Christmas" first broadcast?

(a) 1963
(b) 1964
(c) 1965
(d) 1966

16. In the 1954 movie *White Christmas*, why was the old New England inn in such desperate financial straits?

(a) The previous owner had been subject to a lawsuit, but had concealed this fact from prospective buyers
(b) The town suffered a major blow when a local shoe factory closed
(c) The inn was a ski resort, and there hadn't been any snow for a year
(d) The tourist guides had their doubts about the kitchen help

17. Which of the following Christmas personages did *not* appear in an eponymous animated Christmas special?

(a) Linus van Pelt
(b) Rudolph the Red-Nosed Reindeer
(c) Frosty the Snowman
(d) The Little Match Girl

18. What's the name of the character Bing Crosby plays in *Holiday Inn*?

(a) Winston Smith
(b) Jim Hardy
(c) Charles Foster Kane
(d) Mike Cleary

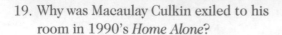

19. Why was Macaulay Culkin exiled to his room in 1990's *Home Alone*?

    (a) He set an elaborate trap in his smug older brother's room
    (b) He was discovered attempting to tape his weird uncle while he, the uncle, was taking a shower
    (c) He had been watching too many old movies on video
    (d) He was being punished for a disastrous kitchen spill

20. Name the two bad guys in the *Home Alone* movies who eventually became famous as the "Wet Bandits."

    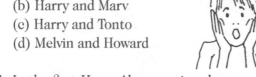

    (a) Joe and Ratso
    (b) Harry and Marv
    (c) Harry and Tonto
    (d) Melvin and Howard

21. In the first *Home Alone* movie, where was the family headed for Christmas?

    (a) Paris
    (b) Barcelona
    (c) Florida
    (d) San Juan

22. How is Joe Pesci disguised as he scopes out the neighborhood in the early scenes of the first *Home Alone* movie?

    (a) As a mobster
    (b) As a policeman
    (c) As a mailman
    (d) As an exterminator

23. In the first *Home Alone* movie, why did Macaulay Culkin head-butt his older brother in the stomach?

    (a) The brother wouldn't let him have a turn with the Nintendo game
    (b) The brother took the last of the cheese pizza
    (c) The brother was threatening to squeal about a lousy grade on a spelling test
    (d) The brother was choking on something

24. What is the name of Macaulay Culkin's character in the *Home Alone* movies?

    (a) Kevin McAllister
    (b) Kevin McReynolds
    (c) Kevin MacArthur
    (d) Kevin McCall

25. What is the name of the scary old guy in the first *Home Alone* movie?

    (a) Cratchit
    (b) Bob
    (c) Marley
    (d) Marlon

26. Who does Macaulay Culkin go to to plead for the return of his family in the first *Home Alone* movie?

    (a) The pigeon lady
    (b) Santa Claus
    (c) A hotel employee
    (d) A policeman

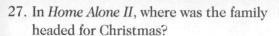

27. In *Home Alone II*, where was the family headed for Christmas?

(a) Paris
(b) Barcelona
(c) Florida
(d) San Juan

28. Which of the following occurs in *Home Alone II*?

(a) Joe Pesci's hair is set on fire
(b) A rope Joe Pesci is climbing is doused with kerosene and set on fire
(c) Joe Pesci is struck in the head by a huge lead pipe
(d) All of the above

29. What is the first image after the opening credits in Frank Capra's 1946 classic *It's a Wonderful Life*?

(a) A sky full of stars, three of which blink as a number of angels speak
(b) George Bailey sledding down a hill on a snow shovel
(c) George's younger brother Harry Bailey sledding down a hill on a snow shovel
(d) A sign reading "You Are Now in Bedford Falls"

30. What is the name of the angel who is assigned the task of saving George Bailey's life in *It's a Wonderful Life*?

(a) Lumen Phosphor
(b) Fluor Candle
(c) Clarence Oddbody
(d) Tom Sawyer

31. Which two characters have this exchange in *It's a Wonderful Life*?

"A lot of these people are out of work!"
"Well, then, foreclose."
"I can't do that. These families have children."
"They're not my children."
"They're *somebody's* children . . . "
"Are you running a business or a charity ward?"

(a) George Bailey and Henry Potter
(b) George Bailey and Uncle Billy
(c) Peter Bailey and Henry Potter
(d) George Bailey and Mr. Gower

32. Had George Bailey, the main character in *It's a Wonderful Life*, never been born, what would Bedford Falls have been called?

(a) Morgantown
(b) Pottersville
(c) Gowerville
(d) Robinwood

33. In *It's a Wonderful Life*, why was young George Bailey hit by his boss?

(a) He was late for work
(b) He'd been neglecting his duties, paying too much attention to the girls at the soda counter
(c) He hadn't delivered a prescription, as he'd been specifically ordered to do
(d) He kept daydreaming about traveling to foreign lands

34. What are the names of the policeman and the taxi driver in *It's a Wonderful Life*?

  (a) Bert and Ernie
  (b) Tom and Jerry
  (c) Mike and Terry
  (d) Billy and Rick

35. Which of the following A-level Hollywood scriptwriters toiled on early drafts of *It's a Wonderful Life*, only to have his work rejected?

  (a) Dalton Trumbo
  (b) Marc Connelley
  (c) Clifford Odets
  (d) All of the above

36. In *It's a Wonderful Life*, what is the nickname of the little girl whose flower-petals wind up in George Bailey's pocket on the night he considers killing himself?

  (a) Daisy
  (b) Zuzu
  (c) Pitter-Pat
  (d) Bunkadoodle

37. What, according to a child in the Bailey family, does it mean when you hear bells ringing?

  (a) You've been knocked out
  (b) You've just won the final round of *Jeopardy*
  (c) You have tinnitus
  (d) An angel has just gotten his wings

38. Who played the lead role in *It Happened One Christmas*, the 1977 television remake of *It's a Wonderful Life*?

  (a) Henry Winkler
  (b) Marlo Thomas
  (c) Jimmy Stewart
  (d) John Denver

39. What actor who would later portray the captain on the pilot episode of *Star Trek* also played Jesus in the controversial 1961 film *King of Kings*, now often aired during the holiday season?

  (a) Jeffrey Hunter
  (b) William Shatner
  (c) Patrick Stewart
  (d) DeForest Kelley

40. In December 1968, James Mason portrayed Franz Gruber in a network television special. Who was Franz Gruber?

  (a) He was a poor German immigrant who brought the tradition of the decorated Christmas tree to the United States
  (b) He was an Austrian immigrant to the United States who wrote dozens of classic Christmas carols
  (c) He was a Swiss war hero who spirited hundreds of Jewish children to safety on Christmas Eve, 1943
  (d) He was an Austrian organist

41. How did Edmund Gwenn (in the role of Kris Kringle in *Miracle on 34th Street*) come to the notice of the management at Macy's?

(a) He answered an advertisement for department store Santas
(b) He saw that the Santa in the store's holiday float was so drunk that he couldn't stand up, and volunteered to replace him
(c) He started handing out presents to children in the store
(d) He showed up at the personnel office dressed in a Santa Claus costume

42. Name the child star whose career was launched by her appearance in *Miracle on 34th Street*.

(a) Shirley Temple
(b) Elizabeth Taylor
(c) Judy Garland
(d) Natalie Wood

43. When was *Miracle on 34th Street* first released in movie theaters?

(a) The late autumn of 1947
(b) The winter of 1948
(c) The late autumn of 1948
(d) The summer of 1947

44. In *Miracle on 34th Street*, whom did Edmund Gwenn list as "next of kin" on his Macy's employment application form?

(a) His invaluable colleague Anna Botelho
(b) Clarence Oddbody
(c) The children of the world
(d) Reindeer

45. In *Miracle on 34th Street*, what precipitated Edmund Gwenn's being committed to Bellevue?

(a) He declared that he was not Santa after all, but rather the Tooth Fairy
(b) He struck a psychiatrist on the head with a cane
(c) He wandered the streets of New York without apparent purpose
(d) He failed a polygraph test administered by the New York City Police Department

46. Name four actors who have portrayed Ebenezer Scrooge in the movies or on television.

47. Who plays Marley's ghost in *Scrooge*, the 1970 adaptation of *A Christmas Carol*?

(a) John Gielgud
(b) Alec Guinness
(c) Jason Robards
(d) Martin Sheen

48. When does the opening sequence of the 1959 classic *Ben-Hur* takes place?

(a) A.D. 33
(b) A.D. 30
(c) A.D. 112
(d) A.D. 1

49. Red Skelton and Vincent Price teamed up in a classic restaurant sketch in the hour-long Christmas special "Red Skelton's Christmas Dinner". What were the names of the characters they played?

   (a) Max and Dan
   (b) Freddy the Freeloader and Professor Humperdue
   (c) Dracula and Dr. Frankenstein
   (d) Bud and Lou

50. Who are Santa's incompetent assistants in the 1934 film *Babes in Toyland*?

   (a) Charlie Chaplin and Buster Keaton
   (b) W.C. Fields and Mae West
   (c) Groucho, Chico, and Harpo Marx
   (d) Stan Laurel and Oliver Hardy

51. In the 1945 film *Christmas in Connecticut*, how does Barbara Stanwyck, as part of a promotional gimmick, convince the world that she's an ideal housewife?

   (a) She rents a house, hires a secret chef, and talks Reginald Gardiner into pretending to be her husband
   (b) She takes out an ad in the *New York Times* that is supposed to have been written by her husband
   (c) She hires her sister-in-law to impersonate her
   (d) She has her picture taken with the children of her neighbor, Shirley Booth

52. Who directed the cable-TV remake of *Christmas in Connecticut*?

   (a) Richard Lester
   (b) Bernardo Bertolucci
   (c) Jonathan Demme
   (d) Arnold Schwarzenegger

53. In 1946, David Lean directed a memorable version of *Great Expectations* that has become a holiday broadcast staple. What is the name of the film's orphan hero?

   (a) Pip Pirrip
   (b) David Copperfield
   (c) Nicholas Nickleby
   (d) Oliver Twist

54. Finish this sentence from the animated classic *The Grinch Who Stole Christmas*.

   "Maybe Christmas," he thought, "doesn't come from a store. Maybe Christmas, perhaps . . ."

   (a) " . . . means cruising in a convertible with four on the floor."
   (b) " . . . is a mail-order package from Land's End at your door."
   (c) " . . . is a new pair of socks in a shade you abhor."
   (d) " . . . means a little bit more."

55. From what town did the Grinch attempt to steal Christmas?

   (a) Bedford Falls
   (b) Whoville
   (c) Schenectady
   (d) Smallville

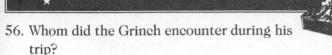

56. Whom did the Grinch encounter during his trip?

(a) Cindy Lou Who
(b) Horton the Elephant
(c) The Cat in the Hat
(d) The Lorax

57. In the 1982 animated feature *The Snowman*, who is the main attraction at the party to which the Snowman brings his young friend?

(a) An elf
(b) The Snow Queen
(c) A baby in swaddling clothes
(d) Santa Claus

58. How do the characters played by Jason Robards and Julie Harris meet in the 1988 HBO special *The Christmas Wife*?

(a) By bumping into one another on a street corner
(b) By being seated in adjoining seats to watch a performance of *The Nutcracker*
(c) Through a lonely hearts agency
(d) Via office e-mail

59. What member of the cast of M*A*S*H also appears in Fred Astaire's classic holiday television movie, *The Man in the Santa Claus Suit*?

(a) Gary Burghoff
(b) Alan Alda
(c) Robert Duvall
(d) Bud Cort

60. 1989 saw a *Married . . . with Children* sendup of *It's a Wonderful Life* called *It's a Bundyful Life*. Who played Al Bundy's guardian angel?

(a) Howard Stern
(b) Bobcat Goldthwait
(c) Sam Kinison
(d) Vincent Price

61. On which classic Christmas story is 1987's *A Miracle Down Under* loosely based?

(a) *The Gift of the Magi*
(b) *The Little Drummer Boy*
(c) *A Christmas Carol*
(d) *A Christmas Memory*

62. The 1990 syndicated movie *The Kid Who Loved Christmas* tells the story of a jazz musician (Michael Warren) who, after becoming a widower, fights to retain custody of his foster child. Which entertainment legend made his final film appearance in this movie?

(a) Michael Landon
(b) Sammy Davis, Jr.
(c) Cary Grant
(d) James Cagney

63. In what year was *Mr. Magoo's Christmas Carol* first broadcast?

(a) 1962
(b) 1963
(c) 1964
(d) 1965

64. Whose voice narrated the animated special *Frosty the Snowman*?

(a) Boris Karloff's
(b) Gene Autry's
(c) Fred Astaire's
(d) Jimmy Durante's

65. Name the actress who played a mannequin who comes to life in the 1990 made-for-TV Christmas movie *A Mom for Christmas*. No multiple-choice here, but we will give you a big, big hint: she starred in the most successful movie musical of all time.

66. Name the members of the group that scored a hit that featured the chorus "Christmas, don't be late" in the early 1960s.

(a) John, Paul, George, and Ringo
(b) Mick, Keith, Charlie, Bill, and Ron
(c) Pete, Roger, John, and Keith
(d) Simon, Theodore, and Alvin

67. Which unlikely duet crooned "The Little Drummer Boy" for a holiday television special?

(a) Janet Jackson and Frank Sinatra
(b) David Bowie and Bing Crosby
(c) Paul McCartney and Elvis Costello
(d) Pat Boone and Little Richard

68. Which group recorded the novelty songs "Plenty of Jam Jars," "Everywhere It's Christmas," and "Christmas Time (Is Here Again)" for special Christmas disks meant for limited distribution to the official members of their fan club?

(a) Spike Jones and His City Slickers
(b) The Beatles
(c) The Partridge Family
(d) The Cowsills

69. Name the lead vocalist on the '80s Christmas hit "2000 Miles."

(a) Deborah Harry
(b) Pat Benatar
(c) Joan Jett
(d) Chrissie Hynde

70. Who recorded the only antiwar holiday song to achieve chart status in the U.S. during the Vietnam War? What was the song?

71. Name the rock star who organized the benefit recording "Do They Know It's Christmas" and won praise for his work on behalf of famine victims.

(a) Bob Geldof
(b) Elton John
(c) Mark Knopfler
(d) Sting

72. This song, composed for a children's Christmas program in the 1940s, sold a million and a half copies in seven weeks when it was released nationally, thereby becoming one of the fastest-selling records in history. Name the song.

(a) "Frosty, the Snowman"
(b) "Winter Wonderland"
(c) "All I Want for Christmas Is My Two Front Teeth"
(d) "Silver Bells"

73. Who recorded the original version of "I Saw Mommy Kissing Santa Claus"?

(a) Jimmy Boyd
(b) Herman Hasswell
(c) Pinky Lee
(d) Michael Jackson

74. How old was this artist when he recorded "I Saw Mommy Kissing Santa Claus"?

(a) 11
(b) 12
(c) 9
(d) 44

75. In what year was Bing Crosby's recording of Irving Berlin's "White Christmas" released?

(a) 1942
(b) 1943
(c) 1944
(d) 1945

76. Who recorded the immortal holiday classic "Grandma Got Run Over by a Reindeer"?

(a) Weird Al Yankovic
(b) Barnes & Barnes
(c) Elmo and Patsy
(d) The Nurk Twins

77. One of the following recordings is fictitious. Which is it?

(a) "Santa Bring My Baby Back to Me," by Elvis Presley
(b) "Santa Claus is Coming to Town," by Bruce Springsteen
(c) "Away in a Manger," by the Brady Bunch
(d) "Santa's Got a Brand New Bag," by James Brown
(e) "Winter Wonderland Experience," by Jimi Hendrix

78. Who was the artist who recorded a chorus of barking dogs singing "Jingle Bells"?

(a) Don Charles
(b) Dr. Demento
(c) David Gilmour
(d) Phillip Glass

79. Who recorded "Santa Claus and His Old Lady?"

(a) John Cougar Mellencamp
(b) John Mellencamp
(c) John Cougar
(d) Cheech and Chong

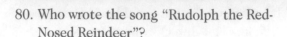

80. Who wrote the song "Rudolph the Red-Nosed Reindeer"?

    (a) Gene Autry
    (b) Johnny Marks
    (c) Kurt Weill
    (d) Harry Warren

81. When was Rudolph's song first released commercially?

    (a) 1947
    (b) 1948
    (c) 1949
    (d) 1950

82. Who wrote the book about Rudolph that is said to have inspired the song?

    (a) E.B. White
    (b) Theodore Geisel
    (c) Robert L. May
    (d) Watty Piper

83. Which figure comes closest to the actual number of "Rudolph the Red-Nosed Reindeer" recordings sold, by all artists recording it, since the song was first released?

    (a) 20 million
    (b) 50 million
    (c) 80 million
    (d) 100 million

84. In the animated special "Rudolph the Red-Nosed Reindeer," who utters the immortal line "His beak blinks like a blinkin' beacon!"?

    (a) Santa
    (b) Prancer
    (c) Comet
    (d) Donner

85. What is the name of Rudolph's dentist friend?

    (a) Marvin
    (b) Newton
    (c) Irving
    (d) Herbie

86. What is the name of Rudolph's explorer friend?

    (a) Barry Lyndon
    (b) Yukon Cornelius
    (c) Yukon Jack
    (d) Jumping Jack Flash

87. What do Bumbles do?

    (a) Bounce
    (b) Make honey
    (c) Rumble
    (d) The Froog

88. This made-for-TV movie was not only the highest-rated Christmas special of the 1988 season—it was the highest-rated TV movie of the year for the network that broadcast it. What was it?

    (a) *The Homecoming at Walton's Mountain*
    (b) *Adventure at Space Mountain: A Christmas Saga*
    (c) *Michael Landon Presents a Little House Christmas*
    (d) *A Very Brady Christmas*

89. Who plays Mary Steenburgen's guardian angel in 1985's *One Magic Christmas*?

    (a) Dennis Hopper
    (b) Harry Dean Stanton
    (c) Burgess Meredith
    (d) Walter Matthau

90. In 1985's *Santa Claus: The Movie*, what did the evil toymaker B.Z. attempt to foist upon the world's children?

(a) A lollipop that would supposedly allow them to fly, but that would be likely to explode when used
(b) The Everlasting Gobstopper
(c) Poisoned candy canes
(d) Fruitcake

91. What is the name of Chevy Chase's character in *National Lampoon's Christmas Vacation*?

(a) Frank Appleton
(b) Clark Griswold
(c) Brad Majors
(d) Ward Cleaver

92. Who plays the Ghost of Christmas Present in 1988's *Scrooged*?

(a) Jack Nicholson
(b) David Johansen
(c) Carol Kane
(d) Jason Robards

93. How does the Ghost of Christmas Present highlight Bill Murray's lesson in *Scrooged*?

(a) Gives him a cookie for every correct answer
(b) Allows him a glimpse at his own gravestone
(c) Causes the headlines in the *Wall Street Journal* to change to odd messages only the two of them would understand
(d) Attacks him with a toaster

94. What is Bill Murray's job in *Scrooged*?

(a) He is a stock-market tycoon
(b) He is president of the IBC television network
(c) He is chief executive officer of the world's largest toy company
(d) He is a writer

95. In *Scrooged*, how does Bill Murray suggest that mice decked out as reindeer should be outfitted?

(a) With antlers stapled to their heads
(b) With tiny candy canes
(c) With fake sleighbells that don't ring
(d) With forty red, white, and blue shoestrings

96. Which of the following animated characters starred in a Christmas holiday special or video?

(a) Bart Simpson
(b) The Jetsons
(c) The Flintstones
(d) Tom & Jerry
(e) All of the above

97. How many feature-length, Christmas-related films had been released by Walt Disney Studios before 1985's *One Magic Christmas*?

(a) Four
(b) Three
(c) Two
(d) Zero

98. Who played Jesus in 1965's *The Greatest Story Ever Told*?

(a) Patrick McGoohan
(b) David McCallum
(c) Robert Reed
(d) Max Von Sydow

99. Jack Jones and Mel Torme joined Judy Garland on her 1963 network television Christmas special. Name the future Academy Award winner who also made an appearance on that program.

100. Who starred in the 1982 American Ballet Theatre production of *The Nutcracker*, now broadcast seemingly every holiday season on PBS?

(a) Mikhail Baryshnikov and Gelsey Kirkland
(b) Rudolf Nureyev and Margot Fonteyn
(c) Leslie Collier and Anthony Dowell
(d) Shari Lewis and Lamb Chop

101. In the episode of *The Brady Bunch* entitled "The Voice of Christmas," why does young Cindy Brady ask Santa to restore her mother's voice?

(a) So Carol Brady can sing at Christmas church services
(b) So Carol Brady can audition for a community production of *The Sound of Music*
(c) So Carol Brady can recite "A Visit from St. Nicholas" to the Brady family as she always does at Christmas time
(d) So Carol Brady can sing about Wesson Oil

102. In the film *Prancer*, what happens when little Jessica first walks within sight of an above-street display of Santa's reindeer?

(a) She has a near-death experience
(b) She sees the ghost of her mother
(c) She watches as one of the reindeer falls to the ground and nearly strikes an automobile
(d) She makes a wish

103. In *Prancer*, why does Jessica's father want to shoot the real reindeer after he sees it standing in the middle of the road?

(a) It's wounded and he wants to put it out of its misery
(b) It's strikingly similar in appearance to an old girlfriend
(c) He's a warped, frustrated old man
(d) He's hallucinating

104. Which Christmas song does Judy Garland sing in *Meet Me in St. Louis*?

(a) "Have Yourself a Merry Little Christmas"
(b) "Winter Wonderland"
(c) "Rudolph the Red-Nosed Reindeer"
(d) "The Christmas Song"

105. How does a Christmas tree figure into the plot of 1973's *The Poseidon Adventure*?

(a) Ernest Borgnine uses it to stop an attacking shark
(b) Terrified passengers climb it in an attempt to reach the "bottom" of the capsized ship
(c) Leslie Nielsen trips on it, causing a concussion that keeps him from responding effectively to the tidal wave bearing down on the ship
(d) Shelley Winters wears a gown that is ripped by it as she passes one of the ornaments

106. Which characters end up dressing as Santa Claus in the Christmas episode of *I Love Lucy* in which the object is to cheer up a distraught Little Ricky?

(a) Lucy
(b) Lucy and Ethel
(c) Lucy, Ethel, and Ricky
(d) Lucy, Ethel, Ricky, and Fred

ANSWERS ⤳

1. d
2. c
3. b
4. b
5. c
6. d
7. d
8. a
9. b
10. a (Poitier appeared in 1963's *Lilies of the Field*, which preceded this feature.)
11. b
12. d
13. d
14. a
15. c
16. c
17. a (This was a trick question; "eponymous" means that the special bears the same name as the character. A futuristic animated version of *The Little Match Girl* aired in 1991.)
18. b
19. d
20. b
21. a
22. b
23. b
24. a
25. c
26. b
27. c
28. d
29. d
30. c
31. c (Peter was George's father.)
32. b
33. c
34. a
35. d
36. b
37. d
38. b
39. a (Hunter played Captain James T. Kirk's predecessor.)
40. d (Another trick question. Gruber's only music credit is the immortal *Silent Night*.)
41. b
42. d
43. d
44. d
45. b
46. Here are six: Reginald Owen (1938), Alistair Sim (1951), Mr. Magoo (1962), Albert Finney (1970), George C. Scott (1982), and Michael Caine (1992). Okay, okay; Magoo is a bit of a stretch. (By the way, Bill Murray is *not* a correct answer; his character's name in *Scrooged* is Frank Cross.)
47. b
48. d (*Ben-Hur* opens with an account of the Nativity.)
49. b
50. d
51. a
52. d
53. a
54. d
55. b
56. a
57. d
58. c
59. a
60. c
61. c
62. b
63. a

64. d

65. Olivia Newton-John. (The megahit musical was, of course, *Grease*.)

66. d

67. b

68. b

69. d

70. "Happy Xmas (War Is Over)" by John Lennon and the Plastic Ono Band.

71. a

72. c

73. a

74. b

75. a

76. c

77. e

78. a

79. d

80. b

81. c

82. c

83. b

84. d (Donner is Rudolph's dad.)

85. d

86. b

87. a

88. d

89. b

90. a

91. b

92. c

93. d

94. b

95. a

96. e

97. d

98. d

99. Judy's seventeen-year-old daughter Liza Minnelli, of course. Liza's siblings Joey Luft and Lorna Luft also appeared.

100. a

101. a

102. c

103. a

104. a

105. b

106. d

YOUR CHRISTMAS VIDEO CHECKLIST ∽

Looking for something good to watch on video? Holiday videos are often hard to track down in December, but if you use this checklist you'll always have something good to ask for when the clerk says, "Sorry, that's out right now."

The vast majority of these videos are suitable for viewing by all members of the family. The most notable exceptions may be found in the *Home Alone* films, which some parents may consider too violent for small children.

How many of the following have *you* seen?

- ☐ *All I Want for Christmas*
- ☐ *Babes in Toyland*
- ☐ *Ben-Hur*
- ☐ *A Charlie Brown Christmas*
- ☐ *A Child's Christmas in Wales*
- ☐ *A Christmas Carol (1938)*
- ☐ *A Christmas Carol (1951)*
- ☐ *A Christmas Story*
- ☐ *A Christmas to Remember*
- ☐ *Christmas in Connecticut*
- ☐ *Christmas Lilies of the Field*
- ☐ *A Disney Christmas Gift*
- ☐ *Ernest Saves Christmas*
- ☐ *For Better or for Worse: The Bestest Present*
- ☐ *Frosty the Snowman*
- ☐ *The Greatest Story Ever Told*
- ☐ *The Grinch Who Stole Christmas*
- ☐ *Hans Brinker*
- ☐ *Holiday Affair*

- ☐ *Holiday Inn*
- ☐ *Home Alone*
- ☐ *Home Alone II*
- ☐ *It Came upon a Midnight Clear*
- ☐ *It's a Wonderful Life*
- ☐ *Jesus of Nazareth*
- ☐ *Jiminy Cricket's Christmas*
- ☐ *The Kid Who Loved Christmas*
- ☐ *King of Kings*
- ☐ *The Little Drummer Boy*
- ☐ *Little House on the Prairie: Christmas at Plum Creek*
- ☐ *The Man in the Santa Claus Suit*
- ☐ *March of the Wooden Soldiers*
- ☐ *Miracle Down Under*
- ☐ *Miracle on 34th Street*
- ☐ *Mister Magoo's Christmas Carol*
- ☐ *The Muppet Christmas Carol*
- ☐ *National Lampoon's Christmas Vacation*
- ☐ *The Night They Saved Christmas*
- ☐ *The Nutcracker*
- ☐ *The Nutcracker Prince*
- ☐ *One Magic Christmas*
- ☐ *Pee-Wee's Playhouse Christmas Special*
- ☐ *Pinnochio's Christmas*
- ☐ *Prancer*
- ☐ *Scrooge*
- ☐ *Scrooged*
- ☐ *The Ten Commandments*
- ☐ *White Christmas*
- ☐ *The Year without a Santa Claus*
- ☐ *Yogi's First Christmas*

EVERYTHING YOU ALWAYS WANTED TO KNOW—AND THEN SOME—ABOUT *IT'S A WONDERFUL LIFE* 〰

If you asked twenty people to name their top ten Christmas films of all time, odds are that nineteen of them would find a place on the list for Frank Capra's 1946 Christmas classic, *It's a Wonderful Life*. But how well did the picture do in its initial release?

During World War II, Capra, who had scored with such hits as *It Happened One Night, Mr. Smith Goes to Washington,* and *Mr. Deeds Goes to Town*, headed the government's Office of War Information, and directed the powerful *Why We Fight* series of documentaries. When the war ended, Capra returned to Hollywood and, with William Wyler, George Stevens, and Samuel Briskin, formed Liberty Pictures—an independent production company in an era of big-studio moviemaking. For his first project, he bought the rights to a short piece by Philip Van Doren Stern called "The Greatest Gift." It told the tale of a man who was afforded the opportunity to see what life would have been like if he had never been born.

Capra asked Jimmy Stewart, who had returned from active duty as an Air Force pilot, to be his leading man. To win Stewart's commitment before any script existed, Capra had to give a verbal summary of the plot he had in mind. According to Stewart, the account was a rambling one that had to do with an angel who didn't have any wings yet, a good man named George Bailey who wanted to see the world but never got to, a savings and loan company, a small town, and a misplaced wad of money—among many, many other things. Although Capra's summary left Stewart more baffled than ever about what the film was actually *about*, he agreed to do the picture. Donna Reed, Lionel Barrymore, and Thomas Mitchell also signed on.

The picture was filmed over the *summer* of 1946. All the snow in the winter scenes is fake; all the actors in overcoats and mittens were sweltering. When the movie was released in late December of 1946, it received generally positive critical notices... but it flopped at the box office. There are a number of theories as to exactly why this occurred.

One argument goes that the film failed because it was Capra's darkest effort to date. *It's a Wonderful Life* includes a child-beating scene, a suicide attempt, and a nightmarish tour of a very seedy, very depressing outpost that could no longer call itself Bedford Falls. It may well be that the many "down" moments of the film were not in tune with the mood of the moviegoing public shortly after World War II. Even though the film features what may be the happiest (or, depending on your perspective, corniest) ending in movie history, that ending is a long time coming, and a war-weary audience may simply have been looking for more unmistakably upbeat product in late 1946 and early 1947.

Another line of reasoning has it that Liberty Films had trouble competing with bigger, better-promoted, and better-distributed studio films. This may well have been the case; even though RKO was handling the distribution of the picture, the number of theaters initially showing the film seems quite low for a major release, and Liberty apparently had trouble collecting from theaters.

The third theory suggests that bad timing was the film's undoing. It was released to a few dozen theaters very late in December, 1946, with broader distribution coming only late in the following January. Not, perhaps, the best way to launch a Christmas movie! Another obstacle may have been the weather: A major blizzard put a huge hole in East Coast movie attendance during the film's run.

Whether it was because of the tone of the film, the competitive pressures from the big studios, the timing, or a combination of all three, *It's a Wonderful Life* was anything but a wonderful experience for the fledgling Liberty Films studio. By the end of the year, that project and others like it had brought the company into serious financial trouble. To avoid personal responsibility for Liberty's debts, Capra and his partners dissolved the studio—and, in so doing, paved the way for the remarkable revival of the story of George Bailey of Bedford Falls.

The irony is that if Liberty had not failed, *It's a Wonderful Life* might never have become a holiday tradition. Television, not the movies, was the medium by which Capra's film became widely known and loved. This was largely because the copyright to the film had fallen into the public domain at a time when broadcasters were hungry for cheap holiday-oriented programming. If you had a copy of the film, you could show it, period. You could also delete as many scenes from it as you pleased in order to accommodate television's insatiable appetite for commercial breaks, a fact that has infuriated many a Capra purist.

Thankfully, the unedited version of the film is available on video-tape (Turner Entertainment, which obtained the RKO library, has the original negative). Steer clear of the bootlegs and the commercial-jammed "edited" versions; head down to your local video emporium and check out a copy of the crystal-clear, uncut *It's a Wonderful Life* for holiday viewing. But get there early—you'll have some competition!

Whoops!

Watch for these film flubs in Capra's holiday masterpiece.

In the dinner scene before the big dance, when Harry Bailey says, "Annie, my sweet, have you got those pies?", the water-pitcher on the table is about one-third full. Later in the scene, without anyone's assistance, the level has mysteriously risen to about one-half.

Shortly after Mary loses her bathrobe and dashes into a nearby bush, she tells George that she's hiding in the hydrangea bush. It's hard to tell what the set designer was getting at with this "plant," but one thing's for certain: It ain't no hydrangea bush. (Then again, perhaps the stress of the moment has gotten to Mary!)

Watch *very* closely after George tosses the robe onto the bush; the robe vanishes in the next shot!

In the scene in which George walks into the Building and Loan carrying a holiday wreath, the wreath magically appears and disappears on his arm in various shots.

After George leaves Mr. Martini's on the night he attempts to commit suicide, he crashes his car into an old tree. Watch the crash closely; the instant before the car hits the tree, the car has no snow to speak of on it, but in the very next shot, noticeable snowdrifts have suddenly appeared on the car's body.

Right before George's bitter line "I wish I'd never been born," Clarence Oddbody is standing with his arms at his side. But in the very next shot, Clarence's arms are crossed.

Near the end of the long final scene of the film, Zuzu reaches for the pocket watch before the stocky man pulls it out of her coat to surprise her with it.

THREE DECADES OF HOLIDAY VIEWING: WHAT WE WERE WATCHING ON CHRISTMAS EVE, 1962-1992 ≈

Christmas Eve, 1962

The Bing Crosby Show
Mary Martin joins Bing in a special holiday celebration.

Black Nativity
A children's special featuring, in the words of a newspaper listing of the day, an "all-Negro cast."

It's a Wonderful Life
Countless broadcasts of Frank Capra's film about a good man who learns the value of his time on earth give viewers a dose of holiday spirit.

Christmas Eve, 1963

The Red Skelton Hour
Red spends a special hour in celebration, complete with carols, comedy, and ballet. In a pantomime sketch, a hobo finds a ragged toy doll that magically comes to life.

Petticoat Junction
The plans for Christmas festivities in Hooterville are in trouble—until a railroad magnate pays a visit to the local folks.

Telephone Hour
Hostess Jane Wyatt welcomes Bill Baird's Marionettes to her Christmas show.

Christmas Eve, 1964

Hazel
Hazel tries to find a way to keep George from acting like Scrooge.

The Burke Family Singers
The Burkes pay a visit to Baroness Maria von Trapp for a special Christmas Eve celebration.

Dr. Kildare
Rip Torn guest stars as a patient whose generosity on Christmas Eve brings unexpected results.

Christmas Eve, 1965

The Smothers Brothers Comedy Hour
The Brothers celebrate their first network Christmas broadcast

Gomer Pyle
Gomer and Sergeant Carter learn a lesson about the spirit of the season.

Sing Along with Mitch Miller
Mitch hosts a festive family reunion.

Christmas Eve, 1966

Bing Crosby's Hollywood Palace Christmas Special
Bing's special guests include Kate Smith, Cyd Charisse, and Bob Newhart.

The Lawrence Welk Show
Welk's Christmas show is a homey affair, with performances of classic Christmas songs by members of his family.

Heart of Christmas
The program features seasonal music from host/conductor Skitch Henderson and harpist Robert Maxwell.

Christmas Eve, 1967

The Ed Sullivan Show
Ed celebrates the holiday season with his guests Arthur Godfrey, Bobbie Gentry, and the Cowsills.

The GI's Christmas Eve Special
American servicemen send messages to their loved ones and show how the season is being observed in Vietnam.

And on Earth, Peace
An hour of Christmas musice native to Central and Eastern Europe, hosted by Margaret Truman.

Christmas Eve, 1968

Julia
In the first American network television series to feature a nonwhite protagonist, star Diahann Carroll is joined by Marc Copage and Michael Link in an episode entitled "I'm Dreaming of a Black Christmas."

That's Life
Robert Morse, Leslie Uggams, and the Doodletown Pipers share thoughts on "Our First Christmas."

60 Minutes
Harry Reasoner offers his essay "What Christ Looked Like."

Christmas Eve, 1969

The Flying Nun
Sally Field stars in the Christmas episode "Winter Wonderland."

Music Hall
Wayne Newton hosts a seasonal celebration with his guests Julie Budd and the Singing Angels.

Space Cantata
A musical special set to official NASA footage from the Apollo 8 mission.

Christmas Eve, 1970

The Flip Wilson Show
Flip and his guests Burl Ives and Sha-Na-Na present a holiday program of comedy and music.

Boughs of Holly
Host Pete Seeger shares some memorable Christmas songs.

Story Theater
Five fairy tales from the works of the Brothers Grimm, staged by the Yale Repertory Theater Company.

Christmas Eve, 1971

J.T.
Jane Wagner and Kevin Hooks star in this drama about a shy black youngster whose closest friends are a cat and a transistor radio.

The Odd Couple
Tony Randall and Jack Klugman star in the Christmas episode "Scrooge Gets an Oscar."

Beethoven's Birthday
Leonard Bernstein and the Vienna Philharmonic celebrate the anniversary of the composer's birth.

Christmas Eve, 1972

Christmas with the King Family
The Kings offer an evening of wholesome musical fun and seasonal celebration.

The Miracles of Christmas
The Mormon Tabernacle Choir offers traditional Christmas favorites.

The Wonderful World of Disney
The Christmas episode "A Present for Donald" is featured.

Christmas Eve, 1973

Gunsmoke
James Arness and Amanda Blake star in the Christmas episode "P.S., Murry Christmas."

An American Christmas in Words and Music
Burt Lancaster hosts this celebration of the American Christmas. His guests are James Earl Jones, Peter Yarrow, and Linda Lavin.

A Dream of Christmas
A southern minister has trouble adjusting to his new home in Los Angeles.

Christmas Eve, 1974

Holy Year Jubilee
Pope Paul VI celebrates Midnight Mass in St. Peter's Basilica

Christmas at Pops
Arthur Fiedler and the Boston Pops Orchestra celebrate the season with the Tanglewood Festival Chorus.

The Joy of Christmas
The Westminster Ensemble joins the Mormon Tabernacle Choir for an evening of seasonal music.

Christmas Eve, 1975

Tony Orlando and Dawn
Carroll O'Connor and the International Children's Choir are guests on the Christmas episode of the popular variety show.

A Bicentennial Christmas
The American Christmas tradition is reviewed in anticipation of the nation's 200th birthday.

The Oral Roberts Christmas Special
Roberts offers inspirational messages for the season.

Christmas Eve, 1976

Donny and Marie
Guests Sonny and Cher, Edgar Bergen, and Paul Lynde help the duo celebrate the season.

The Homecoming: A Christmas Story
Patricia Neal stars as the mother of a rural American family in the 1930s.

The Sounds of Christmas
Doc Severinsen and his orchestra play holiday favorites.

Christmas Eve, 1977

The Jeffersons
In this holiday episode, George is sending gifts and cash to a mysterious address.

A Special Christmas with Mr. Rogers
The children's television personality and his friends—including King Friday and Mr. McFeely—celebrate the season.

Christmas around the World
Seasonal celebrations from several countries are broadcast live via satellite.

Christmas Eve, 1978

The Nutcracker
Mikhail Baryshnikov and Gelsey Kirkland star in Tchaikovsky's classic ballet.

It Happened One Christmas
Cloris Leachman and Wayne Rogers play supporting roles in this remake of Frank Capra's holiday classic *It's a Wonderful Life*.

Amahl and the Night Visitors
Teresa Stratas stars in a new rendition of Menotti's holiday operetta.

Christmas Eve, 1979

A Christmas Special . . . With Love, Mac Davis
Mac is joined by Dolly Parton, Kenny Rogers, Robert Urich, and the choir of St. Mary's Church in Van Nuys, California.

Christmas Eve on Sesame Street
Big Bird and the rest of the gang get together for a celebration of the season.

Family
The holiday spirit takes a turn for the worse when Kate learns that Doug is keeping something from her.

Christmas Eve, 1980

The House without a Christmas Tree
A young girl's desire for a Christmas tree meets with opposition from her no-nonsense father.

A Fat Albert Christmas
The Cosby kids help a family in distress.

Real People
The program profiles "the nation's official Santa Claus." Also: a woman who dresses up as a Christmas tree, and the story of Hanukkah as told by hand puppets.

Christmas Eve, 1981

High Hopes: The Capra Years
Lucille Ball, Carl Reiner, and Burt Reynolds review the career of the man who directed *It's a Wonderful Life* and other classic films.

20/20
Hugh Downs offers a profile on the Salvation Army.

The Man in the Santa Claus Suit
Fred Astaire stars in this film about a mysterious man who changes the lives of three people.

Christmas Eve, 1982

Pinocchio's Christmas
This animated holiday special is based on the classic tale.

The Nativity
Princess Grace of Monaco hosts this recorded musical-drama production set in St. Patrick's Cathedral.

The Muppet Movie
Kermit and Miss Piggy star in a special holiday broadcast of the popular film.

Christmas Eve, 1983

Diff'rent Strokes
Arnold invites a streetcorner Santa home to share the holiday.

Christmas with Luciano Pavarotti
The world-famous tenor sings Christmas classics.

The Love Boat
On Christmas Eve, Mickey Rooney makes an "otherwordly" visit to the ship's passengers.

Christmas Eve, 1984

Sleeping Beauty
Christopher Reeve and Bernadette Peters star in a made-for-cable adaptation.

Cagney and Lacey
Chris, Mary Beth, and company search for a quick exit from work on Christmas Eve.

Scarecrow and Mrs. King
Amanda and Lee find themselves spending the night before Christmas with Soviet agents.

Christmas Eve, 1985

Sing-It-Yourself Messiah
Three thousand San Franciscans join the Conservatory of Music Orchestra at Louise Davies Symphony Hall.

The Black Stallion
Mickey Rooney stars in the network broadcast premiere of this popular family film.

Joyeux Noël: A Cajun Christmas
A celebration of the holiday season, New Orleans style.

Christmas Eve, 1986

The Night They Saved Christmas
Art Carney and Jaclyn Smith strive to keep the North Pole from being blown sky-high.

St. Elsewhere
A rented Santa suffers a coronary while entertaining at the hospital.

Robert Shaw's Christmas Special
Shaw offers two hours of song and celebration.

Christmas Eve, 1987

Bugs Bunny's Looney Christmas Tales
The Warner Bros. gang blows off some holiday steam.

The Magic Flute
David Hockney presents a new rendition of Mozart's classic.

Oprah!
Oprah reviews the year's holiday entertainment offerings.

Christmas Eve, 1988

A Claymation Christmas Celebration
The California Raisins perform in a series of skits ranging from Dickensian London to the Cathedral of Notre Dame in Paris.

Christmas Comes to Willow Creek
Citizens of a poverty-stricken Alaska town learn the true meaning of the season.

The Garfield Christmas Special
The world's most popular cat stars in a half-hour animated special.

Christmas Eve, 1989

A Christmas Carol
George C. Scott delivers the definitive Scrooge of our time in this rebroadcast of the popular special.

A Muppet Family Christmas
Kermit, Miss Piggy, Big Bird, and the rest of the gang celebrate the holiday.

Bill Cosby Salutes Alvin Ailey
Roberta Flack, Anthony Quinn, and others join Bill in a salute to the world-famous choreographer.

Christmas Eve, 1990

A Very Retail Christmas
Ed O'Neill stars as a nasty toymaker.

The New Visions Christmas Special
VH-1, the less raucus music video channel, welcomes Dr. John for an evening of holiday song.

A Child's Christmas in Wales
The Disney Channel presents a new version of Dylan Thomas's classic.

Christmas Eve, 1991

The Little Match Girl
F. Murray Abraham narrates this animated adaptation of the Hans Christian Andersen tale, now set in New York City in 1999.

The Tailor of Gloucester
A musical adaptation of Beatrix Potter's story about a mouse who helps a tailor on Christmas Eve.

Die Fledermaus
The Royal Opera presents this production of the Strauss opera about a maid who masquerades as a countess at a ball. Starring Marilyn Horne, Jean Sutherland, and Luciano Pavarotti.

Christmas Eve, 1992

The Night Before Christmas
Joel Grey narrates a half-hour animated musical version of Clement Moore's poem.

Christmas in Vienna
An hour-long concert of seasonal favorites by Jose Carreras, Diana Ross, and Placido Domingo.

It's a Wonderful Life
Countless broadcasts of Frank Capra's film about a good man who learns the value of his time on earth give viewers a dose of holiday spirit.

CHAPTER ELEVEN

YOUR PART of TOWN

Most towns and cities across America schedule annual holiday festivities of one kind or another. Some are strictly ceremonial; some showcase local merchants; some combine seasonal and commercial celebrations. Local festivals, which are often defined by a region's cultural heritage, feature themes as diverse as the nation itself: Yule Log ceremonies in the Pacific Northwest; Las Posadas in the Southwest; steel band concerts in St. Croix; Victorian festivals in New England; the lighting of the National Christmas Tree in Washington, D.C.

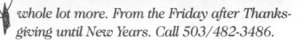

anta Claus is just about everywhere when it comes to these festivals. Other commonalities include decorations of public places, merry music, and, of course, an effort to make things especially joyous for children.

What follows is a sampling of festivals: some big-city events, some historically important celebrations, and some quaint, smaller gatherings that seemed too interesting to omit. This chapter is *not* an exhaustive list of all festivals; that would take up as much space as this entire book allows us! If you would like more information on seasonal celebrations in your area, try calling your local chamber of commerce or visitor's bureau for detailed information about holiday events. Also helpful: your state's division of tourism.

Alexandria, Virginia

Alexandria Community Scottish Christmas Walk
Alexandria's Scottish heritage is saluted with a parade through historic Old Town. Special activities include bagpipes, highland dancers, tours of old homes, and children's events. Early December. Call 703/838-5005.

Annual Woodlawn Plantation Christmas
Carolers, musicians, and costumed actors portraying a family from the past century welcome you to a Christmas party. Wagon rides, a burning yule log, and refreshments provide a taste of the old Virginia Christmas. Early December. Call 703/780-4000.

Civil War Christmas Open House
At the Fort Ward Museum and Historic Site. Mid-December. Call 703/838-4848.

Ashland, Oregon

Come Home for the Holidays
Theatrical events, arts and crafts displays, and a whole lot more. From the Friday after Thanksgiving until New Years. Call 503/482-3486.

Aspen, Colorado

Tree Lighting
The annual lighting of Aspen's tree. At the Sardi House; early December. Call 1-800-262-7736.

Binghamton, New York

Christmas Forest
On display: trees depicting traditional ethnic customs, as well as themed trees. Various dates in December. Call 607/772-0660.

Boothbay Harbor, Maine

Harbor Lights
A seafaring holiday celebration. First Saturday in December. Call 207/633-2353.

Carmel, California

Weihnachtsmarkt
The German Hallowed Eve Market celebration. First Sunday in December. Call 408/624-8886.

Charlottesville, Virginia

Sounds of the Season: A Holiday Concert and Tour
Music and celebration at Ash Lawn-Highland. Late December. Call 804/293-9539.

Chewelah, Washington

Festival of Lights
Free breakfast with Santa (well, nearly free: merchants provide you with tickets) and a lot more. Weekends in December through Christmas. Call 509/935-8991.

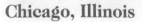

Chicago, Illinois

Caroling to the Animals
Don't knock it until you've tried it. At the Lincoln Park Zoo. Early December. Call 212/935-6700.

City of Chicago Christmas Tree Lighting
The official beginning of the Christmas season in Chicago takes place in Daley Center Plaza. Late November. Call 312/744-3315.

Festival of Lights
A memorable evening at the Swedish American Museum Center. Mid-December. Call 312/728-8111.

Holiday Lights Festival
The sparkling local tradition. On Michigan Avenue from the Chicago River to Oak Street. Mid-November to December 31. Call 312/642-3570.

Skate on State
Ice-skating fun for the whole family. Beginning in November. At State and Randolph streets. Call 312/744-3315

Clermont, New York

Christmas at Clermont Open House
The Livingston House, a state historic site, is decorated for the holidays and offers music for the season. Early December. Call 518/537-4240.

Corona del Mar, California

The Christmas Walk
A street fair in which merchants offer lots of free edibles. First Sunday in December. Call 714/673-4050.

Croton-on-Hudson, New York

Candlelight Tour
A celebration of the early Eighteenth-century English Christmas, complete with carolers, musicians, and a bonfire. At the Van Cortlandt Manor. In December; dates vary. Call 914/631-8200.

Dallas, Texas

The Adolphus Children's Parade
A seasonal parade for all ages. Early December. Call 214/742-8200.

Dallas Christmas Tree Lighting
This event kicks off the holiday season in Dallas; the mayor lights the downtown tree. Early December. Call 214/670-8847.

Christmas at the Arboretum
The stately DeGolyer mansion is decorated for the season. Early December. Call 214/327-8263.

Candlelight Tour
A candlelight holiday festival set among the Victorian and pioneer homes of Old City Park. Mid-December. Call 214/421-5141.

Des Moines, Washington

Christmas in Des Moines
An evening boat parade, a visit from Santa, and a big waffle feed, too. Second weekend in December. Call 206/878-7000.

East Haddam, Connecticut

Victorian Christmas at Gillette Castle
Music and revelry of the era. First weekend after Thanksgiving to the weekend before Christmas. Call 203/526-2336.

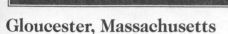

Gloucester, Massachusetts

The Victorian Christmas Festival Weekend
A celebration of the Victorian Christmas, complete with costumed participants, at Hammond Castle. Mid-December. Call 508/283-7673.

Hanover, New Hampshire

Dickens of a Christmas
The author who did more than any other to develop the modern notion of Christmas is celebrated in this two-day event. First weekend in December, beginning Friday. Call 603/643-3115.

Hollywood, California

Hollywood Christmas Parade
Hollywood Boulevard becomes Santa Claus Lane for the season; the parade is held the first Sunday after Thanksgiving. Call 213/469-8311.

Hot Springs, Arkansas

Luminaries
An outdoor Christmas Eve program at Hot Springs National Park. Call 501/624-3383.

Houston, Texas

Astroworld's Holiday in the Park
Christmas festivities at the popular theme park. December. Call 713/799-1234.

Annual Tree Display
Houston's annual tradition. December. Call 713/799-1234.

Hyde Park, New York

A Historic Hyde Park Christmas
Springwood is decorated as it was in 1944, the last holiday season President Roosevelt spent there. November and December; dates vary. Call 914/229-9115.

Jamestown, New York

Tradition of the Trees
Displays of Christmas trees from different eras and nations. At the Fenton Historical Museum. Most of December. Call 716/483-7521.

Kingsburg, California

Santa Lucia Festival of Lights
An enchanting celebration of Swedish Christmas traditions. Day after Thanksgiving. Call 209/897-2925.

Christmas Festival
Arts and crafts, parades, and other enjoyable aspects of the season. Second Saturday in December. Call 209/897-2925.

Leavenworth, Washington

Christmas Lighting Festival
Rides on sleighs, choir performances, and dazzling lights are the highlights of this Cascade Mountain celebration. Call 509/548-5807.

Los Angeles, California

Las Posadas
Olvera Street provides the most prominent Southern California venue of the parade reenacting Mary and Joseph's search for shelter for the Christ Child; from mid-December to Christmas Eve. Call 213/628-4349.

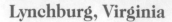

Lynchburg, Virginia

Christmas at the Market Craft Show
Lots of distinctive holiday crafts and other offerings.
At City Armory. Late December. Call 804/847-1499.

Lynden, Washington

Dutch Sinterklaas Celebration
Yes, "Sinterklaas" is an early form of the familiar
"Santa Claus." For a taste of the colorful (and enor-
mously influential) Dutch tradition of observing the
yearly appearance of St. Nicholas, check out this
delightful festival. First Saturday in December. Call
206/354-5995.

Miami, Florida (Metro area)

Holiday and Country Craft Show
Plenty of enchanting holiday craft offerings. On Main
Street in Miami Lakes. November. Call 305/821-1130.

Santa's Enchanted Forest
Why bother trying to recreate the North Pole in south-
ern Florida, anyway? In the Tropical Park, west of
Coral Gables. Mid-November to late January. Call
305/893-0090.

Bayside Marketplace Holiday Celebration
Downtown Miami's annual festival. Late November
to Christmas Day. Call 305/577-0306.

Home for the Holidays Celebration
On Ocean Drive in South Beach. December. Call
305/933-9095.

Minneapolis, Minnesota and environs

Festival of Trees
More Christmas Trees than you can shake a sugar-
plum at. Early December to early January at the
Landscape Arboretum. Call 612/443-2460.

Folkways of Christmas
Lovely music and seasonal celebrations.
Weekends in early December at Historic Murphy's
Landing. Call 612/445-6900.

Holiday Festival at the Mall of America
The season is observed in high style in the largest
mall in the galaxy (also one of the nation's largest
tourist destinations). Mid-November through
December. 612/883-8800.

Holiday Bazaar
A chance to stock up on holiday goodies. Early
December. Call 612/292-3225.

Holiday and Lights
Sparkling! Throughout the month of December at the
Minnesota Zoo. Call 612/431-9000.

Holidazzle
Twenty-seven parades during the month of December
at the Nicollet Mall. Call 612/338-3807.

Victorian Christmas and Gala Ball
Costumed participants provide music and entertain-
ment of the era. First three weekends of December at
the Alexander Ramsey House. Call 612/296-8760.

Monson, Massachusetts

Big Mac Christmas Crafts Show
Seasonal arts and crafts celebration. Begins the
weekend after Thanksgiving. Call 413/283-8143.

Mount Vernon, Virginia

Holidays at Mount Vernon
Historic Mount Vernon Estate is the site for a recrea-
tion of an authentic eighteenth-century holiday season.
Visitors may also tour the mansion's third floor, not
usually open to the public. Early December to Early
January. Call 703/780-2000.

Nantucket, Massachusetts

Christmas Stroll
Local merchants put out festive decorations during this lively festival. First Saturday in December. 508/228-1700.

Nashville, Tennessee

Christmas at Opryland
The event, which features lights, decorations, food, special entertainment, and, town fathers point out proudly, the nation's largest Nativity scene, is held from late November to the end of December. Call 615/889-6611.

Dickens of a Christmas
"Listed as one of the top 20 tourist events in the Southeast," according to the organizers. Christmas carolers in Victorian garb serve up good things to eat and drink and lots of entertainment in a two-day festival. Mid-December. Call 615/790-7094.

Rudolph's Red Nose Run and Nashville Gas Christmas Parade
A 5K race and 1-mile fun run. Early December. Call 615/734-1754.

Newport News, Virginia

Celebration in Lights
Holiday light display. At Newport News Park. December 25-January 1. Call 804/247-8451.

Christmas at the Mariner's Museum
A seasonal event with a nautical twist. Late December; dates vary. Call 804/595-0368.

New York, New York

Christmas Tree Lighting at Rockefeller Center
The big one—at least if you're a New Yorker. Generally the first Monday of December. Call 212/632-3975.

Niagara Falls, New York

Festival of Lights
Outdoor and indoor nighttime activities feature Oxy Lights, animated displays, professional and community entertainment, and, of course, lots and lots of lights. Late November through January 1. Call 716/285-9141.

Nogales, Arizona

Festival of Lights
Families from both Mexico and the U.S. take part in this colorful festival, which is held from late November to early December. Call 602/287-3685.

Norfolk, Virginia

Holidays in the City
The major downtown event of the season. Mid-to-late December. Call 804/623-1757.

Northeast Harbor, Maine

A Northeast Harbor Christmas
Crafts, pageants, music, and more. First weekend in December. Call 207/276-5040.

Old Westbury, New York

Festival of Trees
Designer-decorated trees, mini-villages, and special offerings at local shops. Late November. Call 516/378-2000.

Oroville, California

A Frontier Christmas
Features costumed characters and an emphasis on Gold Rush history. First weekend in December. Call 916/538-2219.

Oxnard, California

Parade of Lights
At the Channel Islands Harbor. Second Saturday in December. Call 805/985-4852.

Philadelphia, Pennsylvania

Fairmount Park House Christmas Tours
Seven historic houses located throughout the park are decorated for the holidays in themes reminiscent of an old-fashioned Christmas. Selected houses are lighted as they were in the eighteenth century. Activities at the Horticulture Center include Christmas craft projects and storytelling. Early December. Call 215/684-7922.

Festival of Trees and Tours
See the Pearl S. Buck House decked out in its holiday finest. Mid-December. Call 215/249-0100.

Toy Parade
Santa hits the City of Brotherly Love on Thanksgiving Day to the beat of local school bands. Call 215/636-1666.

Phoenix, Arizona

Heritage Square Victorian Holiday
Crafts, foods, and other Victoriana. Early December. Call 602/262-5071.

International Christmas
Features dozens of trees decorated in the styles of various cultures. Throughout December. Call 602/221-2900.

Portland, Oregon

Festival of Lights
At the Grotto; early December through New Year's Day. Call 503/452-4505.

Festival of Trees
At the Convention Center; early December. Call 503/452-4505.

Winter's Lights Festival
At the Portland Zoo; throughout the month of December. Call 503/452-4505.

Poulsbo, Washington

Yule Fest
If you've never seen a genuine Yule log ceremony, here's your chance to do so by the waters of Puget Sound. A festive Scandinavian celebration that features costumed Vikings and authentic food from the Sons of Norway. Early December. Also of interest: the Holiday Heritage House. Call 206/779-4848.

Provincetown, Massachusetts

Festival of Lights
This Thanksgiving Eve event marks both that holiday and the beginning of the Christmas season. The Pilgrim Monument, tallest granite structure in America, is strung with countless lights. Call 508/487-3424.

Richmond, Virginia

Joy from the World
At the Science Museum of Virginia. Late December to early January. Call 804/367-1013

Roanoke, Virginia

Festival of Trees
At Dominion Tower. Late December.
Call 703/344-0931.

Roseburg, Oregon

Umpqua Valley Christmas Artfest
Exquisite handmade ornaments and stocking stuffers
are just the beginning. Wine, edibles, music, and other
festive elements mark this popular festival. Opening
reception in late November; festival during first week-
end of December. Call 503/672-2532.

St. Croix, Virgin Islands

Christmas Festival
Steel bands, cool drinks, and tropical winds make for
a very different kind of Christmas celebration.
Generally the last two weeks of December and the
first two weeks of January. Call 809/773-0495.

San Francisco, California

Santa Claus Parade
In the Mission District. Dates determined annually.
Call 415/826-1401.

Seasonal Theater Events
The San Francisco Ballet mounts an annual produc-
tion of The Nutcracker. Call the Ballet at 415/621-
3838. The American Conservatory Theater mounts
an annual production of A Christmas Carol. Call the
ACT at 415/749-2228.

Sanger, California

Trek to the Nation's Christmas Tree
Since 1926 people have celebrated the holiday
beneath the huge (and, yes, officially designated)
General Grant tree in Kings Canyon National Park.
Second Sunday in December. Call 209/875-4575.

Schenectady, New York

Annual Christmas Parade
"Largest nighttime parade in the East," or so town
boosters claim. Bands, lighted floats, over 100 cos-
tumed characters, and, of course, Santa. Late
November. Call 518/372-5656.

Seattle, Washington

Christmas Celebration
Downtown Seattle's annual festival. December; dates
vary. Call 206/623-0340.

Silver City, New Mexico

Festival of Trees
The annual celebration of seasonally decorated trees.
First week in December. Call 505/538-3785.

Soulsbyville, California

Auburn Christmas Crafts and Music Festival
Beat the Christmas rush—and still enjoy the carols.
Veteran's Day weekend. Call 209/533-3473.

Sonora Christmas Crafts and Music Festival
More music and handcrafted goodies. Weekend imme-
diately following Thanksgiving. Call 209/533-3473.

Springfield, Massachusetts

International Holiday
An inclusive festival that celebrates the ways in which the various cultures of the world mark the winter solstice. Early December. Call 413/739-3871, ext. 312.

Stevenson, Washington

Christmas in the Gorge
When it comes to Christmas spectacle, its hard to ignore a celebration that lights up the Columbia Gorge and all the towns nestled along it. Carols and a visit from Santa, too. First Saturday after Thanksgiving. Call 509/427-8911.

Taos, New Mexico

Yuletide in Taos
Local artists and craftspeople—of which there are many in Taos—help make this a colorful and unforgettable festival. Early December. Call 505/758-3873.

Tarrytown, New York

Family Fun Weekend
Special tours, seasonal celebrations, and ideas on preparations for Christmas. Late November. Call 914/631-8200.

Tortugas, New Mexico

Fiesta of Our Lady of Guadalupe
Inspiring festival with strong Catholic and Native American emphasis. Beginning December 10. Call 505/526-8171.

Tucson, Arizona

Fiesta de Guadalupe
Features Las Posadas, the parade commemorating Mary and Joseph's quest for shelter for the Christ Child. Held on the second Sunday of December. Call 602/299-9192.

Vienna, Virginia

Carol Singing
The U.S. Marine Band and local choirs lead the audience in singing Yuletide favorites at Wolf Trap Farm Park. Early December. Call 202/433-4011 or 703/255-1934.

Virginia Beach, Virginia

Yule Log Celebration
The traditional celebration. At the Adam Thoroughgood House. Early December. Call 804/622-1211.

Volcano, California

Motherlode Scots Festival of Lights
A Scottish holiday celebration in old Gold Rush country. Early December. Call 209/223-1510.

Warsaw, Virginia

Holiday Caroling by Candlelight
Locals say this is among the most beautiful celebrations in the area. At the Richmond County Museum. Dates in December vary. Call 804/394-4901.

Washington, D.C.

A Christmas Carol at Ford's Theatre
The historic site is always bustling at this time of year, thanks to the annual stage adaptation of Dickens's holiday classic. Late November to late December. Call 202/347-4833.

Christmas Pageant of Peace
Annual since 1954, the pageant is usually initiated by a member of the First Family lighting the National Christmas Tree. Early December. Call 202/619-7222.

Holiday Celebration Exhibition
At the Smithsonian's National Museum of American History. A spectacular display of Christmas trees, along with other holiday displays. Mid-December through early January. Call 202/357-2700.

People's Christmas Tree Lighting
The magnificent Christmas tree on the west side of the U.S. Capitol is lighted each year the day before the Pageant of Peace begins. Military bands perform in concert. Early December. Call 202/224-3069.

Washington National Cathedral Christmas Open House
Christmas carols, bell ringing, special family activities, and demonstrations of calligraphy, stone carving, and needlework are a few of the highlights. Early December. Call 202/537-6267.

White House Christmas Candlelight Tours
Evening tours of the White House Christmas decorations, aglow with holiday candlelight. Shortly after Christmas. First come, first served; show up early, as the tours are extremely popular. Call 202/456-2200 or 202/619-7222.

Wickenburg, Arizona

Cowboy Christmas Festival: Poetry, Singin', and Pictures
Not what they're used to back East, that's for sure. Gallop into the holiday sunset the first weekend in December. Call 602/684-5479.

Wickford, Rhode Island

Festival of Lights
This historic town, founded in 1662, is site of a delightful celebration of colonial times during the holiday season. First weekend in December (Thursday night through Sunday). Call 401/295-5566.

Willcox, Arizona

Christmas Apple Festival
Held the first Friday and Saturday in December. Call 602/384-2272.

Williamsburg, Virginia

Foods and Feasts in seventeenth-Century Virginia
At the Jamestown Settlement. A rich examination of past traditions. December 24-26. Call 804/229-1607.

Grand Illumination
Lights festival at Colonial Williamsburg. Early December to January 1. Call 804/229-1000.

A Jamestown Christmas
More colonial activities. At the Jamestown Settlement. Through most of December; dates vary. Call 804/229-1607.

Woodstock, Vermont

Woodstock's Wassail Celebration
A ball, a choir, a champagne buffet breakfast at midnight: classy doings. Three-day festival, second weekend in December. Call 802/457-3555.

INDEX BY REGION

If you live in one of the northeastern states, see the listings for:

If you live in one of the southern states, see the listings for:

If you live in one of the Rocky Mountain, southwestern, or midwestern states, see the listings for:

If you live in one of the western states, see the listings for:

Oxnard, California
Portland, Oregon
Poulsbo, Washington
Roseburg, Oregon
San Francisco, California
Sanger, California
Seattle, Washington
Soulsbyville, California
Stevenson, Washington
Volcano, California

CHAPTER TWELVE

HOLIDAY RECIPES

❦

Food is central to the celebration of the Christmas holiday—and no book on the subject of celebrating Christmas would really be complete without a sampling of holiday recipes. Here are ours; some are for Christmas morning, some are for the big meal of the big day, and some can be adapted to other times. (There's even a recipe for coffee liqueur that you begin preparing in November!)

Bon appetit!

❦

Breakfasts, Brunches, and Breads

APPLE CRISP ≈

Exquisite on a cold December morning with a good cup of coffee!

Topping:

    3 tablespoons chilled butter
    ½ cup firmly packed brown sugar
    ⅓ cup all-purpose flour

In a medium bowl, using a pastry blender or 2 knives, mix together brown sugar, flour, and butter until coarse crumbs form.

Filling:

    ½ teaspoon nutmeg
    ½ teaspoon ground cinnamon
    ¼ cup water
    2 tablespoons granulated sugar
    4 cups apples, peeled, cored, and thinly sliced

- Preheat oven to 375 degrees Fahrenheit.
- Grease a 9" pie pan.
- Place apples in prepared pan.
- Mix together sugar, nutmeg, cinnamon, and water. Toss apples with sugar mixture.
- Sprinkle topping over filling.
- Cook until top is golden brown and crispy, approximately 30 minutes.

APPLESAUCE LOAF ≈

If you've never tried this, you're in for a special holiday treat.

    1 cup granulated sugar
    ½ cup butter, softened
    1 large egg, room temperature
    1½ cups all-purpose flour
    1½ teaspoons baking soda
    1 teaspoon ground cinnamon
    ¾ teaspoon nutmeg
    ½ teaspoon salt
    ½ teaspoon ground cloves
    1½ cups unsweetened applesauce
    ½ cup dark raisins
    ½ cup coarsely chopped walnuts
    Confectioners' sugar

- Preheat oven to 350 degrees Fahrenheit. Grease and flour a 9" x 5" loaf pan.
- In a medium bowl, cream butter and sugar together until light and fluffy.
- Beat in eggs.
- In another bowl, mix together flour, baking soda, cinnamon, nutmeg, salt, and cloves. Gradually beat flower mixture into butter mixture.
- Beat in applesauce.
- Stir in raisins and nuts.
- Pour batter into prepared pan.
- Bake loaf for 1 hour, or until a toothpick inserted into the center comes out clean. Transfer pan to wire rack. Cool for 10 minutes. Remove loaf from pan and cool completely.
- Dust with confectioners' sugar.

BAKED FRENCH TOAST WITH WHIPPED CREAM AND STRAWBERRIES ≈

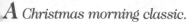

A Christmas morning classic.

2 large eggs
¼ cup milk
1 teaspoon vanilla extract
6 slices day old white bread
3 tablespoons butter
2 tablespoons granulated sugar
½ teaspoon cinnamon
1 cup heavy cream, whipped, or 1 pint vanilla ice cream
3 cups sliced, sweetened strawberries

• Preheat oven to 400 degrees Fahrenheit.
• In a medium bowl, beat eggs, milk, and vanilla.
• Place bread in a shallow dish. Pour egg mixture over bread and let stand for 5 minutes, then turn bread over once with a rubber spatula and let stand for 5 minutes more.
• Melt butter in a 13" x 9" x 2" baking pan in oven for 5 minutes.
• When bread has absorbed egg mixture, transfer bread to baking dish. Sprinkle with cinnamon sugar and bake until golden and puffy, approximately 25 minutes or until well browned and puffy.
• Serve with whipped cream and strawberries.

BLUEBERRY BREAD ≈

Try this with a good cup of coffee on Christmas morning. You'll get a great start on the big day—and you'll probably be back for seconds.

1 cup fresh blueberries
1½ cups all-purpose flour
1 tablespoon flour
½ cup granulated sugar
⅔ cup milk
1 egg
1 heaping teaspoon baking powder

• Preheat oven to 375 degrees. Grease and flour a 9" x 5" loaf pan.
• Sift the dry ingredients together (leaving aside 1 tablespoon flour).
• In a separate bowl, stir together the egg and milk.
• Make a well in the center of the dry ingredients. Add milk mixture to the well all at once, tossing with a fork until just moistened.
• Toss blueberries in 1 tablespoon flour. Add blueberries to batter.
• Spoon batter into prepared pan.
• Bake until a toothpick inserted into the center comes out clean, approximately 30 minutes.
• Transfer to wire rack; let cool.

CRANBERRY BREAD ⁓

A wholesome and delicious holiday treat—and easy to make, too!

2 cups all-purpose flour
1 cup granulated sugar
1½ teaspoons baking powder
½ teaspoon baking soda
1 teaspoon salt
1 cup frozen cranberries, chopped into halves
¼ cup shortening
½ cup orange juice
1 teaspoon grated orange peel
1 large egg, lightly beaten
½ cup chopped walnuts

- Preheat oven to 350 degrees Fahrenheit. Grease a 9" x 5" loaf pan.
- Sift together flour, sugar, baking powder, baking soda and salt.
- Using a pastry blender or 2 knives held together, cut in shortening until coarse crumbs form.
- In a separate bowl, combine orange juice, orange peel, and eggs.
- Make a well in the center of the dry ingredients. Add egg mixture all at once to well, tossing with a fork until just moistened.
- Stir in the nuts and cranberries. Spread batter in prepared pan. Bake until a toothpick inserted in the center comes out clean, approximately 1 hour.
- Remove bread from pan; cool completely.

CRISP WAFFLES FOR CHRISTMAS MORNING ⁓

For a holiday accent, top these with whipped cream and green and red crystal sugar.

2 cups sifted cake flour
4 teaspoons baking powder
¼ teaspoon salt
2 large eggs
1¼ cup plus 1 tablespoon milk
6 tablespoons vegetable oil or melted butter

- Grease and preheat an electric waffle iron.
- Sift together the dry ingredients.
- Beat the eggs with an electric mixer.
- Add milk and dry ingredients alternately until just blended.
- Stir in oil or melted butter.
- Spoon batter onto prepared waffle iron and cook until golden brown and crisp. (Cooking times will vary.)

EGGS A LA BUCKINGHAM ⤳

A great—and easy—preparation for Christmas morning.

5 large eggs, lightly beaten
½ cup milk
½ teaspoon salt
⅓ teaspoon pepper
5 slices toasted white bread
1 tablespoon butter
Grated cheddar cheese to taste

Arrange toast slices in a baking dish or ovenproof platter.
In a large bowl, combine eggs with milk, salt, and pepper.
Melt butter in skillet; cook eggs until just scrambled. (They should appear *slightly undercooked.*)
Spoon eggs over toast; sprinkle with desired amount of grated cheddar cheese.
Bake until cheese melts, approximately five minutes.
Serve immediately.

FANCY NANCY'S CHRISTMAS IRISH BUNDT BREAD ⤳

Unforgettable!

3 cups all-purpose flour
3 teaspoons baking powder
1 egg
1½ cups milk
⅓ cup vegetable oil
¾ cup granulated sugar
1 cup golden raisins, tightly packed
1 tablespoon caraway seeds

For icing:

1 cup confectioner's sugar, sifted
1½ tablespoons hot water or milk
½ teaspoon vanilla flavoring
Green or red food coloring

- Preheat oven to 350 degrees Fahrenheit. Grease and flour an 9-inch Bundt pan.
- In food processor, combine flour, baking powder, and sugar and process.
- In a large bowl, mix together milk, oil, and egg.
- Pour liquid mixture into food processor with flour mixture; pulse until blended and smooth.
- Pour mixture back into mixing bowl. Add raisins and seeds. Mix well.
- Pour batter into prepared pan.
- Bake bread until a toothpick inserted into the center comes out clean, 35-45 minutes. Cool for 25 minutes in pan. Cool for 1 hour on rack.
- Mix icing ingredients together and drizzle over bread.

GERMAN COFFEE CAKE

An old favorite.

1 cup margarine, softened
2 cups granulated sugar
4 large eggs, at room temperature
1 pint sour cream
2 teaspoons vanilla extract
2 teaspoons baking soda
1½ cups all-purpose flour
3 teaspoons baking powder
½ cup walnuts

Topping:

½ cup granulated sugar and 2 teaspoons
cinnamon, mixed together in small bowl

- Preheat oven to 350 degrees Fahrenheit. Grease a 9" x 13" baking pan.
- In a large mixing bowl, cream together margarine and sugar.
- Add eggs, sour cream, baking soda and vanilla.
- Beat in flour and baking powder. Stir in nuts.
- Pour half of batter into a greased 9" x 13" pan.
- Sprinkle half of topping over batter; run a knife once through batter.
- Pour remaining batter into the pan, then run a knife once through batter.
- Bake until a toothpick inserted into the center comes out clean, approximately 40-45 min.
- Transfer baking pan onto a wire rack. Cool for 30 minutes.

HOLIDAY LEMON NUT BREAD ≈

A zesty change of pace for Christmas morning!

2½ cups all-purpose flour
1 cup granulated sugar
3½ teaspoons baking powder
½ teaspoon baking soda
½ teaspoon salt
½ teaspoon grated lemon peel
½ cup water
⅓ cup shortening, melted
2 large eggs, lightly beaten
½ cup fresh lemon juice
1 cup chopped walnuts (or ½ cup nuts and ½ cup raisins)

- Preheat oven to 350 degrees Fahrenheit. Grease and flour a 9" x 5" x 3" loaf pan.
- In a large bowl, sift together flour, sugar, baking powder, baking soda, lemon peel, and salt.
- Combine water, shortening, eggs, and juice; Make a well in the center of the dry ingredients. Pour egg mixture into well, tossing with a fork until dry ingredients are just moistened. Stir in nuts and raisins.
- Spread batter into prepared pan.
- Bake bread until a toothpick inserted into the center comes out clean, approximately 60-75 minutes.

Let cool for 10 minutes; remove from pan. Cool on wire rack for five minutes. Wrap in plastic and refrigerate until ready to serve.

MERRY MOCHA COFFEE MIX ～

Coffee lovers take note! This is a delicious holiday treat you will not soon forget.

16 ounces instant coffee
2 cups cocoa powder
4 teaspoons ground cinnamon
2 teaspoons ground nutmeg
Water (amount will vary depending on number of cups you are preparing)

- In a mixing bowl, stir together dry ingredients.
- Boil required amount of water in a kettle, then pour into medium-sized mugs.
- Add one spoonful of mixture to each mug—or more or less, according to taste.

SAUSAGE QUICHE ～

Tasty and substantial—a magnificent start to the holiday.

1 pound hot sausage
½ cup chopped onion
½ cup chopped green peppers
2 cups grated cheese
4 tablespoons flour
½ teaspoon salt
4 large eggs
1 8 oz. can evaporated milk
2 unbaked pie shells

- Preheat oven to 350 degrees Fahrenheit.
- Saute sausages, onion, and pepper together in a skillet; remove from heat and drain well.
- In a large mixing bowl, mix cheese, flour, and salt.
- In another bowl, beat together eggs and milk.
- Combine all ingredients in a large bowl.
- Pour mixture evenly between 2 unbaked pie shells.
- Bake until top is golden and set, approximately 30-45 minutes.
- Let cool for 10 minutes.

Appetizers

ANTIPASTO ❧

Exquisite!

1 pound American cheese, sliced
½ pound imported ham, sliced
½ pound imported Genoa salami, sliced
½ pound prosciutto, sliced
½ pound mortadella, sliced
1 12 oz. can tuna, packed in oil and undrained
1 full head lettuce
½ pound imported sharp provolone, cut into
  1-inch chunks
1 8 oz. jar pepperoncini
1 8 oz. can green stuffed olives
Olive oil
Red wine vinegar

- Roll slices of meat with American cheese and line along the outside of a large platter, alternating the different kinds of meat.
- Wash, dry, and break up the lettuce and arrange in the center of the plate.
- Spread tuna on top of lettuce, being sure not to drain any oil from the can.
- Arrange provolone around the lettuce.
- Top with olives and peppers.
- Dressing: Mix together three parts olive oil to one part red wine vinegar. Pass separately to guests.

CHRISTMAS FONDUE ❧

Perfect for holiday parties.

1 cup butter
1 cup all-purpose flour
4 cups milk
2 cups Chablis
2 teaspoons chicken flavored bouillon powder
Pieces of cheddar cheese, thinly sliced, about 1½
  pounds

- Melt the butter in a large saucepan. Stir in the flour; cook for several minutes over low heat.
- Add the bouillon, milk, and Chablis; stir frequently until mixture thickens.
- Stir in cheese until melted and smooth. (Use more or less cheese, according to your own taste.)
- Transfer to a fondue pot; keep warm.
- Serve with slices of bread and raw vegetables.

CHRISTMAS PARTY MIX (FOR A BIG PARTY) ≋

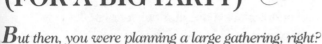

But then, you were planning a large gathering, right? This mix will keep your guests munching happily!

2½ tablespoons Worcestershire sauce
16 cups rice and corn cereals of your choice (Chex, for instance), evenly combined
1½ cups small pretzel sticks
3 cups salted peanuts
2 teaspoons salt
1½ cups margarine, melted

- Preheat oven to 275 degrees Fahrenheit.
- Combine all the ingredients except the butter.
- Drizzle melted butter over cereal mixture, stirring to distribute it evenly.
- Bake in shallow pans for about an hour, stirring occasionally; check often during last fifteen minutes to be sure mixture does not overcook.

CRISPY CHRISTMAS NACHOS ≋

*O*ndele!

½ cup yellow cornmeal
½ teaspoon salt
1¾ cups boiling water
1 teaspoon margarine

- Preheat oven to 425 degrees Fahrenheit. Grease a baking sheet.
- Mix cornmeal and salt in a bowl. Mix in 1 cup of boiling water. Blend.
- Add margarine, stirring until melted; add remaining water; stir.
- Drop mixture by rounded teaspoonful (drop should be a little bigger than a quarter) onto prepared baking sheet.
- Bake nachos until golden and crisp, 12 to 15 minutes or until golden brown. Serve with salsa.

HOLIDAY SHRIMP DIP ≈

Delicious!

3 cans small deveined shrimp, drained
2 8 oz. packages cream cheese, softened
1 12 oz. bottle shrimp sauce
Crackers of your choice
Parsley

- Combine shrimp and cream cheese.
- Add ½ bottle shrimp sauce and mix well. Place shrimp mixture in mold of appropriate size.
- Chill overnight.
- Invert mold onto a platter. Spoon remaining sauce over top as if frosting.
- Garnish with parsley and serve with crackers.

RICK-DIMI-DITTY ≈

A tasty holiday appetizer.

¼ medium-sized onion, finely chopped
1 tablespoon of butter or margarine
1 can condensed tomato soup
½ pound American cheese, sliced fine
1 egg
Crushed red pepper flakes to taste
Salt to taste
1 teaspoon Worcestershire sauce

- In a large saucepan, melt butter; stir in onion.
- Add soup with ½ can water.
- Bring the soup to a boil, stirring often.
- Stir in cheese. Mix well. Lower heat.
- In a small mixing bowl, beat the egg, Worcestershire sauce, salt and pepper. Stir egg mixture into saucepan. Stir constantly.
- Cook until mixture thickens. Do not boil.
- Serve with crackers of your choice.

YULE CRUNCHES

*S*nappy!

1 envelope onion soup mix
1 cup butter or margarine, softened
12 slices white bread, crusts removed

- Preheat oven to 350 degrees.
- Blend butter with onion soup.
- Spread onion soup mixture on each slice.
- Cut each slice into four strips.
- Place bread slices on a baking sheet. Bake for until golden brown, approximately 10 minutes.

Side Dishes

CALIFORNIA YORKSHIRE PUDDING ≈

A new twist on an old favorite.

6 large eggs
1½ teaspoons salt
¼ cup pan drippings reserved from roast beef.
2 cups milk
1½ teaspoons Worcestershire sauce
1½ cups all-purpose flour
2½ cups cooked and cooled wild rice

- Preheat oven to 450 degrees Fahrenheit.
- Pour one teaspoon of the pan drippings into twelve muffin-pan cups. Place muffin pan in prepared oven for two and a half minutes.
- Mix together eggs, milk, salt, and Worcestershire sauce in a large bowl; blend until mixed well. Add flour, stirring until blended.
- Add rice. Pour batter evenly into the hot drippings in prepared pan. Bake until brown and puffy, approximately 25 minutes.

CHEESE LATKES ≈

If you've never tried these, you're in for a pleasant surprise at your holiday meal.

1 cup all-purpose flour
1 teaspoon baking powder
½ teaspoon salt
1 cup dry pot cheese, grated
1 cup milk
3 large eggs, well beaten
Oil for frying

- Sift dry ingredients together in a large mixing bowl.
- Combine milk, cheese, and eggs, stir into dry mixture.
- Blend until smooth.
- Heat oil in a skillet.
- Drop mixture by rounded tablespoon into skillet. Fry, turning once, until brown on both sides.
- Transfer latkes to paper towels to drain.
- Serve with fruit preserves of your choice.

CHEESY CAULIFLOWER WITH WHITE SAUCE ⤳

A holiday favorite at many homes. Timing is important; the sauce must be hot when poured over the tender florets.

2 2-lb. cauliflower, trimmed
Juice of 1 lemon
Water
Salt
1 bay leaf
4 tablespoons butter
3 tablespoons flour
2 cups *cool* milk
2 small onions, peeled, studded with cloves
1 bay leaf
1½ cups shredded cheddar cheese

- Pour water into a large bowl. Place cleaned, washed, and stemmed cauliflower head-down in cold water for about 10-15 minutes. (Water should cover cauliflower.)
- Break cauliflower into florets. Steam, partially covered, in a saucepan with lemon juice and bay leaf.
- Cook until tender, about 10-12 minutes.
- While cauliflower cooks, melt butter over low heat in a saucepan. Stir in flour and cook for approximately 4 minutes, stirring constantly.
- Pour in milk. Mix well.
- Add the onions. Beat until smooth and glossy.
- Remove from heat. Add in cheese, stirring until melted and smooth.
- Place cauliflower florets on a serving dish.
- Cover florets with sauce. Serve immediately.

CHRISTMAS PUMPKIN SOUP ⤳

Used to thinking about pumpkins only as pie filling? Broaden your horizons and try this delicious soup!

4 cups chicken broth
8 cups canned pumpkin puree
5 cups milk, scalded
6 tablespoons butter
6 tablespoons firmly packed brown sugar
1½ cups boiled ham, finely diced
Salt to taste
Parsley
Dash nutmeg

- In a large pot, mix broth and pumpkin until smooth.
- Stir in milk. (If you prefer a creamier soup, add more milk.)
- Stir brown sugar, butter, ham, and salt into pumpkin mixture.
- Heat soup until it simmers. Garnish with parsley and nutmeg.

CREAMY SWEET POTATO SOUFFLE ≈

You'll never think of the humble sweet potato in quite the same way after sampling this holiday treat.

¼ cup butter
¼ cup all-purpose flour
5 large eggs (room temperature), separated
1½ cups half and half
¼ cup grated Cheddar cheese
3 cloves garlic, crushed
1½ teaspoons salt
¼ teaspoon pepper
¼ teaspoon cream of tartar
1½ cups *cold* mashed sweet potatoes

- Preheat oven to 375 degrees Fahrenheit.
- Grease a 2-quart souffle dish with a collar extending 3 inches above the rim.
- Melt butter in a large saucepan. Mix in flour and cook, stirring constantly, for 1 minute. Blend in the half and half; cook over low heat, stirring constantly.
- Stir in egg yolks, 1 at a time. Stir in cheese, salt, garlic, and pepper, beating well after each addition.
- Stir mashed potatoes into the egg mixture.
- In a large bowl, beat the egg whites with cream of tartar until stiff peaks form. Fold egg whites into potato mixture.
- Pour potato mixture into prepared dish.
- Bake souffle until top is puffy and golden, approximately 50 minutes. Serve immediately.

FROZEN CRANBERRY SALAD ≈

A refreshing change of pace.

1 cup heavy cream
1 cup crushed pineapple, drained
1 can whole or jellied cranberry sauce
2 tablespoons mayonnaise
2 tablespoons granulated sugar
2 8 oz. packages cream cheese, softened
¾ cup walnuts, coarsely chopped

- Whip cream in a large mixing bowl.
- Stir pineapple into whipped cream. Set aside.
- In a blender or food processor, process cranberry sauce until blended smooth.
- Add mayonnaise, sugar, and cream cheese and continue to process until well blended. Stir in nuts.
- Fold cranberry mixture into whipped cream. Pour into molding tray of your choice; cover and freeze.
- Let salad stand at room temperature for 15 minutes. Slice and serve on lettuce.

GREEN-AND-RED STUFFED TOMATO TREAT ≈

An elegant accompaniment to the main dish at your Christmas table.

2 heads fresh broccoli
3 teaspoons butter or margarine
3 large ripe tomatoes
4 ounces shredded fontina cheese
¼ teaspoon ground nutmeg
¼ cup heavy cream
1 teaspoon salt
⅛ teaspoon pepper

(Note: depending on the sizes you select, you may need more broccoli or tomatoes; buy extra to be on the safe side.)

- Preheat oven to 350 degrees Fahrenheit.
- Grease a large baking dish.
- Cut off broccoli florets. In a large saucepan, steam them until tender, 5-10 minutes. Drain broccoli. In a blender or food processor, process broccoli until smooth.
- In a large saucepan, melt the butter. Add the broccoli; cook over medium heat for about three minutes or until the broccoli is tender.
- Add cheese, nutmeg, cream, salt, and pepper. Cook, stirring frequently, until cheese melts. Do not overcook. Set the mixture aside.
- Slice tomatoes in half horizontally. Remove seeds and pulp with a spoon, leaving a small indentation.
- Spoon the broccoli mixture evenly into the center of each tomato half.
- Place the tomatoes in prepared baking dish.
- Bake for 8-10 minutes, or until tomatoes are tender.

MEXICAN CHRISTMAS EVE SALAD ≈

A delicious fruit salad from south of the border.

2 medium apples, peeled, cored, and thinly sliced (about 2 cups)
1 medium banana, sliced
Fresh lettuce
Lemon juice, fresh or bottled
2 cups pineapple chunks, drained
1 1-pound can sliced beets, drained
1 cup navel orange sections (about 2 oranges)
½ cup unsalted peanuts
½ cup pomegranate seeds
Nondairy whipped topping to taste

- Line a large serving platter with lettuce leaves.
- In a large bowl, mix together sliced apples and bananas. Sprinkle with a little lemon juice (it keeps them from turning brown).
- Arrange apples, bananas, orange sections, pineapple chunks, and beets over lettuce.
- Sprinkle peanuts and pomegranate seeds over fruit.
- Serve nondairy whipped topping on the side; each guest may use more or less dressing according to taste.

MOCK TURTLE SOUP FOR THE HOLIDAYS ≈

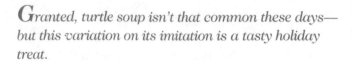

Granted, turtle soup isn't that common these days— but this variation on its imitation is a tasty holiday treat.

Two packages powdered onion soup mix
Water
1¼ cups diced veal cutlets
¼ teaspoon butter
Sour cream
Dried parsley

- In a large saucepan, melt butter.
- Saute veal (which is similar in taste to turtle meat) lightly over low heat approximately 10 minutes, being sure to cook it thoroughly. Remove from heat and set aside.
- Prepare onion soup as package directs.
- When soup is hot, drain off solids and discard them.
- Add cooked veal to prepared broth.
- Garnish with dollops of cold sour cream sprinkled with parsley. Serve immediately.

POTATO LATKES ≈

A delicious side dish.

2 cups raw potatoes, peeled and grated
2 large eggs, well beaten
1 teaspoon salt
2 teaspoons all-purpose flour
¼ teaspoon baking powder
1 onion, grated fine
Oil for frying
Cold sour cream or apple sauce as garnish

- Soak grated raw potatoes in cold water until ready to cook to prevent discoloration.
- Drain potatoes well. In a large mixing bowl, mix together all ingredients except oil.
- In a large frying pan, heat ½ inch oil; drop mixture by heaping tablespoons into *hot* oil.
- Flatten each spoonful with a spatula and fry until golden brown on both sides.
- Transfer latkes to paper towels to drain. Cool on paper towel to remove excess oil.
- Serve with cold sour cream or apple sauce.

SOUTHERN STYLE CHRISTMAS CORN ≈

A tasty variation for the holidays.

1 can chopped corn (whole kernels), drained
2 large eggs, slightly beaten
1 teaspoon salt
⅛ teaspoon pepper
1½ teaspoons melted butter
1 pint scalded milk

- Grease a large microwave-save casserole dish.
- Mix together corn, eggs, salt, and pepper.
- Stir in butter and milk.
- Pour corn mixture into prepared dish.
- Microwave on high in 3-minute sessions for 10-15 minutes or until firm. (Note: Cooking times may vary dramatically by oven.)
- Rotate and check frequently; do not overcook!

SPECIAL GREEN-AND-RED VEGETABLE SALAD ≈

Cool and delicious.

Trimmed florets from 1 head broccoli
Trimmed florets from 1 head cauliflower
1 pound carrots, sliced thin
1 pound fresh mushrooms, washed and sliced into thin segments
1 medium green bell pepper, sliced into strips
1 medium red bell pepper, sliced into strips
2 small zucchini, sliced
4 stalks celery, sliced

Marinade:

¼ cup vegetable oil
¼ cup olive oil
1½ cup tarragon vinegar
2 large cloves garlic, minced
1½ teaspoons prepared mustard
¼ cup granulated sugar
1½ teaspoons salt
1 teaspoon tarragon leaves

- Place vegetables in large salad bowl.
- Combine all marinade ingredients; mix well and pour over vegetables. Toss well.

YORKSHIRE PUDDING

A classic!

1 cup milk
1 cup all-purpose flour
2 large eggs
¼ teaspoon salt
½ cup beef fat from a roast (quantity may vary,
   depending on size of pan you use)

- Preheat oven to 350 degrees Fahrenheit.
- Mix together milk and eggs.
- In a large mixing bowl, mix flour and salt together.
- Stir milk mixture into flour mixture so that it forms a smooth paste.
- Cover bottom of hot pan with beef fat.
- Pour batter over beef fat.
- Bake pudding until golden, approximately twenty minutes.

Main Courses and Accompaniments

BREAD CRUMB STUFFING ∼

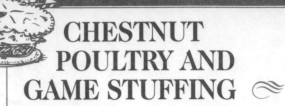

A popular stuffing recipe.

1⅓ tablespoon butter, melted
3 cups seasoned bread crumbs
¾ teaspoon salt
1⅓ tablespoons dried parsley
½ teaspoon pepper
1 large egg, beaten well
8 drops onion juice

- In a large mixing bowl, drizzle butter over bread-crumbs. Toss together with a fork.
- Stir in salt, pepper, dried parsley, and onion juice. Mix well.
- Mix in beaten egg.
- Stuff poultry just prior to cooking. (You may wish to enlarge the quantities in the recipe if you are cooking a particularly large bird.)

CHESTNUT POULTRY AND GAME STUFFING ∼

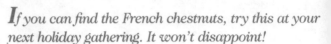

If you can find the French chestnuts, try this at your next holiday gathering. It won't disappoint!

4 cups French chestnuts
1¼ cups ground cracker crumbs
¾ cup butter
⅓ cup heavy cream
1¼ teaspoons salt
¼ teaspoon pepper

- Shell chestnuts.
- Place chestnuts in enough boiling salted water to cover; cook until softened. (Cooking time will depend on size of chestnuts.) Drain and coarsely mash chestnuts.
- Fold cracker crumbs, butter, cream, salt, and pepper into chestnut puree.
- Stuff poultry just prior to cooking. (You may wish to enlarge the quantities in the recipe if you are cooking a particularly large bird.)

CHRISTMAS ALMOND BURGERS ≈

Red and green peppers make these stand out as holiday specials!

1 small red bell pepper, cut into thin strips
1 small green bell pepper, cut into thin strips
¼ cup butter
4 pounds ground beef
2 teaspoons salt
½ pound finely ground blanched almonds
1 teaspoon pepper
4 tablespoons butter

- Preheat oven to 400 degrees Fahrenheit.
- Fold almonds into ground meat.
- Mix in salt and pepper.
- Shape meat into six large patties; place patties in a shallow pan.
- Bake patties for ten minutes. Place a pat of butter evenly on the top of each. Bake for ten more minutes or until done to taste.
- In a saucepan, steam red and green pepper strips until tender.
- Garnish with red and green pepper strips.

CHRISTMAS SWEET AND SOUR MEATBALLS ≈

A memorable holiday entree.

1 pound ground beef, chicken or turkey
1 cup seasoned bread crumbs
1 large egg, lightly beaten
2 tablespoons chopped onion
2 tablespoons milk
¾ teaspoon salt
2 tablespoons solid vegetable shortening
1 8¼ ounce can pineapple chunks, drained (reserve the juice!)
1 tablespoon cornstarch
¼ cup cold water
1 8 ounce can whole or jellied cranberry sauce
Half of a 12 oz. bottle barbecue sauce
¼ teaspoon salt
½ medium green bell pepper, cut in strips

- Mix ground meat, bread crumbs, egg, onion, milk, and salt in a large mixing bowl. Using a tablespoon, shape meat mixture into meatballs.
- In a medium bowl, mix together shortening, pineapple chunks, cranberry sauce, barbecue sauce, and salt.
- In a second bowl, dissolve cornstarch in cold water.
- In a large skillet, cook meatballs until browned. Drain off grease.
- Stir pineapple and cornstarch mixture into the skillet.
- Add pepper strips. Simmer, covered, until peppers are tender, 15 to 20 minutes, making sure peppers become tender. Add reserved pineapple juice a little at a time, until mixture reaches desired consistency.

GLAZED YULE HAM ≋

Not to be missed.

10- to 15-pound uncooked storebought ham
Orange marmalade
1 8-ounce package of cream cheese, softened
Greens of your choice (for garnish)

- Follow package directions for baking ham. (Generally, baking takes 3½ to 4 hours.)
- 30 minutes before ham is done, brush over with orange marmalade.
- Transfer ham to a cutting board. Cool slightly.
- Using a pastry bag fitted with a star tip, pipe cream cheese decoratively on top of ham.
- Slice and garnish with greens.

HERB STUFFING ≋

One of several excellent stuffing recipes to consider for your holiday table.

4 ounces beef suet, finely chopped
1 cup seasoned bread crumbs
1 tablespoon dried parsley
1 tablespoon dried sage
Dash of thyme
1 tablespoon grated lemon rind
Pepper and salt to taste
1 large egg, lightly beaten
2 teaspoons milk

- Mix suet with bread crumbs, parsley, sage, thyme, lemon rind, pepper and salt.
- Stir in beaten egg and milk. (Add more milk if necessary to attain your preferred consistency.)
- Stuff poultry just prior to cooking. (You may wish to enlarge the quantities in the recipe if you are cooking a particularly large bird.)

HOLIDAY MAPLE HAM ≈

The real thing.

1¼ cups firmly packed dark brown sugar
⅓ cup maple syrup
Whole cloves (quantity will depend on size of ham)
Precooked ham (approximately ten pounds),
  trimmed

- Preheat oven to 350 degrees.
- In a medium bowl, combine the brown sugar and the maple syrup.
- Place the ham in a roasting pan. Bake for an hour and ten minutes. Preheat your oven to 350 degrees; set the ham on a rack in a pan, and place the pan in the center rack of the oven.
- Transfer the ham from the oven to the counter; using a kitchen knife, score the surface of the ham in a diamond pattern.
- Insert cloves evenly along top of the ham.
- Brush brown sugar and maple syrup mixture over ham.
- Return ham to oven; bake for 20 minutes more.

HOLIDAY PORK ROAST WITH STRAWBERRY AND PRUNE STUFFING ≈

It takes a little work, but this roast is more than worth the effort.

Boned pork loin (3½ pounds)
4 medium strawberries, sliced
10 pitted prunes
3 large apples, peeled, cored, and sliced
1½ tablespoons dark raisins
¼ cup apple juice
½ teaspoon salt
½ teaspoon ground cinnamon
½ teaspoon pepper
½ teaspoon ground cloves
1½ tablespoons red currant jelly, melted
1 cup plain or seasoned bread crumbs
¼ cup butter, melted

- Preheat oven to 350 degrees.
- In a small bowl, combine salt, pepper, and cloves. Rub over surface of roast. Cover with plastic wrap.
- In a large bowl, combine prunes, apples, raisins, cinnamon, strawberries, and apple juice. Mix well and cover.
- Refrigerate the roast and the fruit mixture for 12 hours.
- Drain and reserve liquid from fruit mixture.
- With a large kitchen knife, cut a long, deep incision along the length of the roast. Carefully remove the core of the roast. (This meat can be cooked and added to a soup later.) Stuff the

(cont.)

opening with the fruit mixture, then sew the opening shut with a large needle; tie off with twine.

- Rub reserved liquid from the fruit mixture onto the exterior of the roast.
- Roast for 40 minutes; remove from oven.
- Spread the melted jelly over roast. Sprinkle bread crumbs evenly over top. Drizzle melted butter over roast.
- Return roast to the oven and cook for 1 hour more. Let stand 10 minutes before serving. (Cooking times may vary depending on your oven and the size of the roast; always be sure pork is cooked thoroughly.)

ROAST TURKEY WITH APRICOT FRUIT STUFFING ∼

Unforgettable!

1½ cups chopped onions
5 tablespoons margarine
2 quarts cubed bread, toasted
¾ pound pitted prunes, sliced
6 dried apricot segments, coarsely chopped
2½ cups tart apples, peeled, cored, and chopped into 1-inch chunks
1 cup apple juice
2 teaspoons dried sage
1 teaspoon dried basil
2¼ teaspoons salt
¼ teaspoon pepper
1 turkey, ready to cook (approximately 13 pounds)

- Preheat oven to 375 degrees Fahrenheit.
- Saute onions in margarine until they are golden brown.
- In a mixing bowl, toss bread with onions, prunes, apples, apricots, apple juice, and seasonings.
- Spoon stuffing into turkey; fasten with poultry pins if necessary.
- Roast for 25 minutes per pound. Scoop out fat from the pan as it gathers. Check regularly near the end of the allotted time; juices should run clear when bird is done. Do not overcook.

SAUSAGE POULTRY AND GAME STUFFING ≈

Another distinctive stuffing recipe.

¾ cup sausage, uncooked, casings removed, crumbled
2½ cups seasoned bread crumbs
1¼ tablespoons dried parsley
1¼ tablespoons dried onion
⅓ cup butter, melted
½ teaspoon pepper
2 large eggs, lightly beaten
4 cups water

- In a skillet, brown sausage lightly. Remove sausage; drain on a paper towel.
- Place breadcrumbs in a large bowl and add four cups of water
- When the breadcrumbs are soft, press out excess liquid by hand.
- In a large bowl, combine sausage with soft bread-crumbs, parsley, onion, pepper, and beaten eggs.
- Drizzle melted butter into sausage mixture.
- Stuff poultry just prior to cooking. (You may wish to enlarge the quantities in the recipe if you are cooking a particularly large bird.)

SWEET AND SOUR CHICKEN ≈

A zesty addition to the holiday table.

3 pounds boneless chicken breast cut into 1-inch pieces
1 8 oz. can chunk pineapple, drained
1 4 oz. jar maraschino cherries
1 green pepper, sliced into strips
1 12 oz. jar prepared sweet and sour sauce
2 tablespoons vegetable oil
¼ teaspoon salt
¼ teaspoon pepper
¼ teaspoon garlic powder
¼ teaspoon parsley flakes

- In a skillet, saute chicken and sliced pepper in oil until chicken turns golden. Drain off grease. Sprinkle with salt, pepper, garlic powder, and parsley.
- Add fruit and sweet and sour sauce to chicken.
- Cook chicken mixture over medium heat until mixture is heated throughout.

Sweets and Desserts

ANISE OVAL COOKIES ⟿

Green and red sensations!

⅔ cup granulated sugar
⅔ cup solid vegetable shortening
2 teaspoons anise flavor extract
2 cups all-purpose flour
2 teaspoons baking powder
2 large eggs
1 cup sifted confectioners' sugar
1–2 tablespoons hot water or milk
½ teaspoon vanilla extract
Green and red food coloring

- Preheat oven to 350 degrees Fahrenheit.
- In a large mixing bowl, cream together sugar and shortening, at medium mixer speed, until light and fluffy.
- Blend in eggs and anise extract.
- At low speed, beat in flour and baking powder.
- Shape dough into 2-inch ovals.
- Place ovals at least 1 inch apart on ungreased cookie sheets.
- Bake cookies until golden brown, approximately 8-10 minutes. Transfer baking sheet to a wire rack to cool.
- For icing: In a large bowl, mix confectioners' sugar, hot water or milk, vanilla extract, and food coloring. Drizzle over the cookies while they are cooling.
- Store cookies wrapped in wax paper in air-tight container.

BANANA SPLIT CAKE ⟿

Live it up for the holidays! Try this with ice cream!

3 sticks butter or margarine
2 cups crushed graham crackers
2 large eggs
2 cups confectioners' sugar
5 bananas, sliced very thin
8 ounces nondairy whipped topping
1 4 oz. jar maraschino cherries, drained
½ cup coarsely chopped pecans
1 20 oz. can crushed pineapple, drained

- Mix 1 stick butter together with graham cracker crumbs. Pat crumb mixture into the bottom of a 9" x 13" pan.
- Beat eggs, remaining butter, the confectioner's sugar, and banana pieces for no less than fifteen minutes.
- Spread batter over prepared crust.
- Cover with whipped topping; sprinkle with nuts and cherries. Spread crushed pineapple over whipped topping.
- Chill overnight.

BRANDY RINGS ≈

A festive and delicious "braided" pastry.

2½ cups sifted all-purpose flour
1 cup butter or margarine
2 tablespoons brandy

- Preheat oven to 350 degrees Fahrenheit.
- Grease 2 large baking sheets.
- Combine flour, margarine, and brandy in a large mixing bowl and blend together to make dough.
- On a lightly floured surface, roll the dough into ropes approximately ½ inch thick.
- Cut the ropes into five-inch strips.
- Twist two pieces together; shape into a ring; pinch ends together to seal.
- Repeat with remaining dough.
- Place rings a good distance apart on prepared baking sheets. Bake rings until golden, approximately 12-15 minutes.

CHOCOLATE CARAMELS ≈

A holiday delight for chocolate lovers.

2½ tablespoons butter
2 cups molasses
1 cup firmly packed dark brown sugar
½ cup milk
3 ounces semisweet chocolate, coarsely chopped
1 teaspoon vanilla extract

- In medium-sized saucepan, melt butter over medium heat.
- Add molasses, brown sugar, vanilla, and milk. Stir until sugar is dissolved.
- Bring mixture to a simmer; add chocolate, stirring until melted and smooth.
- Bring chocolate mixture to a boil. Remove from heat for a moment and test: when a small amount of the mixture is tried in cold water, and a firm ball can be formed, proceed to next step. Do not overcook!
- Pour mixture into medium-sized buttered pan.
- Let stand until cool; cut into small squares.

CHOCOLATE CRINKLES

Chocolate fans take note: This is a Christmas treat worth waiting for!

½ cup vegetable oil
4 ounces unsweetened chocolate, melted
2 cups granulated sugar
4 large eggs
2 teaspoons vanilla
2 cups all-purpose flour
2 teaspoons baking powder
½ teaspoon salt
1 cup confectioner's sugar

- In a large mixing bowl, mix oil, melted chocolate, and granulated sugar.
- Beat in eggs, 1 at a time, beating well after each addition.
- Add vanilla. Beat in flour, baking powder and salt.
- Cover mixing bowl with plastic wrap. Chill for several hours.
- Drop dough by teaspoonfuls into confectioner's sugar. Roll dough in sugar and shape into balls.
- Preheat oven to 350 degrees.
- Grease 2 medium baking sheets.
- Bake cookies on greased baking sheets until set, 10-12 minutes.

CHRISTMAS CUTOUT COOKIES

½ cup butter
½ cup granulated sugar
2 large eggs, lightly beaten
1 teaspoon vanilla extract
¼ cup sliced almonds
2 teaspoons baking powder
2¾ cups all-purpose flour
Green and red colored sugar
Icing (commercially prepared, in tubes)

- Preheat oven to 400 degrees Fahrenheit.
- In a large mixing bowl, beat together butter and sugar until light and fluffy.
- Beat in eggs, vanilla, and almonds.
- Beat in baking powder and flour, ½ cup at a time until blended.
- Wrap dough in plastic wrap and chill for several hours.
- On a floured surface, using a floured rolling pin, roll out dough.
- Using several different shaped cookie cutters, cut out cookies.
- Decorate with colored sugar and icing.
- Bake cookies until just golden, approximately 6-7 minutes.

CHRISTMAS THEME SUGAR COOKIES ≈

As sweet as the time of year they celebrate.

1 cup granulated sugar
1 cup margarine
1 large egg
½ teaspoon almond or vanilla extract
1½ teaspoons baking powder
½ teaspoon salt
2½ cups all-purpose flour
Red and green sugar crystals
Colored jimmies
Small silver ball candies

- In a large mixing bowl, beat together margarine and sugar.
- Beat in egg, extract, baking powder, and salt. Gradually add in flour.
- Add salt and baking powder. Gradually add in flour. Mix well.
- On a floured surface, knead dough by hand and shape into a large ball. Wrap in plastic wrap and chill up to two hours, until firm.
- Roll dough out on floured surface to a ¼" thickness. Cut out shapes with Christmas theme cookie cutters. Gather trimmings; roll out and cut more cookies. Decorate with sugar crystals, jimmies, and candies.
- Preheat oven to 350 degrees; grease a cookie or baking sheet. Bake in batches for 10-12 minutes or until brown.

Note: bake large cookies with large ones and small cookies with small one for best results. Placing cookies of unlike sizes on the same sheet will result in uneven cooking.)

COCONUT WREATH COOKIES ≈

A real sign of the season!

½ cup butter or margarine, softened
½ cup granulated sugar
1 large egg
1 3½ ounce pack of shredded sweetened coconut
1¾ cups all-purpose flour
Red & green candied cherries, sliced

- Preheat oven to 375 degrees Fahrenheit.
- Grease and flour a baking sheet.
- In a large bowl, beat together butter and sugar.
- Blend in egg and coconut. On low speed, add flour, ½ cup at a time, until blended.
- Wrap dough in plastic wrap and chill for several hours.
- On floured surface, roll ⅓ of dough at a time to a ¼" thickness. Using a 2½" doughnut cutter, cut dough into rings. Gather trimmings; roll out dough; cut more cookies.
- Remove any excess coconut from edges; edges of cookes should be smooth.
- Lightly grease and flour large cookie sheet. Place cookies on prepared baking sheet 1 inch apart.
- Arrange cherry slices on cookies to resemble flower petals; press into cookies.
- Bake cookies in batches for 10 minutes or until brown.

CRUNCHY CHRISTMAS CANDY ≈

A favorite with the little ones.

1 cup granulated sugar
½ cup evaporated milk
¼ cup margarine
¼ cup crunchy peanut butter
½ teaspoon vanilla extract
1 cup old-fashioned dry oats
½ cup peanuts

- Bring sugar, evaporated milk, and margarine to a boil, stirring frequently.
- When sugar is dissolved, remove from heat and stir in peanut butter and vanilla.
- Mix in oats and peanuts. Drop mixture by rounded teaspoon onto wax paper so that each morsel has a peak.
- (If mixture is too stiff, add a few drops of milk.)
- Chill candy until firm.

CRUNCHY CHRISTMAS NUT TREATS ≈

Leave some of these out for Santa—you'll be glad you did.

1 cup solid vegetable shortening
¼ cup confectioners' sugar
1 teaspoon vanilla extract
2 cups sifted all-purpose flour
½ cup chopped almonds
½ cup chopped walnuts

- Preheat oven to 300 degrees Fahrenheit.
- In a large bowl, beat together shortening, confectioners' sugar, and vanilla exttract.
- At low speed, beat in flour.
- Stir in nuts.
- Shape dough into round balls and place several inches apart on ungreased baking sheet.
- Bake in batches for 15-18 minutes. Check frequently near end of cooking time; do not scorch.
- Transfer cookies to a wire rack. Roll warm cookies in confectioners' sugar.
- Let stand until cool, 30 minutes.

FIVE LAYER PUDDING ≈

Easier to make than you might think, and a real crowd pleaser. The red and green cherries add a distinctive holiday touch.

Complete list of ingredients (for simplicity in preparation, these are repeated in recipe as required for each layer):

1⅓ cups all-purpose flour
¼ cup margarine
⅓ cup coarsely chopped almonds
1 8 oz. package cream cheese, softened
1 cup confectioners' sugar
1 cup nondairy whipped topping or whipped cream
2 3 oz. packages instant chocolate pudding
Approximately 6 cups milk (see pudding package directions for exact amount)
Nondairy whipped topping or whipped cream
⅛ cup chopped pecans
⅛ cup sliced red cherries
⅛ cup sliced green cherries

First layer:

1⅓ cups all-purpose flour
¼ cup margarine
⅓ cup coarsely chopped almonds

Preheat oven to 300 degrees Fahrenheit.
Melt margarine in 13" x 9" pan in preheated oven.
Remove pan; add flour; mix and press into a crust that covers the bottom of the pan. Sprinkle chopped nuts on top.
Bake crust for about 20 more minutes, or until browned. Set aside to cool.

Second layer:

1 8 oz. package cream cheese, softened
1 cup confectioners' sugar
1 cup nondairy whipped topping or whipped cream

- In a large mixing bowl, beat together sugar, whipped topping, and cream cheese.
- Spread cream cheese mixture over prepared crust.

Third layer:

2 packages (approximately 3 oz. each) instant chocolate pudding
Approximately 6 cups cold milk (see pudding package directions for exact amount)

- Mix pudding according to package directions.
- Pour pudding over cream cheese layer.

Fourth layer:

Nondairy whipped topping or whipped cream

- Spread topping over pudding.

Fifth layer:

⅛ cup chopped pecans
⅛ cup sliced red cherries
⅛ cup sliced green cherries

- Top with chopped pecans and red and green cherries.
- Chill for 90 minutes before serving.

GINGERBREAD FROM HOME ⁓

Real homestyle gingerbread—perfect for holiday snacks!

½ cup firmly packed light brown sugar
⅓ cup butter
½ cup light molasses
1 teaspoon baking soda
1¼ cup all-purpose flour
1 teaspoon ground cinnamon
½ teaspoon ground ginger
1 large egg
½ cup boiling water

- Preheat oven to 325 degrees Fahrenheit.
- Grease and flour an 8" square baking pan.
- In a large bowl, mix together brown sugar and butter. Mix in baking soda and molasses.
- Add flour, cinnamon, and ginger. Mix well.
- Add in egg.
- Add boiling water. Mix well.
- Pour batter into prepared pan; smooth top.
- Bake gingerbread until a toothpick inserted into the center comes out clean, approximately 40 minutes.

GINGERBREAD MEN ⁓

Decorate these men with the season in mind!

2¼ cups all-purpose flour
½ cup granulated sugar
½ cup solid vegetable shortening
½ cup light molasses
1½ teaspoons ground cinnamon
1 teaspoon baking powder
1 teaspoon ground ginger
1 teaspoon ground cloves
½ teaspoon baking soda
½ teaspoon salt
1 large egg
Prepared frosting, green and red

- Preheat oven to 350 degrees Fahrenheit.
- In a large mixing bowl, beat together sugar and shortening.
- Add egg, salt, baking powder, baking soda, ginger, cinnamon, cloves, and molasses. Add flour ½ cup at a time, beating until dough forms.
- Shape dough into a ball, wrap in plastic wrap, and chill for up to two hours or until firm.
- On floured surface, roll dough out to ¼" thickness.
- Using gingerbread man cookie cutter, cut out cookies. Place on ungreased cookie sheet at least 1 inch apart.
- Bake cookies in batches for 8-10 minutes for small men, 12-15 minutes for larger. Transfer baking sheet to a wire rack to cool.
- Spread frosting over cookies. Decorate with candies.

GREEN AND RED CHEWY CHOCOLATE COOKIES ≈

Santa's favorite at many a home.

1¼ cups margarine, softened
2 cups granulated sugar
2 large eggs
2 teaspoons vanilla extract
2 cups all-purpose flour
¾ cup cocoa powder (not instant)
1 teaspoon baking soda
1 teaspoon salt
Green and red candy-coated chocolates to taste
    (we like a lot of them)

- Preheat oven to 350 degrees.
- Beat together margarine and sugar until light and fluffy.
- Add in eggs and vanilla. Beat flour, cocoa, baking soda, and salt into butter mixture.
- Stir in candy-coated chocolates.
- Drop batter by rounded teaspoonfuls onto ungreased baking sheet.
- Cook in batches for 8-10 minutes per sheet of cookies.
- Check cookies near end of baking time. Do not overcook!
- Transfer baking sheet to wire rack to cool.

HERMITS ≈

A classic—and perfect for Christmas morning.

2 cups sifted all-purpose flour
2 teaspoons baking powder
1 teaspoon ground cinnamon
¼ teaspoon nutmeg
1 teaspoon mace
½ cup butter or margarine
½ cup firmly packed dark brown sugar
½ cup granulated sugar
2 large eggs, lightly beaten
2 cups dark raisins
½ cup almonds

- Preheat oven to 350 degrees Fahrenheit.
- Grease a 9" x 13" baking dish.
- Sift flour, baking powder, cinnamon, nutmeg, and mace together. (We suggest 3 times.)
- In a large bowl, beat together butter and sugar until light and fluffy.
- Beat dry ingredients into butter mixture.
- Beat in eggs.
- Stir in raisins and nuts.
- Pour the mixture into prepared dish.
- Bake hermits until browned, approximately 15 minutes.
- Transfer baking pan to a wire rack to cool.

HOLIDAY BAKED CUSTARD ≈

Didn't you love this when you were a kid?

1 cup milk
1 cup evaporated milk
3 large eggs, lightly beaten
¼ cup granulated sugar
¼ teaspoon salt
¼ teaspoon vanilla extract
Water

- Preheat oven to 325 degrees Fahrenheit.
- Combine all ingredients. Mix well.
- Pour into medium-sized baking dish.
- Place filled baking dish in larger pan partially filled with cold water (about 1 inch deep).
- Bake custard until set, approximately 50-60 minutes, checking frequently near end of alloted time. Do not overcook!

HOLIDAY FUDGE ≈

It's the hint of marshmallow that makes the difference in this recipe. And there's no baking!

4½ cups granulated sugar
1 can evaporated milk
¼ cup butter
12 ounces of milk chocolate bar
12 ounces chocolate chips
1 tablespoon vanilla extract
⅛ teaspoon salt
1 pint marshmallow spread
2 cups walnuts, coarsely chopped

- Grease a 13" x 9" pan.
- In a large saucepan, cook sugar, milk, and butter for 5 minutes, stirring constantly.
- Dissolve chocolate bar and chocolate chips in saucepan.
- Mix in vanilla, salt, marshmallow and walnuts.
- Pour fudge into prepared pan.
- Chill overnight.

LEMON BARS ⁓

Simple to make, and always a big hit at family gatherings.

1 cup all-purpose flour
¼ cup confectioners' sugar
½ cup butter, softened
2 large eggs, lightly beaten
¾ cup granulated sugar
3 tablespoons fresh lemon juice
2 tablespoons all-purpose flour
½ teaspoon baking powder
Confectioners' sugar

- Preheat oven to 350 degrees Fahrenheit.
- Grease an 8" x 8" x 2" pan.
- Mix together flour and confectioners' sugar. Using a pastry blender, cut butter into flour mixture until coars crumbs form.
- Pat crumb mixture into prepared pan.
- Bake crust until golden, approximately 10-12 minutes. Set aside.
- In a large bowl, combine beaten eggs with sugar and lemon juice. Beat until thickened.
- Beat in flour and baking powder.
- Pour batter over prepared crust.
- Return pan to oven; bake lemon bars until set, approximately 20-25 minutes.
- Transfer pan to wire rack and let cool.
- Sift confectioners' sugar over top and let cool. Cut into 1 inch squares.

MAPLE BELLS ⁓

One of the perennial symbols of Christmas— and a darned good cookie, too.

4 cups all-purpose flour
1 cup butter or margarine, softened
¾ cup firmly packed light brown sugar
½ cup maple syrup
2 teaspoons cream of tartar
1 teaspoon baking soda
¼ teaspoon salt
2 large eggs

- Preheat oven to 350 degrees Fahrenheit.
- Grease a baking sheet.
- In a large mixing bowl, beat together butter and sugar at medium speed until light and fluffy.
- Beat in eggs and maple syrup. Beat in cream of tartar, baking soda, and salt.
- At low speed, beat in flour until dough forms.
- Shape dough into a ball; wrap in plastic wrap and refrigerate for 1 hour.
- On a floured surface, roll out dough to a ⅛" thickness; using bell-shaped cookie cutters, cut out cookies. Place cookies in batches on prepared baking sheet.
- All large pieces should be baked together, as should all small ones, so that each batch will cook evenly.
- Bake cookies until golden brown, approximately 10 minutes.

MEATLESS MINCE PIE

A real holiday treat!

½ cup cooked rice
½ cup seedless raisins
½ cup currants
½ cup honey
2 tablespoons chopped orange sections
1 tablespoon grated lemon peel
1 tablespoon butter
⅛ teaspoon cinnamon
⅛ teaspoon nutmeg
Sprinkling of granulated sugar
1 large egg white, lightly beaten
Prepared uncooked double layer pastry shell

- Preheat oven to 450 degrees Fahrenheit.
- Grease a medium-sized pie pan.
- Mix together rice, raisins, currants, honey, orange, lemon peel, butter, cinnamon, and nutmeg.
- Fit shell into prepared pie pan. Spoon rice mixture into shell. Cover with remaining dough and press edges together to seal. Brush pie with beaten egg white. Sprinkle with sugar.
- Bake pie until crust is golden, approximately 10 minutes. Reduce temperature to 350 degrees; bake about 30 minutes more. Check frequently; do not scorch or overcook!
- Transfer pan to a wire rack to cool.

MELLOW MIDORI CHRISTMAS TREE CAKE

One of the most enjoyable examples of holiday greenery.

Cake:

1 box yellow cake mix
1 package (approximately 3 oz.) pistachio pudding
4 large eggs
½ cup plain or vanilla yogurt
½ cup vegetable oil
¾ cup Midori brand melon-flavored liqueur
1 teaspoon coconut extract

- Preheat oven to 350 degrees Fahrenheit.
- Grease and flour Christmas tree shaped pan of appropriate size (if available; standard cake pan will do, too).
- In a large bowl, blend and mix all cake ingredients. Beat cake batter for 4-5 minutes at medium speed until blended and smooth .
- Pour batter into prepared pan.
- Bake cake until a toothpick inserted into the center comes out clean, approximately 50-55 minutes.
- Transfer pan to a wire rack; after 15 minutes, turn cake out onto rack and cool thoroughly.

(cont.)

Glaze ingredients:

2 cups confectioners' sugar
½ cup Midori brand melon flavored liqueur
½ cup softened cream cheese
2 tablespoons softened margarine
1 teaspoon coconut extract
Red and green sugar crystals

- In a medium bowl, blend and mix all glaze ingredients. Beat on high speed until smooth. Glaze cake; decorate top with red and green sugar crystals.
- Glazing hint: place wax paper or paper towels under wire rack to catch drippings from glaze.

OLD-FASHIONED CHRISTMAS TEA CAKES

Sometimes the old recipes are the best.

1 cup margarine
1 cup granulated sugar
3 large eggs
1 teaspoon nutmeg
3½ cups all-purpose flour

- Preheat oven to 350 degrees Fahrenheit.
- Grease a baking sheet.
- In a large bowl, beat together sugar and margarine until light and fluffy.
- Beat in eggs and nutmeg. Beat in flour ½ cup at a time, beating until blended and smooth.
- Drop batter by rounded tablespoonful onto floured surface. Roll cakes out to ¼" thickness.
- Place cakes 1 inch apart on prepared baking sheet.
- Bake cakes in batches until golden and set, approximately 10 minutes.
- Transfer baking sheet to a wire rack to cool.

PEANUT POPCORN FUDGE ⤴

An unlikely—but delicious—holiday combination.

2 cups granulated sugar
½ cup smooth peanut butter
½ cup milk
1 tablespoon margarine
Heaping cup of popped popcorn, coarsely chopped
1 teaspoon vanilla extract

- Grease a medium-sized baking dish.
- In medium saucepan, warm peanut butter, milk, and sugar until smooth.
- Add margarine, popcorn, and vanilla.
- Beat until all ingredients are well distributed and mixture is of an even consistency.
- Pour onto prepared baking dish; chill well.

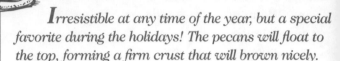

PECAN PIE ⤴

Irresistible at any time of the year, but a special favorite during the holidays! The pecans will float to the top, forming a firm crust that will brown nicely.

Prepared uncooked pie crust to fit your standard pie pan
1 cup dark corn syrup
1 cup coarsely chopped pecan pieces, toasted
½ cup granulated sugar
3 large eggs
1 teaspoon vanilla extract
½ teaspoon salt

- Preheat oven to 350 degrees Fahrenheit.
- Place pie crust in greased pie pan (or, if crust comes in alumium pie pan, use that); put in oven and brown slightly, 5-10 minutes. Remove.
- In a large bowl, beat eggs until foamy. Add sugar, pecans, vanilla, corn syrup, and salt. Mix well.
- Pour filling into prepared crust.
- Bake pie until top is set, approximately 40-45 minutes.
- Transfer pan to a wire rack to cool.

PEPPERMINT FLAVORED CANDY CANE COOKIES ≈

Cool and refreshing.

1¼ cups margarine
1 cup confectioner's sugar
1 teaspoon vanilla extract
¼ teaspoon salt
1 large egg
3½ cups all-purpose flour
¼ teaspoon peppermint extract
Pinch of red food coloring

- Preheat oven to 350 degrees Fahrenheit.
- Grease a baking sheet.
- Beat together margarine and sugar on medium speed until light and fluffy.
- Mix in vanilla, salt, and egg. On low speed, beat in flour ½ cup at a time, until dough forms.
- Shape dough into a ball and divide in half.
- In a small bowl, mix red food coloring and peppermint extract.
- Knead food coloring mixture into one half of dough.
- With lightly floured hands roll 1 teaspoon of plain dough into a 4 inch rope.
- Repeat rolling process with red dough. Braid ropes together and shape as a candy cane. Pinch ends together to seal.
- Repeat with remaining dough.
- Place cookies at least 1 inch apart on on prepared baking sheet. Bake in batches for 10 minutes or until golden brown.
- Transfer baking sheet to a wire rack to cool. Let stand until cool, 20 minutes.

"PERFECT EVERY TIME" TOLL HOUSE COOKIES ≈

Make a lot—they disappear quickly!

2 cups firmly packed dark brown sugar
1 cup granulated sugar
¾ cup butter
1¼ cup solid vegetable shortening
4 large eggs, lightly beaten
6 cups all-purpose flour
2 teaspoons baking soda
1 teaspoon salt
4 teaspoons vanilla extract
1 large bag chocolate chips
2 cups coarsely chopped pecans

- Preheat oven to 375 degrees Fahrenheit.
- Grease a large baking sheet.
- Mix together flour, baking soda, and salt.
- In a large mixing bowl, beat together shortening, sugar, and butter at medium speed, until light and fluffy.
- Beat in vanilla and eggs.
- Using low speed, beat in flour ½ cup at a time, beating until dough forms.
- Stir in chocolate chips and nuts.
- Bake cookies in batches until golden, approximately 10-12 minutes.
- Let stand until cool.

PLUM PUDDING PIE ∽

An update of the classic recipe.

Prepared unbaked pie shell to fit your standard pie
  pan
2 large eggs
1 cup orange marmalade
1 cup pitted dates, coarsely chopped
1 cup shredded sweetened coconut
1 cup crystallized fruit, chopped (preferably
  crystallized plums)
1 cup walnuts, coarsely chopped
¼ cup slivers of ginger-preserved watermelon rind
  (if available)
2 tablespoons milk
1 tablespoon butter

- Preheat oven to 425 degrees Fahrenheit.
- Beat together eggs, add marmalade, dates,
  coconut, crystallized fruit, walnuts, watermelon
  rind, and milk, in that order. Blend well.
- Place pie crust in greased pie pan. (Or, if crust
  comes in aluminum pie pan, use that.) Pour filling
  into prepared crust.
- Dot top with butter.
- Bake for 25 minutes or until crust is golden
  brown.
- (Hint: if pie seems dry during baking, *gently* mix in
  1 tablespoon of orange or pineapple juice.)

POTATO COOKIES ∽

*They sound strange. They taste delicious. What
better time than the holidays to try something exotic?*

1 stick butter or margarine
1 cup granulated sugar
1 large egg, lightly beaten
1 cup instant potato buds
1½ cup prepared biscuit mix
½ cup shredded sweetened coconut
1 tablespoon coconut or vanilla extract
Confectioners' sugar

- Preheat oven to 350 degrees Fahrenheit.
- Grease a large baking sheet.
- In a large bowl, beat together butter and sugar
  until light and fluffy.
- Add egg to batter mixture.
- Mix in potato buds, biscuit mix, shredded coconut,
  and coconut or vanilla extract.
- Drop by rounded teaspoonfuls onto prepared
  cookie sheet. Flatten cookies with the back of a
  fork.
- Bake cookies for 5 minutes.
- Remove baking sheet from oven. Sprinkle with
  powdered sugar.
- Return to oven for 5 minutes more.
- Let stand until cool.

RED VELVET CAKE ≈

Delightful!

Cake:

½ cup solid vegetable shortening
1½ cup granulated sugar
1 teaspoon vanilla extract
2 large eggs
2 ounces red food coloring
2½ cups all-purpose flour
2 tablespoons cocoa powder
1 teaspoon baking soda
1 teaspoon salt
1 cup buttermilk
1 tablespoon white vinegar

- Preheat oven to 350 degrees Fahrenheit.
- Grease 2 8-inch cake pans.
- In a large bowl, beat together shortening, sugar, and vanilla until light and fluffy.
- Add eggs to the mixture one at a time, beating well after each addition.
- Mix in food coloring.
- Mix together flour, cocoa powder, baking soda, and salt in a separate bowl.
- Mix together vinegar and buttermilk. Alternately, beat flour mixture and buttermilk mixture into egg mixture.
- Pour batter into prepared pans; smooth tops.
- Bake cakes until a toothpick inserted into the center comes out clean, approximately 30 minutes.
- Transfer pans to wire racks to cool. After 20 minutes, carefully use a spatula to turn cakes out onto rack to cool completely.
- Slice each layer in half horizontally.

Icing:

1 cup milk
5 tablespoons flour
1 cup sugar
1 cup butter, softened
1 teaspoon vanilla extract

- In top of double boiler, cook milk and flour over medium heat until thick, stirring constantly. Let cool.
- In a medium bowl, beat sugar, butter and vanilla until light and fluffy. Add milk mixture. Mix until combined.
- Cool icing completely before using.
- Spread icing evenly on top and sides of cake.

ST. NICHOLAS DAY CANDIES ≈

Tiny "snow-covered" treats that vanish like magic!

1 cup pitted, chopped dates
1 cup dark seedless raisins
½ cup figs, coarsely chopped
½ cup pitted dried apricots, coarsely chopped
1 cup coarsely chopped walnuts
½ cup orange peel
3 tablespoons fresh orange juice
Shredded sweetened coconut

- In a blender or food processor, process dried fruit and orange peel until ground to a uniform consistency.
- Spoon the fruit mixture into a large bowl; stir in the walnuts and enough orange juice to hold the mix together. (Discard any excess orange juice.)
- When mixture is sturdy enough, roll candy mixture into small balls, approximately 1 inch wide.
- Roll balls into coconut. Wrap each candy individually in green or red plastic wrap and chill completely.

SNOWBALL CAKE ≈

Winter wonderland!

1 package yellow cake mix
3 large eggs
⅓ cup vegetable oil
1¼ cups water
1 teaspoon almond extract
½ cup coarsely chopped crystallized ginger
¾ cups coarsely chopped almonds, toasted
1 12 oz. can prepared white creamy frosting
Shredded sweetened coconut

- Preheat oven to 350 degrees.
- Grease and flour a medium-sized Bundt pan.
- In a large bowl, combine cake mix, eggs, oil, water, and almond extract.
- Mix for 2-3 minutes until mixture attains a uniform consistency; fold in ginger and almonds.
- Pour batter into prepared pan.
- Bake cake until a toothpick inserted into center comes out clean, approximately 50 minutes. Cool in pan 25 minutes. Remove and cool on rack for an additional 2 hours.
- Put in freezer until hard enough to cut. Using either a cake divider or a very long serrated knife, slice cake horizontally into 2 layers. Remove and set aside the top. Hollow out bottom half, leaving ½" to ¾" on the sides and bottom.

(cont.

Filling:

1 8-ounce package cream cheese, softened
½ cup sour cream
3 tablespoons confectioner's sugar
½ teaspoon vanilla extract

- Beat cream cheese, sour cream, confectioners' sugar, and vanilla extract in large bowl until smooth.
- Spoon filling into hollow of cake. Replace top.
- Spread prepared white frosting over top and sides of cake.

SPECIAL CHRISTMAS OATMEAL COOKIES ≈

A classic—but with extra goodies for a special time of year.

1 stick butter or margarine
4 tablespoons solid vegetable shortening
1 cup firmly packed light brown sugar
½ cup granulated sugar
1 large egg
¼ cup water (4 tablespoons)
1 teaspoon vanilla extract
3 cups old-fashioned rolled oats
1 cup all-purpose flour
1 teaspoon salt
½ teaspoon baking soda
1 teaspoon ground cinnamon
½ cup chocolate morsels
Macadamia nuts, walnuts, and raisins in desired amounts.

(Note: The more extra goodies you add to these cookies, the better they are!)

- Preheat oven to 350 degrees Fahrenheit.
- Grease a large baking sheet.
- Beat butter and shortening together until mixture is smooth.
- Beat in sugar, egg, water, and vanilla until light and fluffy.
- Add remaining ingredients. Mix well.
- Drop mixture by rounded teaspoonfuls onto prepared baking sheet.
- Bake cookies in batches until golden, approximately 12-15 minutes.
- Transfer baking sheet to a wire rack to cool.

SWEET POTATO PUDDING ❧

2 cups cooked sweet potatoes
¼ cup unsweetened frozen apple juice
⅓ cup fresh orange juice
1 sliced banana
2 large eggs
1 teaspoon ground cinnamon

- Preheat oven to 350 degrees Fahrenheit.
- Grease a medium-sized pie pan.
- Place all ingredients in a blender and process until smooth.
- Pour mixture into prepared pie pan.
- Bake pudding until top is set, approximately 35 minutes.
- Transfer pan to wire rack; let cool.

TRIFLE ❧

A holiday treat that's likely to become a tradition at your house after the first time you serve it.

1½ dozen ladyfingers, split in half
¼ cup sherry
1 dozen almond macaroon cookies, broken in pieces
¼ cup toasted almond slices
¾ cup fresh strawberries, sliced
¾ cup fresh blueberries, sliced
¾ cup fresh peaches, sliced
1 cup custard (see separate recipe below)
1 pint whipped cream

- In a trifle bowl, arrange ladyfingers.
- Sprinkle sherry over ladyfingers.
- Add one layer of macaroon cookie pieces and half of the toasted almond slices.
- Add one layer of strawberries, peaches, and blueberries. Top with custard and whipped cream. Garnish with more almond slices.

(cont

Custard:

3 large eggs
¼ teaspoon salt
½ stick butter
1¼ cups granulated sugar
1 teaspoon vanilla extract
⅓ cup all-purpose flour
3 cups milk

- Scald milk in top of large double boiler.
- In a mixing bowl, beat eggs, sugar, flour, and salt at medium speed until light and fluffy.
- Add egg mixture to scalded milk: cook over medium heat and stir constantly until thickened.
- Add vanilla and butter.
- Place a piece of wax paper directly over top of surface. Cool for 30 minutes.

WISH COOKIES

You'll wish you'd made more!

10 graham crackers, crushed
½ cup butter or margarine, melted
½ cup chopped almonds
6 ounces chocolate chips
½ cup sweetened shredded coconut
1 can condensed milk

- Preheat oven to 350 degrees Fahrenheit.
- In a large mixing bowl, combine melted butter with graham crackers. Mix well.
- Press crumb mixture into bottom of a 13" x 9" pan.
- Sprinkle nuts, then chocolate chips, and coconut (in that order) over cracker crumbs.
- Gently pour condensed milk over top.
- Bake for 15-20 minutes or until golden brown.
- Let cool before cutting.

Drinks

BRANDY COCOA ∽

A mellow and delicious drink for the holidays.

2 tablespoons unsweetened cocoa powder
⅓ cup granulated sugar
1½ cups boiling water
4 cups whole milk
3 teaspoons brandy

- In a saucepan, scald milk.
- In another saucepan, mix cocoa, sugar, and enough boiling water to make a smooth paste.
- Add remaining water and boil one minute, then add to milk.
- Mix well; add brandy, then beat mixture with egg beater for two minutes.
- Serve in large mugs.

CRANBERRY GLOGG ∽

A New England favorite. It's funny to say, great to drink. This is a warmhearted cup of holiday cheer guaranteed to start even the coldest evening off right.

6 cups cranberry juice cocktail
6 whole cloves
2 cinnamon sticks
Cinnamon schnapps to taste

- Combine juice, cloves, and cinnamon in a large saucepan.
- Warm over a medium heat for 15 minutes. Reduce heat and let sit for 5 minutes.
- Remove cinnamon sticks and cloves.
- Pour into mugs.
- Add schnapps as desired, depending on the amount of warmth you have in mind.

HOMEMADE COFFEE LIQUEUR FOR CHRISTMAS, BEGUN IN NOVEMBER ⬤

The tropical stuff you buy in the store is pretty good, but our guess is you'll get more of a kick out of putting this variation together yourself. Try it. It takes some time, but it's worth it. You may never go back to the labeled version again.

4 cups granulated sugar
2 ounces instant coffee crystals
2 cups water
3 cups vodka
1 vanilla bean, split in half lengthwise

- Mix sugar and coffee in the bottom of a large pitcher.
- Add water.
- Chill for 90 minutes, then add vodka. Mix well.
- Drop the vanilla bean into an empty half-gallon bottle with a screw top.
- Pour the coffee mixture into the bottle, seal, and store for 30 days in a dark place.

HOT CANDY CANE IN A HOLIDAY MUG ⬤

An inspired twist on a peppermint theme.

Two cups hot cocoa
Peppermint liqueur
Whipped cream
Two red maraschino cherries, halved
Two green maraschino cherries, halved

- Pour hot cocoa into 2 large mugs.
- (Note: cocoa made from scratch is best, but prepared mixes to which you add boiling water will serve, too.)
- Add peppermint liqueur to taste.
- Top with whipped cream and red and green maraschino cherries.

HOT CINNAMON STOCKING ≈

The perfect drink for Christmas Eve.

Two cups hot cocoa
Cinnamon-flavored liqueur
Whipped cream
Two red maraschino cherries, halved
Two green maraschino cherries, halved

- Pour hot cocoa into 2 large mugs.
- (Note: cocoa made from scratch is best, but prepared mixes to which you add boiling water will serve, too.)
- Add cinnamon-flavored liqueur to taste.
- Top with whipped cream and red and green maraschino cherries.

PERFECT EGG NOG ≈

Forget the store-bought stuff. The real thing is easy to make and much, much better.

6 large eggs, separated
½ cup granulated sugar
1 pint heavy cream
1 pint milk
1 pint whiskey
2 ounces rum

- Place egg yolks in a large bowl.
- Add sugar to the yolks, beating at medium speed.
- After the yolks have been beaten very stiff, mix the egg whites with the yolk mixture.
- Stir in cream and milk.
- Add whiskey and rum. Stir thoroughly.
- Chill for 2 hours. Serve with grated nutmeg on top.

UNFORGETTABLE CHRISTMAS IRISH CREAM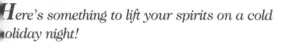

Here's something to lift your spirits on a cold holiday night!

1 12 oz. can condensed milk
8 ounces Irish whiskey
4 large eggs
1 tablespoon chocolate syrup
1 teaspoon vanilla extract
1 teaspoon coconut extract

Mix all ingredients together in a blender. Chill for 1 hour and serve.

WASSAIL

The classic recipe. This drink has warmed many a holiday heart, and will likely be popular for years to come.

2 quarts apple cider
2 cups orange juice
1 cup fresh lemon juice
1 teaspoon cloves
Cinnamon sticks

• Put apple cider, orange juice, and lemon juice into a large saucepan. Add the cloves, and two cinnamon sticks; warm over medium heat for 20 minutes.
• When ready to serve, strain off cloves and cinnamon sticks and pour liquid into mugs.
• Place a new cinnamon stick in each mug and serve.
• (Note: A teaspoon of honey may be substituted for the cloves.)

CHAPTER THIRTEEN

PARTY IDEAS and GAMES

More than any other holiday, Christmas is known for its festivities. For many of us there is nothing quite like the memories of red noses and smoky breaths at parades, sleigh rides, and caroling on starry, crisp evenings. And indoor celebration can hardly be overlooked. Hosting the perfect party on Christmas Eve or reinventing traditional Christmas games are two great ways to get the most from the holiday.

THE IDEAS THAT FOLLOW are offered as suggestions for your holiday get-together. Use them as offered—or adapt them for your own personalized Christmas celebrations. Let your imagination run wild!

SOME PARTY IDEAS FOR THE ADULTS ≈

Food is a must for any party, but especially for a Christmas gathering. Just the mention of the holiday can make many mouths water in anticipation! (In addition to the ideas that follow, you should consult the separate chapter on holiday recipes.)

Christmas tree hors d'oeuvres are always fun. Make a vegetable dip, cut up vegetables, and arrange them to look like a Christmas tree. For example, slices of carrot sticks would form the tree trunk, while the branches could be celery sticks and slices of green pepper; broccoli florets, small tomatoes, and cauliflower florets would serve as decorations. Put the bowl of dip at the base of the tree. Sprinkle the dip with parsley to give an added greeny effect. Another option is to fill the celery with cream cheese and paprika to add even more color.

≈

Songs for your rocking Christmas party playlist: "Jingle Bell Rock," Bill Haley and the Comets; "2000 Miles," The Pretenders; "Happy Xmas (War Is Over)," John Lennon and the Plastic Ono Band; "Wonderful Christmastime," Paul McCartney.

≈

How about dancing to some rocked-up Christmas music, or maybe older, softer Christmas songs for the less energetic groups? A little Christmas waltzing just might warm up all the body parts the egg nog hasn't reached.

Or, if the party spirit begins to flag, get a little silly with a game of Charades using elements that fit the season. Great charade ideas include: Christmas movies (see the video checklist in the mass-media section of this book for ideas); traditional Christmas figures such as Santa Claus, the Little Drummer Boy, or the reindeer; and the names of Christmas songs. Everyone is sure to enjoy this most traditional of party games.

Another classic Christmas party idea involves a *memory game* based on the song "The Twelve Days of Christmas." (It appears in the carols section of this book.) Gather the players into a circle; let each person review the lyrics for a few moments, and appoint one person as judge. The judge takes the lyrics and selects a person to start the song, beginning with the first day. *From memory,* each player must sing a single day—and all the days that preceded it! If you miss a day (or, depending on the harshness of the judge, if you hesitate unduly), you must leave the circle. The judge then reads the correct lyric for the remaining players. When the circle has been reduced to two players, the judge gives each the twelfth day. If both can recite it, the game ends in a tie. If not, the person who gets the furthest through the longest and most difficult day of the song is the winner.

The Secret Santa gift exchange is usually a big hit at parties where the guests are well acquainted.

Christmas is the season of giving (and receiving!) So how about a *secret Santa gift exchange* as a theme for your party? You can adjust the amount of money to be spent according to the income of the guests, but ten to fifteen dollars is usually a good maximum amount to spend on a gift. Secret Santa can be done in a variety of ways, but the easiest is probably to have everyone bring a wrapped gift that will be good for either gender, then draw numbers at the party (number one picks a gift first). Or, if you know for sure who is coming, put all the names in a hat and match people up so that everyone has a special secret Santa.

PARTY IDEAS FOR CHILDREN

If you're looking for a good way to keep children occupied during those long days before the holiday, why not throw a Christmas party? Following are some ideas to use for your festive gathering.

Find a large roll of paper and roll it out across the floor. Assign each child an area and the tools to decorate, and have the group make a giant *holiday banner* for a children's hospital, nursing home, or other charitable institution.

You can also introduce some everyday games with a bit of a festive twist. Play a holiday version of "Pin

the Tail on the Donkey" with *"Pin the Nose on Rudolph"* or *"Pin the Star on the Tree."* Just set up the appropriate poster, and place adhesive tape on the object the child tries to affix to in. Children can play the old game of "Duck, duck, goose," as *"Rudolph, Rudolph, reindeer." "Rudolph in the Middle"* is another nice game: Children form a circle with one child in the middle. The children hold hands and walk in a circle, singing "Rudolph the Red-Nosed Reindeer." On the word "glows," the children all drop to the floor. The child in the middle must tag someone on the outside before he or she sits down; if she succeeds, the tagged player goes to the middle.

These games easily lead into an all-time favorite. *Musical chairs*, played with Christmas songs such as "Jingle Bells," "Santa Claus is Coming to Town," or other such songs, is always a fun and popular option. When playing with very young children, it is often best to have the number of chairs equal the number of children, so that nobody feels left out; for older children, it is more fun to take away the chairs.

Throwing a little education your child's way during school vacation can never hurt—so long as it's done in fun. Have the children learn, discuss, and participate in the *Christmas customs of other countries*. (See the chapter on Christmas around the world for details.)

Your kids will get a kick out of a holiday stocking hunt!

Or, to borrow from another holiday, entertain with a *Christmas Stocking Hunt*. Fill many small stockings with various candies, nuts, crayons, gum, or other small items and then create a Christmas version of an Easter egg hunt, with stockings hidden in various out-of-the way spots around the house.

As part of your party, you might help the children make *greeting cards* for friends and family members who do not live with them, such as aunts, uncles, and grandparents. (Ideas for greeting cards can be found in the chapter on decorations.) When the party is over, the children can deliver the cards in person at home.

The *Stocking Puzzle Game* is another great party activity for children. Using magazines, cut out pictures of toys and trinkets that would be appropriate to put in a stocking. Tape the pictures to cardboard, then cut the cardboard into irregular shapes like a puzzle. Put each puzzle into an envelope and put the envelopes into stockings. (Depending upon the size of the puzzle, you may wish to put more than one in each stocking.) Give each child a stocking and have them complete the puzzles; the one who finishes first gets to pick the first simple prize from a big stocking. (We suggest you have plenty of trinkets on hand—you don't want to leave a player unhappy!)

For a quiet interlude or as a prelude to an afternoon nap, gather the children around for *story time*! Pick out a favorite Christmas reading—the prose and poetry sections of this book should offer plenty of candidates—and share some holiday fun.

PARTY IDEAS FOR ADULTS AND CHILDREN

Noisemakers, Christmas favors for guests, pink champagne, egg nog, or dried figs wrapped around walnuts are the kinds of details that make a party special.

A *Christmas masquerade* can be just what Santa ordered. Suggest that guests dress up as characters from famous holiday films and videos. (Examples might include George Bailey from *It's a Wonderful Life*, Rudolph, or Frosty the Snowman.)

Have one person become *Santa Claus for an evening* and surprise your guests with inexpensive gifts, such as homemade bread or fudge. This could also be a good way to distribute Christmas favors to everybody in attendance.

Put off decorating the tree until your Christmas Eve party, and then let the kids and guests pitch in. When there's plenty of egg nog and music for all, a *tree dressing party* can be lots of fun!

CHAPTER FOURTEEN

CHRISTMAS AROUND The WORLD

~

Do they have Santa Claus in China? What's for Christmas dinner in Sweden? What happens when Christmas falls in the middle of summer vacation?

Not many people are aware of the many different ways the Christmas holiday is observed around the world. From the privacy of a single home to public worship in a cathedral, in the smallest villages and the largest cities, in the jungles and in the deserts, there is Christmas. But the form it takes is often surprising!

~

CHRISTMAS IN EUROPE

As a general rule, the Christmas season in Europe begins in early December and lasts through January. The celebration is marked by beautiful and expansive Nativity scenes, huge feasts, and the observance of Epiphany. Though each ethnic group on the continent has its unique customs and rituals, there are elements that unify the holiday for all within a given country.

France

For the French, the winter holiday (known as Noël) is especially important for children. The season is a time to bask in the innocence and wonder of youth, while remembering and honoring the Holy Child who started it all.

Noël, from an expression meaning "day of birth," begins for most French on December 6, St. Nicholas's Day. St. Nicholas's Day is celebrated most heartily in the provinces, particularly in Lorraine, as it is believed that the Virgin Mary gave Lorraine to Nicholas as a gift; he is their patron saint. He is also, of course, the patron saint of children; little ones leave out their shoes in hopes that St. Nicholas will leave gifts of nuts and candy during his night visit. In Lorraine there is a procession honoring the saint in which the figures of three boys in salt barrels are carted through the streets. These figures stand as a reminder of one of the Saint's more lurid miracles: bringing three murdered boys back to life.

In some provinces of France St. Nicholas can be seen walking in a long red robe with a basket of goodies on his back, accompanied by Père Fouettard (Father Whipper), who dresses in an ugly black robe and takes care of bad children. The Père Fouettard figure is the French entry in the long roster of dark companions of St. Nicholas (or Père Noël, as the French call him).

The signs of the season begin to appear rapidly after St. Nicholas's Day. Homes, streets, shopping malls, cafés, and shops are decorated with lights, colorful decorations, and the image of Père Noël. While not as popular as in America, *sapins* (trees) are sold in outdoor markets; most who take trees home pot them so they will last longer and may be replanted later. The tree is decorated with glass, paper, or crocheted ornaments; a star, angel, or Père Noël is placed on top. While most French families use electric lights, some still use candles.

More important than a tree to the French home is the crèche, or Nativity scene. These scenes range from simple to ornate and can contain traditional elements as well as ones recently made or bought in stores.

The crèches are meant to look as realistic and beautiful as possible. To contribute to the realism, the children of Provence collect moss, pine, and rocks for the background. Some crèches contain *santons* (little saints) representing people in the Nativity. Santons came to France in the 1800s from

Italy by way of Italian merchants; the figures are made of clay and in most cases are clothed with fabric.

The French crèche often depicts a French rather than Judean landscape. This could simply be a case of strong local influence on religious imagery, or it could have something to do with an obscure tradition hearkening back to the time when some areas of France claimed to be the birthplace of Christ. The regions of Provence, Auvergne, and Brittany have all made this claim in past eras. The climate and geography of these areas are considered to be similar to that of the Holy Land, and this coincidence may have something to do with the old claims.

Flowers are another staple decoration in the French home during the holiday season. Lush arrangements of roses, gladioli, carnations, and snapdragons are often found on the table or next to the fireplace, as are Poinsettias, hyacinths, azaleas, and Christmas begonia plants. Some houses assign a special place on the table for the hellebore, or Christmas Rose.

Along with decorating, the preparations for the *reveillon* must be completed by Christmas Eve day. Reveillon (awakening) is the grand Christmas Eve feast that takes place after midnight Mass. The feast may have as many as fifteen courses, ranging from soups, fruits, salads, meats, fish, and chicken to cheese, breads, nuts, pastry, candy—all with plenty of wine. (This is, after all, France.)

The arrival of Christmas Eve sees the infant Jesus finally taking his place in the family crèche after a small family ceremony. Little children are put to bed, left to hope that the gifts they ask for will be left by Père Noël.

Previously, Petit Jesus, or Little Jesus, was the one who came to children on Christmas Eve. Later, the visitor was the spirit of Christmas, Père Noël. In present-day France, most children believe Jesus sends Père Noël in his place.

Unlike the American Santa, Père Noël is tall, dresses in a long red robe, and travels with a sack and a donkey. Though Père Noël is not seen in department stores as often as Santa is in the United States, he too can be contacted by sending letters to the North Pole.

After the children are in bed, the older members of the family head off to midnight Mass. Along the way there are often processions reenacting the Nativity, some of which end in living crèches (where people play out the manger scene). The midnight Mass itself is very important in France, and almost everyone attends. At the Mass's conclusion, all head home to begin the reveillon.

The French feast following Christmas Eve midnight Mass often extends until dawn.

The reveillon often lasts the entire night, with no time for the adults to sleep before the children wander down to open their gifts. The adults wait to exchange their gifts on New Year's Day; some village near the Spanish border mix Spanish and French traditions and open gifts on January 6.

The remainder of the vacation time surrounding this holiday is often spent either skiing in the French Alps or visiting the Riviera.

Belgium

St. Nicholas arrives in Belgium on December 4 to take a look around and gauge children's behavior. On December 6 he delivers special treats to good children—and switches to bad ones. The children leave out hay and water for his horse or donkey along with their shoes as an added measure of goodness.

An area of the country known as Flanders is famous for its Nativity plays, which are performed with great care and attention to tradition. Three men who are chosen for their good behavior during the year dress as Magi and walk through the town. They sing songs at each house and are rewarded with snacks.

Everywhere in Belgium there are extensive processions on Christmas Eve. Each procession winds through the town, picking up members as it flows, until it reaches the church for midnight Mass.

Italy

Italy is the birthplace of the manger scene, or *presepio*, and it rightfully holds a place of distinction in the Italian Christmas. The presepio is filled with clay figures called *pastori* (which the French, as we have seen, call *santons*). All who come to the home kneel to pray or sing before the presepio.

~

Italy is the birthplace of the manger scene.

~

In the days before Christmas, children visit homes and read Christmas selections, receiving a money reward. Over the twenty-four hours prior to Christmas Eve a strict fast is observed, followed by a great meal. A unique feature of this evening is the "Urn of Fate," a bowl filled with both presents and empty boxes. Each person picks to see whether he or she is "fated" to receive a gift—although no one ever really goes away empty-handed.

Italian children receive gifts twice during this season. The Christ Child is said to bring small gifts on Christmas Eve, but the more anticipated gift giving is from La Befana, who comes down the chimney on Epiphany Eve to leave goodies in shoes. Legend has it that La Befana was the woman who declined the Wise Men's offer to accompany them on their journey to see the Christ Child. Regretting her decision later, she set out to bring the Child gifts, but, as she never found Him, she leaves gifts for other children instead. (The tradition has variants in many other countries, as well.)

Throughout the season, houses, stores, and streets are decorated in traditional ways, and there is much music and singing. The *ceppo* is an Italian version of the Christmas tree. Made of wood, the ceppo gives the appearance of a ladder, with shelves linking two sides. The bottom shelf always contains a presepio; other shelves contain gifts and decorations.

As part of an older tradition, shepherds (*pifferai*) often come in from neighboring villages to play their horns and bagpipes before all the holy shrines, and before carpenter's shops, in honor of Joseph. In a role similar to that of the American Santa Claus, women dressed as La Befana collect for charities like the Red Cross.

Christmas morning is occupied with the church Mass. As they have done for hundreds of years, Italian churches compete to see who has the most beautiful presepio. Popular opinion generally assigns that honor to the presepio of the Ara Coeli Church in Rome.

Spain

The Christmas season in Spain begins on December 8 with the Feast of the Immaculate Conception. An interesting feature of this feast is known as *Los Seises*, the Dance of Six, an ancient custom whereby boys perform a dance around the altar that symbolizes Christ's birth. Although the dance is still known as Los Seises, it is now performed by ten boys.

It is no surprise that the manger scene or *nacimiento* has a place of reverence in the Spanish Christmas. This manger scene contains all the traditional elements, with a few distinctly Spanish ones thrown in. Among the animals watching over Christ is a Spanish bull, and a stream of water is always included. Sometimes bullfighters are part of the onlooking crowd. These scenes are set up in public squares and in homes, taking precedence over Christmas trees, which are not common.

The Spanish refer to Christmas Eve as Noche Buena *(Good Night).*

On Christmas Eve, family members gather in the room containing the nacimiento to sing hymns and pray. Late in the evening the *Misa de Gallo* (Mass of the Rooster) is attended. Many Hispanic countries refer to midnight Mass as the Mass of the Rooster; it has been said that the only time a rooster ever crowed at midnight was the moment when Christ was born. After Mass, a big meal is consumed.

Adults exchange gifts on Christmas Day. Another treat is the "Urn of Fate," a bowl filled with the names of everyone present. Two names are picked out at once; those whose names are chosen together are supposed to enjoy a lasting friendship or romance.

There is much dancing and other festivities through Epiphany, the day that children receive presents in their shoes from the Three Wise Men. (There is no Santa Claus figure.) Sometimes three men dress as the Magi and wander the streets singing before visiting the public nacimiento.

England

While the great traditions of the Yule log and boar's head are no longer commonly observed in England, in the minds of many they are an integral feature of the old-fashioned English Christmas. Dyed-in-the-wool traditionalists may substitute roast pig for the boar's head, but the modern fireplace is far too small to accommodate the massive Yule logs of times past. Even the great English roast beef has been replaced by turkey. Mince pie and plum pudding are still favorites, however, and the land that gave us the Christmas card is still sending them by the millions.

In England the Christmas tree has been widespread since Prince Albert introduced the custom in 1841. Caroling and bell ringing are very popular, as well. Father Christmas, so similar in many ways to the American Santa Claus, leaves gifts for children. Letters to him are not mailed, but rather thrown in the fire; if they fly up the chimney, the desired gift is considered as good as brought.

Children hang up their stockings on Christmas Eve. After the children are in bed, parents decorate the tree; the house is filled with holly, ivy, and mistletoe. Afterward, many go to a midnight Christmas service, where there is a great deal of caroling and bell ringing. In the morning children open their gifts, and all sit down to that turkey in the afternoon.

An additional observance at this time of year is Boxing Day, held on December 26. The name is taken from the old custom of opening the alms boxes in church the day after Christmas to give money to the needy. The idea expanded to servants and tradesmen, who expect to be tipped for the year's service.

Wales

Carol singing in Wales has become an art form. Nowhere in the world are Christmas carols more carefully crafted and lovingly sung. Each village has a trained choir and great gatherings for group singing.

The Christmas season is also the time for the Mari Llywd to appear. This odd creature is represented by a man wearing a sheet and carrying a horse's skull (or wearing a fake horse head). The "creature" dances around in public and tries to bite people with the horse's jaws. If he manages to bite you, you must give him money!

The Christmas service is called Plygain and goes from 4:00 A.M. until sunrise on Christmas morn. Pulling taffy is one way to spend the day; in Wales, taffy is as much a part of Christmas fare as candy canes are in America.

Ireland

Christmas in Ireland is more religious and less festive than in other parts of Europe. Lit candles are

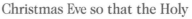

left in the windows on Christmas Eve to light the Holy Family's way, but there are seldom many other decorations. The door to the home is left open on Christmas Eve so that the Holy Family may partake of the bread and milk left out on the table. Father Christmas is the gift giver here, and some presents are given out. For a treat, three special puddings are made during this season: one for Christmas, one for New Year's, and one for Twelfth Night.

In parts of Great Britain, on the day after Christmas (St. Stephen's Day) many engage in "hunting the wren." This old tradition called for the killing of a wren to symbolize the death of the old year and the birth of the new. The dead wren was put on a stick so the hunters could parade with it from house to house, singing carols. The homeowner would give the hunters some goodies for their troubles, and they would give him or her a feather for good luck. Areas that still observe this custom today use a fake stuffed wren.

Scotland

Christmas was not celebrated in Scotland until the 1960s; the once-outlawed holiday was long seen as just another workday. Things have gradually changed, but Christmas is still not, to the Scots, the major event that is to many other peoples. New Year's Day is still the more important celebration.

Germany

Germany, perhaps more than any other country, has influenced the way Christmas is celebrated around the world. It is from Germany that we get some of the most popular ideas associated with the Christmas season and the Christmas spirit, as well as such welcome innovations as the Christmas cookie. (For more information on specific German contributions to the holiday, see the chapter on Christmas customs.)

Things get started on St. Nicholas's Day (December 6). Advent wreaths and calendars make their appearance, and this day marks the beginning of the German Christmas season.

It is said that the tradition of the Christmas tree began in Germany, and most modern families there would consider it unthinkable to pass the holiday without a tree. The tree is usually trimmed by the mother, who decorates with balls, tinsel, stars, cookies, marzipan, and so on. No one else is allowed to see the tree until Christmas Eve.

After Mass or church on Christmas Eve, the *Christkind* or Kris Kringle—not St. Nicholas—brings the gifts. At first, the Christkind was meant to be the Baby Jesus; later the name came to stand for a more angelic figure that embodies the spirit of the Christ Child. The Christkind wears a flowing white robe, a white veil, and gold wings. He often enters by an open window and rings a bell when gifts have been left. The name later evolved into Kris Kringle; it is in no way a pseudonym for Santa Claus. Like St. Nicholas, Kris Kringle is accompanied by a nasty companion called Knecht Rupprecht, Pelznickle, or Ru-Klas.

Austria

St. Nicholas's Day opens the Christmas season in Austria. Called SanterKlausen, the saint arrives not with a nasty helper for the holidays, but with the devil himself! (This is an extreme, but not uncommon, variation on the "dark companion" theme.) Both figures test the children, and the good ones get presents.

In Austria, the Nativity scene is displayed around the family tree, which is decorated with cookies as well as ornaments. There are processions known as "Showing the Christ Child." Nativity plays are also performed; similar to the Spanish posadas, they dramatize the Holy Family's journey.

On Christmas Eve, many enjoy music from the *Turmblasen*, a brass band that plays carols from church steeples or building towers. Later there is midnight Mass.

Both December 25 and 26 are legal holidays. The days are spent relaxing, socializing, and feasting on carp, ham, goose, pastry, and the like.

One of Austria's most important contributions to the celebration of Christmas is a song sung by church choirs and carolers around the world: "Silent Night." On Christmas Eve, 1818, organist Franz Gruber composed the music to accompany Josef Mohr's poem. The carol was Gruber's only published musical work. Today, it is certainly hard to imagine Christmas without that song.

Switzerland

As Switzerland is populated by four distinct groups of people, it has no dominant holiday tradition. Those with French backgrounds follow French customs; Germans, Italians, and Romansh speakers likewise follow their own traditions. Regardless of nationality, however, all in Switzerland celebrate with mangers and trees.

Switzerland (a nation with four official languages) has multiple Christmas traditions, with no single approach to observing the holiday dominating.

In some parts of Switzerland great care is taken to emphasize the holiday's religious significance before its festive side. Children are not allowed to open their gifts until all have gathered around the tree to sing songs and read the story of the Nativity from the Bible. Presents are brought by the *Christkindli*; the angelic figure arrives in town on a sleigh loaded with goodies and pulled by six reindeer.

Churches in Switzerland are famous for their bells, and bell-ringing competitions are held in some areas, such as Valais, on Christmas Eve.

St. Stephen's Day, December 26, has become an extension of the Christmas celebration in Switzerland.

Holland

Of all the countries in the world that celebrate St. Nicholas's Day, Holland is the one in which old Nick truly can be said to reign supreme. Arriving by steamer on the last Saturday in November, the saint is greeted by huge crowds of people, including dignitaries. After parading through the streets in full bishop's regalia, Nicholas and his companion Black Peter take up residence in a hotel and begin preparations for St. Nicholas's Eve. In the time between his arrival and the holiday, St. Nicholas visits schools, hospitals, and shopping malls. The presents he leaves in children's shoes on St. Nicholas's Eve are disguised and come with catchy poems; Black Peter leaves switches for misbehaving children. Children often have St. Nicholas parties.

Double play: In Holland, as in some other countries, both December 25 and the following day—known as Second Christmas—are legal holidays.

For Christmas there are church services and much eating and merriment. Boiled chestnuts are among the popular snacks. The houses are decorated with holly and pine, and there are Christmas trees. December 26, also a legal holiday, is referred to as Second Christmas, but is usually an opportunity for resting up from the previous day's activities. One nice feature of this day is the abundance of music that can be heard from a variety of choirs, radio broadcasts, and other performances.

Denmark

In Denmark, Santa is not alone. There is a mysterious creature lurking about during the Christmas season, the mischievous *Julnisse*.

Dressed in gray with a red bonnet, red socks, and white clogs, the Julnisse hides in farmhouse lofts or in barnyards. Unless appeased with a treat he may play tricks, but if properly taken care of, he'll watch over the family's animals for the upcoming year. The figure is quite popular, and is often featured on collector's plates made specially for Christmas.

Apparently, the tradition of collecting such plates began years ago, when rich families would give their servants plates of goodies for the Christmas holiday. The plates, considered far better than the servants' everyday dishes, were set aside by servants. The custom caught on and now the Christmas plate—with or without a Julnisse—is a popular collectible.

Danish children's letters to Santa are sent to Greenland, where they are answered by members of the Danish Tourists Association.

What occupies most plates during the Danish Christmas meal is roast goose, red cabbage, potatoes, and pastry. Food is a major element of the Danish celebration. One custom (common to other Scandinavian countries, as well) involves hiding an almond in the rice pudding. Whichever child has the portion with the almond gets a prize.

Norway

Norwegians, like other Scandinavian peoples, believe in sharing Christmas with the animals. On Christmas Eve day, a sheaf of grain or "Bird Tree" is hung out in the yard so that the birds may feast too.

By four o'clock on Christmas Eve, all work has ceased; all are dressed in their best clothes to begin the festivities, and other Scandinavian customs are observed. The rice pudding is eaten; whoever finds the magic almond is given a treat. Of course, some rice pudding must also be given to the barnyard elf to ensure he'll protect the animals and not pull pranks.

For the children there is *Julesvenn* to bring gifts on Christmas Eve—like the Danish Julnisse, a holdover from an ancient Jul feast. Between Christmas and the season's end on January 13, there are many parties for children and adults, including the *Julebukk*, a Halloween-like celebration named after Thor's goat. Children wear costumes and knock on neighbors' doors asking for treats.

Sweden

Although St. Lucia's Day on December 13 is observed in other Scandinavian countries, it is celebrated on a grand scale in Sweden. St. Lucia, who was martyred in A.D. 304 for being a Christian, is important to the Swedes because, legend says, she brought food to Sweden during a time of famine. In the wee hours of December 13, thousands of young girls in a white robes, acting the part of St. Lucia, serve pastry and coffee to their parents while they are in bed. (More than one visiting American parent, recalling bleary-eyed Christmas mornings past, has observed that this laudable custom would probably be just as meaningful if adopted to the U.S. Christmas celebration, but that's another story.) Special buns are made with an "X" on them

to symbolize Christ. There is also an official St. Lucia parade in Stockholm.

On Christmas Eve day the family gathers in the kitchen for a ritual known as *doppa i grytan* (dipping in the kettle). A kettle is filled with drippings—corned beef, pork, and sausage. Each person dips a piece of dark bread in the kettle until it is soaked through, then eats it. This ritual is meant to remind each family member of those who are less fortunate, and to encourage thankfulness.

The Swedish also have the Scandinavian tradition of the rice pudding with the hidden almond, only here the finder of the almond is destined to be married within a year. And like other Scandinavians, the Swedes have their gnome, known as Jultomten, who must be appeased. *Jultomten* is also the one to put presents under the tree on Christmas Eve, presents that come with poems and are disguised. Jultomten rides the *Julbock*, a straw goat modeled after the one Thor had.

On December 25, the first of two Christmas Days, there is an early-morning church service. The day is filled with visiting and other religious observances. On December 26, the Second Day of Christmas, men ride through the villages to waken all early, and animals are given extra food.

Twelfth Night (Epiphany) is observed on January 6. Villagers dress up as Biblical characters and go from home to home singing hymns.

As King Knut had once declared that the Christmas should be celebrated for twenty days, the season doesn't officially end until January 13, Saint Knut's Day. (King Knut IV ruled from 1080-1086 and is honored as a saint for his virtue and generosity.)

The days between Christmas and Saint Knut's Day are filled with parties for children and adults. After this day, trees are taken down to mark the official close of the season.

Finland

Christmas in Finland encompasses most of the Scandinavian traditions already described, with some unique Finnish customs added for good measure. One is visiting the steam baths before Christmas Eve, presumably to get squeaky clean for the holiday. Finns also sprinkle straw around the family Christmas tree—and sometimes on the dinner table—to remind all of the circumstances of Jesus' birth.

Greece

In the Greek tradition, Christmas is not as important a holiday as Easter, so the celebration is on a smaller scale than some might expect. December 6 marks St. Nicholas's Day, but emphasizes his role as the patron saint of sailors; December is a time of rough seas around Greece, so prayers are for safety rather than gifts.

Make no mistake, though, Christmas itself is celebrated merrily. Children wander the streets singing carols and playing little drums or triangles; they are rewarded with candy, nuts, or money. There are no Christmas trees, however, and gift giving is reserved for St. Basil's Day (January 1).

Featured among the Christmas meal is the *Christopsomo*, or Christ Bread. The bread is usually decorated with a symbol indicating the family's occupation. Some traditions call for giving the first piece to a beggar; a second Christopsomo is usually baked for the animals in hopes of a prosperous year. Pork or chicken is also on the holiday menu.

To light the evenings, the *skarkantzalos*—similar to a Yule log—burns from Christmas Eve to Epiphany.

Among the highlights of the Greek Orthodox Christmas observance is the Blessing of the Water.

Because the Greek Church is an Eastern church, it celebrates Christ's birth on January 6. Known as Greek Cross Day, it is the day on which the Blessing of the Water takes place. In this ceremony, a priest dips a crucifix in a lake, river, or stream. The water, called Baptismal Water, is now considered holy and is used by the faithful for its healing powers. In some cases the crucifix is tossed into the water, and young men dive in to retrieve it. The one who finds the crucifix is considered especially blessed and is treated as king for a day, even getting special gifts. This Blessing of the Water is also done in Syrian and Coptic churches, as well as in some parts of Russia and the United States.

Russia

Perhaps the best way to look at the Russian Christmas is to go back to the customs of pre-Revolutionary Russia, when Christianity flourished. Father Frost was a staple of the old tradition, and presents were brought by Babushka, Russia's version of the old woman who was supposed to have declined to join the Wise Men. There was also a girl dressed in white called Kolyada who would visit houses, singing carols and giving treats. Christmas trees were decorated.

Members of the Russian Orthodox church would fast until after church services on Christmas Eve. Some communities engaged in the Blessing of the Water; sometimes a priest would go through the village with this water to bless the houses.

In the years following the Revolution, many of the customs of Christmas were hard to track down, as they were for all intents and purposes illegal—or at least counter to the official pronouncements of the Party. Now that the Communist regime has passed, it is a good bet that many of those traditions will come back into prominence.

Poland

During the Christmas season, the letters C, M, and B are the most important in Poland. Representing the initials of the Three Wise Men (Casper, Melchior, and Balthazar), the letters are painted on the doors of homes along with three crosses in hopes of insuring a good year.

Lucky children in Poland receive gifts twice during the Christmas season. St. Nicholas brings the first round on St. Nicholas's Day; the Star Man, accompanied by Star Boys, brings the second round on Christmas Eve.

The Star of Bethlehem is very important to the Poles. Its sighting—or, at any rate, the sighting of the first star seen on Christmas Eve—marks the end of Advent and of fasting.

On Christmas Eve, after the first star has appeared in the sky, the head of the household breaks a wafer called *oplatek* and shares it with every person in the house. These wafers, which bear images of the Nativity, have been blessed by a priest. Oplatek are also given to the animals as a gesture of blessing and good will.

Wilia, the Christmas Eve meal, has thirteen courses, one for Jesus and each of the Apostles. Hay is placed under the tablecloth as a reminder that Christ was born in a manger.

The Christmas tree usually has its own room. It is decorated with fruit, nuts, colorful paper, and homemade ornaments.

The midnight Mass in Poland is called *Pasterka*, the Mass of the Shepherds. It is believed that on this night the animals bow in reverence and receive the power to speak.

The Czech Republic

The Czech Republic sets aside both December 24 and 25 for Christmas, which are known as First and Second Christmas. The season opens with *Svatej Nikulus* (St. Nicholas's) Day on December 6, and ends with the visit of the *Tri Kralu* (Three Kings) on January 6. Svatej Nikulus has a bag of goodies for nice children; his companion for the trip is the devil, who carries switches for the bad ones.

The manger scene, or *Jeslicky*, is a must in churches and homes. There are Christmas trees, which are lit Christmas Eve; dinner consists of carp, pudding, and fruit stew. A seat at dinner is left empty for the Christ Child. Later, *Pasterka* (midnight Mass) will be attended.

CHRISTMAS IN CENTRAL AMERICA AND THE WEST INDIES

Christmas in Central America and the West Indies is characterized not by snow and sleighbells but warm weather and bright flowers. For the most part the countries in this area adhere to the traditions of the midnight Mass and Nativity scenes. On Christmas Eve there are often processions with people wearing costumes and carrying the manger; large festive meals are eaten on either Christmas Eve or Christmas Day. On Christmas Day there are picnics, bullfights, and other good times. A small number of Christmas trees are imported from the United States, and Santa is seen on occasion, but not to bring gifts. Gifts are put in children's shoes by the Three Kings or the Christ Child on January 6th.

These are the common aspects of the holiday; there are also a number of customs unique to individual countries.

Mexico

The Christmas season in Mexico begins on December 16, the first day of *posadas*. Posada is the Mexican word for a tradition popular among many Hispanic countries, the commemoration of the Holy Family's pilgrimage. Posadas take place over a period of nine days before Christmas; in each posada, the faithful act out Mary and Joseph's search for lodging. People travel to one another's homes, taking

on the roles of Holy Pilgrims or nasty inn-keepers. The ritual culminates in celebration and prayer around the family altar, on which is placed a crèche and a covering of pine branches and moss. The houses are decorated with Spanish moss, evergreens, and paper lanterns. Also present are "The Flowers of the Holy Night," or poinsettias. After the religious portion of the posada is over, there is much merriment, with food, fireworks, and pinatas. The final and most important posada takes place on Christmas Eve. The Baby Jesus is placed in the cradle amid prayer and song. Afterward, everyone attends midnight Mass.

Protestant and Catholic Christmas celebrations in Mexico may differ markedly.

For Catholics the festivities end here. Christmas Day is quiet, and there is no Santa Claus figure. Children will receive their gifts on Epiphany. For Protestants, however, the posadas are a bit different. There is more outdoor caroling, and children receive a gift bag from Santa during a church service early on Christmas Eve.

Honduras

Hondurans have their own version of posadas. For nine days before Christmas, the faithful act out Mary and Joseph's search for lodging. One house in the village is chosen to be the place of shelter, where people go to sing and pray. As there are many poor, the missions are important in providing holiday festivities for children. Tamales are served, dances and fireworks displays are held, and people visit each other's crèches.

Costa Rica

In Costa Rica the Nativity scene is given its own room, not just a spot in a corner or on a table. In accordance with the climate, the decorations consist of brilliantly colored flowers and wreaths of cypress leaves and red coffee berries. Children put out their shoes for the Christ Child to fill, as their parents did, but Santa is beginning to show up more and more.

Nicaragua

By late November, festivities have started in Nicaragua. Children gather in the streets with bouquets to honor the Virgin Mary with song. This portion of the holiday ends on December 8 with the Feast of the Immaculate Conception. On December 16, the Novena to the Holy Child begins; another kind of posada, it concludes on Christmas Eve at midnight Mass.

Panama

Schoolchildren in Panama engage in pre-Christmas activities much like the ones enjoyed by American children. Decorations and cards are made, gifts are exchanged, and there are plays. Requests for gifts are sent to Baby Jesus in Heaven, however, not to Santa Claus.

Puerto Rico

Understandably, there is a large American influence on the Puerto Rican Christmas, which features a mixture of Spanish and American traditions. Puerto Ricans have Santa Claus and a tree, but receive gifts on both Christmas and Epiphany. Before Christmas there is a great deal of neighborhood caroling, with people dressing up as they believe the Magi did. Nine days before Christmas, a kind of posada begins in the form of the Mass of the Cards, which is held every day at 5:30 A.M.

A fun Christmas Eve tradition is *Asalto*, in which a band of people appear on someone's lawn to shout, sing carols, and plead for goodies. The owner usually opens up his or her house to them; after a small party, the group moves on to another house.

CHRISTMAS IN SOUTH AMERICA

The celebration of Christmas in South America is similar to that in Central America because of the warm climate and the religious aspects of the holiday. As with most countries of Hispanic origin, children receive gifts on Epiphany rather than Christmas; the *nacimiento* (crèche) and midnight Mass are essential, but posadas are not as popular as in other areas.

Chile

Christmas in Chile is observed in accordance with most of the region, but features two unique events. In Andacollo there is a grand festival honoring the Virgin Mary. Another festival, resembling a county fair, features horse racing. The gift giver here is *Viejo Pascuero*, Old Man Christmas, and oddly enough, he too has reindeer.

Peru

Sport is also a feature of Christmas Day in Lima, Peru, for it is on that day that the biggest bullfight of the year is held.

Colombia

Part of the Colombian Christmas ritual very closely resembles the American Halloween. On Christmas Eve, people dress up in costume and roam the streets; those who guess the true identity behind a mask are given a gift. Colombia is also one of the rare Hispanic countries in which children receive gifts brought by the Christ Child on Christmas Eve, not Epiphany.

Venezuela

An interesting tradition in the area of Merida, in Venezuela, is the Standing up of the Christ Child, *La Paradura del Niño*. According to the rules, the figurine of the Child must be stood up on New Year's Day to indicate his maturity. Any Child found lying down in its manger at that time is likely to be "kidnapped" and kept in a special place of honor until the ransom is paid. Ransom is a *paradura* party. But before the party can begin, "godparents" must be chosen; later, they lead a procession to where the Child is kept. After the godparents return the figurine to the manger setting and stand it up, children offer gifts, and there is much food and dancing.

Many Venezuelans travel to midnight Mass via rollerskates!

Brazil

Brazil is one South American country that has incorporated some American ideas for Christmas. Brazilians have a Santa equivalent called Papa Noël, lighted Christmas trees, and similar gift-giving traditions. The manger, or *pesebre,* is still very important, however. On Christmas Eve a meal is laid out before the household attends midnight Mass, so that the Holy Family may eat if they wish. Children put out shoes for Papa Noël to fill.

Because of the warm climate, Christmas Day is often filled with picnics and sport.

CHRISTMAS IN AFRICA

In most African countries Christians make up only a small part of the population, so Christmas is usually not celebrated on a grand scale. But it is celebrated!

Although Christmas has been a tradition in Ethiopia for quite some time, observance in most other countries is limited to areas with established missions. In these areas Christmas is observed

simply, in a way that many feel reflects the true meaning of the day. The missions provide homes and schools for the young children and hospitals for the ill; during Christmastime, the efforts of all are concentrated on helping those in need, and on the spiritual aspects of the holiday. There are no Santas or trees, and very little gift giving, except to the poor. In some places, lucky children receive sugar, grains, or fruit.

As a general rule, Christmas is a low-key affair in Africa; its observance is usually limited to relatively small Christian populations. The emphasis is typically on charitable acts and simple presents, rather than the purchase of expensive gifts.

In Algiers there are a number of Catholic churches that celebrate midnight Mass. Streets are colorfully decorated.

The Christian church in Ethiopia is the Coptic church. Believers there still abide by an older calendar, which places Christmas on January 7.

Things stray from the norm a bit in Ghana. Here Christmas evergreen or palm trees are seen, but only in churches, and there is a Father Christmas who comes out of the jungle. Children have school pageants, and there is more gift giving. Early Christmas morning, a group enacts the story of the shepherds and angels heralding Christ's birth, traveling the streets and singing songs. This band is often rewarded with gifts.

In Liberia, mission schools give gifts and decorate palm trees.

It's fair to say that, in most African countries, Christmas could be ignored entirely without changing the cultural landscape much. One exception to this, however, is found in South Africa. Christmas there falls in the midst of summer vacation, so the festivities are adapted to the warmer weather. In the European sections of the country, shops are decorated and streets are lit. Father Christmas puts gifts in the children's stockings. After a church service on Christmas Day, the Christmas feast is eaten outside. The non-European sections have feasts, carnivals, and parades.

CHRISTMAS IN THE MIDDLE EAST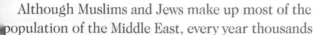

Although Muslims and Jews make up most of the population of the Middle East, every year thousands of Christians from around the world make pilgrimages to the Holy Land, especially Bethlehem, in the West Bank.

They come to visit the place where, according to the Gospels, it all began. Not surprisingly, this is the time of the year when Bethlehem is most popular.

Each year thousands of Christians make the pilgrimage to Bethlehem for what is perhaps the most moving Christmas celebration of them all.

The festivities in the "little town" center on the Church of the Nativity and the Shepherds' Fields. The Church of the Nativity is believed to stand on the place where Christ was born; under the church, within a small cave, a star on the floor marks the place where Mary gave birth to Jesus. The

Shepherds' Fields is said to represent the fields where the angels announced the arrival of Christ.

Among the indigenous Christians in Bethlehem, there are three groups. The Roman Catholics celebrate Christmas on December 25, the Greek Orthodox on January 6, and the Armenian Christians on January 18. Representatives protecting the interests of these three groups sit on a board that "governs" the Church of the Nativity, so that no group will be favored or slighted. No services are held within the church itself, but rather in an adjoining building. Services on Christmas Eve are by invitation only, but are televised to the crowds outside. Afterward, most venture to the Shepherds' Fields, which are also divided into three sections.

With the obvious exception of Israel, the peoples of the Middle East are predominantly Muslim. Some of these Muslim countries do have Christian sections, and in those sections Christmas is observed, although the observance is usually more strictly religious, as in Africa. Some countries, however, have indigenous Christian populations that have been celebrating Christmas for centuries.

In Armenia it is believed that Christmas should be celebrated on the day of Christ's baptism, which is January 6 in most church calendars. However, the Armenian Church follows the old Julian Calendar, which marks this date as January 19. One week before Christmas there is a fast, during which no meat, eggs, cheese, or milk may be eaten. Religious services are held on Christmas Eve and Christmas Day. Afterward, children go onto the roofs with handkerchiefs and sing carols; often the handkerchiefs are later filled with fruit, grain, or money.

In Iraq, the reputed home of the Magi, Christmas

is known as the Little Feast (Easter being the Great Feast). Christians here fast from December 1 until Christmas Eve, consuming no meat, eggs, milk, or cheese. After the evening church service, a great feast begins, but there is no gift exchange.

Syria celebrates Christmas longer than most Middle Eastern countries, beginning on December 4, St. Barbara's Day, and lasting through Epiphany, January 6. Children receive gifts on Epiphany from the Camel of Jesus. A tradition left over from the days of religious persecution is locking the outside gate of the house on Christmas Eve. This is to remind all that they once had to practice their religion behind closed doors. The father lights a great fire in the courtyard, and the youngest son reads from the Gospel. The way the fire burns is said to predict the family's fortune's for the upcoming year. Hymns are sung. After the fire has been reduced to embers, family members make a wish and jump over them.

Epiphany Eve is known in Syria as *Lilat-al-Kadr* (Night of Destiny). A Magic Mule brings presents to children on this night. The mule's magic powers came from when he was caught up as the trees bowed at midnight on the night of Christ's birth.

In Pakistan, many aspects of the Christmas celebration are similar to those in America. There's even a Santa Claus!

In neighboring India, the Christmas trees for the churches are made out of straw. The straw is twisted into shape and coated with mud; later, greens are applied, and then candles. In some instances, banana trees are also decorated.

In some Middle Eastern countries, such as Saudi Arabia, the Christian population is made up largely of foreign oil workers. Here, Christmas is celebrated with decorations, carols, and imported food. An altar is built in the home, and the Nativity scene is often played out.

CHRISTMAS IN THE FAR EAST

In the Far East there are perhaps fewer Christians than there are in the Middle East. As in Africa, the existence of a Christian population here is largely due to missionary work.

China

China was only opened to the West four hundred years ago, so, relatively speaking, Christians and Christmas have not been around for long. A minute portion of the Christian population celebrates a Christmas heavily influenced by the missionaries. Christmas is referred to as *Sheng Dan Jieh*, or the Holy Birth Festival. There are trees, called "trees of light," and paper lanterns are intermingled with holly for decoration. Stockings are hung, and there is a version of Santa known as *Lam Khoong-Khoong* (nice old father), or *Dun Che Lao Ren* (Christmas old man). Gift giving has some formal rules. Jewelry and other more valuable gifts are only given to the immediate family; other gifts are given to relatives and friends.

More important to the majority of Chinese is the New Year, referred to as the Spring Festival, which is celebrated in late January. New toys and clothes are given and feasts are held. The spiritual aspects concern ancestor worship, and portraits of ancestors are displayed on New Year's Eve. This is not, strictly speaking, a Christmas celebration, but it is a festive and popular seasonal undertaking.

Japan

Japan has roughly the same proportion of Christians to non-Christians as China. Christmas there is celebrated by a large number of people—including a good many who follow other religions. For the Japanese, Christmas is a strictly secular celebration, considered a time for fun and gifts. There are Japanese versions of American Christmas carols; department stores have Christmas trees and special Christmas sales; holly, bells, and other decorations

are everywhere. Some believe that the Japanese awareness of Christmas is due in part to their large manufacturing interests in America; since so many of their own products are bought as Christmas gifts, the argument goes, the Japanese are interested in the holiday as an economic and social event.

The Japanese Christmas, which grows more popular each year, is seen primarily as a secular occasion for gift giving. Outside of the relatively small Japanese Christian community, there are few religious elements associated with the holiday.

The religious aspects of the Japanese Christmas are confined to the areas touched by missionary work. In these parts Christmas is celebrated with services, hymns, children's pageants (with Japanese dress), visits to hospitals, and other services to the needy. Often, Japanese cakes are given out to those attending church.

Korea

Typical for this part of the world, Korea has a small pocket of Christians who celebrate Christmas with traditional religious services. Schoolchildren put on pageants, and there is a great effort put into helping the needy. For the actual Christmas service, a group of adults and children stay awake in the church on Christmas Eve. At around 2:00 A.M. they go out into the neighborhood singing, and they are often invited into homes for a treat. Religious services are held in the morning, and there is much caroling as people make their way there.

For the country as a whole, Christmas is a non-working holiday, although the majority of the population is Buddhist. Some families have trees, and children are given small gifts.

OTHER PARTS OF THE WORLD 🎵

Canada

Christmas is celebrated in many different ways in Canada. The country is made up of a variety of ethnic groups, most of which celebrate Christmas in accordance with their own traditions.

Vancouver, on the western end of Canada, is illuminated with lights, especially in the harbor area, and trees are lit in homes. In Montreal, Masses are celebrated in the many beautiful cathedrals, and in Nova Scotia old carols are sung at home and in church. In Newfoundland, the inhabitants' fishing skills are put to work for the church. During Christmas week the daily catch is given to the church so that it can be sold to raise money for the church's work.

Australia

As in South Africa, Christmas falls during summer vacation down under. Because of the climate, flowers are the most important Christmas decoration, particularly the Christmas Bush and the Christmas Bell. Father Christmas and Santa exist side by side—like siblings, which they certainly are. Gifts are exchanged on Christmas morning before attending church. Typically, the afternoon is spent at the beach or engaging in sports.

Australia is also the home of "Carols by Candlelight," a tradition started by radio announcer Norman Banks in 1937. After Banks saw a woman listening to carols alone by candlelight, he decided to do something to relieve the loneliness and isolation some feel during the holidays. He announced a community carol sing for anyone who wanted to join in. The concept has grown in popularity over the years, and the recorded program is now broadcast the world over.

The United States

Because American culture and media have had such a disproportionate impact on the development of Christmas traditions elsewhere in this century, a detailed look at the development of the holiday in the United States seems worthwhile here.

Columbus' s 1492 voyage to the New World ended when he ran aground on Christmas Eve. (He and his men were rescued by native peoples.) His was, of course, the first of many such expeditions to what would eventually be called the Americas. Later explorers found the inhabitants of these unfamiliar lands engaging in end-of-the-year festivals just as people did back in Europe. Peoples in the Pacific Northwest and Alaska had winter celebrations; a tribe in North Dakota hung gifts on cedar trees.

Despite these fascinating parallels with Christmas traditions, it would certainly be overstating the case to say that Native Americans played any significant role in the shaping of the Christmas celebration in the United States. The main influence, of course, was European, and the first wave of European settlers to the colonies were of English, Dutch, and Germanic origins. These groups, representing a variety of churches and religious affiliations, organized communities according to the traditions and values of their heritage. Among other religious, cultural, and political differences manifest during the colonial period was the question of Christmas. In this case there was scant middle ground: Some were completely for it, some completely opposed.

Those communities with strong Separatist or Puritan ties thought about Christmas only long enough to object to it—and in many colonies (most notably in New England) these strict "low-church" denominations represented the majority. Excerpts from the diary of Governor Bradford of Plymouth Colony give a dismal description of Christmas in 1621, describing only work and the discouragement of celebration. At first the laws forbade only public celebration, not private, but in 1659 a law was passed prohibiting the celebration of Christmas entirely, with offenders to pay a five-shilling fine or be whipped.

A steady influx of moderates from overseas brought about the repeal of the law in 1681, and the first Christmas services were held in Boston Town Hall in 1686. Still, even when it was no longer illegal, Christmas remained a workday in Boston. Although Alabama declared Christmas a legal holiday in 1836, the first state to do so, the same was not done in Boston until 1856, and children there were attending school on Christmas Day until 1870.

Americans owe the Christmas tree—and a great deal more of their Christmas celebration—to German immigrants.

Hessian troops at Trenton, unwilling to forsake their customary celebrations during the Christmas season of 1776, were taken by surprise by General Washington in one of the turning points of the Revolutionary War. As it happens, Hessians, who came from central Germany, are believed to have been the first to set up a Christmas tree on American soil. They were also the first part of a wave of Christmas-loving Germans who would profoundly influence the American holiday.

In the nineteenth century, it seemed that wherever Germans settled in America, they brought Christmas cheer. In Pennsylvania, in New York, in Virginia, and elsewhere, they kept their love of Christmas alive. In some places they were surrounded by some of the holiday's staunchest opponents, but they carried on anyway, and gradually gained converts to their merry ways.

But there were other voices for Christmas in America's youth. In Virginia, the Cavaliers (seventeenth-century English royalists) observed Christmas by ringing bells, decorating evergreens, and feasting. The Dutch founders of present-day New York celebrated similarly; they also brought St. Nicholas with them, the man who would eventually be known in America as Santa.

An infusion of Victorian Christmas spirit that began in the middle of the nineteenth century, coupled with the continued dedication to the holiday of German immigrants and their descendants, brought about the beginning of the holiday Americans recognize. In 1890 Oklahoma, the last contiguous state or territory that did not officially recognize Christmas as a holiday, saw the error of its ways. The country was now celebrating from sea to shining sea, gradually incorporating customs and traditions from all over the world. Although it had a late start, the American Christmas, because of its ancestry, rivals any other in richness and variety. And if some of its variations—say, overcommercialization—seem suspect when considered in terms of the holiday's deeper meanings, others—such as the elimination of St. Nick's sometimes terrifying "dark companion"—may be welcome in many homes.

The Christmas of Santa Claus, of wrapped presents beneath the tree, of family gatherings for television broadcasts of *It's a Wonderful Life*—that Christmas is alive and well because it has, like the country in which it grew, been assembled from bits and pieces of what worked elsewhere, combined with new ideas, and transformed into a colorful whole. Christmas in America is a glorious hodgepodge, a sometimes chaotic blend of disparate elements, and all the more magnificent for its variety.

CHAPTER FIFTEEN

MULTICULTURAL CELEBRATIONS

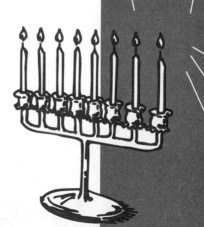

In addition to Christmas, there are other notable observances that take place during the winter solstice. Two of them are Hanukkah and Kwanzaa, both of them meaningful and popular in the diverse world in which we live. In this chapter, we explore the background and evolution of these important celebrations.

HANUKKAH ≈

HANUKKAH, MEANING "DEDICATION," is a Jewish holiday commemorating the rededication of the Temple in Jerusalem in 165 B.C. The eight-day "Festival of Light" or "Feast of Dedication" begins on the twenty-fifth day of the Hebrew month called Kislev, which usually falls in late November or December. Because Christmas and Hanukkah occur around the same time of the year, many people think of Hanukkah as a sort of "Jewish Christmas," but that is far from the case.

The meaning and significance of Hanukkah is individual, steeped in Jewish tradition and experience. What the two holidays do have in common, however, is a complex history, and the use of ritual and symbolism in their celebration.

The Roots of the Festival

The legend of Hanukkah is a familiar one to most: upon the defeat of the Syrian army at the hands of the Maccabees, the Jewish people were able to reclaim the Temple in Jerusalem. When worshipers went to light the Temple lamps as part of the rededication ceremony, however, they found only enough undefiled oil to burn for one day. Miraculously, the lamps burned for eight days, which was enough time to prepare new oil. The eight days of Hanukkah commemorate this miracle. But this is only part of the story; there is much more to Hanukkah.

Hanukkah, like Christmas, is a midwinter festival, and like Christmas, marks a single event but uses rituals and customs from other holidays and festivals. More than remembering the miracle of the oil, Hanukkah is a celebration of Jewish victory and survival in the face of great odds, especially the survival of religious freedom. The oil and the candles are merely symbols of this greater miracle.

To understand Hanukkah fully, it is necessary to go back hundreds of years before the events that inspired it, to see how the situation was created.

In ancient times, the people of Judea (Southern Palestine, including Jerusalem) were the subjects of various kings and empires. As subjects they paid their taxes and obeyed the laws of the land, but otherwise lived as they chose, going about their business peacefully.

In time the people of Judea became subjects of the Greek empire. When Alexander the Great came to rule the empire, he sought to spread Greek culture, known as Hellenic culture, to the world, beginning with his occupied territories. Thus began the so-called Hellenization of the Jewish people, a peaceful cultural exchange that even included intermarriage between occupying soldiers and local women; the children born of these marriages further mixed the cultures. The Jewish people did not seem to have much objection to this Hellenization; when Alexander came to Jerusalem in 332 B.C., the people promised to name all male children born in the first year of his reign after him.

When Alexander died, his kingdom was divided up between two generals, Ptolemy and Seleucis. The area handed over to Ptolemy was called the Ptolemaic kingdom and consisted of Egyptian lands. The Seleucid referred to Seleucis's domain, Asia Minor and Syria. At this time, Rome had taken over Italy and was on the rise.

For more than a hundred years the Jewish people and their lands were part of the Ptolemaic Empire, paying their taxes but retaining their religious and cultural freedom and even some rights of self-government. Hellenization went on but it was not forced. Although people knew the Greek language, took Greek names, and wore Greek styles, they were ultimately faithful to the Mosaic life and never gave up the hope of controlling their own destiny someday. And while most saw no threat in Hellenization, a group called the Hasidim did see a problem: the eventual disappearance of the Jewish people.

Thirty-four years before the Maccabean revolt, the Jewish lands came under the Seleucid Empire, which was headed by Antiochus III. At first things went on as they had, but as Rome began to threaten more and more, Antiochus concluded that a unification of his territories would make his empire less vulnerable. The Hellenization was intensified. This time religion was also a target, with Antiochus putting statues of Greek gods in public places and synagogues, including the Temple in Jerusalem.

As it happened, however, the Jewish people were not at all happy about this new development, and Antiochus, not wanting internal dissent, decided not to push the issue any further. Antiochus's successor, Seleucis IV, kept the same policy as his father, but Antiochus IV, the next ruler in line, felt differently.

An unstable man and probably something of an egomaniac, Antiochus began an attempt to enforce strict Hellenization policies, and even went so far as to issue formal bans against the Jewish Sabbath and circumcision. To aid him on the religious end, Antiochus appointed a man named Jason, a Hellenizer of Jewish descent, to be the new high priest. Hellinization under Jason continued to pick up speed, yet a policy of permitting some traditional Jewish practices remained in effect. As a practical matter, those who wished to could still follow the old ways.

This leniency came to an end with the ouster of Jason, who was replaced by Menelaus. Menelaus had no regard for Jewish ways, and was a very strict Hellenizer.

Around this time, Antiochus, thinking all was well with his properties, went off to challenge Rome in Egypt. Rumors of his death came back to Judea, giving confidence to the discontented. The displaced Jason joined forces with members of the Hasidim and staged a revolt that ousted Menelaus from power. As soon as Menelaus was gone, the victorious Hasidim removed all the statues of Greek gods and Antiochus.

But Antiochus was not dead; having suffered humiliation at the hands of the Romans, he was prepared for an opportunity take out his frustrations and wield his still-considerable military power. His target became Judea, where he unleashed his army to kill and pillage. The army killed more than ten thousand people and restored the statues of the gods and Antiochus.

Opposition in Judea

The Jewish people, even those formerly tolerant of Hellenization, now banned together against Antiochus and became sympathetic to the Hasidim. But there was little they could do to save themselves, as they were unarmed, untrained, and would not fight on the Sabbath. It seemed the most a person could do to show his or her dissent was to die as a martyr.

The Greek soldiers continued to pillage and rape forcing people to participate in Greek sacrificial rituals; those who would not were slain. This went on throughout the country, until a small village called Modi'in struck back.

Modi'in was occupied by a priest named Mattathias, who along with his five sons (Johanan, Simon, Judah, Eleazar, and Jonathan), mounted an opposition to the forces of Anitochus. The soldiers were taken by surprise and beaten handily by the small band of rebels. The rebels took whatever weapons they could from the slain soldiers and retreated to the hills to plan strategy. The success of this band, known collectively as the Maccabees, gave their compatriots hope, and soon new recruits from all over were making their way to the hills to train.

Over the next three years the Maccabees achieved victory after victory; they were patient and smart, often catching the larger army off-guard. When Mattathias died, Judah took over and led the Maccabees to the ultimate success: the reclaiming of the Temple in Jerusalem.

This victory over a much larger, better trained, and better equipped army is, quite understandably, considered a miracle by the Jewish people. The people, we are told, rejoiced for eight days, singing, dancing, eating, and worshipping; the miracle of the oil and the lamps is among the most prominent features of the accounts of this first festival.

The Evolution of the Festival

After that first celebration in the Temple, Judah decreed that the miracle of the Jewish victory should be commemorated every year in the same fashion. Over the centuries, borrowing a bit from other Jewish festivals and inspiring some customs of its own, Hanukkah has evolved into the holiday we recognize today.

There are several explanations for the festival's eight-day duration. The most widely accepted is that it is in commemoration of the eight days that the lamps stayed lit. There is also a legend that Judah and his followers found eight enemy spears in the Temple, which they made into a lamp stand. Some observers think that the eight days are the result of combining the Hanukkah festivities with other Jewish festivals of similar length.

In the years immediately following the Maccabean victory, having these legends to fall back on became increasingly important to the survival of Hanukkah. Within thirty years the Jewish lands came under Roman rule, and a holiday that rejoiced in Jewish battle success and nationalism would not have been tolerated. So the legend of the oil moved to the forefront, thereby masking the deeper reasons behind Hanukkah until it was safe for them to come to prominence again.

During the tragedies of World War II and the subsequent struggle to retain a Jewish homeland, Hanukkah's undertones of Jewish pride and survival became more important than ever.

Today in the United States, Hanukkah is celebrated for the most part quietly at home, with family and friends. Though observance of the holiday may vary from house to house, the Menorah is the central element of any Hanukkah celebration. On the first night of Hanukkah, one candle on the candelabrum is lit by the *shamash*, or servant, the ninth candle that lights all others. Each night after the first, an additional candle is lit, until all eight are aglow on the final night.

Hanukkah is a happy holiday, full of food and good cheer. On the fifth night of Hanukkah, many families engage in a formal gathering known as the Night of the Fifth Candle dinner. This is typically the time during the festival when family members and friends from far away make a special effort to gather with their loved ones. These days, this special gathering is not always restricted to the fifth night of Hanukkah, but may take place on the night during the festival that the most people can attend.

While food selections for Passover and other Jewish holidays arise from strict observances of religious law and ritual, the specific items of Hanukkah fare have evolved, in no small measure, under the influence of later customs. The oil in the potato latkes served, for instance, is meant to symbolize the miracle oil that kept the Temple lamps burning for eight days. Dairy products are prevalent as a result of the legend of Judith, daughter of the Maccabees. It is said that Judith once entertained an enemy leader by feeding him large quantities of cheese. The man became so thirsty that he had to drink more wine than he should have, which dulled his senses and made him an easy capture.

Food is not the only entertainment during Hanukkah, however. The *dreidel*, a top with four raised sides, is by far the most popular Hanukkah toy. Each side of the dreidel contains a Hebrew letter representing the words in the sentence "A great miracle happened there." As the top spins and comes to rest, nuts, sweets, or pennies are traded among the players.

Money given during Hanukkah is called Hanukkah *gelt*. In older times, this money was given to children so they could buy a gift for their Hebrew school teacher. These days, they are allowed to keep most, if not all, of the money for themselves. Hanukkah gelt remains one of the more popular Hanukkah gifts.

Katowes are popular among older children. These brain twisters are puzzles and riddles of sorts; all of the answers to these puzzles must be in numbers that equal forty-four, which is the total number of candles lit during the Hanukkah festival. Adults may pass the time playing checkers or chess. (There are chess sets that pit the Maccabees against the forces of Antiochus!)

Over the course of the eight days, families usually entertain friends at home, eating, drinking, singing, and generally being merry. Songs echo through the halls, and small gifts are exchanged on many nights. Depending on the family's preference, the custom of giving one small gift per night can be modified to one or two larger gifts given on only a few nights.

Hanukkah observances in the synagogue consist of reading passages from the Torah on each of the eight days. Psalms 113 through 118 and the prayer of Al Ha-Nissim may also be read. Many temples and synagogues sponsor Hanukkah festivals, as do schools and community centers. Most of the activity is geared towards children, featuring plays, concerts, parties, and food.

Though not the most important holiday on the Jewish calendar, Hanukkah stands out as a time of great merriment. Hanukkah is important to the Jewish people as a reminder of a miraculous time in their history, but it can be a valuable reminder to all of the potential of the human spirit.

KWANZAA

KWANZAA IS A CELEBRATION of African-American heritage, unity, and values that takes place from December 26 through New Year's Day. Originated by Maulana Karenga in 1966, Kwanzaa, meaning "first fruits of the harvest" in Swahili, is a nonreligious ceremony that strives to promote a feeling of pride and cultural awareness. Each of the seven days is assigned a principle which is explored on that day. The principles are known by both their English and Swahili names: *Umoja* (unity), *Kujichagulia* (self-determination), *Ujima* (collective work and responsibility), *Ujamaa* (cooperative economics), *Nia* (purpose), *Kuumba* (creativity), and *Imani* (faith). Each night a candle is lit on a *kinara*, a seven-branched candelabrum, as a way to mark awareness of the principle. After the candle is lit, the prescribed part of the evening is over. As with most of Kwanzaa, it is up to the individual to decide how he or she would best like to explore the principles,

nd the festival as a whole. Some give examples of the principle at work in their daily life, others read stories or poems by African or African-American authors; still others play music or dance.

Fruits and vegetables are an important part of Kwanzaa, as they symbolize unified effort, as in harvesting. Other tools of the festival include ears of corn to represent every child in the family, and straw mats that stand for respect for tradition. Sometimes the items are displayed through the week on a Kwanzaa table.

The week is also highlighted with special African or African-American foods, such as black-eyed peas salad, *Yassa* (chicken marinated in onion sauce), groundnut soup, sweet potato pie, collard greens, brown rice, cornbread, fish, and African stew. Sometimes parties are given, particularly on the last day.

In the early days, observance of Kwanzaa was limited, but it has gradually gained popularity over time. As the festival enters its twenty-sixth year, an estimated fifteen million people in the United States are celebrating it in some way. There are many books out on the subject, and museums and other institutions are host to Kwanzaa-related poetry readings and music performances. The Smithsonian features an exhibit on Kwanzaa activities, and Manhattan's American Museum of Natural History has a Kwanzaa program.

With popularity, of course, comes a measure of commercialism. While giving small gifts is sometimes part of Kwanzaa, traditionally Christmas-sized gifts such as Nintendo sets and bicycles are now being given to children. Recently there has been an attempt to give Kwanzaa its own Santa figure, Nia Umoja. Meant to represent a wise man, Nia Umoja travels around asking children about Kwanzaa.

Though it more closely resemble, the Jewish Hanukkah with its candles and its duration, and the American Thanksgiving in tone and theme, many people incorrectly assume Kwanzaa is meant to be an alternative to Christmas. While it does take place during the same season, Kwanzaa is in no way meant to usurp Christmas, and many people celebrate both events.

BIBLIOGRAPHY ∿

Barnett, James H. *The American Christmas*. New York: Macmillan, 1954.

Bartlett, John. *Bartlett's Familiar Quotations*. 14th ed. Edited by Emily Morison. Boston: Little, Brown and Company, 1968.

Chernow, Barbara A., and George A. Vallasi. *The Columbia Encyclopedia*, Fifth Edition. Boston: Houghton Mifflin, 1993.

Coffin, Tristram P. *The Illustrated Book of Christmas Folklore*. New York: Seabury Press, 1973.

Count, Earl W. *4000 Years of Christmas*. New York: Henry Schuman, 1948.

Crippen, Thomas G. *Christmas and Christmas Lore*. New York: Gordon Press, 1976.

Dawson, W.F. *Christmas, Its Origins and Associations*. New York: Omnigraphics, 1990.

Hadfield, Miles, and John Hadfield. *The Twelve Days of Christmas*. London: Cassell, 1961.

The Home Book of Quotations. Edited by Burton Stevenson. New York: Dodd, Mead, and Company, 1944.

Jones, E. Willis. *The Santa Claus Book*. New York: Walker & Company, 1976.

Editors of the Reader's Digest. *Treasury of Modern Quotations*. New York: Thomas Y. Crowell Company, 1975.

Rice, Sara. *Holiday Selections*. New York: Ayer, n.d.

Sanson, William. *A Book of Christmas*. New York: McGraw-Hill, 1968.

Smith, Elva Shophronia, and Alice Isabel Hazeltine. *The Christmas Book of Legends and Stories*. New York: Lothrop, Lee & Shepard Company, 1944.

Snyder, Phillip. *December 25th: The Joys of Christmas Past*. New York: Dodd, Mead, and Company, 1985.

Weil, Lisl. *Santa Claus Around the World*. New York: Holiday, 1987.

INDEX ~

Hermits, 375
Herrick, Robert, "Ceremonies for Christmas," 197
Holiday Baked Custard, 376
Holiday Banner, as a Christmas decoration, 398
Holiday Fudge, 376
Holiday Lemon Nut Bread, 342
Holiday Maple Ham, 363
Holiday placemats, instructions for, 265
Holiday Pork Roast with Strawberry and Prune Stuffing, 363
Holiday Shrimp Dip, 348
Holiday Wave Bottles, 263
Holland, and Christmas traditions, 409
"Holly and the Ivy, The," 193
Holly
    decorations for, 261
    history of, 30
Hollywood, California, 325
Homemade Coffee Liqueur for Christmas, Begun in November, 391
Honduras, and Christmas traditions, 414
Hors d'oeuvres, for a party, 397
Hot Candy Cane in a Holiday Mug, 391
Hot Cinnamon Stocking, 392
Hot Springs, Arkansas, 325
Houston, Texas, 325
Hyde Park, New York, 325

— I —
"I Saw Three Ships," 229
Immigrants, and Christmas, 281
Ireland, and Christmas traditions, 407
Irish Cream, 393
Irish, Mary, *Poems for Christmas*: "Christmas Lights," "Merry Christmas," " The Merry Day," " Christmas Secrets," 198
"It Came upon a Midnight Clear," 230
It's a Wonderful Life, history and trivia of, 312
Italy, and Christmas traditions, 405
Ivy, history of, 30

— J —
Jamestown, New York, 325
Japan, and Christmas traditions, 419
"Jingle Bells," 231
"Joy To The World," 232
Judea, and Hanukkah, 425-427

— K —
Katowes, as Hanukkah custom, 428
Kinara, as Kwanzaa custom, 428
King Henry III, and gift giving, 285
Kingsburg, California, 325
Kissing Bough, history of, 31
Korea, and Christmas traditions, 419
Kringle, Kris, explanation of, 20
Kwanzaa
    celebration of, 428
    Kinara, 428
    Yassa, 429

— L —
La Befana, legend and origin of, 23
Lagerlof, Selma, "The Legend of the Christmas Rose," 152-158
Last-Minute Shoppers, and the 1920s, 274
Latkes
    cheese, 352
    potato, 356
Leavenworth, Washington, 325
"Legend of the Christmas Rose, The," (Selma Lagerlof), 152-158
Lemon Bars, 377
"Letter from Santa Claus, A," (Mark Twain), 183-185
Letters
    from Santa, 183-185
    to Santa, 60-61, 272, 410
Liqueur, coffee, 391
"Little Match Girl, The," (Hans Christian Anderson), 44-46
Little Orphan Annie, and the Depression, 275
Little Women's Christmas, The, (Louise May Alcott), 37-43
"Lo, How a Rose E'Er Blooming," 233
Longfellow, Henry Wadsworth, "Christmas—1863," 199
Lord of Misrule, origin of, 22
Los Angeles, California, 325
"Lully, Lullay," 234
Luther, Martin, and Christmas, 28
Lynchburg, Virginia, 326
Lynden, Washington, 326

— M —
Main Courses, and accompaniments, 359-366
Maple Bells, 377

"Markheim," (Robert Louis Stevenson), 171-182
Masquerade, as Christmas party, 399
Meatless Mince Pie, 378
Mellow Midori Christmas Tree Cake, 378
Menelaus, 426
"Merry Christmas, Everyone!," 194
Merry Mocha Coffee Mix, 343
Mexican Christmas Eve Salad, 355
Mexico, and Christmas traditions, 413
Miami, Florida (Metro Area), 326
Middle Ages
    and Christmas, 8-11
    and Henry VIII, 9
Middle East, and Christmas traditions, 417
Midnight Mass, origin of, 23
Minneapolis, Minnesota and environs, 326
"Mistletoe," (Walter De La Mare), 194
Mistletoe, history of, 30
Mock Turtle Soup for the Holidays, 356
Monson, Massachusetts, 326
Moore, Clement C.
    "A Visit From St. Nicholas" ("Twas The Night Before Christmas"), 200-201
    and Santa Claus, 255
Morgan, J.P, and Christmas bonuses, 271
Morley, Christopher, "The Worst Christmas Story," 159-165
Mount Vernon, Virginia, 326
Mummers, origin of, 22

— N —
Nachos, 347
Nantucket, Massachusetts, 327
Nashville, Tennessee, 327
Nast, Thomas, and Santa Claus, 256
Nativity Scenes, explanation of, 19
New Year's Day, and gift giving, 286
New York, New York, 327
Newport News, Virginia, 327
Nia Umoja, and Kwanzaa, 429
Niagara Falls, New York, 327
Nicaragua, and Christmas traditions, 414
"No Room in the Inn," 235
Nogales, Arizona, 327

Shakespeare, William, 10
   "Bird of Dawning," 203
   "Hamlet" and Christmas legends, 25
Shamash, as Hanukkah custom, 427
Side dishes, 351-358
"Silent Night," 242
Silver City, New Mexico, 329
Snowball Cake, 384
Songs, for Christmas parties, 397
Soulsbyville, California, 329
Soup
   mock turtle, 356
   pumpkin, 353
South America, and Christmas
   traditions, 415
Southern plantation, at Christmas, 26
Southern Style Christmas Corn, 357
Spain, and Christmas traditions, 406
Special Christmas Oatmeal Cookies, 385
Special Green-And-Red Vegetable
   Salad, 357
Springfield, Massachusetts, 329
St. Croix, Virgin Islands, 329
St. Nicholas Day Candies, 384
St. Nicholas
   as Pere Noel, 403
   legend of, 251
   origin of, 253
   reputation of, 253
Stamps
   Christmas history of, 32
   trading and the 1960s, 279
Stars
   Christmas explanation of, 25
   of Bethlehem in Poland, 412
Stevenson, Robert Louis
   "Christmas At Sea," 204-205
   "Markheim," 171-182
Stevenson, Washington, 329
Stocking Hunt, as children's game, 398
Stockings
   as a puzzle game, 399
   as children's treasure hunt, 398
   origins of, 24
Stuffing
   apricot fruit, 364
   bread crumb, 360
   chestnut poultry and game, 360
   herb, 362

sausage poultry and game, 365
strawberry and prune, 363
Styrofoam, decorating with, 264
Sweden, and Christmas traditions, 410
Sweet and Sour Chicken, 365
Sweet Potato Pudding, 386
Switzerland, and Christmas traditions, 409

— T —

Taos, New Mexico, 329
Tarrytown, New Mexico, 330
Tennyson, Lord, Alfred, "Christmas
   and New Year Bells," 206-207
Tips, employee, Christmas history of, 32
Tomato, stuffed, 355
Tortuga, New Mexico, 330
Toy Boom, after World War II, 288
Traditions, Christmas around the
   world, 401-422
Trifle, 386
Trivia Quiz
   of the mass media, 295-308
   answers to, 309
Truman, Harry, and Independence
   message, 278
"Truth from Above, The," 243
Tucson, Arizona, 330
Turkey, roasted with apricot fruit
   stuffing, 364
Twain, Mark, "A Letter from Santa
   Claus," 183-185
"'Twas the Night Before Christmas,"
   (Clement Moore), 200-201
"Twelve Days of Christmas, The," 244
   as a memory game, 397

— U —

Unforgettable Christmas Irish Cream, 393
United States, and Christmas
   Traditions, 420

— V —

Venezuela, and Christmas traditions, 415
Victorian Christmas, description of, 14
Vienna, Virginia, 330
Virginia Beach, Virginia, 330
Volcano, California, 330

— W —

Waffles, crisp, 340
Wales, and Christmas traditions, 407
Warsaw, Virginia, 330
Washington, D.C., 330
Wassail, 393
   origin of, 25
Watergate, and Christmas, 280
"We Three Kings of Orient Are," 246
"We Wish You a Merry Christmas," 247
"What Child Is This?," 248
Wickenburg, Arizona, 331
Wickford, Rhode Island, 331
Willcox, Arizona, 331
Williamsburg, Virginia, 331
Wish Cookies, 387
Woodstock, Vermont, 331
"Worst Christmas Story, The,"
   (Christopher Morley), 159-165
Would That It Were So, and the 1920s, 273
Wreaths, decorations for, 261
Wrens, custom of, 407

— X —

Xmas, explanation of, 19

— Y —

Yassa, as a Kwanzaa custom, 429
"'Yes, Virginia, There Is a Santa
   Claus,'" (Francis P. Church), 60-61
Yorkshire Pudding, 358
Yule Crunchies, 349
Yule Log, explanation of, 25
Yuppies, and Christmas, 282